COMMANDING THE *LEXINGTON* DURING THE BATTLE OF THE CORAL SEA

I saw the enemy torpedo planes coming in on both bows. The air was full of antiaircraft bursts and the din was terrific. I motioned to the helmsman for a hard left rudder, just as the enemy planes started disgorging their fish.

The water in all directions seemed full of torpedo wakes. Bombs were dropping all around us. Great geysers of water from near misses were going up higher than our masts, and the ship shuddered from the explosions of the ones that hit.

The enemy planes split up to fire on both bows, the hardest maneuver for us to counter. Then I remember seeing two wakes coming straight for our port beam, and there was nothing I could do about them. The wakes approached the ship's side, and I braced myself for the explosion. . . .

COMBAT COMMAND

THE BANTAM WAR BOOK SERIES

This series of books is about a world on fire.

The carefully chosen volumes in the Bantam War Book Series cover the full dramatic sweep of World War II. Many are eyewitness accounts by the men who fought in a global conflict as the world's future hung in the balance. Fighter pilots, tank commanders and infantry captains, among many others, recount exploits of individual courage. They present vivid portraits of brave men, true stories of gallantry, moving sagas of survival and stark tragedies of untimely death.

In 1933 Nazi Germany marched to become an empire that was to last a thousand years. In only twelve years that empire was destroyed, and ever since, the country has been bisected by her conquerors. Italy relinquished her colonial lands, as did Japan. These were the losers. The winners also lost the empires they had so painfully seized over the centuries. And one, Russia, lost over twenty million dead.

Those wartime 1940s were a simple, even a hopeful time. Hats came in only two colors, white and black, and after an initial battering the Allied nations started on a long and laborious march toward victory. It was a time when sane men believed the world would evolve into a decent place, but, as with all futures, there was no one then who could really forecast the world that we know now.

There are many ways to think about that war. It has always been hard to understand the motivations and braveries of Axis soldiers fighting to enslave and dominate their neighbors. Yet it is impossible to know the hammer without the anvil, and to comprehend ourselves we must know the people we once fought against.

Through these books we can discover what it was like to take part in the war that was a final experience for nearly fifty million human beings. In so doing we may discover the strength to make a world as good as the one contained in those dreams and aspirations once believed by heroic men. We must understand our past as an honor to those dead who can no longer choose. They exchanged their lives in a hope for this future that we now inhabit. Though the fight took place many years ago, each of us remains as a living part of it.

COMBAT COMMAND

The American Aircraft Carriers in the Pacific War

ADMIRAL FREDERICK C. SHERMAN, U.S.N., (RTD.)

BANTAM BOOKS
TORONTO · NEW YORK · LONDON · SYDNEY

COMBAT COMMAND

*A Bantam Book / published by arrangement with
E. P. Dutton Inc.*

PRINTING HISTORY

*Dutton edition published in 1950
Bantam edition / November 1982*

Illustrations by Greg Beecham and Tom Beecham.

Maps by Alan McKnight.

*Bantam Books are published by Bantam Books, Inc. Its trade-
mark, consisting of the words "Bantam Books" and the por-
trayal of a rooster, is Registered in U.S. Patent and Trademark
Office and in other countries. Marca Registrada. Bantam
Books, Inc., 666 Fifth Avenue, New York, New York 10103.*

*To the Memory
of those
American officers and men
who gave their lives
to win the Victory
in the Pacific*

CONTENTS

	PREFACE	ix
	INTRODUCTION	xiii
1	THE STAGE IS SET	1
2	PEARL HARBOR	11
3	DEFEAT, RETREAT AND FRUSTRATION	22
4	MOLDING THE TEAM	47
5	THE BATTLE OF THE CORAL SEA	69
6	THE BATTLE OF MIDWAY	94
7	STALEMATE	110
8	LIMITED OFFENSIVE FOR GUADALCANAL	129
9	THE TIDE TURNS: FROM GUADALCANAL TO BOUGAINVILLE	154
10	THE RISING TIDE	178
11	THE GILBERTS AND MARSHALLS	185
12	SEVEN-LEAGUE BOOTS: *The First Battle of the Philippine Sea—Saipan, Tinian, Guam*	197
13	THE PALAUS	223
14	SWEEPING THE SEAS: THE CARRIERS CLOSE IN	228
15	LEYTE AND THE BATTLE FOR LEYTE GULF	238
16	MASTERS OF THE PACIFIC	268
17	IWO JIMA	283
18	OKINAWA AND THE FLEET THAT CAME TO STAY	293
19	BOMBING JAPAN	310

20 THE SURRENDER AT TOKYO   320
21 CONCLUSIONS AND LESSONS   327
    BIBLIOGRAPHY   335
    INDEX   338

PREFACE

Combat Command is fascinating reading. It is essentially an account of the Navy's efforts in the Pacific during World War II. The arrangement is attractive. Starting with Pearl Harbor, in chronological order, chapter by chapter, it unfolds the principal naval campaigns in the Pacific.

Ted Sherman, by training and experience, is well qualified to spin this yarn. He has served in practically all types of naval vessels, and has had training in two specialties of the naval Service. These specialties, the submarines and the naval air forces, had potent and direct bearing on the final victory. Ted had wide combat experience from the commencement of the war. His entire combat service was in connection with carrier-based air.

I have always felt that the attack his task force made during the first carrier raid on Rabaul was one of the decisive actions of the Pacific War, and saved the day for our embattled forces. We had just secured and held a precarious and narrow beachhead at Empress Augusta Bay, on Bougainville. We knew the Japanese had sent a large force of cruisers and destroyers to Rabaul. Their intentions were obvious. They planned to bombard and attempt to destroy our forces on and near that island. Admiral "Tip" Merrill's cruisers were short of ammunition and sleep after days of continuous and heavy fighting. They were hopelessly outnumbered by the enemy. It was imperative that they be withdrawn. The only force available was the large carrier *Saratoga* and the smaller carrier *Princeton*, with accompanying destroyers. After fueling this force in waters within range of Japanese planes, we directed them to a position where they could make continuous attacks on the enemy. Our shore-based dive bombers and torpedo planes could not make continuous attacks because of the distance of our bases and the difficulty of furnishing fighter support. We had not had too much success with horizontal bombing against shipping. When it was decided to send in these two carriers, I fully expected that they would be lost. The results were beyond our fondest hopes. The Japanese attack was completely disrupted, and the *Saratoga* and *Princeton* escaped unscathed. Had our attack failed, the Solomons campaign might have been delayed for months, with a consequent delay in the Central Pacific campaign, then about to be launched. I recommended this Force for a Navy Unit Citation — but it was not approved. This was a perfect attack, and it had a tremendous bearing on the over-all strategic picture. The fact that our ships were not attacked, proved its success. An attack by an inferior force which completely disrupts the plans of a superior force, deserves recognition.

One story of Ted and his return to Coronado after the *Lexington* had been sunk. He had lost all his belongings. His loaned khaki was not in the best of shape and his general appearance was not too dandified. He entered a drugstore and started ordering various necessary and missing toilet articles. The saleswoman looked at him with a bit of disdain and some suspicion, until she saw he had money to pay for his purchases. He requested a bag in which to carry his toilet articles. With withering sarcasm, she said: "Ain't you heard there's a war on?" What price glory?

Ted is very forthright and, like all forthright people, has decided opinions. The conclusions he reaches will not be well received by many whom he criticizes. His opinions and conclusions express his point of view, and deserve study by historians and students of naval strategy and tactics. It is the duty of historians and students to seek to know how active combat commanders think and reason. After weighing all factors carefully, they must reach their own conclusions. This book is a valuable contribution to naval writing. It presents an intimate picture of the thoughts, reasonings, actions and reactions of a combat commander.

My refusal to bring the carriers into Tokyo Bay at the time of the surrender was not snap judgment. It was the result of cool and protracted discussion and reasoning. We did not trust the Japanese. The carriers could not operate in Tokyo Bay. We kept them at sea with their powerful air forces "just in case." As soon as we felt confident that the Japanese intended to behave, we brought the carriers in and gave all hands a chance to "looksee."

The writer of this preface is at variance with some of Ted Sherman's opinions and conclusions. That does not prevent my giving careful thought to his point of view, and in some cases being influenced thereby. These are minor points in the big, over-all picture. They add zest to the story.

WILLIAM F. HALSEY
Fleet Admiral, U. S .N., Retired

INTRODUCTION

The waging of the war in the Pacific Ocean was entirely separate from the fighting in Europe. The vast distances involved, the immense areas fought over by the armed forces, the diversity of the many islands embraced in the conflict, made it almost like a war on another planet. Primarily naval in character, the Pacific war was fought under such unprecedented conditions that new methods and tactics had to be evolved as the fighting proceeded. The development of air warfare produced a problem the United States Navy had never before faced save in fleet tactical exercises, and then only on a limited scale. The decision to give the war against Germany priority in man power and matériel put the Pacific forces under a terrific handicap at the start. For more than two years, they fought a tough and fanatical enemy with a minimum of supplies and men. During this period, the Navy had to stand mute when the nation asked, "Where is the Pacific Fleet?"

The story told in this book is one of daring, courage and hardships; of ruthless combat in the air, on the sea, under the sea, and on the ground, with much of the latter in steaming jungles. It is a story of long, slender supply lines, of toeholds on distant beachheads, of aircraft carriers ranging the wide spaces of the Pacific destroying the navy of Japan and her land-based air forces as well. Led by the planes of our carriers, which spearheaded the advance, amphibious expeditions landed to seize island after island, as air bases and staging stations for further conquests, until at last the war was brought to the door of Tokyo itself.

This story has never been told as one continuous narrative. It was covered by many able correspondents, but theirs were necessarily piecemeal accounts. Many dispatches the censors held back for months. Official reports released since the end of the war are tedious and stilted. Some are subject to question, at least as to certain details. Human nature being what it is, no commander turns in a report reflecting upon himself, if he can avoid it. My endeavor has been to eliminate inaccuracies and to tell the story as it really happened.

Since this book is primarily focused upon the carriers and the war at sea, the story of the ground actions has necessarily been abbreviated. The Navy had to get the troops to the beachheads, to land them and support them after they got ashore. While our strategy in the Pacific was principally naval, victory was won by the teamwork of all the Allies and all branches of the armed forces. At times, there were minor disagreements and friction between the Army and Navy. In general, cooperation between the two services, under the able direction of the Joint Chiefs of Staff, was of the highest order. The greatest single factor in our success was this magnificent teamwork.

Thus the war in the Pacific, as a whole, reflected great credit upon its participants. Countless deeds of individual valor, courage and devotion to duty will never be recorded. After some mistakes at the beginning, our top leaders proved themselves both steadfast and intelligent, executing sound plans and orders for the new kind of action required by the advent of air power and by the geography of the Pacific area. Our combat commanders were aggressive, keen and able. Nevertheless, they were human beings, and they would be the first to decry any attempt to portray them as supermen. I have attempted to show them as they were, in both their errors and their successes, as they played their roles in the greatest war in history.

Whereas this work features the story of our aircraft carriers in the Pacific, it is not only a personal memoir, but a study of the Pacific war as a whole. While I participated in many of the engagements, the story would be incomplete were it limited to only those actions. My sources have been, in addition to my own papers and observations, numerous official reports and documents of all kinds; other publications, both official and unofficial; and last but not least, many off-the-record conversations with officers and men of all ranks, especially as to those engagements at which I was not personally present.

In addition to presenting the facts accurately, I have sought to interpret them, to analyze the record, to give events their proper emphasis, and to fit them together so as to provide the reader with a clear and comprehensive picture of the war.

Those who have generously given valuable assistance in assembling the material, in preparing the maps and illustrations, and in giving criticism and suggestions, are too numerous to mention individually. I am deeply grateful to them all. I am indebted to Fleet Admiral William F. Halsey, my beloved boss during much of the fighting, and to McGraw-Hill Book Co., Inc., for permission to quote from his book, *Admiral Halsey's Story*.

This publication is in no sense official, nor is it in any way sponsored by the Navy Department. It was prepared after my retirement from active service, and the views and opinions expressed in it are my own. I hope it may contribute in some small measure to the American public's knowledge of the part played by our Navy, and especially our aircraft carriers, in the destruction of Japan's empire in the Pacific, and will dispose America to look well to its naval security in future years.

FREDERICK C. SHERMAN
Admiral, U.S.N., Retired

July 1, 1949

1

THE STAGE IS SET

"Air attack on Pearl Harbor. This is no drill. Repeat. This is no drill." This electrifying message was flashed to the bridge of my command, the aircraft carrier *Lexington*. It was 7:58 on Sunday morning, December 7, 1941. That clear morning found the *Lexington* 600 miles west of Pearl Harbor, as part of a task force proceeding toward Midway. Although we had been feverishly training and preparing for a possible outbreak of war against Japan, the actual event came as a shock. Few had dreamed that the attack would come at our mid-Pacific base only 2,000 miles from San Francisco and almost 3,500 miles from Tokyo.

Nevertheless, the possibility of such an attack had been recognized by naval aviators and by the Secretary of the Navy, the late Colonel Frank Knox. Ten months before, on January 24, 1941, the Secretary had sent a message to Secretary of War Henry L. Stimson, with copies to the Commander in Chief of the Pacific Fleet, Admiral J. O. Richardson, and the Commandant of the 14th Naval District (Hawaiian Area), Admiral C. C. Bloch. Knox's message read in part:

> The security of the U. S. Pacific Fleet while in Pearl Harbor, and of the Pearl Harbor Naval Base itself, has been under renewed study by the Navy Dept. and forces afloat for the past several weeks. This re-examination has been in part prompted by the increased gravity of the situation with respect to Japan, and by reports from abroad of successful bombing and torpedo plane attacks on ships while in bases. If war eventuates with Japan, it is believed

1

easily possible that hostilities would be initiated by surprise attack on the fleet or the Naval base at Pearl Harbor. . . .

In my opinion, the inherent possibilities of a major disaster to the fleet or Naval base warrant taking every step, as rapidly as can be done, that will increase the joint readiness of the Army and Navy to withstand a raid of the character mentioned above. The dangers envisaged, in the order of their importance and probability, are considered to be:
1. Air bombing attack.
2. Air torpedo attack. . . .

This letter was seen by Admiral Husband E. Kimmel shortly after he relieved Admiral Richardson as commander of the Pacific Fleet in February, 1941.

Few officers, however, at this time recognized aviation as the mighty weapon of destruction it later proved to be. The battleship, most nonaviation officers still believed, was the dominant factor in naval warfare. Our carrier aircraft had made many surprise attacks in practice exercises, on ships at sea as well as on the Pearl Harbor base, and even on the Panama Canal. But these were "dry runs." No actual bombs or torpedoes were dropped and no actual shots were fired by the defending antiaircraft guns. The battleship admirals doubted that planes could accomplish any serious damage in the face of real antiaircraft fire. They admitted that the Navy's aircraft were a valuable adjunct of the fleet, but considered their primary usefulness to be for scouting and observation. Planes were generously described by the top-echelon officers of that time, who claimed in fact to be "air-minded," as "the eyes of the fleet." They failed completely to realize that air power was destined to become the dominant weapon in fighting at sea, that the long rule of the battleship as the mistress of the seas was over, that in the coming war, planes would sink the mightiest battleships afloat without assistance from any surface ships, and that soon no vessels except submarines would dare to move during daylight in a combat area without air cover. A new era in naval warfare was about to dawn.

There were other warnings which should have indicated the possibility of a surprise air attack on the fleet at Pearl Harbor. Major General Frederick L. Martin and Rear Admiral Patrick N. L. Bellinger, commanders of the Army and Navy Air Forces on Oahu, had submitted on April 9, 1941, an estimate stating that Japan might make a fast carrier raid on Hawaii which, if successful, might prevent for a long period effective defensive action by our forces in the Western Pacific. They forecast that the most likely and dangerous form of raid would be an air attack launched from one or more carriers within 300 miles of their objective, and that there was a high probability that the onslaught might be delivered as a complete surprise. This estimate proved uncannily prophetic. General Martin and Admiral Bellinger could not have predicted the attack more accurately had they had the Japanese operation orders before them.

Why, then, were no precautions taken to guard against such an attack? The answer to this question is not simple. Admiral Kimmel, Admiral Bloch, and Major General Walter C. Short, the Army commander in Hawaii, were capable and conscientious officers who would not consciously omit any action necessary to safeguard the forces under their command. It can only be concluded that they failed to appreciate both the imminence of a carrier raid on Pearl Harbor and the tragic effectiveness such an attack would have against our fleet and planes.

This state of mind was not confined to those officers alone. It typified the thinking of a great many officers and was prevalent in the higher ranks in Washington. A "wolf, wolf" psychology had grown up due to repeated alarms, over many years, of imminent war with Japan. The Navy had had so many warnings that it had become dulled to the fact that the current "war scene" was the real thing.

When British carrier planes had attacked the Italian fleet at anchor at Taranto in November, 1940,* the question of the practicability of launching torpedoes from aircraft in the shallow waters of Pearl Harbor had been reexamined. Admiral H. R. Stark, Chief of Naval Operations, wrote to Admiral Kimmel: "It is considered that the relatively shallow depth of water limits the need for antitorpedo nets in Pearl Harbor. A minimum depth of 75 feet may be assumed necessary to successfully drop torpedoes from planes; 150 feet of water is

---

*For the full story of this devastating raid read *To War in a Stringbag* by Commander Charles Lamb. Another volume in THE BANTAM WAR BOOK SERIES.

desired." Stark's letter went on to say that the depth of water in which torpedoes were launched in the attack at Taranto was between 84 and 90 feet. The depth in Pearl Harbor was 30 feet or less, except in the channels, where it was 45 feet. This was thought to be too shallow for a torpedo plane attack on our fleet. Yet, an intelligence report circulated in the Navy Department in April, 1941, described tests in England in which torpedoes equipped with special devices had been launched in 42 feet of water, about the same depth as in Pearl Harbor. For Japan to use similar devices against our Hawaiian base was apparently not considered within the capabilities of the Oriental enemy.

Admiral Kimmel's standing order governing the security of fleet units in the Hawaiian area was furnished to me as Commanding Officer of the *Lexington*. This order was revised from time to time and the latest version was dated October 14, 1941. It assumed that no responsible foreign power would promote war by attacking our fleet or base, but that irresponsible and misguided nationals of such powers might attempt, among other things, sabotage, blocking of the harbor entrance, mine laying, or a "surprise attack on ships in Pearl Harbor." In the measures prescribed, no provision was made for ships or planes to search or patrol against a carrier raid. Most of the precautions directed were for the purpose of guarding against submarine attack. Our own carriers had made many practice air strikes against Hawaii and other bases without being detected until the planes were over the target. Yet nothing was done to guard against such a raid by the Japanese. Our high command was soon to become aware of the deadly effectiveness of an attack by carrier planes.

The events leading up to Pearl Harbor went back many years. In 1907, during the administration of Theodore Roosevelt, there had been a threat of war over immigration legislation which offended the Japanese. Again in 1913, the passage of laws against Japanese owning land in California had aroused war possibilities. Then came World War I, in which Japan was a somewhat unwelcome and uncertain member of the allied and associated powers through her alliance with Great Britain. She used this opportunity to clear the Germans out of Tsingtao and the Shantung Peninsula and to seize the German held islands in the Central Pacific. Her announced policy of "Asia for Asiatics," the so-called "Monroe Doctrine of the Orient," was a definite indication of her aggressive intentions in the Far East.

After World War I, the Washington Naval Disarmament Conference of 1922 gave further evidence of Japanese imperialism. Japan would agree to arms limitation only on terms giving her supremacy in naval strength in the Far East. She furthermore forced an agreement that British and American bases between Hawaii and Singapore would not be further strengthened. These demands were strong indications that Japan was preparing for eventual war even with the United States. Our acquiescence in them gave her the domination of the Asiatic area necessary in her vision of conquest.

In 1910 the Japanese had laid aside the pretense of their protectorate over Korea and bluntly annexed that country; in 1931 they moved into and occupied Manchuria. This latter act violated the Nine Power Treaty and other agreements covering the Pacific area, made at the 1922 Disarmament Conference. The League of Nations sent the Lytton Commission to investigate this aggression. Although that body condemned the Japanese action in drastic terms, the League was powerless to do anything about it. Mr. Stimson, then Secretary of State, sent Japan a series of sharp notes protesting her action and almost threatening war unless she withdrew from Manchuria. The policy of "nonrecognition" of these accessions of territory was adopted. Public opinion in the United States was unwilling to back up Stimson's notes with force and President Hoover declined to take any strong measures.

In 1937 the Japanese militarists created the "incident" at the Marco Polo Bridge just outside Peiping which opened formal hostilities between China and Japan. American support of China resulted in strained relations between Japan and the United States, and that same year Japanese aviators deliberately bombed one of our gunboats, the *Panay*, on the Yangtze River, sinking her with considerable loss of American lives. By promptly disavowing this act and paying an indemnity, the Japanese Government avoided hostilities at that time.

The start of World War II in Europe in 1939 found Japan officially neutral but openly sympathetic to the Axis. She became more aggressive in her attitude in the Orient and more intolerant of the rights of other nations with interests there. She considered that the European powers' preoccupation with Germany removed any restriction on her acts in that area. Although the United States was not involved in Europe, Japan believed that our reluctance to go to war would deter us from any military action to interfere with her conquest of China.

With the outbreak of the European war, a large part of our Pacific Fleet, known as the Hawaiian Detachment, was permanently stationed in the Hawaiian Islands and augmented from time to time by "maneuvers" of the entire Fleet in that area. This was a diplomatic reminder to Japan of the existence of our naval force, and a warning that we did not approve her policy of aggression. I became part of the Hawaiian Detachment as Commanding Officer of the *Lexington* in May, 1940.

Diplomatic notes regarding their conflicts in foreign policy had been exchanged between Japan and the United States almost continuously from 1931 to the autumn of 1941. Never had any semblance of a basis of agreement been reached. Internal forces in Japan, consisting of civilian businessmen on the one hand and militarists on the other, were battling for control of the government. The militarists were in the ascendancy and had achieved almost complete power. As American-Japanese relations approached a climax, peace advocates in Japan proposed a meeting between Prime Minister Konoye and President Roosevelt for a frank exchange of views. This proposal was turned down by our government on the grounds that it would be useless unless a preliminary agreement on principles had first been reached. Then, in November, 1941, Saburo Kurusu was sent to Washington to assist Ambassador Nomura in conversations with our State Department in what was apparently a last effort to prevent war. With the militarists in complete control, it is doubtful that the Japanese Government ever considered these talks as more than a smoke screen behind which the final arrangements and preparations for the projected war could be conducted.

As early as January, 1941, Ambassador Grew had reported to the State Department that there were reports from many sources, including one Japanese, that the military forces of Japan planned a surprise mass attack at Pearl Harbor in case of "trouble" with the United States. Most of our high naval officials discounted this report as fantastic.

In the meantime, in Washington, the War and Navy Departments had collaborated in breaking the Japanese diplomatic code. From the intercepted and decoded messages, a wealth of intelligence concerning the Japanese intentions was available. The information obtained, general in character, did not specifically mention Pearl Harbor, but indicated strongly that negotiations were approaching a crisis. As early as November 5, 1941, a message from Japan to the envoys in Washington was copied, which stated, "It is absolutely necessary that all arrangements for signing this agreement be completed by the 25th of this month." Again, on November 11, came the instructions: "The date set forth in my previous message is absolutely immovable under present conditions. It is a definite deadline and therefore it is essential that settlement be reached by about that time." On November 22, 1941, the deadline was extended until November 29 in the following terms: "If the signing can be completed by the 29th, we have decided to wait until that date; after that, things are automatically going to happen." There were other indications that the negotiations were to be a pretense to gain time for some definitely scheduled operation. The last part of a fourteen-part message was intercepted and decoded late on the night of December 6, approximately twelve hours before the attack on Pearl Harbor. It definitely broke off the conversations and stipulated that a note to this effect was to be delivered at 1:00 P.M., Washington time. The important significance of the time designated was that it was just after daylight in Honolulu. It was a clear indication that hostilities were to be initiated at that hour.

When this message was intercepted, the authorities in Washington took no immediate action by way of sending a special warning to the Army and Navy commanders in Hawaii. The next morning (Sunday), about 11:00 A.M., Washington time, the Army Chief of Staff, General George C. Marshall, attempted to send such a warning to Hawaii, but it was sent by ordinary commercial cable (although long-distance telephone was available) and was not received at Pearl Harbor until long after the attack was all over.

During the year, there had been several predictions that if the Japanese started hostilities it would be on a Saturday, a Sunday or a national holiday, because of our custom of knocking off work on these days. The Navy Department had sent a message to the District Commandants calling attention to this probability and directing that proper watches and precautions be kept in effect during such periods.

Other information received during November showed that the Japanese were recalling their merchant vessels and instructing their foreign representatives to destroy their codes. This intelligence was furnished to Admiral Kimmel at Pearl Harbor. But much additional information received in Washington from the intercepted and decoded dispatches was not sent him, on the erroneous assumption that it was also being decoded in Hawaii. On November 27, the Chief of Naval Operations sent to all Fleet Commanders a message stating in part, "This dispatch is to be considered a war warning. Negotiations with Japan looking toward stabilization of conditions in the Pacific have ceased and an aggressive move by Japan is expected in the next few days. . . . Japanese future action unpredictable but hostile actions possible at any moment."

On the same date, the War Department sent a similar message to Major General Walter C. Short, the Commanding General of the Hawaiian Department, but added: "If hostilities cannot be avoided, the United States desires that Japan commit the first overt act. This policy should not be construed as restricting you to a course of action that might jeopardize your defense. Prior to hostile Japanese action you are directed to undertake such reconnaissance and other measures as you deem necessary, but these measures should be carried out so as not to alarm civil population or disclose intent. Report measures taken." In reply, General Short reported, "Department alerted to prevent sabotage." This message received scant attention in Washington and no action was taken to improve or increase the state of alertness reported. General Marshall, before the Congressional Investigating Committee after the war, accepted full responsibility for this failure.

In Hawaii, the Fleet went about its routine business. The Army Air Force assembled its planes in neat, orderly rows in restricted parking areas to facilitate guarding against sabotage. No special warning was sent out to ships or units. The usual week-end leave and liberty were granted. As it happened, the carrier *Enterprise* had just delivered a squadron of Marine fighter planes to Wake Island and was now about 200 miles west of Pearl Harbor. The only other carrier in the area was the *Lexington,* with accompanying cruisers and destroyers, about 300 miles southeast of Midway and 600 miles west of Pearl Harbor. We were about to deliver a squadron of Marine dive bombers to Midway. We had received no special war warning prior to sailing from Hawaii. The rest of the Fleet, battleships, cruisers and destroyers, were moored in the crowded waters of Pearl Harbor. No special alert had been set, and some of the ships had their watertight doors and hatches open, getting ready for Sunday morning inspection. No air reconnaissance was out to detect the possible approach of Japanese carriers. The fleet commander believed in battleships as the dominant factor in war. He was little concerned over the striking power of airplanes.

Thus was the stage set for the tragedy of Pearl Harbor. The shock to the American people resulted in a postwar Congressional investigation to determine responsibility for the surprise which caught our defenses napping and resulted in such serious damage to our fleet and aircraft.

The majority report of the investigating committee exonerated the President, the Secretary of State, the Secretary of War, and the Secretary of the Navy from the charge of having "tricked, provoked, incited, cajoled, or coerced Japan into attacking this nation." It found that the disaster was due to the failure of the Army and Navy to institute measures designed to detect an approaching hostile force and to effect a state of readiness commensurate with the realization that war was at hand. Specifically, the Hawaiian Commands were charged with failure to integrate and mutually coordinate their facilities for defense or to employ the resources at their command in repelling the Japanese raiders. In addition, the War Plans Division of the War Department and the Intelligence and War Plans Divisions of the Navy Department were found responsible for having failed to evaluate properly the intercepted messages from Japan or to supply the Hawaiian commanders with this information.

The minority report of the investigating committee, in contradiction to the majority report, placed direct responsibility on the President and the Cabinet, as well as on the Army and Navy heads in Washington, but did not exonerate the commanders in Hawaii.

I have frequently been asked for my opinion as to the responsibility for the Pearl Harbor disaster. I was in command of the *Lexington* for eighteen months before the Pearl Harbor attack and for six months afterward. The carrier spent much of that time in Hawaiian waters. It is my opinion that the stationing of the Pacific Fleet at Pearl Harbor from 1940 on was a matter of diplomacy under the discretion of the President and the Secretary of State. If the elected head of the government desired to use the Navy for this purpose, the Naval Command, after pointing out the danger, must accept the decision as a matter of government policy beyond its authority to question. However, the Navy, fully realizing the hazards of the situation, was responsible for seeing that proper defense measures were taken, that the required alert was set, and that the Navy's guard was kept up at all times. These measures were not taken. The responsibility for this failure rests primarily both upon the Naval Command in Washington and upon the Commander in Chief of the Pacific Fleet in Hawaii.

Why were proper measures for security not taken? The reasons were mainly psychological. First, the top command of the Navy, both in Washington and in the Fleet, consisted of battleship-minded officers who little appreciated the terrible destructive power of a mass air attack. The second psychological cause was the series of immediate war alarms going back so many years that naval minds were dulled to indications that war was actually at hand. Had this been fully appreciated, there can be little doubt that Admiral Kimmel would have sent the available planes out on reconnaissance rather than giving priority to training, as he actually did. Even though Washington failed to give Kimmel valuable information to which he was entitled as Commander, the knowledge he had of the existing situation should have impelled him to take all available measures to insure the safety of the fleet under his command. That was his first duty and responsibility.

Had a proper air search been maintained in the northwest quadrant from Pearl Harbor in those crucial days before December 7, the attack might have been a disaster for the Japanese instead of for us. As fate decreed, the stage was now set. The Japanese carrier raiding force had approached to within 200 miles northwest of Pearl Harbor without being detected. The attack which shook America was about to begin.

2

PEARL HARBOR

Dawn appeared over Pearl Harbor on December 7, 1941, with its usual tropical brilliance, but there were few people awake to greet it. It was Sunday morning and the Fleet was "in," except, that is, for its carriers, some cruisers, and accompanying destroyers. The officers and men were looking forward to holiday routine. Normal port watches were set with a few additional but perfunctory skeleton crews at their posts around the antiaircraft guns. The stationing of these men was generally considered to be for the purpose of training rather than preparedness for an actual attack. Most of the ammunition was stowed down below in the magazines. Late reveille was sounded as was customary on a holiday. Breakfast was served to the crews at 7:30 A.M. and, for the officers in the wardrooms who could take theirs in more leisurely style, at any time up to 8:30. Preparations were being made on several ships for Sunday morning inspection at 9:30, and some of the forehanded men were opening up watertight doors and hatches for ready access. First call for colors was sounded at 7:55 as usual.

Just as the bugle notes were dying away, strange planes appeared high over Ford Island in the middle of Pearl Harbor. A few seconds later, others unexpectedly swung in from various directions. To the amazement of the lookouts, they bore the Rising Sun markings of Japan. Without hesitating, the planes suddenly began dropping bombs and torpedoes on the heavy ships alongside the docks and moorings. The watchers could hardly believe their eyes. Nine of the planes dived on the Naval Air Station on Ford Island and concentrated on the aircraft parked in orderly fashion on the concrete parking areas near the launching ramps, while the remainder directed their attention to the ships.

At the same time, 18 to 24 single-seater fighter planes

were hitting the Marine air base at Ewa, only two miles southwest of Ford Island. These planes swooped in from the northwest and strafed the field with machine guns from an altitude of only 20 to 25 feet above the ground. They threaded back and forth until all the Marine tactical aircraft had been set on fire or shot up and then turned their guns on Navy utility aircraft, planes under repair, and on the Marines themselves.

While the enemy planes were working over Ford Island and Ewa, another formation struck at the Naval Air Station on Kaneohe, on the other side of Oahu. These attackers flew low and viciously machine-gunned the seaplanes moored on the water. Burning and sinking PBY flying boats soon dotted the area. Following up swiftly, a squadron of light bombers appeared and commenced bombing and strafing the airfield and surrounding buildings. Hangers and planes were soon burning all along the water front. Although guns were immediately manned and the personnel performed many acts of

Japanese Zero

heroism, only six planes of the 33 at the station escaped destruction, and these were badly shot up. As a base from which seaplanes could be operated for searches or counterattacks, Kaneohe was completely useless.

In the meantime other planes were attacking the Army installations at Hickam Field, adjacent to Pearl Harbor, and at Wheeler Field in the central plains area. The Army aircraft parked close together on the aprons for greater security against sabotage, made easy targets. The Japanese burned hangars and planes by dive bombing, horizontal bombing and strafing. Practically the entire Army Air Force in the Hawaiian area was destroyed in the first few minutes. Of its major forces, only the Navy's two carriers, which were at sea, escaped the scourge.

While the airfields were receiving their holocaust of fire, 50 horizontal bombers, 40 torpedo planes, and 81 dive bombers were blasting ships of the fleet at their moorings in Pearl Harbor. Before considering this part of the action in detail, however, let us see how the Japanese task force was organized and how its approach was made.

The attack on Pearl Harbor was conceived by Admiral Isoroku Yamamoto, Commander in Chief of the Japanese Combined Fleet. Preliminary study of the operation was undertaken in January, 1941, and final details were worked out in September. The purpose of the raid was to immobilize our Pacific Fleet in order to gain time and ensure freedom of action for the Japanese invasions of the Philippines and the Netherlands East Indies. No landing in Hawaii was ever contemplated in connection with the attack. Designed solely as a hit-and-run affair, it depended for its success upon surprise. Invasion of this bastion of the mid-Pacific at this time was beyond Japanese capabilities.

The combat units of the Japanese carrier task force, commanded by Vice-Admiral Churichi Nagumo, consisted of six aircraft carriers, the *Akagi, Kaga, Soryu, Zuikaku, Hiryu* and *Shokaku;* the battleships *Hiei* and *Kirishima;* the heavy cruisers *Tone* and *Chikuma;* the light cruiser *Abukuma;* and nine destroyers. The Japanese high command expected to lose one-third of its forces in carrying out the raid. In order to avoid detection, it was considered necessary to keep the unit small, at the same time providing the most powerful air attack possible. The carrier air groups had been reinforced with highly trained pilots, and special training had brought them to the peak of efficiency. The ships were selected for their long cruising range and the commanders of all units especially chosen for efficiency.

In view of the shallow and restricted waters of Pearl Harbor, special stabilizers were attached to the Japanese torpedoes to prevent their taking deep initial dives. The torpedo was correctly estimated to be the most effective of all weapons for putting warships out of commission for a considerable period of time. Fighter planes were to be used to destroy American planes in the air and on the ground and prevent them from counterattacking.

A northern course passing between Midway and the Aleutians was selected for the approach of the task force, in preference to a central or southern course, since this involved the least danger of meeting commercial vessels or of detection by land-based search planes. If discovered prior to X-minus-two day (two days before the date scheduled for the attack), the force was to return to Japan. If discovered on X-minus-two day, the decision as to what action to take was left to the discretion of the force commander. If discovered on X-minus-one day, or on the morning of X day, the attack was to be pressed home regardless. If at any time during the approach to Pearl Harbor, the American fleet attempted to intercept the task force, the Japanese planned to counterattack. If our fleet was not found in Pearl Harbor, they were to search over a 300-mile radius around Oahu and attack if contact was made, but otherwise to withdraw.

The enemy expedition sortied from Hitokappu Bay in the Kuriles at 6 A.M. on November 26. On December 2, instructions were received to the effect that negotiations had failed and that December 8 (Tokyo date) was designated as X day. The task force refueled at sea from tankers on December 3. During its approach, forces in Japan carried on deceptive radio communications to indicate that the carrier fleet was still in home waters. The force arrived at the launching point 200 miles north of Oahu at the appointed hour, 6:00 A.M. on December 7 (Hawaii date).

The aircraft in the first attack unit took off immediately, as the carriers headed into the wind, and the second group 75 minutes later. They flew at 10,000 feet, above a dense cloud cover which became broken as they approached the islands from slightly east of north. Fleecy clouds were nestling on the tops of the mountains as the peaceful scenery of Pearl

Harbor and the island of Oahu was unveiled beneath them. With no hostile planes to interfere, they checked their positions and broke their cruising disposition to carry out their work of destruction.

Seven of our battleships were moored in a double line alongside Ford Island, in what was known as "Battleship Row." The eighth, the *Pennsylvania*, was in dry dock across the channel at the Naval Station. On the opposite side of Ford Island, the ex-battleship *Utah*, which had been converted to a target vessel, was lying next to the vacant berth of the absent *Lexington*. Adjacent to her were the cruiser *Raleigh* and the seaplane tender *Curtiss*. Nine cruisers, 20 destroyers, five submarines, and one hospital ship, plus supply and repair ships, tugs, and gunboats—86 combat and service ships in all—were scattered about the harbor. Five of the battleships were in p...·s, with the *Oklahoma* secured outboard of the *Maryland*, the *West Virginia* outboard of the *Tennessee* and the repair ship *Vestal* alongside the *Arizona*. The *California* was moored alone near the oil dock and the *Nevada* was moored singly astern of the *Arizona*.

As the enemy torpedo planes and dive bombers concentrated their attack on the heavy ships, all the outboard battleships were hit in the first blow by one or more torpedoes. Simultaneously, the dive bombers rained their deadly missiles on the big ships and one bomb went down one of the *Arizona*'s stacks. Suddenly her forward boilers, and then a magazine, blew sky-high. Oil from her fuel tanks ignited and covered the water around the ship with towering flames, endangering the near-by *Tennessee*. Dense black smoke from the burning ships billowed upward to the heavens.

Four torpedoes and two heavy bombs struck the *West Virginia*. She began to settle by the stern and a huge fire started in a forward fuel tank. The *California* was hit by two torpedoes and almost at once took an eight-degree list and began to settle. Fires sprang up intermittently throughout the ship, filling the spaces with noxious fumes and gases. She remained afloat for three days but continued to flood, until she finally rested on the bottom with only her superstructure exposed.

On the *Oklahoma*, there was no time to close all the open doors and hatches or to seal the compartments against damage. She was immediately hit by four torpedoes on her port side and at once began to list in that direction. She

slowly rolled clear over, with only the starboard side and a portion of the keel and starboard propeller shaft above the surface. She had rotated through an arc of approximately 150 degrees, and that portion of the ship which remained above the surface was supported by the vessel's masts, thrust into the mud of the harbor bottom. Most of the men below were trapped, but 32 were saved through holes cut into the bottom of the capsized hull. Some 400 bodies were still in the ship when it was refloated by salvage operations many months later.

The *Pennsylvania* was in dry dock at the Naval Station with the destroyers *Cassin* and *Downs*. Both destroyers were struck by bombs which detonated the magazines and started tremendous oil fires, but by flooding the dry-dock they were eventually extinguished. The *Cassin* had slipped her blocks and capsized against the *Downs* in a crazy mass of twisted metal. The picture was one of utter destruction, yet both the *Cassin* and *Downs* were eventually repaired and saw further service. The *Pennsylvania*, *Maryland* and *Tennessee*, though heavily damaged by bombs, remained afloat and shortly after the attack were able to proceed to the Pacific coast under their own power.

The *Nevada*, which had been moored alone, was the only battleship to get under way during the attack. Lieutenant Commander Francis J. Thomas was senior officer aboard at the beginning of the raid. He decided at once that he would have a better chance of saving the vessel if he could get her to the open sea where she could maneuver. Without waiting to make the usual preparations, the stately ship gathered way and started moving out. Clearing the burning *Arizona* and the repair ship *Vestal* by about 40 feet, she turned into the channel just as the Japanese dive bombers became aware of her intentions. This was a golden opportunity to sink the ship in the channel, thereby bottling up the entire harbor, and they turned their fury on her. Majestically steaming for the harbor entrance, the slowly moving battleship sent out a hail of antiaircraft fire as bomb after bomb exploded in the water within a few hundred feet of her. Hit by six bombs, which caused extensive flooding, she also received severe damage from strafing. Her injuries forced her to go aground near the dry dock in which the *Pennsylvania* rested, and she gradually settled, taking in water through gaping holes in her side. Afterward she was moved by tugs and grounded across from Hospital Point to avoid blocking the channel.

The destroyer *Shaw* was in Floating Dry Dock No. 2 in the Navy Yard. Three bombs struck this destroyer, ruptured an oil-storage tank and blasted flaming oil throughout the forward part of the ship. One of the magazines went up with a roar and the ship broke in two just ahead of No. 1 stack. Marvelous to relate, this destroyer later returned to the Pacific coast under her own power and was fitted with a new bow.

In addition to the aircraft, from 10 to 12 Japanese I-class submarines participated in the attack. Five carried midget submarines, handled by two-man crews, on deck abaft their conning towers. Some of them had preceded the enemy carrier task force as lookouts and others had sailed direct from Japan to Hawaii. The use of the midgets was admittedly an experiment, but it was thought they would be of some use to the task force and might themselves make effective torpedo attacks. One was able to report by radio the results of the air attack as observed on the night of the 7th. Another reported attacking one or more vessels inside Pearl Harbor. American forces destroyed and subsequently raised one midget in the harbor. Another was sunk near the entrance. A third ran aground on the far side of the island, near Bellows Field, and the ensign in command was captured. The fate of the remaining two tiny submarines is unknown.

Of the large submarines, one was lost, time and place unknown. Another was damaged by depth charges near the entrance to Pearl Harbor, but escaped and returned to its base. The others operated in the vicinity of Hawaii until January, then proceeded to the west coast of the United States.

Totally unprepared for the attack, our ships in Pearl Harbor had suffered tremendous damage. Of the eight battleships present, the *Arizona, California, West Virginia* and *Oklahoma* were sunk; the *Nevada* was aground, heavily damaged; and the *Maryland, Pennsylvania* and *Tennessee* were hurt, though less seriously. The cruisers *Helena, Honolulu* and *Raleigh* were damaged, as were the destroyers *Shaw, Cassin* and *Downs.* Of the auxiliaries, the minelayer *Oglala* and the ex-battleship *Utah* capsized and sank. The repair ship *Vestal* and the seaplane tender *Curtiss* were also hit. The battleship fleet, considered by so many the backbone of the

Navy, in little over an hour had been rendered incapable of action for many months. Eventually all ships except the *Arizona* and *Oklahoma* were salvaged and reconditioned for service, but at great cost in critical labor and materials. It is questionable whether this expense was justified in a time of grave man-power and steel shortage, for subsequent events were to reveal the dominance of aircraft and carriers in the new naval warfare.

The American carrier *Enterprise*, about 200 miles west of Oahu at the time of the raid, as a routine matter had launched eight scout bombers at dawn to scout ahead and then to land at Ewa Airfield on Oahu. As they approached the island, they sighted bursting antiaircraft shells and to their amazement ran into Japanese planes. In furious dog-fights with the faster and more maneuverable enemy fighters, five of the *Enterprise* planes were shot down by the enemy aircraft and by our own antiaircraft guns. Many of the pilots mistook the enemy for friendly planes and realized their hostile character only when they received a stream of machine-gun bullets from a supposed friend.

The *Enterprise* remained at sea until the next day conducting a fruitless search for the enemy fleet. Late in the afternoon a group of six fighters, which had been out on this quest, flew in to land at Ford Island after dark. In spite of notification to all ships that friendly planes were coming in, itchy trigger fingers on the damaged battleship *Pennsylvania* opened fire on them as they passed overhead to approach the landing circle. Four of them were shot down in flames by our own guns before the tragic error could be corrected.

The *Lexington*, approximately 400 miles southeast of Midway as part of a task force under command of Rear Admiral John H. Newton, was approaching the designated launching point for the Midway-bound planes. When we received the flash, "Air attack on Pearl Harbor," General Quarters was immediately set clanging on all ships, and battle stations were manned as all watertight doors and hatches were closed. Admiral Newton ordered the task force to reverse course and we headed back for Pearl Harbor, our mission of delivering the Marine planes to Midway laid aside in the excitement of the moment.

Air searches were immediately launched from the *Lexington* and the remaining planes were ready on deck for an instant attack if the enemy carriers were located. Later a dispatch addressed to our task force directed: "Intercept and destroy enemy. Believed retreating on a course between Pearl and Jaluit. Intercept and destroy." Upon receipt of this message, we headed southward and increased speed. The estimated enemy course between Pearl Harbor and Jaluit, in the Marshall Islands, was well to the south of our location.

This message deprived us of any chance of intercepting the enemy striking force, for the Japanese carriers were actually at the time retreating to the northwest. The *Lexington*, being west of Pearl Harbor, was in an ideal position for intercepting the enemy whether north or south of Oahu. Had we maintained our central position until the direction of the Japanese withdrawal was known, we could certainly have intercepted them. Furthermore, with actual hostilities upon us, the completion of the delivery of the planes to Midway was more important than before. As it was, we carried these planes around with us as excess baggage during our unsuccessful search for the Japanese carriers, and eventually returned them to Pearl Harbor. They could have been launched for the flight to Midway at any time after the news of the attack on Pearl Harbor was received.

Admiral Halsey told me later that he was responsible for the decision to send us south to look for the enemy, and that it was due to conflicting and confusing messages which were afterward attributed to enemy sources. Halsey believed this diversion might have been just as well, as he was concerned as to what would have happened to the lone *Lexington* had we contacted the six Japanese carriers.

When the attack on Pearl Harbor was over, shortly after 9:20 A.M., and the last Japanese planes had departed, the Navy and Marine Corps had suffered a total of 2,835 casualties, including 2,086 officers and men killed or fatally wounded. Army casualties amounted to 600, of whom 194 were killed and 364 wounded. In addition to the damage to ships and hangars, the Navy had 92 planes destroyed and 31 damaged, and the Army lost 96 planes. The Japanese lost only 29 planes, in addition to one fleet submarine and five midget submarines. The difference in losses indicates the gravity of what has been called the greatest naval disaster in our nation's history.

From a purely military standpoint, however, this attack was not the disaster it has been represented to be. Our naval high command at that time little realized that control of the sea was dependent on the air power of carriers and not upon the obsolete battleships which were put out of action at Pearl Harbor. Nothing could have impressed this lesson upon them more forcefully than this carrier raid on our ships in their defended base.

Only by the fortunes of war were our carriers out at sea when the attack came in. Had the *Enterprise* and the *Lexington* been at their regular berths there is little doubt that they too would have been totally destroyed. As it was, the portion of our sea power which was put out of action was the part that was already obsolete in the new era of fighting.

What rendered the Japanese carrier attack on Pearl Harbor a justifiable risk, from the enemy viewpoint, was the fact that at the opening of the war they had 10 carriers to our seven, of which we had only three in the Pacific. This disparity was the main factor in forcing us to take the defensive in the early part of the war, and not the loss of our battleships, as popularly believed.

Accurate information as to the direction of approach and retirement of the enemy planes was available through radar detection. Had it been utilized, both the *Enterprise* and the *Lexington* could have been directed to attack the enemy carriers. But our fighting forces were not yet indoctrinated in obtaining and evaluating such information. As it was, the efforts of the carriers were dissipated in futile searches to the southward and to the eastward.

Thus the war came to us. The end was almost four years away. It was destined to take us far afield, into little-known parts of the Pacific, and to demonstrate new methods of naval warfare of which the world had never dreamed.

3

DEFEAT, RETREAT AND FRUSTRATION

With the destruction at Pearl Harbor of the main strength of our battleship fleet, the Navy's plans for fighting a war against Japan became unworkable. Strategy against Japan in the Pacific had been discussed by the Navy high command for many years, and war plans had been frequently revised. Never had such planning considered the possibility of the loss of so large a percentage of our battleships as had occurred in the initial blow.

In annual war games at the Naval War College at Newport, the "American" and "Japanese" fleets had been pitted against each other. In 1940, I had commanded the "Japanese" fleet. For years, there had been two schools of thought on the proper conduct of a Pacific campaign. One school argued for a quick dash by our fleet across the Pacific to relieve Manila or seize a suitable base in that vicinity as swiftly as possible, leaving Japanese bases in the Marshalls, Marianas and Carolines to be taken later. Under this plan, it was essential that the fleet leave Hawaii within thirty days after the start of hostilities. General MacArthur estimated that he could hold the fortress of Corregidor, in Manila Bay, for sixty days, but the fleet must arrive within that time to lift the siege. This plan assumed that without control of the sea overseas conquest was impossible, and that such control depended upon battleships.

The other school advocated the so-called "step-by-step" method. Under this plan, the fleet, with its Marine force, first advanced to the Marshall Islands, established a base there, and then by similar steps advanced across the Pacific to Manila. Under this scheme, the defenses of the Philippines were to be strengthened to enable Corregidor to hold out for six months or more, until the fleet should arrive with its rear communications secured by the occupation of a system of bases and the neutralization or capture of those held by the enemy.

B-17

The quick-dash method, daring in conception, staked everything on an early, decisive naval battle between the two fleets, for we believed the Japanese would not permit us to reach Manila without a fight. In the battles on the game board, our fleet was almost universally successful in this theoretical naval action, although it always suffered serious losses in achieving victory. These results were attained because the relative fighting strength of the two forces was supposed to rest on their gun power, in which feature our battleship strength was much superior to that of the Japanese. Air power was not recognized as a decisive factor. Airplanes were considered useful primarily for scouting and observation.

The "step-by-step" plan, less hazardous than the quick dash, kept the fleet always within range of an advanced operating base as it moved across the Pacific. It had the virtue of not risking everything in one battle far from our supporting bases. This plan simplified the logistic problem, since the fleet need not be accompanied at all times by its supply train.

The war plan currently in effect in 1941 was essentially a variation of the "step-by-step" method. We were building up our defensive forces in the Philippines with additional troops and more fighters, bombers and patrol planes. Thus, it was hoped, Corregidor could hold out at least six months, and perhaps indefinitely. It was estimated that the reinforcing would be completed by February, 1942. This was one reason why the military and naval leaders had urged the President and State Department to delay a showdown with Japan until we were more nearly ready.

The war plan further provided that our fleet in Hawaiian waters would make harassing raids on Japanese bases in the Marshalls to relieve enemy pressure on Singapore and the Dutch East Indies until the Navy was strong enough to seize fleet bases in the Marshalls area.

The Pearl Harbor attack knocked these plans into a cocked hat. A defensive war in the Pacific was forced upon us, whether we wished it or not. When the stab in the back came, we had only three aircraft carriers in the Pacific to oppose Japan's ten. Counting those in the Atlantic, we had a total of only seven. On the expiration of the Disarmament Treaties in 1936, we had shortsightedly allowed the Japanese to outbuild us and achieve superiority in this paramount class of warships.

At Manila, far to the westward of Pearl Harbor, it was two in the morning of December 8 (East Longitude date), when the war opened in Hawaii. Lieutenant General Lewis H. Brereton, Commanding General of the Far Eastern Air Force, writes (*The Brereton Diaries*) that he was awakened by a telephone call from General Richard K. Sutherland, General MacArthur's Chief of Staff, informing him that the Japanese had bombed Pearl Harbor and a state of war existed.

Brereton ordered his air units readied for action. Expecting a Japanese air attack any time after dawn, he asked permission to bomb Formosa immediately with all available B-17's. Sutherland said he would obtain MacArthur's authority for the attack. For some reason, still unexplained, MacArthur's permission was not received until about 10:00 A.M.

While awaiting it, many of the planes were sent out on scouting missions. When the permission finally came through, they were recalled for loading with bombs, and reservicing. They were still on the ground when the enemy attack came in about noon. MacArthur stated after the war that he had no recollection of receiving Brereton's request and that his headquarters had no record of it. Whatever the circumstances, the report was current in Navy circles that the request had been made but that MacArthur had not approved it because he had not been officially notified of the Pearl Harbor attack or of the existence of a state of war.

Seversky P-35

A heavy fog in Formosa, however, delayed the Japanese attack, and not until 10:05 could planes of the 21st and 23rd naval air flotillas be launched. Upon arrival over their targets, the enemy pilots were astonished to find our heavy bombers and most of our fighters still on the ground. The highly trained Japanese delivered an effective 90-minute assault on all aircraft and facilities in the Manila area, destroying half of the heavy bombers and one-third of the fighters of the U.S. Far Eastern Air Force, and heavily damaging many more. American planes were afire all over Clark Field, in a welter of flames and black smoke. Only 17 B-17's, 15 P-35's and 55 P-40's remained available for combat after the tragic day.

To the eastward, in the Gulf of Davao, was part of Navy Patrol Wing Ten with its tender, the converted destroyer *Preston*, its planes patrolling the eastern approaches to the Celebes Sea. At the southeastern tip of Palawan Island, four light planes based on the *Heron* scouted the western approaches. The planes left at Manila searched to the westward as far as the coast of Indo-China. At 7:10 A.M. on December 8, the *Preston* reported an attack by Japanese planes from their base on Palau Island, to the eastward. Two of our patrol planes, moored on the water, were sunk by strafing. The Navy's war in the Philippines had begun.

Somewhat later, four Japanese destroyers entered the Gulf of Davao. The *Preston* remained hidden in a small cove and slipped out to sea after the enemy ships had passed out of sight. Patrol Wing Ten now began a hunted existence, trying to keep one step ahead of the numerically superior enemy. Its planes were scattered in lakes, swamps and coves, wherever facilities were available. Taking advantage of hideout areas and gasoline supplies previously planted throughout the Philippines, they searched the seas to provide information for our Asiatic Fleet as it retired southward in accordance with the war plan.

On December 10, the Japanese bombed and practically wiped out the Navy Yard at Cavite, damaging the submarine *Sea Lion* and the destroyer *Peary*, which were there under repair. The *Sea Lion* was later destroyed by our own forces to prevent its capture. On the same date, enemy troops landed at Aparri and Vigan in northern Luzon. Throughout the day, our weakened Army Air Forces made ineffectual attempts to bomb and strafe the Japanese transports and landing barges.

Meanwhile the enemy, enjoying almost complete control of the skies, maintained their attacks on our airfields.

In addition, December 10 saw the end of the British battleship *Prince of Wales* and the battle cruiser *Repulse*, which had been sent out to strengthen British naval forces in the Orient. The *Prince of Wales* was a super-modern battleship of 35,000 tons displacement, completed in 1940. Heavily armored, she carried ten 14-inch guns in her turrets, was capable of a speed of more than 30 knots and fairly bristled with antiaircraft guns. The *Repulse*, built during World War I, had been modernized in 1936. She carried six 15-inch guns in her main battery and heavy AA armament. The two battleships arrived at Singapore on December 2 and passed majestically up the channel to the naval base. There was no secrecy. One of the reasons for their presence was to bluff the Japanese from further advances.

Three days after their arrival, Vice-Admiral Sir Tom Phillips, British Naval Commander in Chief in the Far East, flew to Manila for a conference with Admiral Thomas C. Hart, our Asiatic Commander in Chief. Phillips reported that the carrier *Ark Royal*, assigned to his forces, had been sunk in the Mediterranean, and that the *Indomitable*, which was to have replaced her, had gone aground in the West Indies. The battleships *Revenge* and *Royal Sovereign*, intended for his command, had also not arrived. But these deficiencies did not disturb the Royal Navy's confidence that it could handle the situation. Estimates of Japanese capabilities at that time were modest. Shortly after Phillips' return to his headquarters at Singapore, the Pearl Harbor raid was a matter of history. Manila was being attacked and Japanese forces were reported moving toward the Malay Peninsula.

At dusk on December 8, the British battle squadron left Singapore for a sweep northward to attack Japanese convoys reported to be landing troops on the north coast of Malaya. The force consisted of the *Prince of Wales*, the *Repulse*, and the destroyers *Electra*, *Vampire*, *Tenedos* and *Express*. The weather on the 9th was overcast, and Phillips disdained to call on the shore-based planes at Singapore for air cover. Japanese submarines sighted the British ships during the afternoon and flashed their position, course and speed to the 22nd Naval Flotilla at Saïgon, which had been expecting the report. Consisting of 117 torpedo planes and bombers manned by well-trained pilots, the flotilla's mission was to protect the transports against British interference.

December 10 broke fair and clear over the British ships, an ideal day for air attack. The clouds had gone and the blue tropical sea danced with the sun's reflections. The British ships plowed along with an appearance of invulnerability. It was 11:10 in the morning when nine Japanese bombers approached from ahead, flying at 12,000 feet. Without swerving, they aimed their bombs at the two great warships below. Phillips radioed his base for fighter-plane cover, but it was too late. No fighters ever arrived. The *Repulse* received a bomb hit in the first salvo which started a fire below decks. Although a tremendous volume of projectiles from the British antiaircraft guns poured into the sky, the attacking planes were little affected.

Just behind the bombers came a flock of torpedo planes which concentrated on the *Prince of Wales*. A torpedo struck her near the stern, seriously damaging her steering gear.

Half an hour later a second wave of torpedo planes appeared. Maneuvering desperately, the *Repulse* avoided 19 torpedoes, but the crippled *Prince of Wales*, hampered by her injury, took another broadside hit. Water poured into her hull and she listed heavily. Soon another torpedo smashed her stern so completely that she was unmaneuverable.

The sky seemed full of enemy aircraft. The torpedo planes brazenly maneuvered just out of gun range, at an altitude of about 1,000 feet, taking position on all four quarters of the doomed ships. Then they came roaring straight in, dropping to only 300 feet above the water and releasing their torpedoes as close as 300 yards from their targets. Although antiaircraft bursts were all around them, they dropped their missiles, banked steeply, and were soon out of range. Another flight of nine more bombers came in at 10,000 feet. The *Prince of Wales* was now dead in the water and took additional hits. Within a few minutes, she heeled over and capsized. The rounded underbody reared above the surface, then the great hull slowly sank from sight.

About the same time the *Repulse* was hit by torpedoes on both sides. She took a heavy list. The ship was still turning sluggishly when over the loudspeakers came the order "Abandon ship! God be with you." With men pouring down her side, the stern of the *Repulse* rose vertically and then was swallowed by the sea. Crew members jumped from the masts and superstructure, others slid down the sloping side. Some jumped astern, where the propellers were still turning over, to be caught in the threshing blades.

Destroyers rescued many survivors from the water, but of a total complement in the two ships of 170 officers and 2,755 men, 40 officers and 555 men were lost. Admiral Sir Tom Phillips was among them.

The *Prince of Wales* and the *Repulse* were the first capital ships in World War II to be sunk by airpower alone while under way and in a state of readiness at sea. It was apparent that not even heavily armored battleships were immune from the deadly power of aircraft.

While this battle was going on far to the south, the situation in Manila was rapidly worsening. On December 26, Admiral Hart left by submarine to shift his headquarters to Soerabaja, arriving there about January 1. Another submarine evacuated President Manuel Quezon and some of his entourage to the southern Philippines, which he later left by P-T boat for Australia, arriving there with his family on March 27. High Commissioner Francis B. Sayre also left by submarine. The ground forces by this time had been withdrawn to the Bataan Peninsula and Corregidor. On March 11, General MacArthur, on orders from President Roosevelt, left Manila Bay by P-T boat for Mindanao and from there was flown to Australia, where he arrived on March 17.

Although Admiral Hart had been named Commander of the American, Dutch and British naval forces, the theater lacked a supreme commander with authority over all ground, air and sea components. The naval units of different nationalities had never trained together. They had different conceptions of naval tactics, and in the case of the Dutch, the language difficulty caused additional trouble.

When war came, the submarines of our Asiatic Fleet were operating in defense of the Philippines. A number were on patrol north of Luzon. Eight were in reserve at Manila, ready to attack enemy ships whenever located. But this was a confusing and disillusioning period for our submarines. Allied air reconnaissance was practically nil and the performance of our torpedoes was disappointing. The "tin fish" ran ten feet deeper than set. Often they exploded prematurely, or, when they did hit the target, failed to explode. Moreover, their explosive force was too weak to cause much damage.

The submarine *Stingray*, off northern Luzon, made the

contact report on December 21 which first indicated that enemy invading forces were entering Lingayen Gulf. A number of submarines were ordered to penetrate the gulf and attack the enemy transports. Only the S-38, under Lieutenant W. G. Chappell, was able to get inside and stay long enough in the shallow waters to inflict damage. Shortly after dawn on December 22, she fired four torpedoes at four different targets, all of which missed. While she was submerged to reload, an enemy destroyer dropped three depth

PT Boat

charges close aboard. About an hour and a half later, she came to periscope depth and fired two more torpedoes which sank the loaded transport *Hayo Maru*. Harried by depth charges and aerial bombs, the S-38 finally escaped from the gulf three days later and returned, damaged, to Manila.

Save for the submarines and Lieutenant John D. Bulkeley's fast, daring P-T boats, our naval vessels in Philippine waters had all withdrawn southward. Hong Kong fell on Christmas Day. Japanese expeditions from Davao and Jolo took Tarakan,

in Borneo, and Menado, in the Celebes, on January 11. Efforts by our submarines to frustrate these landings failed largely for lack of air reconnaissance. On the Malay Peninsula, the Japanese, in tanks, in planes and on bicycles, were swinging toward Singapore, which surrendered on February 15. Burma was being overrun, and on February 24 the garrison withdrew from Rangoon. The Japanese spearhead threatened, unless quickly stopped, to reach Australia.

On January 10, General Sir Archibald Wavell arrived at Soerabaja and assumed supreme command of all forces in that theater. His command was known as ABDACOM (American-British-Dutch-Australian Command). Admiral Hart became subordinate to Wavell as Commander of the Allied Naval Forces, comprising cruisers, destroyers and submarines. Unity of command over the flotilla was only nominal. Each nation used its ships independently for escorting troop transports or merchant shipping, disregarding the necessity of concentrating the Allied forces to halt the Japanese advance.

On the night of January 24, 1942, the cruisers *Boise* and *Marblehead*, under Rear Admiral W. A. Glassford, were ordered to support Destroyer Division 59, under Commander Paul H. Talbot and comprising the *John D. Ford*, *Pope*, *Parrott* and *Paul Jones*, in a night torpedo attack on a large Japanese convoy heading southward toward Balikpapan. Thus occurred the Battle of Makassar Straits.

Glassford's flagship, the *Boise*, struck an uncharted pinnacle rock on the way north and had to turn back. She managed to get to a south Java port and thence to India for repairs and finally back to the United States. Glassford transferred to the *Marblehead* but a turbine casualty slowed her to 15 knots, insufficient for accompanying a high-speed destroyer attack. The destroyers under Talbot, a cool, determined and capable officer, went on by themselves. Dutch planes and Patrol Wing Ten had been reporting the movements of the Japanese convoy. It contained four cruisers, 13 destroyers, and at least five armed transports.

At 25 knots, later increased to 27, Talbot set a course for the coast of Borneo. Although their engines badly needed overhaul, the old destroyers somehow maintained the speed. They made contact with the enemy formation off Balikpapan at 2:45 in the morning.

Aided by the light of gigantic fires on shore, where the Dutch were burning everything possible to deny it to the

Japanese, the little formation of four destroyers suddenly appeared in the midst of the enemy ships. Wisely limiting their fire to torpedoes until those weapons were expended, the American attackers had the Japanese in complete confusion. At first they thought they were undergoing a submarine attack. They mistook the destroyers for units of their own force. Four times the American vessels threaded through the convoy, firing torpedoes on both sides at transports loaded with troops. The night was ablaze with burning ships and the water was covered with swimming Japanese and lifeboats. After all torpedoes were expended, gunfire was opened on targets looming out of the dark at ranges of 500 to 1,500 yards, using the illumination of the burning vessels. Talbot's control and direction of our ships were excellent. Frantically the Japanese began returning the fire but in the confusion, in many instances, fired on their own vessels. Just before dawn, our four daring destroyers withdrew to the south without any pursuit by the enemy.

These ships had performed the almost incredible feat of steaming back and forth through a vastly superior enemy force for more than an hour. They had achieved a clear-cut victory over the Japanese, the first in the whole campaign. Their own damage was negligible. Eenmy records after the war established the Japanese losses as four transports sunk; no information was found as to those damaged. It was estimated that enemy casualties ran into the thousands.

Attempting to repeat the Balikpapan success, a mixed force of four cruisers and eight destroyers on February 3 were discovered by Japanese aircraft before they could reach striking position. Heavily attacked by air the following day, the *Marblehead* was permanently disabled, the heavy cruiser *Houston* suffered major damage and the Dutch cruiser *De Ruyter* was temporarily put out of action. It was necessary to cancel the operation. This force was under command of Rear Admiral Karel W. F. H. Doorman of Holland.

On a chance, six submarines were stationed in Makassar Straits and three off Ambon, south of Molukka Passage, along the line of the enemy's next probable thrust. Although one of them managed to get in an attack, no confirmed sinking could be established. Then the submarines were stationed off Kema, where the enemy were next expected. Only the S-37 was in the path of the subsequent invasion move toward Makassar City. Enemy records confirmed that she sank the 1,500-ton destroyer *Natsuhio* on February 8th. She was the first American submarine in history to sink an enemy destroyer.

The Japanese advance continued relentlessly at widely dispersed points. They were extending their holdings on Borneo and had landed at Rabaul in New Britain, Kavieng in New Ireland, and Kendari and Staring Bay on the southeast coast of Celebes. Early in February, 1942, they occupied Ceram and Amboina. From the new bases, enemy planes began intensive bombing of Soerabaja and other Java points, as well as Timor, within bombing range of the Australian mainland. With Soerabaja no longer tenable as a naval base, American naval headquarters was transferred to Tjilatjap on the south coast of Java. The enemy controlled all the northern approaches to the Dutch East Indies.

In mid-February, Admiral Hart returned to the United States and command of the Allied naval forces passed to Vice-Admiral Conrad E. L. Helfrich of the Royal Netherlands Navy. Admiral King states in his report that the shift was by previous agreement with the Dutch. On February 24, General Wavell left Java on a British motor sloop to set up new headquarters in India, turning over the Allied forces in Java to Dutch commanders. It was evident that the fall of Java was not far off.

After the air action of February 4, the damaged *Houston* and *Marblehead* returned to Tjilatjap, where the Dutch before hostilities had wisely placed a small floating drydock. The *Houston* was patched up with railroad rails so that she could fight again. Her commander, Captain Alfred H. Rooks, reported that although one turret had been put permanently out of action, she was "still quite a fighting ship." The *Marblehead* could not be made entirely watertight nor could her damaged rudder be made operable. Air attack could be expected at any time, and the *Marblehead* steamed out in a barely seaworthy condition. She eventually reached the United States after a voyage that was a heroic struggle of men against the sea.

On February 15 the Japanese occupied Palembang, on Sumatra, to threaten Java from the west. At Batavia, where he had taken the Dutch ships after the air battle on the 4th, Admiral Doorman had the cruisers *Java* and *DeRuyter* and the smaller *Tromp*. These ships had been reinforced by the British heavy cruiser *Exeter* and the Australian light cruiser *Hobart*. On February 14 this force, which also contained six

American, three Dutch and several British destroyers, sailed to attack a Japanese convoy in Bangka Strait, east of southern Sumatra. On the way the Dutch destroyer *Van Ghent* ran fast aground and was lost. The rest of the force were again driven off by air attacks, but managed to return to their base without suffering actual damage.

A trickle of supplies was now beginning to come through from Australia. A fast troop convoy left Darwin on February 15 to reinforce the garrison on Timor, a ferry station for fighter planes on their way to Java. It was escorted by the *Houston* and the destroyer *Peary*. On the 16th, the familiar story of air attack was repeated. By radical maneuvering and dispersal, the convoy avoided any direct hits but all four transports sustained leaks from near misses and strafing. The convoy returned to Darwin. Next day the *Houston* headed west to rejoin Doorman's striking force and thus avoided the disaster which was about to fall on the northern Australia base. The *Peary*, delayed by fueling operations, remained in the harbor.

On February 19 a large group of Japanese carrier planes suddenly appeared over Darwin. The same carrier striking force which had attacked Pearl Harbor was now operating from Staring Bay in Celebes. The docks were the first targets and the British ships *Zealandia* and *Neptuna*, unloading ammunition, were hit and exploded violently. Fires started over a wide area. Meeting no opposition, the enemy pilots first concentrated on the transports and naval ships, then took the merchant vessels in succession. For more than two hours they kept up amazingly accurate attacks, until nothing was left. At the airfield, two hangars were burned, grounded planes destroyed and runways cratered. The destroyer *Peary* was hit five times, one bomb setting off an ammunition magazine and another exploding in an engine room. Although her guns continued to fire until the attack was over, she sank at one o'clock, stern first. Only one officer and 52 men of her crew survived.

At dawn on February 18, the Japanese landed on the southern shore of Bali, just east of Java. The island contained an airfield and controlled the exit from the Java Sea at that point. Learning of the assemblage of transports in Badoeng Strait, east of Bali, Admiral Doorman decided to attack on the night of the 19th. This was the action known as the Battle of Badoeng Strait. An attack was organized in three waves, the first consisting of the Dutch cruisers *De Ruyter* and *Java*, the modern Dutch destroyer *Piet Hein*, and the two old American destroyers *Pope* and *Ford*. The second wave included the Dutch cruiser *Tromp* and the American destroyers *Stewart*, *Parrott*, *Edwards* and *Pillsbury*. The third attack was to be made by Dutch destroyers.

The first wave alerted the Japanese when the leading *De Ruyter* turned her searchlights on an enemy ship in the darkness. In the succeeding melee, the *Java* was hit and the destroyers, bringing up the rear, ran into an avalanche of fire. The *Piet Hein* was sunk but the *Ford* and the *Pope* fired torpedoes at an enemy cruiser on which they claimed hits. Under the murderous fire, they retired to the southeast. The *De Ruyter* and *Java* continued on through the strait into the Java Sea. Gun flashes and explosions among the Japanese ships indicated that they were firing on each other in the confusion.

About two and a half hours later, the second wave went in, destroyers leading. Our ships were silhouetted against the starlit sky while the Japs were obscured against the land. All hell broke loose as the small ships and the *Tromp* charged into the maze of vessels, their searchlights stabbing the night and tracers and flashes of gunfire interlacing the darkness around them. Firing their torpedoes as they made their way through the strait, the *Tromp* and *Stewart* were hit and so badly damaged that they could not be repaired before the invasion of Java, and rendered no further service. The third wave of Dutch destroyers later made their run through the narrow passage. The United States Strategic Bombing Survey stated after the war that the Japanese lost no combat ships in this battle, but had one destroyer damaged. There were no transport losses.

About this time the converted carrier *Langley* and the British aircraft tender *Seawitch* arrived in Australia bound for Ceylon, and carrying fighter planes with their flight crews embarked. Admiral Helfrich obtained their diversion to Java to bolster his defense. On February 27 the *Langley* was met by the American destroyers *Whipple* and *Edsall*, some 100 miles south of Tjilatjap, for escort into that port. Japanese carrier planes found them. Diving out of the sky, the bombers landed a salvo of five direct hits and three damaging near misses on the carrier. Flaming from many fires, with her parked aircraft burning and her water mains ruptured, the

Langley was finally abandoned about four hours later and sunk by gunfire from the *Whipple*. Her complement, except 11 who were missing, were rescued by the *Whipple* and *Edsall*.

Badly neded in Java, the destroyers transferred the *Langley*'s survivors to the Navy tanker *Pecos* in the lee of Christmas Island, not far westward, on February 29. The destroyers then headed back for Java and the *Pecos* started without escort for Ceylon. A little after noon the lone *Pecos* was spotted and attacked by planes from the ever-menacing Japanese carrier striking force. Hit repeatedly, she slowly settled and then plunged, bow first, into the sea. The bobbing heads of the survivors in the water were used by the Japanese pilots for machine-gun practice. A distress signal had been flashed which fortunately was picked up by the recently departed *Whipple*. She reached the scene about 10 that night and trailed cargo nets and life lines for the exhausted survivors to climb aboard. When 220 had been picked up, an enemy submarine contact was reported and the *Whipple* discontinued her rescue operation. The rest of the 700 men of the *Langley* and *Pecos* were left to their fate. None of them was ever recovered.

The *Seawitch* arrived safely at Tjilatjap, but too late for her planes to be used. It was only hoped that the Dutch would destroy them before they fell into the hands of the advancing Japanese.

The enemy was now poised at Bali on the east and Sumatra on the west for the assault on Java. Admiral Helfrich did his best with what he had to stop the invasion. The British urged him to withdraw the naval forces to preserve them for future use elsewhere; but the Dutch were determined to fight to the bitter end. It was not far off. The overwhelming force of the Japanese air power was the primary weapon in their irresistible advances. The surface ships were helpless to halt it.

With fuel supplies almost nonexistent, Helfrich finally consented to the withdrawal on February 27 of the British cruisers *Dragon* and *Danae* and destroyers *Tenedos* and *Scout* and the Australian cruiser *Hobart*. Of the original 13 American destroyers only four were left ready for action. The damaged cruiser *Houston* was also available. The British had the cruiser *Exeter* (veteran of the sinking of the *Graf Spee* off the River Plate), the Australian *Perth*, and three destroyers.

The Dutch had the *De Ruyter*, the *Java*, and two destroyers. Except for submarines and a few remaining aircraft, this was all the naval force left to stop the enemy juggernaut. Admiral Doorman commanded all our forces afloat.

In the afternoon of February 26, information was received of a large enemy convoy heading southwest off the coast of Borneo. This indicated a landing attempt on the north shore of Java itself. Admiral Doorman's heterogeneous little striking force was ordered to sea with instructions to make a night attack, then retire in Tandjoeng Priok near the western end of Java. The order ended, "You must continue attacks until the enemy is destroyed." It was utterly beyond the capabilities of the ships employed.

The action which followed was later designated the Battle of the Java Sea. The squadron departed from Soerabaja on the afternoon of the 26th. Next morning they were bombed. No damage was inflicted, but about noon, Doorman reported by radio, "Personnel have now reached point of exhaustion." Evidently the men were being kept continually at their battle stations. The ships headed back to Soerabaja for the crews to get some rest.

Just as the ships were entering the harbor, Doorman received information that a force of 29 to 45 transports, escorted by two or three cruisers and eight to 12 destroyers, was approximately 60 miles north of Soerabaja, with a strong enemy covering force only about 40 miles away. The Dutch admiral reversed the course of his flagship in the channel and signaled to the other ships, "Am proceeding to intercept enemy unit. Follow me. Details later." Thus they proceeded to their last battle, dead tired, ships of four different nationalities, with no adequate communications with each other and no prearranged plan of action.

The striking force went out on a northwest course in a sea choppy from a 15-knot easterly wind. Visibility was good and soon enemy planes began to shadow the Allied ships. Bombs were dropped ineffectively at 3:30 P.M. and Doorman asked for fighter protection from shore, but it could not be provided.

The Allied cruisers were in column with the *De Ruyter* in the lead, followed by the *Exeter*, *Houston*, *Perth* and *Java* in that order. The British destroyer *Electra* was ahead of the column, with *Jupiter* to starboard, and the *Encounter* to port of the *De Ruyter*. The American destroyers were in column astern and the two Dutch destroyers about 4,000 yards to port of them. This disposition was not effective for battle as the destroyers should be placed in a screen ahead of the heavier ships, both for outpost duties and to be in good torpedo attack position in case of enemy contact. In explanation, it has been stated that the Dutch destroyers were trying to work up to the van and the Americans had contradictory orders not to pass ahead of the Dutch. With their worn-out machinery, leaky condensers, and foul bottoms, all were having difficulty making more than 24 knots. It would have been better if Doorman had slowed down the rest of his ships in order to let the destroyers take their proper positions.

The enemy was contacted about 4 o'clock, slightly on the starboard bow. The force was reported to consist of four to seven cruisers, two heavier ships and 13 destroyers. Fire was opened by the Japanese ships at extreme range at 4:16 P.M. and the Allied cruisers changed course to the left to bring all their guns to bear. The opposing battle lines moved along on generally westerly courses, with the Japanese slightly ahead and the range gradually decreasing during the engagement. Accepting action at this time was contrary to Admiral Doorman's orders, which had directed him to fight a night action.

During this phase, Japanese salvos were landing around our cruisers without doing much damage and our destroyers reported that we appeared to be getting hits on the enemy ships. Then the Japanese destroyers fired torpedoes at long range. Our ships turned away to the south to avoid them and shortly afterward the *Java* received a shell hit. Gunfire at long range continued to be exchanged until about 5:10 P.M. when the enemy destroyers made another torpedo attack. While maneuvering to avoid these torpedoes, the *Exeter* received an 8-inch shell in her engine room and was reduced to 15 knots. The Dutch destroyer *Kortenaer* was struck by a torpedo and sank within 60 seconds of the explosion. The Allied cruisers again turned individually to the south to dodge torpedoes but the *De Ruyter* lagged behind, apparently to close her gun range to the enemy.

The Australian light cruiser *Perth* and the destroyers *Electra* and *Encounter* delayed long enough to lay a smoke screen between the enemy and the damaged *Exeter*. About this time, Doorman signaled "Counterattack." The *Electra* entered the smoke she had just laid to carry out this order, and was met by three Japanese destroyers which immediately opened fire at point-blank range. She was smothered with hits and sank in a few minutes. The *Jupiter* followed the *Electra* into the smoke, but by this time the enemy ships had turned away and disappeared in the failing light. The Dutch destroyer *Witte De With* was damaged when one of her own depth charges accidentally fell overboard and went off under her stern.

Doorman had now gathered his cruisers together and turned back north to renew the engagement. They emerged from the smoke at a range of about 18,000 yards from the Japanese cruisers. The *De Ruyter*'s radio had been damaged and flashing light signals were now Doorman's only means of communicating with his force. The voice radio on the *Houston* was also out of commission.

At 6:06 the *De Ruyter* again flashed "Counterattack;" a few minutes later came a signal, "Cancel counterattack," then "Make smoke." While laying this smoke, the destroyers received the order, "Cover my retirement." The Americans had no idea just what was meant by this order, but they executed a long-range torpedo attack, forcing the Japanese line to turn away in the gathering darkness.

At 6:31 Doorman signaled "Follow me" and headed northeast. The destroyers trailed, with no idea of the Admiral's plans or what the Japanese were doing. After a brief encounter with enemy cruisers in the darkness, the force again turned south and appeared to be retiring to Soerabaja. Eenmy planes kept track of the disposition by dropping occasional flares during the night. About 9 o'clock, as they neared the coast of Java, the American destroyers were running out of fuel after 24 hours of high-speed steaming. Having expended all their torpedoes, Commander Thomas H. Binford, their commander, decided to retire to Soerabaja for fuel. There they found the *Exeter* with the *Witte De With*, which had withdrawn after the engagement. This left only the British destroyers *Jupiter* and *Encounter* at sea with the four cruisers, still seeking the enemy in the darkness.

Cruising along in the black night, the *Jupiter*, without warning, suffered an underwater explosion at 9:25 P.M., attributed to a submarine torpedo. She sank at 1:30 in the morning. The cruisers turned north and shortly thereafter came across survivors of the *Kortenaer*, sunk that afternoon. The *Encounter* was instructed to pick them up, which she did, afterward returning with them to Soerabaja. This left the four cruisers with no attending destroyers. Despite the enemy planes which continued to follow them with flares, Doorman was grimly determined to carry out his orders to "attack until the enemy is destroyed."

The enemy cruisers were again encountered about 11:15 P.M. and in the ensuing action the *De Ruyter* received a hit aft which caused her to turn away. As the *Java* followed, she was hit by a torpedo and within a few seconds was enveloped in flames. Almost immediately the *De Ruyter* took a torpedo and also caught fire. Amid exploding ammunition, her crew were seen to be abandoning ship, and she sank within a few minutes. The *Java* was not actually seen to sink but must have gone down shortly thereafter. This left the *Houston* and *Perth*. Having expended most of their ammunition, they retired to Tandjoeng Priok in accordance with their original orders before the battle.

The Japanese landed on the north shore of Java during the night, and expeditions were reported moving toward the south coast, escorted by two battleships. It was apparent that there was no safe haven on the island for the Allied ships. Admiral Glassford had orders to retire to Australia when it became impossible to remain in Java. Admiral Palliser, the British naval commander, had similar orders from the Admiralty. The time to move had now come, and it was necessary to move fast. Binford, commanding the destroyers at Soerabaja, telephoned to Glassford as to the "vital necessity of leaving Soerabaja that day and no later." But Helfrich would not admit defeat. He planned to continue fighting from Tjilatjap, on the south coast. He ordered the crippled British cruiser *Exeter*, the British destroyer *Encounter* and the American *Pope* to proceed to Tjilatjap via Sunda Strait. Attempting to skirt the south coast of Borneo by daylight and dash through the strait at night, they were intercepted by three Japanese cruisers at noon. The *Exeter* and *Encounter* were smothered with gunfire and went down fighting. The *Pope* was slowed down by a bomb from a seaplane and later overtaken and sunk by enemy cruisers.

Glassford ordered Captain Rooks of the *Houston* to leave Tandjoeng Priok the same night, 28th, for Tjilatjap via Sunda Strait, accompanied by the light cruiser *Perth* and the Dutch destroyer *Evertsen*. The cruisers left two hours before midnight, but the destroyer did not get away until an hour later and hence was not with them when they encountered the enemy. The *Evertsen* reported by radio about midnight that she could see a sea battle in the vicinity of St. Nicholas Point, whereupon Helfrich addressed a message to the *Houston, Perth* and *Evertsen:* "If any of addressees is engaged with enemy, others render assistance as possible." Later the *Evertsen*'s captain radioed that he had been intercepted by two enemy cruisers and had beached his vessel in a sinking condition on Seboekoe Island. Nothing further was heard from any of the three ships until after the war, when prisoners from the *Houston* were recovered from Japan.

These survivors reported that 20 miles south of St. Nicholas Point, the *Houston* and *Perth* had run into a large Japanese convoy of transports, escorted by five cruisers and nine destroyers. In the succeeding engagement, the *Perth* went down in 20 minutes from torpedo hits and gunfire, but the *Houston* fought on for an hour and a half. She remained afloat until her ammunition was expended and all her turrets had been put out of action. As her gunfire ceased, the Japanese ships closed to within 1,500 yards and blasted her unmercifully. Shortly after giving the order to abandon ship, Captain Rooks was fatally wounded by shrapnel. A motor torpedo boat was reported to have delivered the final blow, after which the ill-fated *Houston* rolled over on her beam and sank about 2 A.M. on March 1. The Japanese machine-gunned men on her decks and in the water. One officer stated that 368 survivors were known to have reached the Javanese shore, but only 250 survived the tortures and hardships of the Japanese prison camps. When she went into her last action, the *Houston*'s complement was 982 officers and men. The survivors thought they had sunk many enemy ships before the cruiser went down, but information obtained from Japan after the war indicated that the Japanese suffered only one cruiser lightly damaged, though some transports may have been sunk.

The four American destroyers left in Soerabaja sortied about 5 P.M. on the 28th, after undergoing aerial bombing raids all day. They escaped through Bali Strait by hugging the shore in the bright moonlight, and were not discovered by the enemy until they emerged from the southern end. After a short brush in which they were under fire and simulated a torpedo attack, they escaped at high speed and made for Australia, where they arrived four days later. They were the only ships inside the Malay Barrier to escape destruction by the Japanese.

Five submarines were stationed in the Java Sea during the last days of February and the first days of March, but their campaign was a further story of frustration and ineffectiveness. The S-38 conducted a gun bombardment of Bawean Island and rescued 54 survivors of the *Electra*, sunk in the Battle of the Java Sea. The S-37 rescued two American sailors who were survivors of the *De Ruyter*, and supplied a boatload of Dutch survivors with five days' provisions. The submarine *Seal* sank a merchantman in Lombok Strait on March 1. But the enemy's countermeasures, coupled with the faulty performance of our torpedoes, effectively prevented our submarines from inflicting any serious losses. The *Sargo* during this period fired 13 torpedoes, under ideal conditions, and obtained no hits. Repeated experiences of this kind forced the Bureau of Ordinance to begin tests which ultimately produced marked improvement in this weapon. But the Bureau has a great deal to answer for in the initial ineffectiveness of the torpedoes issued to submarines, destroyers and aircraft.

The ships still at Tjilatjap were ordered to clear for Australia. The destroyers *Pillsbury* and *Edsall* were sunk by Japanese planes on March 1. Two days later the gunboat *Asheville* was sunk south of Java. The rest arrived safely. On the morning of March 1, Helfrich informed Glassford and Palliser that the Allied Naval Command was dissolved as of that moment, and Glassford left Bandoeng by automobile for Tjilatjap, from whence he proceeded by air to Australia. The naval part of the defense of the Netherlands East Indies was over.

During this period of defeat and retreat, submarines evacuated personnel from Corregidor and brought in ammunition and supplies for that fortress until its fall on May 6. Navy Patrol Wing Ten, under command of Captain (later Rear Admiral) Frank D. Wagner, had also been doing heroic work. But its big, cumbersome seaplanes lacked armor, heavy machine-gun defense, and leak-proof gas tanks. Their mission was reconnaissance and various utility assignments. They were not built for combat. Contact with a Japanese fighter usually meant that the patrol plane was doomed. Despite these handicaps, Patrol Wing Ten carried on until its remnants had to be withdrawn to Australia, where it later did valuable work. With the destruction of the bulk of the Army air forces on December 8, there was little chance of fighter protection for the PBYs while carrying out their missions. With the help of Dutch PBYs, they attempted bombing attacks, but without success against the airtight Japanese defenses. Some personnel of the Wing remaining on Bataan fought on foot with the Army. The Wing flew small amounts of essential supplies to Corregidor, and assisted in evacuating personnel from the fortress.

Six planes stationed at Ambon, in the Ceram group, on December 26 made a bombing attack on two Japanese cruisers, two destroyers and 13 transports at Jolo, in the Philippines. Crew members claimed hits on a cruiser and a transport, but four planes were shot down. Survivors were eventually rescued after thrilling experiences; friendly natives cared for them and passed them by outrigger canoe down the long Sulu chain to Tarakan and thence to Soerabaja, which they reached on January 10.

In the weeks before the withdrawal from Java, Patrol Wing Ten claimed eight and possibly 12 enemy aircraft shot down, and reported in the neighborhood of 300 bombing, reconnaissance, rescue and utility missions flown, in addition to many administrative and supply flights. They lost 15 PBYs

PBY

shot down in the air and 17 destroyed on the water. The heroic performance of these planes, unsuitable as they were for combat, was one of the high lights of the campaign. "No praise could be too high for the work of Patrol Wing Ten," Admiral Glassford stated.

On March 6, Batavia, capital of the Dutch East Indies, fell, and on March 10 all the defending Dutch, British and American troops on Java unconditionally surrendered. Bataan, in the Philippines, held out until April 9 when General Wainwright withdrew into Corregidor. The surrender of that stronghold, after heroic resistance, came on May 6, while the Battle of the Coral Sea was being fought. The Japanese conquest of an empire was now complete.

During the entire campaign, and including withdrawals from the Philippines to Australia, the Allies lost:

2 battleships (*Prince of Wales* and *Repulse*)
5 cruisers (*Houston, Exeter, Perth, De Ruyter* and *Java*)
14 destroyers (*Edsall, Peary, Pillsbury, Pope, Stewart, Electra, Encounter, Jupiter, Evertsen, Kortenaer, Piet Hein, Van Ghent, Witte De With* and *Banckert*)
1 seaplane tender (*Langley*)
4 submarines (*Perch, S-36, Sealion* and *Shark*)
4 mine sweepers (*Bittern, Finch, Quail* and *Tanager*)
3 gunboats (*Asheville, Oahu* and *Wake*)
1 tanker (*Pecos*)

In contrast, except for some transports, the Japanese lost one destroyer sunk by a mine and two by submarine attack. Slightly damaged were four cruisers, two mine layers and six destroyers, but all these ships were soon repaired and back in action. It was one of the cheapest conquests in history.

The ease with which this vast territory had been seized was astounding. Japanese plans had been carefully made before hostilities started, and their well-coordinated forces moved as relentlessly as a steam roller over the vast areas they had marked out for occupation. They had correctly analyzed the importance of air power and used it to great advantage. With the destruction of most of our Army air potential on Oahu and Luzon on December 7, any possibility of stopping the Japanese movement, or even seriously delaying it, was gone. Japanese air forces alone could have destroyed all the naval forces inside the Malay Barrier, as they did the *Prince of Wales* and the *Repulse*, but their great superiority in surface types made this unnecessary. Wherever used, their carrier air groups brought death and destruction to the objects of their attacks. Under their cover, the surface ships and transports moved to their assigned objectives with little hindrance and completed their conquest with comparative ease.

The Japanese carrier striking force had conducted operations from Pearl Harbor to the Indian Ocean. After sinking most of the American battleships at Pearl Harbor, they rendezvoused in the Palaus and at Staring Bay in Celebes and conducted the strikes on Darwin and Ambon. They then proceeded into the Indian Ocean south of Java and in addition to sinking the *Langley* and *Pecos*, hit Colombo and Trincomalee on Ceylon on the 5th and 9th of April respectively. They returned to Japan at the end of April. Never before had operations of a single force been conducted over such a wide range of the earth's surface in so short a time.

The biggest error in our defense of this area was the failure to disperse our Army air forces on Luzon fields prior to the opening of hostilities. It was a tragic error that the offensive bombing mission against Formosa was so delayed on the day Pearl Harbor was attacked that most of the aircraft were caught on the ground.

Even had we escaped heavy initial air losses, however, it is probable that the end result would have been the same. The great disparity between our air forces and those of the enemy would eventually have brought about the gradual elimination of the Allied air strength. However, our planes would have been more effective in slowing up the advance, and their support and cover for our surface and submarine forces would have enabled those ships to have engaged under more favorable conditions.

The primary strategic conceptions of the high command at the time were not yet in accordance with the changes brought about in naval warfare by the advent of the airplane. The mad dash of the *Prince of Wales* and *Repulse*, without air cover, was a fatal mistake and prevented a later concentration of surface forces which would have constituted a strong threat to the Japanese invasions. The unified Allied command was not in effect long enough to become really effective.

Tactical handling of the combined forces in many cases

left much to be desired. Admiral Doorman's dispositions of his forces were such as to invite disaster. In war, it is not enough simply to have the will to fight; technical skill in utilizing different types of naval units is also essential. Much of our effort was dissipated in providing escorts for shipping in widely separated areas instead of concentrating our strength at the decisive points of contact.

In view of the complete failure to stop or even delay the Japanese advance, the question arises whether our losses were justified. That question must be answered with reference to the morale effect of our resistance. In the longer perspective, that factor has untold value. The heroism of the dogged defenders of Bataan and Corregidor, of the gallant officers and men of the *Houston*, the *Marblehead*, the submarines and other ships of our small Asiatic Fleet, of Patrol Wing Ten, will go down in history as notable examples of courage and devotion to duty against heavy odds. The spectacle of their fighting had far-reaching influence in keeping the Chinese actively in the war and in maintaining for the Allies the respect of the natives of the Pacific regions, an asset which was to be so valuable at later stages in the conflict. In addition to their example, the survivors who escaped brought back valuable experience in fighting the Japanese which was to prove its worth in subsequent engagements on the way back to Tokyo.

Heartbreaking as it was, in bracing the morale of the free nations and in the experience it gained, the attempt to keep the Japanese out of the Philippines and the Dutch East Indies was worth many times its cost. That was proved a few months later, after the Battle of Midway, when the turning point came.

4

MOLDING THE TEAM

As stated in the previous chapter, the Japanese attack on Pearl Harbor completely disrupted the existing war plans for the Pacific Fleet. The Navy had been serenely unprepared mentally for such a catastrophe. Its plans, based on battleships as the supreme weapon at sea, became about as realistic as Grimm's fairy tales. Most of the "backbone" of the Fleet was at the bottom of Pearl Harbor, a mass of useless junk. The complacency of the Navy hierarchy was shaken to its foundations.

This was the atmosphere in which the Pacific Fleet began operations after the Japanese had struck the initial blow. The impression I received at Fleet Headquarters, when the *Lexington* returned from its fruitless search for the enemy carriers, was that the predominant psychology was fear of another attack. Ships were being kept at sea for the sole purpose of avoiding a possible raid in port; only one carrier at a time was allowed to be in Pearl Harbor, to prevent losing more than one should another attack occur, and then only when it was absolutely necessary to take on fuel or supplies. Ships were kept at sea with no particular mission except to be at sea. They spent their time aimlessly cruising, at the same time continually running the risk of an attack by enemy submarines.

The Japanese carriers had planned an air attack on Midway while returning from Pearl Harbor, but after the war they reported that bad weather had prevented their carrying it out. Possibly they were so well pleased with the success already achieved that they decided not to linger, but to proceed immediately to carry out their plans in the Dutch East Indies. Two destroyers, the *Akebone* and *Ushio*, left Tokyo on December 1, and on the night of December 7, bombarded Midway. Their salvos did only minor damage.

At Wake Island, about a thousand miles southwest of Midway and across the international date line, it was December 8, and still dark, when the attack came on Pearl Harbor. The *Enterprise* had delivered Marine Fighter Squadron 21, consisting of twelve Grumman Wildcat fighter planes, to the island just three days before. These were the only planes available to the defenders. Commander Winfield Scott Cunningham was in over-all command of the base, with Major James P. S. Devereaux commanding the garrison Marines, and Major Paul Putnam commanding the aviation unit. The defense problem was complicated by the presence of 1,200 civilians at work on the installations.

A V-shaped atoll, Wake consists of three small islands,

Wake, Wilkes and Peale, surrounding a lagoon and all circled by an outlying reef. The defenders were stationed on all three islands, though the air strip was on Wake, at the point of the V. On getting word of the attack on Pearl Harbor, the little command promptly went to battle stations in anticipation of a visit from the Sons of Heaven. They had not long to wait. Before noon, a formation of 36 heavy bombers from the Marshall Islands, approaching through a rain squall along the south coast, emerged almost on top of the air strip. They came over at 3,000 feet and dropped 100-pound fragmentation bombs with deadly accuracy, also strafing with their machine guns. The first attack destroyed seven planes, killed 25 men and wounded seven others. The whole aviation area was blazing from the fire of a 25,000-gallon gasoline tank which had been hit in the first few minutes, as well as scattered fuel drums. More bombing raids were made on the 9th and 10th. Casualties were fewer on these days; the personnel had learned to take better shelter.

Time after time the pitifully few fighter planes remaining after the first attack went aloft to meet the enemy bombers. Some were shot down, others damaged beyond repair. Eventually none were left.

In the meantime, preparations had been made at Pearl Harbor for the relief of Wake. Troop reinforcements, additional fighter aircraft and other defense equipment, including radar, were assembled for disptach to the hard-pressed outpost. The expedition, commanded by Rear Admiral Frank J. Fletcher, consisted of the carrier *Saratoga*, three heavy cruis-

Grumman Wildcat

ers, nine destroyers, and the seaplane tender *Tangier* to transport troops and equipment. A slow fleet oiler, the *Neches*, was assigned to furnish fuel oil. On December 15 the relief expedition sailed from Pearl Harbor. A second task force, built around the *Lexington* and headed by Vice-Admiral Wilson Brown, was directed to strike enemy forces at Jaluit, 814 miles south of Wake, to divert the attention of the Japanese from Wake.

At daylight on December 11, the enemy at Wake made their first landing attempt. Their force consisted of three light cruisers, six destroyers, two destroyer transports and two merchantmen transports, carrying a landing force of only 450 men. As the expedition approached the atoll, the Marines withheld their fire until the enemy ships were within 5,000 yards range, then suddenly opened up with their 5-inch guns. Within a few minutes the leading cruiser, the *Yubari*, was hit just above the water line amidships. With her whole side engulfed in smoke, she turned away from the deadly shore guns. The destroyer *Hayate* was hit and blew up in a violent explosion. As the smoke cleared away, the gunners saw her broken in two and disappearing from sight. Other ships were hit and damaged.

In great haste, the Japanese reversed course and retired, Rear Admiral Kajioka ordering a general retreat to Kwajalein. During the withdrawal four Marine fighter planes inflicted heavy casualties on the Japanese. One destroyer, the *Kisaragi*, which they bombed, blew up and sank from the explosion of a deckload of depth charges. In all, two destroyers were sunk and three cruisers, two destroyers and one transport were damaged by the garrison in repelling this attack.

Following this failure, the Japanese renewed their daily bombing attacks and organized a new landing attempt for December 23. This time their forces were augmented with two aircraft carriers, the *Soryu* and *Hiryu*, which had participated in the Pearl Harbor attack, and six heavy cruisers.

The American relief force, under Admiral Fletcher, was proceeding slowly westward from Pearl Harbor. Its speed was reduced so that its slow tanker, the old *Neches*, which could make only 12 knots, could keep up. On December 22, the force fueled its destroyers from the *Neches* on a course to the northward which took it farther away from its destination. That night it again turned westward. At 8 the next morning, when only 425 miles from Wake, it received orders to return to Pearl Harbor.

Back in Pearl Harbor, Vice-Admiral William S. Pye had relieved Admiral Kimmel as Commander in Chief, pending the arrival of Admiral Nimitz from Washington. Pye became apprehensive that the relief force might be overwhelmed before it could accomplish its mission. Early in the morning, he decided to recall it. With this decision went Wake's last hope of relief. Had the relief force arrived a day or two earlier the island might have been held.

Aboard the relief ships there was astonishment, shame and anger. On the *Lexington*, far to the south, we had been directed on the 20th to cancel our strike on Jaluit and instead to support the *Saratoga* operations near Wake. We were proceeding to that locality at our best speed when the order came to cancel our mission and return to Pearl Harbor. We, too, were sick at having to turn back.

The new Japanese plan provided for landing under cover of darkness. As the expedition approached about 2 o'clock on the morning of December 23, the weather was stormy and the vessels rolled and pitched in the swells, their decks wet with spray. In the blackness of the night, the Japanese troops of the special landing force clambered down the transports' sides to their landing craft. The two heavily loaded patrol boats, when close to the shore, rang up full speed ahead to run aground on the island. They struck the outer reef in a smother of breakers and foam, swept across on the next swell, and hit the shore just opposite the west end of the landing strip.

Alert to the landing attempt, the defending garrison illuminated the grounded patrol boats with their searchlights and opened a deadly fire as the Japanese waded through the breakers onto dry ground. Both vessels were set on fire but most of the men managed to reach the sandy coral beach.

About this time, Major Devereaux' telephone communications were cut by either the landing parties or by gunfire. A considerable number of men had reached shore both on the south coast of Wake and on Wilkes. The defending Marines were isolated in a number of machine-gun positions and the Japs were scattered under the cover of the underbrush. In this no man's land the enemy continued to infiltrate and to expand their beachhead. Major Devereaux was unable to get more than fragmentary information as to the situation. About 3:30 the Japanese cruisers shelled the island and the Marine reserves, a pathetically small force of 40, were committed to counterattack.

It was at this time that Commander Cunningham sent his famous dispatch: "Enemy on island—issue in doubt."

From shortly after daybreak, swarms of aircraft from the *Soryu* and *Hiryu*, some 250 miles away, swooped down on the tiny island in unceasing air strikes. Every position occupied by our troops was repeatedly hit.

With the atoll ringed by enemy ships, Devereaux notified Cunningham of the seriousness of the situation and inquired whether any reinforcements were available. Cunningham replied in the negative. All hopes of holding out were clearly vain. Under instructions from the island commander, Devereaux, bearing a white flag, moved southward down the shore to surrender Wake.

The events following the surrender are soon told. At the American hospital, the enemy drove the patients outside, bound their hands behind their backs with telephone wire, and placed nooses about their necks. Inside the hospital, they also fired among the patients, killing one and wounding another. There was some difficulty getting word of the surrender to isolated Marine groups, who received the news with incredulity. At one outpost, a Marine tried to persuade the officer in charge not to give in. "Don't surrender, Lieutenant," he begged. "Marines never surrender. It's a hoax."

Had the *Saratoga* group not been so dilatory by remaining with the *Neches* and stopping to refuel destroyers, it could have delivered its reinforcements on the 21st, two days before the Japanese attacked. Furthermore, had an adequate air search been made, the *Soryu* and *Hiryu* were open to attack by our carrier planes, and those valuable enemy vessels might have been destroyed. This is speculation, but the whole future course of the war might have been changed had we been able to hold Wake, and had two of the enemy's best carriers been destroyed so early in the war.

The fall of Wake was a tragedy, but one that reflected glory on the island's defenders. While they suffered 20 per cent casualties, the Marines had inflicted many times that number on the enemy, had sunk four enemy warships and inflicted appreciable damage on eight more. Twenty-one enemy aircraft had been shot down by our Wildcat fighters or by antiaircraft fire over the atoll. Had substantial reinforcements been rushed out to Wake immediately after the attack on Pearl Harbor, the story might have had a very different ending.

Fifteen hundred miles southwest of Wake lay Guam, an American possession since the Spanish-American War and a stopping point on the air route to the Orient. Virtually surrounded as the island was by the Japanese-mandated Marianas and Carolines, no effort had ever been made to fortify it. Appropriations had been sought to improve its Apra harbor, but they had been refused by Congress on the ground that the development might "provoke" Japan.

Japanese planes repeatedly bombed the almost defenseless island for two days after the attack on Pearl Harbor. At 3:30 on the morning of December 10, enemy forces landed for the assault. By daylight the few defenders had been killed or taken prisoner and the flag of the Rising Sun went up on the station flag staff. A few Americans escaped to the hills, but the Japanese announced that all resistance had ceased on December 22. Five American nurses who had remained on the island were returned to the United States six months later on the S.S. *Gripsholm*. One of them reported that some of the men who had surrendered had been forced to strip to their shorts and kneel at the feet of the Japanese, and had then been bayoneted in the back. Any of the natives who got in the conqueror's way had been bayoneted without regard to age or sex.

More aggressive policies were presaged when on December 30 Admiral Ernest J. King, a naval aviator, became Commander in Chief of the United States Fleet, with headquarters in Washington, and on the last day of 1941 Admiral Chester W. Nimitz took command of the Pacific Fleet.

One of the provisions for strengthening the Fleet was the assignment to it of the new aircraft carrier *Yorktown*, which was transferred from the Atlantic. Proceeding through the Panama Canal, she escorted troop transports to Samoa, far to the south, and became the nucleus of a carrier task force under command of Rear Admiral Frank Jack Fletcher. Samoa was vital to the supply routes from the West Coast of the United States and Panama to Australia. Our effort now was to hold that line and stop the Japanese advance until we could build up strength enough to take the offensive.

At the time of Pearl Harbor, our carriers were equipped with F2A fighter planes, called the "Buffalo" and made by Brewster; with Douglas SBD "Dauntless" dive bombers; and the TBD torpedo plane, the "Devastator," also manufactured by Douglas. The "Buffalo" was a single-seater with a top speed of about 280 miles per hour, and was armed with four 50-caliber machineguns. The "Dauntless," a two-seater, in addition to one 1,000-pound or two 500-pound bombs, carried two 50-caliber machineguns in the fuselage, firing forward, and a 30-caliber swivel or "free" gun fired from the rear seat. The big "Devastator" torpedo bomber, manned by a crew of three, carried in addition to its torpedo one fixed 30-caliber gun firing forward and one "free" 30-caliber firing aft from the rear seat.

None of these planes was initially equipped with armor protection for the pilots or with leak-proof gasoline tanks to prevent the fuel from escaping in case of puncture by a bullet or shell fragment and catching fire. These protections, however, were added almost immediately, though at some cost to the bomb-carrying capacity and range of the planes.

The "Buffaloes" were replaced very shortly after Pearl Harbor by the Grumman F4F "Wildcats," which carried four

F2A Brewster "Buffalo"

50-caliber guns, later increased to six. The "Wildcats" were well protected by armor as well as leak-proof tanks. The Japanese "Zero," the enemy's contemporary fighter, was faster and could outclimb the "Wildcats," but had no armor or sealing for the fuel tanks, and flamed readily when hit. Commander Jimmie Thatch, my fighter squadron commander, answered criticism of the "Wildcat" as compared with the "Zero" by remarking that any pilot who preferred the latter because of its maneuverability ought to have his head examined.

Admiral William F. Halsey, on the *Enterprise*, was ordered south to join Admiral Fletcher to assist in covering the movement of troops to Samoa and after their safe arrival, to take command of the two carrier task forces for a raid on enemy establishments in the Gilbert and Marshall Islands. This operation was to have far-reaching effects.

The *Enterprise* and *Yorktown* task forces departed from Samoa on January 25, 1942, and fueled at sea on the 28th. They then separated, the *Yorktown*, with the cruisers *Louisville* and *St. Louis* and the destroyers *Hughes*, *Sims*, *Russell* and *Walke*, being assigned to hit Jaluit and Mille in the southern Marshalls and Makin in the northern Gilberts on February 1. The *Enterprise* was assigned Taroa, Maloelap, Roi, and Kwajalein in the northern Marshalls. She was accompanied by the cruisers *Northampton*, *Salt Lake City*, and *Chester*, and the destroyers *Dunlap*, *Balch*, *Maury*, *Ralph Talbot*, *Blue* and *McCall*.

Admiral Fletcher's task force ran into bad weather off Jaluit. Despite the additional hazard, 28 planes were launched in the dark so as to reach the target at dawn. They roared down the flight deck in the pitch blackness and tried to rendezvous among storm clouds, rain squalls and lightning. Those which finally got together departed for their objectives in ragged formation, below a cloud ceiling barely 500 feet above the water. With their radios jammed by static, they were unable to accomplish much, but they attacked an 8,000-ton ship found at anchor. Hampered by the low ceiling, rain, and fogging of their windshields and bomb sights, they reported making three hits and leaving her afire amidships and sinking by the stern. No air opposition and little ack-ack were encountered. Six planes failed to return, and it was common talk among the fliers that most of them had been lost in collisions as they tried to rendezvous in the dark.

Fortunately better conditions prevailed later for the take-off of nine planes for Makin and five for Mille. At Makin the bombers found a large seaplane tender with two four-engine flying boats alongside. Likewise hampered by rain and clouds, they reported setting the planes on fire and hitting the tender, which was thought to be capsizing. The bombers assigned to Mille found no worthwhile targets but bombed some small structures found on the island. The task force combat air patrol shot down a four-engine enemy bomber during its retirement that afternoon.

Hunting was better in the area assigned to the *Enterprise*. Halsey had assigned two cruiser-destroyer groups for the gun bombardment of Wotje and Taroa, in addition to the air attacks on all the target atolls. Under command of Rear Admiral Raymond A. Spruance, the cruisers *Northampton* and *Salt Lake City* and the destroyer *Dunlap* bombarded Wotje. The cruiser *Chester* and the destroyers *Balch* and *Maury*, commanded by Captain Thomas M. Shock, bombarded Taroa. The *Enterprise* retained with her only three destroyers, the *Ralph Talbot, Blue* and *McCall*, for plane guards, antisubmarine patrol and antiaircraft protection. It was a daring division of forces. The planes were launched before dawn, only 26 miles from Wotje. In this area the Japanese had well-developed air fields and intense opposition was to be expected. At Roi two of our planes were shot down by enemy combat planes and two more by antiaircraft gunfire. But our airmen shot down three Japanese Zero fighters and seven bombers, destroyed two large hangars, blew up an ammunition dump, smashed the radio building and leveled other buildings on the island.

At Kwajalein, at the other end of the atoll, no Zeros were found in the air but a wealth of shipping targets were spotted at anchor. Among them were five submarines moored alongside a tanker. The Dauntlesses planted a bomb on a cruiser and hit two of the submarines, one of which blew up, the other sinking immediately. Following the bombers, our Douglas TBD Devastator torpedo planes put a "tin fish" apiece into the cruiser and three large oilers. Five more merchant-type ships were damaged and a small gunboat was forced to beach itself to prevent sinking. Against a hail of ack-ack, not one of our planes was lost and no personnel were injured. It was the first successful counterattack by the Pacific Fleet, and the prelude to the great carrier raids which were to characterize the subsequent fighting of our naval forces.

Five of our fighters arriving at Taroa, found a beautiful air field with runways two miles long. Near the strip were many parked planes. Our pilots roared down on the planes, but they would not burn. Our guns were not then equipped with incendiary bullets. A few minutes later the *Chester* raked the island with salvo after salvo from her 8-inch guns. In a second air attack, seven grounded enemy bombers caught fire and went up in smoke. A third attack met fighter opposition, and in sharp dogfights three enemy planes were shot down for the loss of one Dauntless. With the runways cratered and many planes and buildings a mass of flames, our planes withdrew to the *Enterprise*:

Wotje was the fourth target of the *Enterprise* air group. Six fighters assigned to this target strafed the shore installations and covered the operations of the bombarding surface ships. They met a number of Japanese fighters in the air but the enemy pilots were not eager for combat, and no sure kills were reported.

The surface vessels which had been bombarding the islands rejoined the *Enterprise* at noon, and the task force headed back to Pearl Harbor. At 1:30, five enemy bombers suddenly broke out of the clouds astern and dived on the retiring carrier. Amid a stream of antiaircraft projectiles more spectacular than effective, the planes swept in to drop their bombs. Although almost hidden by towering splashes, the *Enterprise* was not hit, the nearest bombs landing only 30 feet away. Fragments spattered holes along the water line and

Douglas TBD "Devastator"

one sailor manning a machine gun died two hours later from wounds. One plane tried a suicide dive on the deck but missed by inches. It sheared the tail off the rearmost parked plane and left one of its own wings on the port gun gallery as it crashed into the sea close alongside. Later in the afternoon other attacks were made, one by a twin-float seaplane and a second by two large bombers. Our antiaircraft gunners shot down two and our fighters one. Under cover of a weather front, the task force returned to Pearl Harbor without further attack.

These raids had effects far greater than the material damage they inflicted. They proved our opponents were no supermen. They gave a boost to the morale of the whole nation and showed the Sons of Heaven we still had power to strike back.

While the *Enterprise* and *Yorktown* were on their strikes, the *Lexington* task force, under Vice-Admiral Wilson Brown, left the Hawaiian Islands for the far South Pacific below the equator, where Vice-Admiral Herbert F. Leary was area commander. Bsides the *Lexington*, the force was composed of the heavy cruisers *Minneapolis*, *Indianapolis*, *Pensacola*, and *San Francisco*, and the destroyers *Clark*, *Patterson*, *Phelps*, *Dewey*, *MacDonough*, *Hull*, *Aylwin*, *Dale*, *Bagley* and *Drayton*. Our orders were to raid Rabaul on New Britain, where the Japanese had landed early in January, 1942, and were busily developing a great base. Plentiful shipping targets were expected. We planned a surprise attack from north of the Solomons, with the planes approaching Rabaul over the intervening island of New Ireland and a simultaneous cruiser bombardment of the ships in the harbor.

All went well until about 11 in the morning of February 20, when a "bogie" (unidentified plane on the radar screen) was reported and a large four-engine enemy plane was sighted disappearing into a cloud on the horizon. Although we on the *Lexington* had had many false alarms, it was our first sight of a real enemy since the war started. After many false starts, we were this time destined to get our baptism of fire. We had a combat air patrol of fighters in the air and a section led by Lieutenant Commander Jimmie Thatch, commander of Fighting Squadron Two, was directed toward the contact.

The enemy plane was cagey and kept dodging in and out of a convenient cloud. Finally Thatch decided that the only way to catch him was to go into the cloud after him. The next time the enemy plane came out of the cloud, our plane was on its tail. A few bursts of machine gun fire and the Japanese plane was out of control and, burning furiously, plummeted into the water. It was the *Lexington*'s first victory of the war and the rising column of smoke, easily visible from the ships, was a thrilling sight.

Shortly thereafter another plane of the same type was picked up on the starboard bow. Another pair of fighters went after it and shot it down, leaving a second column of smoke on the horizon. But the contacts had a disturbing aspect. They meant that enemy scouts had sighted us and had probably reported us to their base at Rabaul. We had lost the chance to arrive at our launching position without being detected, and to make our attack a surprise. But we continued on our course on the chance that the planes might have been unable to get off a radio message. We were soon to learn otherwise.

About 3 P.M., the radar indicated a large formation of planes approaching from the direction of Rabaul. Turning into the wind, we launched all our fighters and prepared for attack. Our radar, one of the first in the Fleet, did not show the altitude of planes it detected. Without this, fighter direction was difficult. Nevertheless, our planes intercepted a group of nine twin-engined bombers at 12,000 feet in the last stages of their bombing approach. Our doctrine was that when enemy planes got within range of the antiaircraft guns, the latter would open fire and the friendly fighters would pull out and leave the job to the guns.

The sky was clear of clouds and it was a perfect day for bombing, with the oncoming planes easily visible from the bridge. The sky was dotted with our antiaircraft bursts, but none of the bombers were knocked down, though our fighters damaged two before the guns took over. When the enemy bombers were in the position where I estimated they would drop their eggs, I ordered "hard right rudder" to turn the ship and spoil their aim. Then we could see the bombs falling from the planes. It seemed an eternity before they hit the water about 100 yards off our port quarter, throwing up enormous geysers of water as they exploded. Our maneuver had prevented them from hitting.

Our fighter planes resumed their attack as soon as the enemy bombers were out of range of the ack-ack guns, and in fierce passes soon shot them all down. Just at this time, a second group of nine bombers came in undetected behind the first. Only two of our fighters, a section led by Lieutenant "Butch" O'Hare, were in a position to intercept them, and as they started to attack, the wing plane's guns jammed. All alone, O'Hare dived on the enemy planes with his guns blazing, although he was exposed to the concentrated machine-gun fire of the entire formation. Beginning with the rear plane, he shot down five before he ran out of ammunition. It was an amazing demonstration of courage and marksmanship. O'Hare was later awarded the Congressional Medal of Honor for this exploit, and promoted to the rank of Lieutenant Commander.

Five of this second group of planes survived long enough to drop their bombs. Again they missed the *Lexington* by a short distance as we dodged them by a similar maneuver. Two of the planes, damaged but not out of control, attempted suicide attacks. From the bridge, I watched one of them flying straight in for the bridge from about 2,000 yards abeam and at only 200 feet altitude. Its guns were pouring a stream

Douglas SBD "Dauntless"

of machine-gun bullets at us and at the same time it was receiving the concentrated fire of every gun on the starboard side of the *Lexington*. It seemed to be impervious to the tremendous fire, and still kept coming on. Finally I saw one of its engines start smoking and I breathed easier. Even then it crashed into the sea only 50 yards from our side. The heat of its burning remains could be felt on board. On the other side of the ship, the second would-be suicider was shot down by the screening destroyers about a thousand yards away. Of the planes which attacked us all were shot down except one which was damaged and may have gotten away. Even the returning scouts, the valiant SBD's, participated in the fighting and wiped out some of the attackers. The *Lexington* lost two fighters in the action, but we had destroyed two enemy four-engine search planes and 17 two-engine bombers.

We had now certainly lost the element of surprise in our projected attack on Rabaul. Admiral Brown decided that the chance of finding profitable targets would be slight and that therefore the risk was not justified. We steamed on until dark to mislead any scouting planes that might be around, and then reluctantly reversed course for a rendezvous with our tankers. On the night before the action, the Battle of Badoeng Strait had occurred in the Java area. Within a week, the *Langley* was destroyed and the Battle of the Java Sea was to mark the end of resistance in the Dutch East Indies.

But the action of Bougainville was only the start of the *Lexington*'s activities against the enemy in the Coral Sea area. After the Marshall Islands raid, the *Yorktown* task force, with the cruisers *Astoria* and *Louisville* and six destroyers, was sent south to augment Vice-Admiral Brown's force. HMAS *Australia* also joined up. The combined task force now contained eight cruisers, 14 destroyers, and the two large carriers. Admiral Brown designated me as air commander, my unit consisting of the *Lexington*, the *Yorktown* and their air groups. For the first time, two carriers would act together tactically as one unit in combat. They would become the model of the multicarrier task groups which functioned so successfully later in the war.

The situation was discussed at a conference on board the *Lexington*. Admiral Brown still desired to attack Rabaul, but this time from a launching point south of the Solomons. The Japanese were now established at Gasmata, in southern New Britain, and had considerable air forces there as well as at

Rabaul. To strike Rabaul from the south meant passing through restricted waters between the Louisiades and the Solomons and coming within range of air attack from Gasmata as well as from Rabaul. I recommended a dawn attack on both places to reduce the chances of counterattack. The plan was adopted, and we proceeded westward through the Coral Sea toward the contemplated launching position.

Shortly after this decision was reached, however, we got information that enemy ships had been sighted off Buna, just around the corner of New Guinea from Port Moresby, and, later, that troops were landing from many transports at Salamaua and near-by Lae, somewhat farther to the north along the same coast. This concentration seemed to promise a better objective than the ones we had chosen. To get within range of Salamaua and Lae from the Coral Sea side, however, we would have to penetrate to the north of the Louisiades and subject ourselves to air counterattack from Gasmata and Rabaul on our flank. There was one other alternative. From the northern tip of the Gulf of Papua, our planes could reach their targets by flying over the Owen Stanley Mountains of New Guinea to the Salamaua area while our carriers remained out of range of the enemy.

There were drawbacks to this plan. We had little information as to the height of the mountains and it was doubtful that our sea-level torpedo planes could clear them. Our intelligence data was extremely meager. Our charts showed the coast line but no details of the interior. Furthermore, our chart of the Gulf of Papua was marked "Surveyed in 1894" and "Area contains many coral heads which grow from year to year and whose position is unknown." It was not a very pleasant prospect for a navigator.

To supplement our meager information, I sent two planes under Commander Walton W. Smith, of Admiral Brown's staff, to Townsville, Australia, and two under Commander William B. Ault, the *Lexington's* Air Group Commander, to Port Moresby to pick up what information they could concerning the route of the projected flight. Commander Ault landed at Port Moresby between two Japanese air raids, a frequent occurrence which indicated their intention of capturing that base. Both he and Smith brought back valuable information. The towering peaks of the Owen Stanley Mountains rise as high as 13,000 feet, a much greater altitude than our loaded torpedo planes could attain. Between these sum-

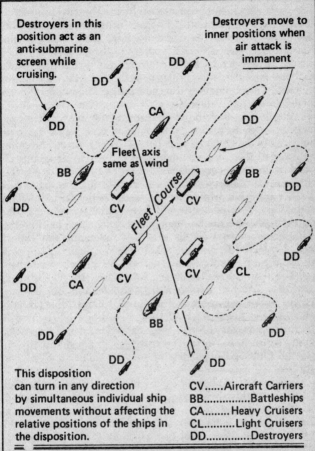

Destroyers in this position act as an anti-submarine screen while cruising.

Destroyers move to inner positions when air attack is immanent

DD

DD

CA

DD

Fleet axis same as wind

BB

Fleet Course

BB

DD

DD

CV

CV

CV

CV

CL

DD

DD

CA

DD

BB

DD

DD

DD

This disposition can turn in any direction by simultaneous individual ship movements without affecting the relative positions of the ships in the disposition.

CV......Aircraft Carriers
BB...............Battleships
CA........Heavy Cruisers
CL..........Light Cruisers
DD..............Destroyers

TYPICAL CARRIER GROUP DISPOSITION
AS USED IN THE PACIFIC WAR

This shows a disposition of 4 carriers, 3 battleships, 2 heavy cruisers, 1 light cruiser and 12 destroyers. Note the concentrated ring of ships around the carriers during an air attack. Attacking planes are faced with an enormous volume of anti-aircraft fire.

mits, however, my officers learned, was one pass at 7,500 feet, through which our planes could go. Though shrouded in clouds most of the time, the pass occasionally cleared for about two hours in the early morning. That would be just time enough, we estimated, for our planes to reach their objectives and get back. The terrain over which they would be flying was classed as "tiger country"—a wild, unexplored region of dense jungle and jagged peaks, inhabited by fierce head-hunters and cannibals.

We determined to attack through this pass. There was danger that if our planes got through on their way out, clouds might close in behind them before their return, shrouding the pass. In that case we might lose two whole air groups. To guard against this contingency, I decided to detail one plane, with an experienced officer, to remain in the pass as a weather observer while the rest were on the far side of the mountains. This officer would have authority to recall the planes if he saw the weather starting to close in. For this assignment, in view of his excellent judgment and experience, I selected Commander Ault. He was badly disappointed, since he naturally wanted to lead his planes in combat.

The date set for the attack was March 10. The cruisers *Australia*, *Chicago*, *Astoria* and *Louisville*, and four destroyers, all under the command of Rear Admiral John Gregory Crace, of the Royal Navy, were detached and left behind to guard the passages through the Louisiades Islands against an enemy sortie in our rear. The rest of us proceeded westward into the Gulf of Papua, passing only 60 miles south of Port Moresby.

It was shortly after daylight when we arrived in the Gulf of Papua. In this sheltered area, we found little or no wind, and we could see that the pass through the mountains was clear. We kept within 15 miles of the coast, despite the numerous forbidding coral heads plainly visible in the clear water. Steaming at full speed to get sufficient wind over our decks, we launched our heavily loaded torpedo planes and dive bombers, with escorting fighter units.

Struggling to gain altitude, Lieutenant Commander Jimmie Brett's torpedo squadron, at the last minute, received the benefit of an updraft of air and cleared the pass with a bare 500 feet to spare. When the groups sighted Salamaua and Lae, they saw two enemy cruisers and four destroyers in the harbors, with five transports and two cargo ships busily unloading supplies onto the beaches. Farther out, another Japanese task force was approaching. It contained an additional cruiser and five destroyers, six transports, and a seaplane tender of the *Kamoi* class. Until they heard the roar of engines and saw the flight swooping down from the mountains, the Japanese had no idea American planes were anywhere within miles of them.

To the enemy's complete surprise, our torpedo planes and bombers swept into the harbors and the dive bombers pushed over in their attacks. When it was all over, five transports or cargo ships had been sunk, a destroyer had blown up, a mine layer was apparently sinking, and a 1,000-pound bomb had landed on each of two cruisers. Two additional destroyers were reported as dead in the water. Antiaircraft fire had been light, but one scout bomber of the *Lexington* group had been shot down. An enemy float plane which had tried to oppose the attack was picked off by Lieutenant Noel Gaylor of the *Lexington*, who sent it flaming into the sea. Another had been driven off, trailing smoke.

After the return of our planes through the pass, we were elated as we counted them and saw that all but one were present. As soon as all were safely aboard, we headed east for our fueling rendezvous and to rejoin our rear-guard cruisers. It had been a most successful attack and had demonstrated that two or more carriers could work together in combat as a team. It delayed the enemy's plans for the capture of Port Moresby and began the attrition of his shipping that was eventually to be a major cause of his downfall. Admiral Nimitz congratulated Admiral Brown on a raid "well planned and well executed."

In the meantime, Admiral Halsey's task force built around the carrier *Enterprise* had not been idle. When the *Yorktown* had been sent south, the *Enterprise* proceeded westward for an attack on Wake Island. Following his previous tactics, Halsey detached two cruisers and two destroyers for surface-ship bombardment in conjunction with the air attacks. This group was again under the command of Admiral Spruance. On the appointed day, the *Enterprise* ran into miserable weather. Attempting to launch in the dark before daylight, one plane crashed, and others that got into the air were unable to rendezvous in the rain squalls and low ceiling. Halsey then suspended launching until dawn and the attack finally got under way an hour later. Due to this delay,

Spruance's ships opened up on the shore installations before the planes arrived. Their shells set numerous fires, including one in what appeared to be a large gasoline depot, just as our planes showed up. No opposition rose from the fine air strip the Japanese had captured from us. The American planes plastered the adjacent buildings and runways with bombs. A four-motored bomber encountered in the air was shot down. "It was just a matter of going in and unloading your bombs," one pilot reported. The raid destroyed three large aircraft, seven large gasoline-storage tanks, a fuel dump, several ammunition magazines, and numerous buildings. It undoubtedly hampered the enemy in their work of building up Wake as an operating base.

Homeward bound again, Admiral Halsey received startling orders from the Commander in Chief. He was to go farther west and attack the little island of Marcus, only 1,200 miles from Tokyo. The force swung about and headed west. Leaving his destroyers behind, Admiral Halsey dashed in on March 4, 1942, with only the *Enterprise, Northampton* and *Salt Lake City*. The attack on Marcus was made entirely by air, with no surface-ship bombardment. It was conducted by moonlight, shortly before dawn. Although no enemy aircraft were seen, intense antiaircraft fire was received and one of our planes was shot down. The occupants were seen to get into their rubber boat near the island and were presumed to have been taken prisoner. Accurate observations were impossible in the moonlight, but the flyers estimated that they had destroyed a group of large gasoline tanks and the radio system and set numerous fires in hangars and other buildings. The raid again demonstrated the feasibility of air attacks on hostile bases wherever the carrier air strength was superior to that of the enemy. It gave us new information about Marcus. And it may have influenced the Japanese in their subsequent decision to attempt to capture Midway, which later produced one of the most decisive battles of the war.

But another stirring event was about to unfold. The carrier *Hornet*, under the command of Captain Marc A. Mitscher, had arrived in the Pacific from the Atlantic and was destined to team with the *Enterprise* in the most daring action yet undertaken. Japan itself was to be bombed.

In February, 1942, on the East Coast, the *Hornet* had taken aboard two Army B-25 medium bombers and Navy pilots in a test had flown them off successfully. Then she sailed for the Pacific. At Alameda, California, she took aboard a deckload of Army B-25's, with their pilots and flight crews, commanded by Lieutenant Colonel James H. Doolittle. The utmost secrecy was maintained as to their destination and most of the crew believed they were simply bound for some distant Army base. Sixteen of the big planes, too large to go down the *Hornet*'s elevators to the hangar deck, were parked on the flight deck. Most of the carrier's own planes were left behind.

For weeks the Army pilots had been training under Navy Lieutenant Henry L. Miller, on landing fields, to get into the air with the shortest practicable take-off run. They were going to have to take off from the carrier deck in only 300 feet, which was considered to be an impossible feat. To many of the Army fliers it seemed an utterly impractical undertaking.

After leaving San Francisco, the *Hornet* and her escorts joined the *Enterprise* at sea about 400 miles north of Wake. The expedition under Halsey now consisted of the *Enterprise* and *Hornet*, the cruisers *Northampton, Salt Lake City, Vincennes*, and *Nashville*, under the command of Spruance, and eight destroyers, the *Balch, Benham, Ellet, Fanning, Grayson, Gwin, Meredith* and *Monssen*. A cheer went up when the ships' companies heard the announcement that the destination of the Army planes was Tokyo.

It had been planned to launch the B-25's at night from a point about 400 miles from the Japanese coast so that the attack would be made under cover of darkness. They were to fly on to friendly airfields in unoccupied China. If launched from this distance, it did not look like too difficult an operation, or one that involved suicidal risks for the airmen. However, on the morning of April 18, while still roughly 700 miles from Japan, the group ran into a number of fishing boats, or possibly pickets. Although the Japanese craft were

B-25 "Mitchell"

promptly sunk by *Enterprise* planes or ships' gunfire, Halsey and Doolittle considered that they might have sent radio word of the presence of the task force. If so, heavy air attacks on the carriers could be expected, perhaps before the bombers could be launched. In addition, there would probably be a hot reception over Japan. The decision was made to launch the planes immediately, even though the distance was too great for them to reach the China bases.

With the deck pitching in the heavy sea, but with a strong wind to assist the take-off, Colonel Doolittle was the first to go. All the big bombers got off without mishap, although several almost dipped into the water before they picked up sufficient air speed to gain altitude with their heavy loads. With a message of "Good luck and God bless you" to Doolittle and his gallant command from Halsey, the task force turned eastward at high speed to withdraw from dangerous waters. No air attack on the ships eventuated and they safely returned to Pearl Harbor.

Winging their way westward, heading into a strong head wind which unfortunately used up more of their precious gasoline, the audacious bombers arrived over Tokyo shortly after noon. In the clear weather, they had no trouble locating the exact targets assigned to each plane. The Japanese had received no advance warning of the raid and there was little hostile reaction. Not more than 30 enemy fighters were sighted during the flight and these were entirely ineffective. Skimming over house tops, except when zooming to 1,500 feet to drop their bombs, the raiders attacked at will. One of the targets was the Navy Yard at Yokosuka, where a direct hit was claimed on a new cruiser or battleship under construction. Others included aircraft factories, power plants, and oil refineries. The flyers had been specifically instructed not to bomb the Imperial Palace or its grounds so as not to make a martyr of the Emperor and cause his people to fight harder than ever.

After the attack, all the bombers headed for the China coast. One got off its course and landed near Khabarovsk in Siberia, where the Russians interned its crew. Not one landed intact on an airfield in Free China. Some crashed into the sea or in enemy-occupied zones, a few in friendly Chinese territory. Eight men were captured by the Japanese and some of them were wantonly beheaded. Of the remaining flight personnel, 64 were smuggled through to freedom by the

Chinese guerrillas and eventually reached the United States. Among them was Doolittle, who was destined to achieve great fame in other theaters and to rise to the rank of Lieutenant General.

The Tokyo raid cost the lives of 11 men and the loss of 16 planes. It electrified the world when it was disclosed, and for months there was a great mystery as to where the flight had originated. President Roosevelt announced that the raiders had come from mysterious "Shangri-La." The unimaginative Japanese must have busily searched their atlases to find that fictional locality.

But these minor actions were but skirmishes preliminary to the vital and dramatic events about to unfold. As hit-and-run raids, they were important in "blooding" our fliers and ships in actual combat and in schooling them to the stern tests that lay ahead. The time had come when vital and decisive sea battles would vividly demonstrate the revolution in naval warfare brought about by aviation, and show beyond further doubt that the battleship, with its heavy guns, would henceforth be relegated to auxiliary roles. These battles between fleets would be fought entirely by aircraft. No surface ships would even sight each other during the engagements.

5

THE BATTLE OF THE CORAL SEA

Despite our successful raids on the Marshalls, Salamaua, Lae, and Tokyo, the war in the Pacific had not been going well for the democracies. The Japanese were proceeding with their conquest of New Guinea, Bataan had fallen on April 9, Corregidor was about to surrender, and the American General Joseph W. Stilwell was being driven out of Burma, taking, as he called it, "a terrible licking." Where the Japanese march would be halted was still unpredictable.

After the Salamaua-Lae raid, the *Yorktown* task force had refueled from tankers well to the eastward. Food was short, but Admiral King in Washington suggested that the task force "live on hardtack and beans," and they remained in the South Pacific. The *Lexington* group took the long trail back to Pearl Harbor to receive additional 1.1 inch antiaircraft guns and for removal of the carrier's 8-inch turrets, which had been proved to be of little use. Their removal would give more deck space for the parking of planes.

At Pearl Harbor, Rear Admiral W. Fitch relieved Vice-Admiral Wilson Brown in command of the task force, which put to sea for routine training on April 16. Before this could be started, however, Admiral Nimitz ordered us to proceed south to the Coral Sea and rejoin the *Yorktown* group under Admiral Fletcher, who would head the combined task force.

The two forces made contact on May 1, but did not immediately join up, Fletcher directing Fitch to go on farther to a fueling rendezvous with the tanker *Tippecanoe*, the cruiser *Chicago* and the destroyer *Perkins*. The *Yorktown* group fueled from the *Neosho* on May 2; the *Lexington* and her screening ships began fueling the next day.

On April 30, a Japanese striking force and support force had departed from Truk to cover the capture and occupation of Tulagi in the Solomons, opposite Guadalcanal, and of Port Moresby in southeastern New Guinea. The enemy's actual invasion forces sailed from Rabaul. After Tulagi was occupied on May 3, the support forces proceeded through the Solomons Sea toward Port Moresby. The transports of the Port Moresby invasion force were to enter the Coral Sea through the Jomard Passage, between the Louisiades and New Guinea, while the striking force, including the big carriers *Shokaku* and *Zuikaku*, remained in the eastern Coral Sea to prevent interference by our carriers. The support force consisted of the light carrier *Shoho;* the heavy cruisers *Aoba, Kinugasa, Kako* and *Furataka;* the light cruisers *Tenryu, Tatsuta* and *Yubari;* and nine destroyers. The Port Moresby invasion force contained nine transports. The striking force comprised in addition to the carriers, the heavy cruisers *Myoko, Haguro,* and *Ashigara,* and six destroyers. The Japanese commander, Vice-Admiral Takagi, knew we had a carrier force near by, but not its strength or exact location.

Admiral Fletcher ordered an immediate attack with the *Yorktown* planes on the enemy shipping at Tulagi, leaving the *Lexington* group to finish fueling the next day. With the *Yorktown* were the heavy cruisers *Astoria, Chester,* and *Portland*

and the destroyers *Hammann*, *Anderson*, *Perkins*, *Walke*, *Morris*, and *Sims*.

From 100 miles southwest of Guadalcanal, at 7:00 A.M., May 4, 12 torpedo planes, 13 scout planes, and 15 dive bombers were launched for the attack. All of the *Yorktown*'s 18 fighter planes were kept over the ships for their own defense. This was a serious mistake. It required the attack squadrons to operate without fighter cover. Furthermore, no orders were issued directing the bombers and torpedo planes to make a coordinated attack.

Therefore the attack was not well organized even by the standards of those early days. The scout bombers arrived first over Tulagi and adjacent Gavutu Harbor. They found there two large transports or cargo ships, two destroyers, a light cruiser, a large seaplane tender, and many small craft. Diving through heavy antiaircraft fire, they claimed four sure hits. Showing up a short time later, some of the torpedo planes aimed at two destroyers and a light cruiser, but estimated only three hits. Others aimed at a cargo ship, but missed. The third group, consisting of bombers, attacked various targets about ten minutes later, and claimed only one hit on the seaplane tender.

These squadrons made additional strikes in the late forenoon and early afternoon. They made their runs with no attempt at coordination, and without fighter cover or strafing against the flak. Enemy seaplanes had interfered with the second attack and four fighters were sent to destroy them. They promptly shot down three seaplanes and strafed a destroyer escaping at high speed, leaving it trailing oil. Our second and third attacks by the torpedo and bomber planes accomplished little more than the first. The pilots reported hitting and blowing up two small gunboats and additional hits on the seaplane tender.

The results of this strike were quite disappointing. Although two destroyers, one cargo ship and four gunboats were estimated sunk, reports obtained from Japan after the war established that their only losses were one old destroyer and four landing barges sunk. These sources also stated that one old destroyer was damaged by strafing, the captain and other personnel being killed. We lost two fighter planes and one torpedo plane to antiaircraft fire, but both fighter pilots were rescued. The poor results were attributed at the time to lack of training. However, coordinated and simultaneous mass

THE BATTLE OF THE
CORAL SEA

SURFACE FORCES
AIR ATTACKS
Nautical miles
0 30 60 90 120   180   240

JAPANESE
STRIKE
FORCE

SHOKAKU
ZUIKAKU
2400
May 4

Bougainville

SOLOMON ISLANDS

2400
May 5

THE SLOT

JAPANESE
SUPPORT
FORCE

Tulagi

Malaita I.

2400 May 8

Guadalcanal

S E A

2400
May 5

2400
May 6

2400
May 7

Rennell I.

2400
May3

Shokaku
damaged

2400
May 6

2400
May 4

YORKTOWN

AMERICAN
CARRIER
FORCE

Sims sunk

Neosho sunk

2400
May 5

LEXINGTON

attacks by dive bombers and torpedo planes, with fighters strafing the antiaircraft guns, would probably have given better results. Such attacks later became standard practice.

The *Yorktown* task force returned to the fueling rendezvous at 8:45 A.M. on May 5 and there joined the *Lexington* group to form one task force. Two Australian cruisers, the *Australia* and *Hobart*, had also reported, so that the force was now as follows:

ATTACK GROUP, REAR ADMIRAL THOMAS C. KINKAID

CRUISERS, *Rear Admiral William W. Smith*
Minneapolis, Capt. Frank J. Lowry
New Orleans, Capt. Howard H. Good
Astoria, Capt. Francis W. Scanland
Chester, Capt. Thomas M. Shock
Portland, Capt. Benjamin Perlman

DESTROYERS, *Capt. Alexander R. Early*
Phelps, Lt. Comdr. Edward L. Beck
Dewey, Lt. Comdr. Charles F. Chillingworth, Jr.
Farragut, Lt. Comdr. George P. Hunter
Aylwin, Lt. Comdr. Robert H. Rogers
Monaghan, Lt. Comdr. William P. Burford

SUPPORT GROUP, REAR ADMIRAL J. G. CRACE, RN

CRUISERS
Australia, Capt. H.B. Farncom, RAN
Chicago, Capt. Howard D. Bode
Hobart, Capt. H. L. Howden, RAN

DESTROYERS, *Comdr. Francis X. McInerny*
Perkins, Lt. Comdr. Walter C. Ford
Walke, Lt. Comdr. Thomas E. Fraser

AIR GROUP, REAR ADMIRAL AUBREY W. FITCH

CARRIERS
Lexington, Capt. Frederick C. Sherman
Yorktown, Capt. Elliott Buckmaster

DESTROYERS, *Capt. Gilbert C. Hoover*
Morris, Comdr. Harry B. Jarrett
Anderson, Lt. Comdr. John K. B. Ginder

Hammann, Comdr. Arnold True
Russell, Lt. Comdr. Glenn R. Hartwig

Fitch had his flag on the *Lexington* and had designated me as his "ex officio" chief of staff, in addition to my duties as captain of the *Lexington*. As the senior naval aviator in the force, he was designated "Commander, Air," in charge of all the air operations, under Fletcher's direction. The orders from Nimitz read "to destroy enemy ships, shipping, and aircraft at favorable opportunities in order to assist in checking the advances by the enemy in the New Guinea-Solomons area."

The combined task force fueled from the *Neosho* on May 5 and 6, after which the tanker and the destroyer *Sims* were sent to cruise about 300 miles to the southeast. The task force headed west into the Coral Sea.

Intelligence of the enemy was very sketchy. Long-range patrol bombers operating out of Townsville, northern Australia, and from Port Moresby, were attempting a long-range search over the Solomons Sea as far as Rabaul, but it was only slightly effective. The weather in the area was difficult, with many tropical rain squalls, and the Army pilots were still relatively inexperienced in recognizing and evaluating types of enemy ships sighted. Whatever they saw, whether a transport, tug, or destroyer, was apt to be reported as either a battleship or a carrier. In the difficult weather, their navigation was often inaccurate. We could rely on neither the positions nor the identifications given in their few reports. Navy patrol planes based at Noumea endeavored against similar handicaps to search between New Caledonia and the eastern Solomons.

By the afternoon of May 6, meager reports from the scouting planes indicated a large number of enemy ships in the New Guinea-New Britain-Solomons area. Their direction of movement seemed to be toward Port Moresby, although what channel they would take to enter the Coral Sea was not apparent. Our task force headed northwest into this critical area without any real information as to the enemy's position, course, strength or destination.

Our carriers alternated in carrying out daily air searches, the remaining planes of both carriers standing by to attack any targets located. Thus one carrier was always left with a

depleted attack group, the other with a full complement. The
fighter squadrons were divided equally, so that the attack
groups had fighter escort while the task force retained the
remainder for its own defense. These early actions were to
show the need for a higher percentage of fighters on our
carriers.

The *Yorktown* had the scouting duty on May 7. At
daylight her scout bombers were launched to search the
northern semicircle to a distance of 275 miles. At the same
time Fletcher sent Crace's cruiser group, plus the destroyer
Farragut, to take station at the southern end of Jomard

U.S.S. Sims

Passage to intercept any enemy ships trying to come through it.

All hands were eagerly waiting when one of the search planes flashed a report of an enemy carrier just north of Misima Island, near the northern entrance to Jomard Passage, and heading southeast. Other reports from the land-based planes at Townsville came in, indicating many ships in the Solomons Sea, all moving in the general direction of Port Moresby. The time to strike had come.

Our remaining scouts returned, reporting no contacts. In one sector to the eastward, they had turned back when they

ran into a rain squall 150 miles out instead of continuing to the designated distance. This was unfortunate, as after events proved that the large carriers *Zuikaku* and *Shokaku* were in this sector. They were not located until the next morning.

Fortune favored the attack groups winging their way toward the reported position of the enemy carrier near Misima Island. The *Lexington* group, leading the way and anxiously scanning the water below, suddenly spotted a vessel. It was the small carrier *Shoho*, escorted by several cruisers and destroyers.

With clocklike precision, the *Lexington* bombers went into their dives, closely followed by the torpedo planes at low altitude. The *Yorktown* planes went in almost simultaneously. Our fighter escorts encountered a number of defending Nakajima 97 fighters, an efficient plane but not as effective as the better-known Zero. When the 97's attempted to break up the dive-bomber formation, our fighters shot down seven of them. Within a few minutes, the *Shoho* had received thirteen bomb hits and seven torpedo hits. Burning from stem to stern and with black smoke pouring out, she blew up and sank fifteen minutes later. Our pilots watched her go down. They reported that her casualties must have been enormous.

Returning from the attack, Lieutenant Commander Bob Dixon, Commander of Scouting Squadron Two, coined a new word which has since become a standard designation for a carrier. His radio message was simply, "Scratch one flattop." They were the most thrilling words we had heard since Pearl Harbor.

Our air groups were back aboard by 1:45 P.M., except for three planes which had been shot down in the attack. With plenty of daylight left, Fitch, on the *Lexington*, immediately planned to send off another strike on other targets in the same general locality as the *Shoho*. Fletcher countermanded this plan, afterwards giving as his reason the fact that the large Japanese carriers, known to be in the vicinity, had not been located. Accepting this as sound, it was then essential to send out another search, but by the time this decision was reached, after exchange of signals between the *Yorktown* and the *Lexington*, it was too late in the afternoon to do either.

While our planes were attacking the *Shoho*, the Japanese carriers *Zuikaku* and *Shokaku*, to the eastward, had been unable to locate our task force amidst the rain squalls. About 300 miles southeast of us, however, they found our tanker, the *Neosho*, which one of their scouts reported as a carrier. Their air groups attacked this helpless auxiliary and her escort destroyer, the *Sims*. The *Neosho* was soon a mass of flames and the *Sims* went down after being hit by several bombs. Although waterlogged, the oiler's tanks kept her afloat until May 11, when she was sunk by torpedoes from the *Henley*, one of our destroyers which had come out from Noumea to rescue survivors.

The cruiser group which had been sent to watch Jomard Passage was attacked at 2:34 P.M., after being shadowed by enemy scouts from 8:40 in the morning, by 10 to 14 twin-engine planes from Rabaul, armed with torpedoes. No hits were made and the cruisers claimed to have shot down four to six of the aircraft. A short time later a formation of high-level bombers loosed a salvo of bombs which straddled the *Australia* but made no hits. Soon thereafter, another group of planes dropped bombs, all of which missed. One of the destroyer commanders identified the last attackers as U.S. Army B-26's.

This was too much for the British admiral. He sent urgent messages asking for fighter cover, which could not be given to him. He therefore reported that he was withdrawing from the area and headed in the general direction of Australia. His ships from then on played no further part in the battle.

On May 7, while we were in and out of rain squalls, various "bogeys" (unidentified planes on the radar screen) were reported. It was hard for our planes to intercept them in the poor visibility, but at 11:14 A.M. a section of *Yorktown* fighters caught up with a four-engined flying boat about 40

B-26 "Marauder"

miles from the task force and shot it down. *Yorktown* planes were not equipped with IFF (Identification of Friendly Forces) and many interceptions were made on planes which proved to be friendly. Others couldn't be contacted because of clouds and mist.

Late in the afternoon, several large groups of planes appeared on the radar screen and the *Lexington* fighters found one of them in an opening in the clouds. It consisted of eight Zero fighters. Our pilots shot down five in a sharp action in which we lost one plane. *Yorktown* fighters downed several additional planes identified as dive bombers. Clearly the enemy carriers were somewhere near by.

It was well after sunset when we began landing our last patrols. About half of these had been taken aboard in the gathering dusk when our lookouts discovered more planes in the landing circle than we could account for. Moreover, contrary to our practice, they were burning running lights. Then they were suddenly identified as Japanese planes trying to land on our decks. They had mistaken our carriers for their own. Some of our ships started shooting at the hostile visitors, but were unable to distinguish friend from foe. They were shooting indiscriminately. Our aircraft disappeared into the darkness like a flock of birds flushed by hunters. The enemy planes turned off their running lights and did likewise.

After the excitement died down, we opened up on our radios to call our own planes back, and landed all but one which was unable to find us in the now complete darkness and was never heard of again. Our radars followed the enemy and tracked them 30 miles to the eastward, where they orbited and one by one went off the screen. This indicated that they were landing on their own carrier only 30 miles away. We reported this to Fletcher, but he was inclined to discredit it. It was confirmed after the war that the Japanese carriers were very close to us that night. It might have been an excellent opportunity for a night torpedo attack by our destroyers or by the *Lexington* torpedo plane squadron, which was trained in night landings. But instead, Fletcher decided to head south to avoid a chance contact with the enemy during the hours of darkness. The Japanese headed north, and the decision unfortunately put us the next morning in a clear area of unlimited ceiling and visibility. Thus we were at a disadvantage compared to the enemy, who remained under the cover of the weather front which had been around us the previous day.

The *Lexington* had the scouting duty. At daybreak we sent out a search in all directions. It was possible that the Japanese might have headed south and passed us during the night. Our planes covered 360 degrees of the compass, 150 miles to the south and 300 miles to the north. All hands were tense as we waited for the decisive action we were sure the day would bring.

At 8:22 came the expected contact report. Lieutenant (j.g.) Joseph Smith of Scouting Two had sighted the enemy formation 190 miles northeast of us. It was thrilling news—the first sighting of the large Japanese carriers by either land-based or carrier planes. In addition to the *Shokaku* and *Zuikaku*, their disposition contained three heavy cruisers and a number of destroyers.

About two minutes after receiving this report, we intercepted a radio transmission from a Japanese plane which we deduced was a contact report of our position. The first carrier duel in history was about to begin. I remarked on the bridge of the *Lexington* that from their distance at the time of contact the attack would probably come in on us at 11 A.M., and that it was possible for the carriers on both sides to be sunk by the simultaneous onslaught of the opposing air groups. We prepared for a fight to the finish.

The weather in the vicinity of the enemy was typical of the tropical front we had experienced the previous day, flyable but full of rain squalls offering good hiding places for surface ships trying to avoid an air attack. Bob Dixon, of "scratch one flattop" fame, upon intercepting the contact report, proceeded to the position of the enemy location to assist in tracking their movements. He stayed in their vicinity for over two hours, dodging in and out of clouds to avoid enemy fighters bent on shooting him down, and gave us excellent information until fuel shortage forced his return.

Both our carriers promptly launched their air-attack groups, the *Yorktown* being designated to lead, reversing the order of the previous day. This group consisted of 24 dive bombers, nine torpedo planes, and six fighters; the *Lexington* sent out 22 dive bombers, twelve torpedo planes and nine fighters, for a total from the two groups of 82 planes.

By the time the planes were launched, the distance to

the enemy had been reduced to about 165 miles, which was still a little long for the torpedo bombers to cover, out and back. We had planned to shorten the return trip still further by heading in their direction while they were in the air. Circumstances beyond our control were to render this impossible.

During their flight to the targets, the two air groups became hopelessly separated. To keep together in the existing weather was impossible. The dive bombers climbed to 17,000 feet to be in position for their attack; the torpedo planes had to make their runs at low altitude and in any case could do little climbing with their heavy loads. In addition, the *Lexington* dive bombers got separated from the rest of their own group. Three of their escorting fighters also went astray in the poor visibility. Thus the *Lexington* group, under Commander Bill Ault, when it finally found the enemy consisted of only four dive bombers, twelve torpedo planes and six fighters.

The *Yorktown* attack group was first to sight the Japanese force, at 10:32, and waited for the slower torpedo planes to get into position. The two enemy carriers, they reported, had separated so that they were now some six or eight miles apart, with one group making for a rain squall and the other heading into the easterly wind and launching its planes. The *Yorktown* group at 10:58 A.M. dived down in a coordinated attack on the latter carrier.

Enemy fighters attacked the bombers during their dives, and our pilots were hampered by fogging of bomb sights and windshields. Nevertheless, they claimed six sure hits which started fires aboard the carrier. Unmolested, the torpedo craft loosed their "tin fish" and, upon their return, claimed three sure hits. In the engagement with the enemy fighters, the two bomber squadrons reported eleven Zeros shot down, while their fighter cover claimed kills on three Zeros, one scout, and a torpedo plane. Making use of the cloud cover for rendezvousing and retiring, all the *Yorktown* planes returned safely.

When the *Lexington* group, minus the dive-bombing squadron, arrived at the spot where they expected to find the enemy, nothing was in sight but rain squalls. Ault directed the torpedo squadron to "fly a square" while he went on with the four dive bombers of his section to look for the Japanese carriers. He found one of them 20 miles away, partly hidden by a squall. Unable to contact the rest of the dive bombers by radio, he ordered a coordinated attack by the torpedo group and his own section of four dive bombers. Zeros engaged in hot combat the six fighters accompanying the torpedo group.

Roaring down in their power dives to 2,500 feet, the bombers released their missiles, with the torpedo planes at the same time flying in just off the water. The pilots subsequently reported two 1,000-pound bomb hits and five torpedo hits. There were vicious dogfights between our own and the enemy fighters, from which two of our fliers failed to return. How many Japanese planes were shot down could not be determined in the poor visibility.

Only one of the four bombers returned to the carrier. Pulling out of their dives, they were unable to reassemble in the mist and rain. One plane, Ensign Haschke, fell in with one of our fighters, Lieutenant Noel Gaylor, and the two came back together. Commander Ault was in touch with the *Lexington* by radio and reported both his radio man and himself wounded. Unable to fix his position after the melee, he requested directions back to the ship. In spite of every effort to distinguish his plane from the dozens of others on the radar screen, the attempts to coach him back were unsuccessful. In his last message Ault told us he was landing on the water. "Remember we got a 1,000-pound hit on the flattop," his voice said, "and one other plane got one too." Probably he became unconscious from his wounds shortly thereafter, and crashed. An unknown spot in the Coral Sea was the end of the trail for this gallant and courageous officer.

Lieutenant Commander Jimmie Brett's torpedo squadron rendezvoused after its attack and took a defensive formation, knowing enemy fighters would soon be after them. They had a long road back home to the carrier. Every ounce of gasoline had to be conserved. In ensuing attacks, they shot down two Japanese fighters and fought off many others. One plane went down into the water, out of gas, just as it got within sight of the *Lexington*. Diligent search later failed to locate its men. When we sighted this group returning about 2 P.M., we had about given them up for lost. They had been out an hour longer than the time when our figures said their gas should have been exhausted. Short of fuel and unable to maneuver for recognition purposes, their one thought was to get into the landing circle as quickly as possible. They came straight in. The *Yorktown* opened fire on them, not realizing they were *Lexington* planes, before we could stop her. Luckily none were hit and we soon had them on board, some of their gasless engines conking out as they hit the deck. They were landed while the *Lexington* was fighting tremendous fires below decks from the internal gasoline-vapor explosion I shall describe a little later.

According to the logs of the returning fliers, the *Lexington* group had attacked at 10:57, the *Yorktown* group at 10:58. Neither had encountered the other during the attacks and it was established that the two enemy carriers had separated on first sighting our planes. A difference of opinion arose as to whether both had attacked the same target, or each a different carrier. When interviewed after the war, Admiral Takagi and other Japanese survivors of the action reported that the *Shokaku* had sustained moderate damage in this attack, but were positive that the *Zuikaku* was not hit. This testimony was given from memory since no Japanese records were available. The informants' recollection of these events which had taken place years before must have been somewhat dimmed by subsequent momentous happenings. It is still my opinion that both enemy carriers were seriously damaged. In any case, both lost the bulk of their planes and pilots, and although they returned to Japan, neither vessel was in shape to take part a month later in the Battle of Midway, for which the Japanese had scheduled them. This may have been the deciding factor in our victory at Midway.

Aboard the *Lexington*, after our attack planes had departed, we had made full preparations for the onslaught we expected from the Japanese. Our returning scouts were landed, serviced, and launched again for defense against low-flying torpedo bombers. Although the SBD's were not intended for use as fighters, their two fixed 50-caliber machine guns in the nose and swivel 30-caliber rear guns might prove useful against the equally slow enemy torpedo planes. Nine of the *Lexington*'s 18 fighters were escorting the attack group, leaving nine others for defense around the carriers.

We landed and serviced our combat patrols. At 11 A.M., all our planes were in the air with full tanks of gas. Then we went to battle stations and "buttoned up" the ship—closed all watertight doors and hatches, stowed all unnecessary gear, had all fire hoses ready, drained our gasoline filling lines, and distributed first-aid equipment throughout the vessel. At eleven o'clock we were as ready as humanly possible to give the enemy planes a hot reception and to withstand whatever damage we might suffer.

At 10:14 a *Yorktown* fighter on combat patrol spotted a Kawanishi four-engine flying boat and promptly shot it down. At 10:55 the radar showed a large group of enemy planes approaching from the northeast. At 11:13 the *Lexington*'s lookouts sighted the first of the attackers. The battle was on.

The weather was bright and sunny, with hardly a cloud in the sky. The Japanese had no difficulty in finding us. On the sparkling, tropical sea, we were visible from miles away. Our move to the south the night before had given the enemy this advantage, but it also meant that they had no cloud cover to mask their approach. The clear visibility gave our antiaircraft guns full play.

Fighter direction was still in its early stage of development. Control was on board the *Lexington* for all the fighters in the air. There were 17 in all, eight from the *Yorktown* plus the *Lexington*'s nine, with Lieutenant "Red" Gill as fighter-direction officer. The single, early model radar we had on

Kawanishi H6K5 "Mavis"

board picked up the enemy aircraft at a distance of 68 miles, but gave no indication of their altitude. On those old radars it was also difficult to distinguish friendly from enemy planes. We felt that if our fighters were sent far out on interception, they might miss the contact, owing to differences in altitude, and thus be wasted. We were also influenced by the belief that the torpedo planes represented the greater hazard and that they would come in low. Accordingly, we kept our fighters close in overhead, at 10,000 feet, ready to attack when the enemy groups arrived at their "push-over" point. The Dauntless dive bombers on anti-torpedo-plane patrol were stationed at 2,000 feet, 6,000 yards out. We learned in this battle that to break up an air attack it was necessary to intercept it at a much greater distance from the carriers. It must be remembered that this was the first carrier duel in history, and we were learning our tactics by experience. Nevertheless, our defending planes did a magnificent job.

Five *Lexington* fighters were vectored out at 11:02 to intercept the oncoming craft. They made contact 20 miles away and reported one group of 50 to 60 planes stacked in layers from 10,000 to 13,000 feet, with torpedo planes in the lowest level, then fighters, then dive bombers, then more fighters. There were approximately 18 torpedo planes, 18 dive bombers, and 24 fighters in this group.

Two of our five fighters had been sent low to look for torpedo planes. The other three fighters in the intercepting unit climbed madly for altitude and dashed in to attack. Engaged by the Zeros, they shot down several but were unable to stop the bombers before they started their dives. The two low fighters attacked the torpedo planes as they dropped down for their part in the battle, but were unsuccessful in stopping them.

The air fighting now became a melee. Our own planes were mixed in with the enemy and the sky was black with flak bursts. The Japanese spent no time in maneuvering, but dived straight in for the kill. The huge *Lexington* dwarfed the other ships in the formation and bore the brunt of the attack.

It was beautifully coordinated. From my bridge I saw bombers roaring down in steep dives from many points in the sky, and torpedo planes coming in on both bows almost simultaneously. There was nothing I could do about the bombers, but I could do something to avoid the torpedoes. As I saw a bomb leave one of the planes, it seemed to be coming straight for where I stood on the bridge. Had I better duck behind the thin armored shield? If it had my name on it, I thought, there was no use dodging, and if not, there was no need to worry. At any rate, I had work to do to try to evade the torpedoes.

The ideal way to drop torpedoes was for groups of planes to let go simultaneously on both bows. In this method, if the target ship turned toward one group to parallel its torpedoes, it presented its broadside to the other. The timing was vital. The enormous *Lexington* was very slow in turning. It took 30 to 40 seconds just to put the rudder hard over. When she did start to turn, she moved majestically and ponderously in a large circle. Maneuverability was greatly improved in later carriers.

As I saw the enemy torpedo planes coming in on both bows, it seemed to me that those to port were closer than those to starboard. They were approaching in steep glides, faster than we considered practicable for torpedo dropping. The air was full of antiaircraft bursts and the din was terrific. When the planes to port were about 1,000 yards away, I motioned to the helmsman, Chief Quartermaster McKenzie, for hard left rudder. It seemed an eternity before the bow started to turn, just as the enemy planes started disgorging their fish.

The water in all directions seemed full of torpedo wakes. Bombs were also dropping all around us. Great geysers of water from near misses were going up higher than our masts, and occasionally the ship shuddered from the explosions of the ones that hit.

In less than a minute, the first torpedoes had passed astern. We quickly shifted rudder to head for the second group of planes. These split up to fire on both bows, the hardest maneuver for us to counter. Then it became a matter of wriggling and twisting as best we could to avoid the deadly weapons heading our way. I remember seeing two wakes coming straight for our port beam, and there was nothing I could do about them. The wakes approached the ship's side, and I braced myself for the explosion. Nothing happened. I rushed to the starboard bridge, and there were the wakes emerging from that side. The torpedoes were running too deep and had passed completely under the ship.

My air officer on the bridge was Commander H. S. Duckworth. "Don't change course, Captain!" he exclaimed.

"There's a torpedo on each side of us running parallel!" We held our course with a torpedo 50 yards on either beam and both finally disappeared without hitting.

Enemy planes were being shot down right and left, and the water around us was dotted with the towering flames of their burning carcasses. One plane turned upside down as it hit the water, its torpedo still slung on its belly. Before it sank, we noticed a peculiar wooden framework around the missile's nose and propeller mechanism. This explained why the Japanese were able to drop their torpedoes at such high speeds and altitudes. The cushioning devices permitted them to enter the water without excessive shock to the delicate machinery. It was a scheme still undeveloped by our ordnance experts, and gave the Japanese at least a temporary superiority in torpedo warfare.

Five bombs had landed on the *Lexington*. Two torpedoes exploded against our port side. The water spouts of three near misses which splashed water on the deck were also thought at first to be from torpedoes, but subsequent examination showed only two actual hits by this weapon.

One bomb had hit the port gun gallery just outside the Admiral's cabin. It wiped out most of the gun crews in that vicinity, and started fires. In addition, it killed Commander Gilmore, our paymaster, and Commander Trojalkowski, our dentist, who were in the passageway just inboard, and communications men in an adjacent room.

Bombs started fires in other parts of the ship, but none was especially serious. Fragments killed men in one of the fire-control stations aloft. One bomb passed between the bridge and the funnel and severed the wire pull on the siren, setting it off to add its sorrowful wail to the ear-shattering din.

Suddenly all was quiet again. It was as though some hidden director had signaled for silence. The Japanese planes were no longer in sight, the guns had stopped shooting for lack of targets. The sea was still dotted with burning planes; our own aircraft were seen in the distance, assembling to be ready for further action. But the enemy were through.

I looked at my watch. The entire attack had lasted just nine minutes. It seemed hours since we had first sighted the enemy planes.

Off in the distance to the southeastward, we could see the *Yorktown*, a column of black smoke rising from her flight deck. Evidently she too had been damaged. She had been attacked by both torpedo planes and dive bombers, but with her greater maneuverability had managed to evade all torpedoes and was hit only by one large bomb, which had penetrated the flight deck and exploded in a storeroom down below. It had killed 37 men outright and wounded many others. Near misses had caused several fragment holes in the hull along the water line. Otherwise the *Yorktown* was undamaged.

Taking stock on the *Lexington*, we found things not so bad as they might have been. The small firest down below were being fought by the damage-control parties, who reported that they would soon have them under control. No smoke from the flames was showing above decks. The ship had taken only a seven-degree list from the torpedo hits, and this was rapidly being corrected by shifting water ballast. The engine room reported full power and speed available if I wanted it. Our flight deck was intact. We felt like throwing out our chests at our condition after the attack. But our satisfaction was soon to be changed to apprehension.

We proceeded to land our planes which were in the vicinity, and out of ammunition or gas after their air battles. We replenished the ammunition of our guns and refilled the ammunition hoists to be ready for another attack should one come. Lieutenant Commander H. R. ("Pop") Healy, our Damage Control Officer, was down in Central Station, below the armored deck, where directions for all damage control were issued and reports received. He had just phoned the bridge to inform me that all damage was under control. "If we have another attack," he said, "I'd like to take it on the starboard side, since both torpedo hits were to port."

At 12:47, the *Lexington* was suddenly shaken by a terrific internal explosion which seemed to come from the bottom of the ship. It rocked the huge structure more violently than had anything we had received during the battle. Smoke began emerging from around the edges of the elevator on the flight deck.

We called Central Station on the telephone but found the connection broken. The rudder indicator on the bridge was also out. All telephones were dead except a sound-powered one to the engine room. However, reports of huge fires breaking out in the vicinity of Central Station were soon received. The station itself was an inferno. A few men had escaped from it; others were rescued by volunteers who risked their lives in the flames, but the majority, including Healy, had been killed outright by the terrific explosion. Its cause was later established as the insidious accumulation of gasoline vapor, leaking unsuspected from our gasoline storage tanks, which had been weakened by the torpedo hits. It was an unexpected blow, but as yet we had no idea that it was to cost us the ship.

Raging fires, fed by gasoline, broke out from ruptured vents and risers. The water main was broken in the area of the explosion, making the work of combating the flames extremely difficult. Long hoses had to be led from the far after part of the ship, and only very low water pressure could be maintained. It was a losing battle from the beginning, but we did not know it then. We fully expected to save the carrier.

I remained on the bridge to direct the handling of the ship and to receive reports. Commander Mort Seligman, the executive officer, was everywhere, advising and encouraging the fire fighters. Small explosions of ammunition were occurring frequently in the vicinity of the fires, and Seligman was more than once blown like a cork out of a bottle from watertight doors through which he was passing. He brought to the bridge frequent reports of conditions down below. All lights were out and the damage-control men toiled in complete darkness except for hand flashlights. The decks where they were working would grow hot from fires on the decks beneath.

Despite the loss of our rudder indicator on the bridge, we were able to steer from there for a while. It was during this period that we landed the torpedo squadron which returned so late and which we had feared was lost. Then the electric steering gear went completely out and we had to steer by maneuvering the engines, giving orders to the engine room over the one telephone still working. We were unable to use the hand steering in the station below for lack of communications to give the steersman there his course.

The fire continued to spread. More frequent explosions were occurring, and the surface of the elevator in the flight deck was beginning to glow a dull red. A report came from the engine control room that the forward engine-room bulkhead was getting white hot, and that the temperature in that vicinity had risen to 160 degrees. They asked permission, which I promptly granted, to abandon the forward engine room and use only the after engine-room space.

Then the one telephone began to get weaker. It was apparent that it was only a matter of time until it would go out completely. When it did, I realized, there would be no way of getting the men out of the engine rooms. Unless I ordered them to leave, they would stay there, trapped by fire all around them, and hemmed in by red-hot bulkheads, until they perished. Over the weakening phone, I ordered these men to secure the engineering plant and get up on deck. Although we were unable to hear any reply, presently the sound of steam escaping from the safety valves assured me they had received the message. Eventually all of them found their way through the encircling fires to safety on the topside.

We now had no power and the ship lay dead in the water. Without pressure on the main, we were helpless even to fight the fire. I called a destroyer alongside to send over its hoses, but the fire pumps on the small vessels in those early days were of such low capacity that only a trickle of water could be obtained from this source. It seemed outrageous that we could do nothing to put out the fire and save our ship.

At this time, about 5:00 P.M., Admiral Fitch, unperturbed and efficient, leaned over the flag bridge and told me I had better "get the boys off the ship." It was heartbreaking, but it seemed to be the only thing left to do. Reluctantly I gave the order to abandon ship. It was the hardest thing I have ever done. Nevertheless, if we could not prevent the loss of the *Lexington*, saving the lives of her crew was of utmost importance.

The officers and men were as reluctant to leave as I was. We had to order them to go. Most of the wounded were lowered to a destroyer alongside, the remainder going directly into small boats from the other ships. Some of the crew, while waiting to disembark, went below to the service store, which was not in the fire area. They filled their helmets with ice cream and stood around on the flight deck eating it. Knotted ropes were dropped over the side for the men to slide down into the water. Some of them lined up their shoes in orderly fashion on the deck before they left, as if they expected to return. There was not the slightest panic or disorder. I was proud of them.

I noticed one crowd waiting to go over the side at the port after gun gallery. As I approached to see what was delaying them, the men, led by Marine Sergeant Peyton, gave "three cheers for the Captain." Their loyalty was inspiring.

Finally, just after sunset, all the crew were off. The water around the ship was black with the bobbing heads of swimmers. Small boats from our escorts, cruisers and destroyers were busy picking men out of the water and transferring them to the other ships. After making a last inspection to insure that there were no stragglers, I stood with Commander Seligman at the stern. I directed him to leave, as it was my duty and privilege to be the last one to go. He went down into the water. I stood on the great ship alone.

While I was pausing there, a tremendous explosion took place amidships by the elevator. Planes and debris of all kinds went high into the air. Ducking under the edge of the flight deck to avoid the falling pieces, I decided it was time to go, and slid down the rope to do my stint of swimming until my turn came to be picked up by the rescue boats.

It was dark when I arrived on the cruiser *Minneapolis*. The burning *Lexington* was an awe-inspiring sight. All the survivors had by then been taken out of the water and were safe on board our cruisers and destroyers. Fletcher directed the *Phelps* to sink the *Lexington* by torpedoes. The great ship was lit up by her flames in the gathering darkness. The *Phelps* stood off and fired four torpedoes. They hit and exploded with dull booms. The stricken vessel started getting deeper in the water, slowly going down, as if she too was reluctant to give up the battle. With her colors proudly flying and the last signal flags, reading "I am abandoning ship," still waving at the yardarm, she went under on an even keel, like the lady she always was. As she disappeared from sight, there was a tremendous underwater explosion from her magazines. It was the end of the *Lexington*.

During the afternoon the task force had remained in our vicinity and the *Yorktown* had repaired the damage caused by her bomb hit. When we had lost propulsive power, our planes remaining in the air had landed on her deck. She had her own air group practically intact, plus the *Lexington* planes she had recovered. In spite of this, no further search was made for the enemy carriers nor were any additional attacks sent off. No Japanese aircraft came near us during the afternoon.

As soon as all the *Lexington* survivors were on board,

Admiral Fletcher decided to withdraw from further action. We proceeded southward during the night, transferring excess survivors on some ships to others not so crowded.

The next day scouts sent out the rear reported two Japanese carriers to the northward, pursuing us. It turned out to be a false alarm, the search planes having mistaken large rocks of the Australian Barrier Reef, with the surf breaking over them, for carriers. Before the error was discovered, a warning to beware of an enemy carrier raid was flashed to Townsville, and we continued southward at increased speed. We did not know then that the Japanese had called off their attempt to capture Port Moresby by sea and were withdrawing to the north.

Later we turned eastward and some of our ships put into Noumea on New Caledonia, while the rest went on to Tonga Tabu, in the Friendly Islands. There we all assembled a few days later for reorganization and redistribution. The *Lexington* survivors embarked on two transports for return to the United States, escorted by the cruiser *Chester*, on which Admiral Fitch and myself were given passage. The *Yorktown* and most of the cruisers went back to Pearl Harbor preparatory to taking part in the Battle of Midway, which was to occur less than a month later, and in which the *Yorktown* was to meet her end.

The Battle of the Coral Sea was a tactical and strategic victory, despite the loss of the *Lexington*. It was the first decisive naval battle in history in which surface ships did not exchange a shot. It was fought entirely by aircraft. As a result of this battle, the Japanese withdrew from their attempt to expand their southern conquests by amphibious attacks from the sea, and retreated with their forces badly punished. Never before had the modern Japanese Navy been defeated.

In this action, the Japanese lost one carrier and 105 planes, and approximately 90 additional aircraft severely damaged. But the most serious effect was the loss of the bulk of their participating carrier pilots, which marked the beginning of the attrition in these skilled fighters that was eventually to be a major cause of Japan's downfall. We lost one carrier, the *Lexington*, the tanker *Neosho*, the destroyer *Sims*, 81 aircraft and 543 men.

The Battle of the Coral Sea was a turning point in the war and a milestone in history. It proved the dominance of the aircraft carrier. As significant as the battle between the *Monitor* and the *Merrimac* in 1862, it ushered in a new era in fighting at sea, and ended the period of Japanese advance.

We learned a lot from this battle. We learned that it was necessary greatly to improve the fire-fighting equipment on our combat vessels. We learned that our carrier complement should include more fighter aircraft. We learned that we must improve our fighter-direction methods and intercept attacking aircraft at greater distances from our ships. All these lessons were to prove invaluable in the actions to come.

6

THE BATTLE OF MIDWAY

Encouraged by their easy conquests in the Southwest Pacific, the Japanese strategists decided to extend their defensive perimeter beyond the line originally contemplated. The Doolittle raid on Tokyo had convinced them that their homeland would not be safe without a foothold in the Aleutians and possession of the island of Midway. Accordingly, several weeks before the battle of the Coral Sea was fought, plans had been adopted to seize these new objectives.

The first phase of the Japanese plans for fighting the war had been completed with their occupation of the rich area of Malaya, Burma and the Dutch East Indies. Their only naval losses in these operations had been three destroyers sunk and a few other ships damaged. Never before had history recorded such vast conquests at such trifling cost. The bulk of the Allied forces in the Far East, on the other hand, had been destroyed. It is not surprising that the Japanese became overconfident and made the fatal error of underestimating their enemy.

Their original basic plans had not included expansion beyond the line, Kuriles, Marshalls, Bismarcks, Timor, Java, Sumatra, Malaya, and Burma. Succeeding operations were to be only for the purposes of consolidating and strengthening this defensive perimeter. Now, however, the enemy made ambitious new plans to extend their control farther east, north and south. These plans provided for:

(1) Capture of Port Moresby to strengthen the southern end of the line in New Guinea and the Bismarcks.

(2) Capture of Midway to strengthen their Central Pacific defenses and force a decisive engagement with the United States fleet.

(3) Invasion of the western Aleutians to strengthen the defenses of the northern area.

(4) Seizure of New Caledonia, Fiji, and Samoa to cut the communication lines between the United States and Australia. This step was contingent on success in the other three.

The loss of the Battle of the Coral Sea did not cause the Japanese to abandon their plan to occupy Port Moresby. They merely changed it to provide for proceeding there overland, across the Owen Stanley Mountains. Although the large carriers *Shokaku* and *Zuikaku* had been intended for the Midway operation, they and their assigned air groups had been so badly mauled in the Coral Sea action that they were not available. Nevertheless, the rest of the fleet was intact, and the operations to capture Midway and occupy the western Aleutians proceeded, both to be undertaken simultaneously.

The landings at Midway and in the Aleutians were to be on June 6, 1942. The total force to be used included seven carriers, 11 battleships, 24 cruisers, and 66 destroyers, in addition to 17 transports and other auxiliaries.

Against this great armada, we had only three carriers, eight cruisers and 14 destroyers. Our battleships afloat after Pearl Harbor were based at San Francisco, to be safe from bombing raids. They were ordered out to the combat area by their commander while the Midway operations were going on, but they played no part in the battle.

Our ships were organized into two task forces:

TASK FORCE 16

CARRIERS
    Enterprise (flagship of Rear Admiral Raymond A. Spruance), *Hornet*

CRUISERS

    Pensacola (flagship of Rear Admiral T. C. Kinkaid), *Northampton, Vincennes, Minneapolis, New Orleans, Atlanta*

DESTROYERS

    Phelps (Capt. A. R. Early), *Balch, Benham, Worden, Aylwin, Monaghan, Ellet, Maury, Conyngham*

TASK FORCE 17

CARRIER

    Yorktown (flagship of Rear Admiral Frank J. Fletcher)

CRUISERS

    Astoria (flagship of Rear Admiral W. W. Smith), *Portland*

DESTROYERS

    Hammann (Capt. A. E. True), *Morris, Russell, Anderson, Hughes*

By existing conceptions of fighting strength, whereby ships' guns were considered to be the decisive weapons, the Japanese fleet was in overwhelming force in comparison to the American. In carriers, they had a superiority of seven to three. But there was another factor destined to play a vital part, and of which the enemy were unaware. Our communications experts had succeeded in breaking the Japanese codes, and from interception of their radio messages Admiral Nimitz in Pearl Harbor had a good idea of what the enemy was up to. In fact, he had fairly complete information as to the composition of their forces and where they would strike. It was evident that the main blow would come at Midway and a secondary one in the Aleutians. Even so, there was considerable anxiety at Fleet Headquarters as to whether the deciphered messages might not have been planted deliberately to lure our defenses to those areas, while the actual blow was struck elsewhere. Nevertheless, upon evaluation of this information, preparations were rushed to strengthen the defenses of Midway. Improvements were made to the airfield, a squadron of Army B-17 Flying Fortresses was stationed there, and the Marine air group was brought up to a strength of 28 fighters and 34 dive bombers. Two squadrons of Navy patrol planes were also based on the island and gasoline and ammunition supplies were greatly increased. Besides the two Task Forces,

25 submarines were stationed on patrol to guard the sea approaches to the threatened base.

When Admiral Halsey was sent home to recuperate from a skin infection which placed him on the sick list, Admiral Spruance had succeeded him in command of Task Force 16. This force sailed from Pearl Harbor on May 28, 1942, to take station northeast of Midway. Task Force 17, under Admiral Fletcher, sailed two days later for the same general area, where the two forces were to operate under Fletcher's command. The *Saratoga,* which had received a torpedo hit from a Japanese submarine off Pearl Harbor on January 11, had been under repair on Puget Sound. The work having been rushed to completion, she picked up her planes at San Diego and hurried westward, but arrived too late for the battle.

The enemy armada advanced toward Midway in three groups, the Main Force from the west; the Occupation Force from the southwest; and the Mobile Force, containing the carriers, from the northwest under cover of a weather front. Lying in wait for them were our carriers northeast of Midway, as well as our planes and ground defenses on the island.

A long-range Navy patrol plane, searching far to the westward, made the first contact. On June 3, 1942, about 9 A.M., it sighted many transports and escorting vessels 500 miles southwest of Midway. It was the Occupation Force. A short time later, the Main Force, containing many battleships and cruisers, was reported 700 miles west of the island. No carriers were identified with this detachment, although the small carrier *Zuiho* was originally with the Main Force. With the Occupation Force were its two seaplane tenders. Our planes searching to the northwest were turned back by the weather front and made no contact with the enemy's Mobile Force and its four large aircraft carriers.

The Japanese transports were too far away, when first sighted, to be attacked by any planes except the Army B-17's. A squadron of the Flying Fortresses, under Lieutenant Colonel Walter C. Sweeney, took off shortly after noon to strike the first blow. After a long over-water flight, they found the enemy transports at 4:23 in the afternoon and made their horizontal bombing attacks through intense antiaircraft fire thrown up by the Japanese ships. No enemy planes opposed them as their three sections went in at altitudes of 8,000, 10,000 and 12,000 feet respectively, and dropped their bombs.

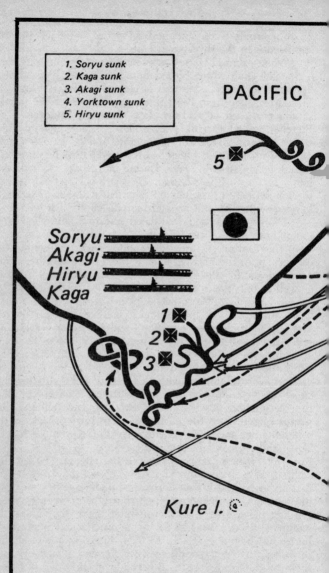

1. Soryu sunk
2. Kaga sunk
3. Akagi sunk
4. Yorktown sunk
5. Hiryu sunk

PACIFIC

Soryu
Akagi
Hiryu
Kaga

Kure I.

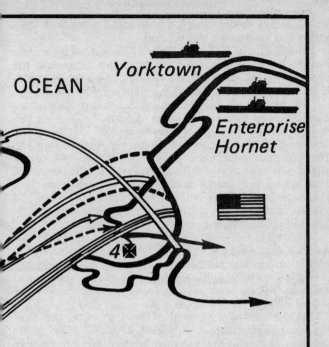

OCEAN

Yorktown

Enterprise
Hornet

4

N
W — E
S

BATTLE OF MIDWAY
June 4, 1942
Nautical Miles

0   25   50   100

Surface forces
Torpedo bombers
Dive bombers

Midway Is.

Pearl &
Hermes Reef

Although they thought hits had been made, actually all were misses and no damage was inflicted.

That night, at 9:15, four Navy PBY's took off for a night torpedo attack against the transports. One plane lost the formation in the darkness and returned. Shortly after midnight, the other three located the ships on their radar.

Throttling back their engines, they reached the torpedo-dropping point before they were discovered. Then all hell broke loose in the way of antiaircraft fire. As the huge, lumbering seaplanes attacked upmoon, the semidarkness was split with tracers and shell bursts. At full speed the planes passed over the targets, strafing as they went. They launched three torpedoes at shapes dimly silhouetted by the moon, but were unable to determine the results. Actually they had seriously damaged one transport by a torpedo hit and lightly damaged others by strafing.

That night there was considerable anxiety on Midway, on our Task Force flagships, and at Pearl Harbor, because the enemy carriers had not been located. They might be in the area of low visibility to the northwest, preparing to launch an attack on Midway at dawn. Our search Catalinas went off at earliest light in that direction.

At 5:45 on the morning of June 4, came the most important contact report of the whole battle. One of the Catalinas radioed, "Many planes heading Midway, bearing 320 degrees, distance 150 miles." Shortly thereafter the Midway radar picked them up 93 miles away, altitude 11,000 feet. By six o'clock every plane able to leave the ground had taken off, either for combat or to avoid being caught on the field.

The first blow at the approaching enemy planes was dealt by Marine Fighter Squadron 221. Flying 24 Buffaloes and Wildcats, the leathernecks intercepted only 30 miles away 71 carrier bombers escorted by 36 Zero-type fighters. Outnumbered, and flying planes inferior in performance to the Zeros, the Marines resolutely tore into the Japanese formation. It was a furious battle. No sooner had the Marines attacked the bombers than they were engaged by the fighters. They later estimated they had downed 23 bombers and eight fighters, but 14 of our 24 planes failed to return. The remaining enemy bombers continued on their way and dropped their eggs on Midway with calm precision. Heavy damage was done to the installations, though the Japanese avoided bombing the runways. Evidently they wanted them for their own use later.

Shortly after reporting the aircraft heading for Midway, the same patrol plane spotted the enemy carriers approximately 180 miles northwest of the island. They had emerged from the weather front and the location of all the enemy detachments was now disclosed. The Mobile Force constituted the greatest threat. Should control of the air be lost, nothing could stop the oncoming enemy. The Japanese were still unaware, however, that our carriers were in the combat area. They thought they had only to deal with the air units based on the island itself. Four Army B-26's carrying torpedoes, and six Navy TBF's of Torpedo Squadron Eight, left Midway without fighter cover to attempt to pierce the strong fighter screen around the enemy carriers. Two of the B-36's and all but one TBF were shot down. The Army flyers who came back thought they had damaged one carrier with two torpedo hits, but information obtained after the war showed that no hits were made in these costly attacks.

Next to attempt to destroy the enemy carriers was Marine Dive Bombing Squadron 24, also without accompany-

Grumman TBF "Avenger"

ing fighters. Again the Japanese defense was airtight. Twelve of the bombers were shot down; of the 16 returning to base, only 11 were fit for further service. The squadron claimed three hits on a large *Kaga* class carrier, but Japanese records show that actually none were made.

Then, at 8:35 A.M., an attack was made by 14 Army B-17's at altitudes ranging from 20,000 to 23,000 feet. Again no bombs struck the targets, according to enemy records. These planes all returned safely, although a few Japanese fighters and inaccurate antiaircraft fire were encountered.

Midway's shore-based fighters, torpedo planes and dive and horizontal bombers had now shot their bolts. They had accomplished nothing, and had taken terrific losses. The enemy carriers were undamaged. In the meantime, about 7:30 A.M. their air scouts had located our carriers. Thenceforth the battle became a carrier duel.

Our waiting carrier task forces had been cruising about 200 miles northeast of Midway, the two forces about 10 miles apart. They had received the early morning contact report giving the location of the enemy flattops, and the *Enterprise* and *Hornet* began sending off planes about an hour later. The commander of the *Enterprise* was Captain (later Vice-Admiral) George D. Murray; the *Hornet* was commanded by Captain (later Admiral) Marc A. Mitscher. The *Yorktown*, commanded by Captain Elliott Buckmaster, delayed launching her planes until 9:05 A.M.

The distance to the enemy was approximately 200 miles— too far for the carrier planes to go and return on their gasoline supply, especially the torpedo planes. Nevertheless, Mitscher told me later, Commander John C. Waldron begged that his Torpedo Squadron Eight be permitted to go. Mitscher reluctantly yielded.

The *Enterprise* and *Hornet* air groups proceeded to the reported location of the enemy. On arriving at the estimated enemy position, they found a bare ocean. Not a ship was in sight. They were almost at the limit of their cruising endurance and had no idea where the enemy might be. In the dilemma, each squadron made its own decision as to where to look. Short of gas after milling around, the *Hornet* planes, except for Torpedo Squadron Eight, returned without sighting the enemy, 14 of them landing at Midway while the rest reached their ship.

Torpedo Eight, at low altitude on their outward course,

discovered the enemy carriers about 25 miles to the northwest. They were the *Akagi*, *Kaga*, and *Soryu*, close together, with the *Hiryu* some distance off to the north. Around them were their surface escorts. Without reporting its find to the other units, the torpedo squadron emulated the charge of the Light Brigade and flew in to attack without fighter cover or dive-bomber coordination, against hopeless odds. Dozens of enemy fighters were patrolling the air over the carriers. Engaged by the swarming fighters and met by pitiless antiaircraft fire, every plane was shot down into the sea. A few managed to drop torpedoes, but none made any hits. It was a gallant but useless sacrifice. Nevertheless, the tradition of Torpedo Eight will live long in naval annals.

Only one man lived to tell the tale. Ensign G. H. Gay survived the crash of the plane he was piloting and clung to a seat cushion to keep himself afloat. From this grandstand seat, he witnessed the later attacks which finally destroyed the enemy carriers. He was rescued by our forces the following day.

Between 9:40 and 9:58, Torpedo Squadron Six, from the *Enterprise*, arrived on the scene. It, too, had neither fighter cover nor dive-bomber support. In a grim struggle, with planes flaming and shrapnel bursting, some of the planes managed to drop their torpedoes. Only six of the squadron returned. Like Torpedo Eight, they made no hits. We were not only paying a heavy penalty for not coordinating our attacks, but in addition we were getting no results.

Torpedo Squadron Three, from the *Yorktown*, sighted the enemy carriers at 10 A.M. It was escorted by six fighters but bored in without waiting to coordinate its attack with the dive bombers. In a storm of flak, and pounded by enemy fighters, most of the planes were shot down in the approach. Five launched torpedoes. None hit its target, and only two planes survived to return to their carrier.

All our Midway-based planes, Army, Navy and Marine, had suffered tremendous losses, and now our three carrier torpedo squadrons had been practically wiped out. Yet, with these sacrifices, the enemy carriers had suffered no damage, though they had lost a considerable number of planes. But our carrier-based dive bombers had not yet made their attacks.

At 10:24 on that historic morning, as the bright sun shone down on a sparkling sea whipped into whitecaps by a brisk easterly breeze, the Japanese carriers had landed some of their planes and were busily reservicing them for attack on our carriers, which they now knew were off to the east. They contemplated a final blow at the "Yanquis" that would put them forever out of the war. It was the chance they had been seeking when they undertook the capture of Midway.

Just at this time, the dive bombers of the *Enterprise* and *Yorktown*, each squadron unaware of the other's presence, appeared simultaneously high overhead, like specks in the sky. Most of the enemy fighters had been drawn down to low altitude by the torpedo-plane attacks, but our dive bombers were not to be denied. In perfect visibility, they pushed over and went down at terrific speed in almost vertical dives through a hail of flak. Nothing could stop them as they roared down, at terminal velocity, from 17,000 feet to 2,500, to drop their bombs. Entirely by chance, the two groups had selected different targets. When they pulled out, the *Enterprise* planes had planted three 1,000-pound bombs square on the *Soryu* and four on the *Kaga*. The *Yorktown* squadron had plastered the *Akagi* with two. Fourteen *Enterprise* planes were lost in this attack, many of them by landing in the water, out of gas. All of the *Yorktown* planes returned safely.

The results were decisive. The three stricken carriers were soon burning furiously. The planes they had been rearming never got off their decks again, nor did any more ever land there. The *Hiryu*, farther north, escaped undamaged. This was later to prove costly.

Unable to control the fire raging on board, the *Kaga* later in the afternoon suffered a tremendous internal explosion from her gasoline tanks, and at 7:25 P.M., she sank. Nearby, the flaming *Soryu* was encountered at 1:59 P.M. by our patrolling submarine *Nautilus*, which had been seeking contact all morning. Despite a screening Japanese destroyer, the submarine fired her torpedoes. Three exploded against the *Soryu*. She remained afloat until 7:10 P.M., when she sank beneath the sea.

The *Akagi* burned all night. Giving up the struggle to save her at five the next morning, her crew abandoned her and she was torpedoed and sunk by the destroyers *Ayashi* and *Nowake*.

The *Soryu* had gone down with all her planes on board, the *Kaga* with 50, and the *Akagi* with 40. The loss of life was heavy, and particularly costly in the trained carrier pilots for whom the Japanese had no replacements. From this deficiency they were to suffer throughout the rest of the war.

In the meantime, planes from the undamaged *Hiryu*, which had escaped to the north at the time of the *Yorktown* and *Enterprise* dive-bombing attacks, were launched for an attack on our task forces. They found the *Yorktown* in Task Force 17, but had been picked up by our radar. Twelve fighters intercepted the attacking planes at 11:59 and, roaring in to attack, shot nearly all of them down. However, eight dive bombers got through to drop their bombs on the carrier before they were destroyed by either flak or the fighters. Three bombs hit the veteran of the Coral Sea battle. Two went through her flight deck and exploded on the hangar deck, setting planes reservicing there afire. The other exploded inside the funnel, the concussion putting out the fires in the boilers. Although the *Yorktown* lost speed for a while, the fires and damages were soon under control. By 1:50 P.M., the wounded carrier was making 19 knots and the hangar fire was out. The landing and launching of planes was resumed.

A second enemy air strike was detected coming in at 2:27 P.M. This group contained torpedo planes and fighters, but no bombers. In another vicious melee, our fighters sent more of them to join their ancestors, but five dropped their torpedoes before meeting their end. Two torpedoes plumped into the side of the *Yorktown* at 2:43 P.M. Her plates torn away, her engines stopped, the great ship heeled over at an angle which gradually increased to 23 degrees. Without power and with smoke pouring from her side, she was abandoned by her crew at 3:00 P.M. and the Task Force departed to the eastward, leaving her at the mercy of the wind and waves. Several hours later, Fletcher directed the destroyer *Hughes* to return and stand by the *Yorktown*, with orders to sink her if necessary to prevent capture by the enemy.

While all this was going on, a *Yorktown* scout plane had located the *Hiryu* only 72 miles away to the northwest. She had a screen of two battleships, three cruisers, and four destroyers. Receiving this contact report, the *Enterprise* and *Hornet* dive-bomber squadrons, which had now returned to their parent carriers and been reserviced, set out to finish off this still undamaged enemy carrier, which by now was in full retreat to the northwest.

The attackers reached her vicinity just before five in the

afternoon. By this time fighter opposition had been considerably reduced, although a fierce antiaircraft barrage had to be penetrated. The few enemy planes in the air, the last of the great swarm that had been present earlier in the day, were quickly disposed of by our fighters as the bombers went into their dives. The *Enterprise* group attacked first and obtained eight hits on the last enemy carrier in the powerful Mobile Force which had started the day so successfully. She was left a mass of flames like her consorts.

Seeing the *Hiryu* burning fiercely, the *Hornet* group diverted its attack to the battleship *Haruna* and the cruisers *Tone* and *Chikuma*, but failed to hit them. Later, a little after six o'clock, eight Army B-17 Flying Fortresses from Midway attacked the *Haruna* and *Chikuma*, but made no hits either. Like the *Akagi*, the *Hiryu* became unnavigable and burned throughout the night. She was torpedoed by the destroyers *Makigumo* and *Yugumo* at 5 A.M., to complete the destruction of the four carriers of the mighty Japanese fleet.

The situation at this time gave the small American carrier force effective control of the sea; we had abandoned the *Yorktown*, but the *Enterprise* and *Hornet* had not been touched. We were complete masters of the air, which meant domination of the surface. Realizing the hopelessness of further operations, and appreciating the significance of the loss of his four carriers, Admiral Yamamoto ordered the retirement of his great armada. The attempt to capture Midway was over. Two undamaged American carriers now reigned supreme over the combat area.

To give his retiring forces a measure of protection against air attacks from Midway, Yamamoto ordered the cruisers *Mogami* and *Mikuma* to bombard the air strip during the night. On their way in, they made a contact in the darkness with our submarine *Tambor*, and while maneuvering to avoid her, the cruisers collided. Damaged, the two ships abandoned their mission and turned westward to join the rest in the retreat to Japan. Only a lone enemy submarine fired a few shells at Midway during the night.

When the *Enterprise* and *Hornet* had recovered their planes from the final attack on the *Hiryu*, as well as the *Yorktown* planes still in the air, Spruance ordered the task force to retire eastward during the hours of darkness. Fletcher had yielded command of both forces when he abandoned the *Yorktown*, informing Spruance that he would conform to his movements. The latter, in his official report, stated, "I did not feel justified in risking a night encounter with possibly superior enemy forces, but on the other hand, I did not want to be too far away from Midway in the morning. I wished to have a position from which to follow up retreating enemy forces or to break up a landing attack on Midway. At this time, the possibility of the enemy having a fifth carrier somewhere in the area... still existed." As a matter of fact, the Japanese originally had had a fifth carrier, the small *Zuiho*, with the main body of battleships, but had transferred her to the Aleutian force.

Our retirement to the eastward during the night permitted the bulk of the enemy forces to escape. By morning, when our ships turned to pursue, the Japanese fleet was too far away to be intercepted. Spruance thus lost the golden opportunity which lay before him to use his now dominant air power to annihilate the remaining enemy forces.

All day, on June 5, the American task force plowed westward in search of the retiring Japanese, but was unable to make any contact. The chase continued during the night, and long-range searches went out again at dawn. This time they had better luck. Late in the forenoon they located the crippled *Mogami* and *Mikuma*, trailing oil and straggling behind the rest of the retreating fleet. These two cruisers and their escorting destroyers had been attacked earlier by dive bombers and B-17's from Midway. Attacking from long range, dive bombers from the *Enterprise* and *Hornet* made numerous hits on the two cruisers. There were no fighters to oppose them, but the ever-present flak hampered their efforts. With her hull already punctured by the collision, the *Mikuma* capsized and sank. The *Mogami* was left a battered hulk, one turret smashed, her mast gone, and her superstructure a shambles. Miraculously, she eventually reached port to fight again. The destroyers *Asashio* and *Arashio* were also severely punished, but managed to reach their base.

This ended the attacks on the powerful armada that had come out with such high hopes of occupying Midway and seeking a decisive engagement with the United States fleet.

The *Yorktown*, which had been left abandoned by her crew at three o'clock on the afternoon of June 4, was found on the morning of the 5th by the small American tug *Vireo*, which had been directed to her assistance by Pearl Harbor. The listing carrier was being guarded by the *Hughes*, which had been sent back the night before for this purpose. No fire was visible, and she seemed in no imminent danger of sinking. While Task Force 16 was pursuing the Japanese far to the west, the little *Vireo* put a party on board the *Yorktown*, secured a towline and started to tow the huge carrier toward Pearl Harbor. She was unable to make much speed but she was doing her best.

When the higher command found out what was going on, the captain of the *Yorktown* was ordered back to his ship with a salvage party of about 250 men to make temporary repairs and assist in getting her back to port. This party set out from Task Force 17 on the destroyer *Hammann*, accompanied by the *Balch* and *Benham* from a position 200 miles to the eastward at sunset on June 5. They reached the *Yorktown* at 2:00 A.M. on the 6th.

The salvage party boarded the carrier. Prospects of getting her on an even keel and restoring power to the main engines appeared good. The fire was out and the damage did not seem insurmountable. But fate then took a hand.

The Japanese submarine I-168, sent out to look for a damaged carrier after bombarding Midway the night of the 4th, sighted the *Yorktown* stopped dead in the water, and fired a salvo of torpedoes at her point-blank range. One of them hit the *Hammann*, fast alongside, and she went down in three minutes. Two others struck the carrier. It was 1:36 in the afternoon of June 6th.

As the *Hammann* sank, about 150 men on her topside were thrown into the water, where rescue could normally be expected. But the destroyer's depth charges, although set on "safe," went off when they reached a depth of about 150 feet, and the concussion killed the men in the water. Ordnance experts have been unable to explain this tragic accident.

The two additional torpedo hits finished the *Yorktown*. At 2:10 the *Vireo* cut the main towline, the salvage crew was removed and the *Yorktown* was again abandoned, although the screening destroyer remained with her. Nevertheless, she continued to float. Finally, at five the next morning, almost three days after she was first stricken, the huge carrier slowly rolled over and went quietly to her watery grave.

Thus ended the Battle of Midway. The American forces had lost the *Yorktown*, the destroyer *Hammann*, 132 aircraft, and 307 officers and men. The Japanese lost four large carriers, one cruiser, 234 aircraft and 2,500 officers and men.

This battle will go down in history as the most decisive of the Pacific war. It was the second important action in which surface vessels played no part. All the vital combat was carried out by carrier planes, and the actual sinking of the enemy ships was due entirely to our carrier dive bombers.

Perhaps the greatest lesson learned from this fleet engagement was the necessity of providing fighter protection for bombing and torpedo planes when attacking against air opposition. The great necessity of teamwork in the air groups was also emphasized. Dive bombers and torpedo planes and fighters, all working in coordination, constituted a weapon that could effectively sink ships, whereas each unit by itself could accomplish nothing. Failure to respect this principle had cost us practically all our gallant torpedo planes, with nothing to show for their sacrifice.

Analysts may criticize Admiral Spruance's retirement to the eastward during the night of June 4, arguing that many more enemy ships could have been sunk had he maintained his position or even steamed farther west toward the enemy. Such a view fails to take into consideration the stress of battle, the lack of complete information as to the enemy's condition, and the possibility of a surprise contact during the night with greatly superior enemy forces. From the facts in Spruance's possession at the time, the decision was entirely sound.

Another lesson of this battle was the extreme difficulty of hitting moving ships at sea, even at medium altitudes, by horizontal bombing. The air enthusiasts who had predicted that with the new secret bomb sights horizontal bombers at high altitudes could drop their bombs "in a pickle barrel," were shown to be false prophets. Future tactics had to be planned accordingly.

The Japanese made the fatal mistake of approaching Midway without adequate advance air scouting to warn them of what lay ahead. Had they located and attacked our carrier task force before attacking the island, it is possible that the battle might have had another outcome. At the least, their chances of defeating our smaller number of carriers would have been much greater. Despite the fact that one of their avowed objectives was to seek a decisive engagement with our fleet, the Japanese blindly charged across the sea without taking steps to find out what ships of ours were in the area. This inexcusable error cost them the battle. When they lost at Midway their superiority in carriers, together with hundreds of irreplaceable trained pilots, they lost the command of the Pacific and, eventually, the war.

7

STALEMATE

The battle of Midway ended a distinct phase of the Pacific War. Until that action, the Japanese, through their superiority in aircraft carriers, had been in a position to dominate the sea, at least the part west of the international date line. With their ten carriers greatly outnumbering our three in the Pacific at the beginning of the war, our strategy had to be a defensive one while we built up our strength. The Japanese, on the other hand, had ranged far and wide; their conquests were stopped only just short of Australia, New Caledonia, and New Zealand. During this period, we had doubled our original carrier strength from three to six by transferring three from the Atlantic.

The Japanese had lost five carriers, one in the Coral Sea and four at Midway. We had lost only two, the *Lexington* and *Yorktown*, which left us with four, the *Saratoga*, *Enterprise*, *Hornet* and *Wasp*. (The small *Ranger* remained in the Atlantic.) The 4-5 ratio now existing in the Pacific was a distinct improvement over the original one. The *Shokaku* and *Zuikaku* had lost most of their trained pilots in the Coral Sea battle and were not yet ready to operate. Thus the new situation represented approximate equality in carrier strength. Under these circumstances, neither opponent could afford to open a large-scale offensive, an undertaking which requires superiority to insure success.

Our top strategists recognized that the carrier had become the dominant factor in control of the sea. However, a large element in our high command, the die-hard battleship adherents, still believed that eventually the air components of the belligerents would neutralize each other, and that the issue would then have to be settled by the old-fashioned, orthodox, battle-line engagement. They were further convinced that planes would be ineffective in unfavorable flying weather, such as would be encountered to some extent in all areas and particularly in the Aleutians and Alaska. They insisted that the battleship fleet must be resurrected as soon as possible to be ready to save the day when our aviation could no longer function. They still considered the "fly-fly" boys and the flying "contraptions" as weapons of opportunity which would peter out in the end. Then, they fondly believed, the battleships would have to take over. In their thinking, the best role of aircraft was to protect the dreadnaughts against air attack so that they could get within range of the enemy fleet and settle things with their heavy guns. Impressed, nevertheless, by the destruction wrought at Pearl Harbor and the sinking of the *Prince of Wales* and *Repulse*, they were now prepared to admit that airplanes *could* sink battleships under favorable conditions.

Statistical analysis revealed that thousands of rounds of antiaircraft ammunition had been fired for each enemy plane shot down. This fact established that antiaircraft guns could not alone stop an air attack and that the most effective protection for ships was by fighter planes. Additional antiaircraft batteries were installed on all vessels, however, until every available topside space was utilized for the sky guns.

The period of stalemate following the Battle of Midway, on June 4, 1942, lasted more than a year, or until the fall of 1943. During this time, both sides devoted most of their efforts to consolidating their positions and building up their forces. Both nations were feverishly building aircraft carriers, though we were also giving top priority to amphibious landing craft. The United States fortunately had ready for production a new class of carriers which would replace the battleship as the mistress of the seas in the new naval warfare. This was the *Essex* class, of 27,000 tons displacement in light condition, and incorporating many new improvements. They could carry more planes than the larger *Saratoga* and *Lexington*, and operate them more efficiently. They could, figuratively speaking, turn on a dime. Although they were destined to go through many battles and a number of them would be badly damaged, not one would be sunk or lost during the war. The *Essex* class carriers were among the most successful ships ever constructed by the Navy.

To augment the carrier force still further, nine cruiser

hulls on the building ways were changed over and completed as carriers. They became the *Independence* class of light carriers and were of considerable value in fast operations, although they carried only 36 planes as compared to 103 by the *Essex* type. The *Independence* type carriers also took less time to build.

The vastly greater industrial capacity of the United States gave us a great advantage in this race. Whereas Japan had obtained unlimited resources in oil, tin, rubber, and food supplies by her conquest of the Dutch East Indies, she had not appreciably enlarged her steel production and was in no position to compete with the United States in this category. Despite her severe handicap, however, Japan went ahead converting merchant hulls to carriers and constructing new ones. She had a total of 36 built or building by the end of the war.

The grand planning of the Pacific campaign was being carried out by the Joint Chiefs of Staff in Washington. This body consisted of Admiral W. D. Leahy, President Roosevelt's personal Chief of Staff; Admiral Ernest J. King, Chief of Naval Operations; General George C. Marshall, Chief of Staff of the Army; and General H. H. ("Hap") Arnold, Chief of Staff of the Army Air Force. When the group met with the British for coordination, the organization was called the Combined Chiefs of Staff to show its two-nation character.

The Combined Chiefs of Staff decided the broad features of strategy; designated areas of responsibility of the United States, Great Britain, and Canada; and determined the components of joint forces which each nation would furnish. The American Joint Chiefs of Staff made more detailed plans of operations for which the United States was responsible. Admiral King undertook further planning, through his War Plans Division, for the missions assigned to the Navy. He then issued directives to the appropriate Theater Commanders. In the Pacific Area, Admiral Nimitz, Commander in Chief of the Pacific Fleet and the Pacific Ocean Area, with headquarters at Pearl Harbor, made out still more detailed plans and issued the final orders to the task force commanders involved. General MacArthur, as Commander in Chief of the Southwest Pacific Theater, functioned similarly at his headquarters in Australia for operations in his zone.

In the Battle of Midway, part of the Japanese plan had been the occupation of outposts in the Aleutians as a diversion to aid the main thrust farther south by drawing a substantial part of the Pacific Fleet to the Aleutians area. Thanks to deciphered enemy dispatches, Admiral Nimitz avoided this snare and concentrated his carriers at Midway.

For the invasion of Alaskan waters, the Japanese assembled a force of two aircraft carriers, the *Ryujo* and *Junyo;* seven cruisers, the *Nachi* (flagship of Vice-Admiral Moshiro Hosogaya), *Takao, Maya, Abukuma, Kiso, Tama* and the converted light cruiser *Asaka Maru;* and 14 destroyers; plus transports, tankers, colliers, three gunboats, seven or eight subchasers, six submarines, a seaplane tender with float planes, and several cargo ships.

The Japanese plan was to land on Adak, destroy any military installations there, and then withdraw to Kiska and Attu, which were to be held only until fall to avoid the onset of severe winter weather. From their experience in the Kuriles, the Japanese believed the Aleutian weather would preclude all winter operations. It will be recalled that many of our own officers believed aircraft would be unable to function in this area, and that surface ships would dominate. Events were to prove that even here, aircraft would be the major weapons.

The principal American bases in the Aleutians consisted of a naval base and airfield at Kodiak, a seaplane base at Dutch Harbor on Unalaska, and a new airfield on Umnak, from which the 11th Army Air Force operated. All were under construction and still in a primitive state. Navy Patrol Wing Four, equipped with PBY amphibious bombers, had been moved north from Seattle and was handling the air-search mission in the area.

For defense of the Alaskan area, Rear Admiral R. A. Theobald had been assigned over-all command in the North Pacific, including both Army and Navy units. His forces included five cruisers, 11 destroyers, and six submarines; Patrol Wing Four with 20 amphibious flying boats; three Army fighter squadrons; one Army heavy-bomber squadron; one Army medium-bomber squadron; one Navy fighter squadron; one Canadian fighter squadron; one Canadian reconnaissance squadron; and miscellaneous patrol vessels and auxiliaries. Captain Leslie E. Gehres was in command of the naval air contingent and Brigadier General W. C. Butler of the Army Air Force units.

On June 3, 1942, the day before the scheduled strike

against Midway, the enemy fleet, which was called the Second Mobile Force, launched an air attack on Dutch Harbor from the carriers *Ryujo* and *Junyo*. Two-thirds of the planes turned back because of bad weather, but six fighters and 13 attack planes reached the target. Diving suddenly out of the overcast, they did considerable damage to barracks and Quonset huts and destroyed one PBY in the harbor. Next day another attack, by 32 planes this time, inflicted heavy damage on fuel tanks and oil supplies and caused many casualties.

An Army pilot made the first contact with the enemy carriers, and radioed that he had seen a large carrier with bombers on deck. He was never heard from again. Seven hours later a PBY succeeded in sighting the enemy ships and gave their position.

Two PBY's made separate unsuccessful attacks, but the foggy weather prevented the main Army Air Force striking group from finding the hostile vessels. The Aleutians have been described as having the worst flying weather in the world. There is almost continuous fog, and clouds both low and high. Icing conditions may be experienced at any time and flying is difficult and hazardous. Williwaws, or squalls of gale force, are frequently encountered with no previous warning.

Returning from the second day's attack, the enemy planes from the *Junyo* by chance chose to rendezvous directly over the newly built Army airfield on Umnak. The Japanese were still unaware that such a field existed. A group of Army fighters took off and in the ensuing melee, and by antiaircraft fire, four enemy planes were shot down before the rest disappeared in the mists.

The Japanese carriers then retired. Enemy troops on June 6 and 7 occupied Kiska and Attu without opposition, but because of their defeat at Midway, Admiral Yamamoto canceled the landing schedule for Adak. It was not until June 10 that two of our patrol planes discovered the enemy's ships and installations on these bleak islands near the extreme end of the Aleutian chain.

A few Aleuts looked on in amazement as the Japanese landed at Attu, and an elderly white couple were taken prisoner. They were Mr. and Mrs. Charles F. Jones, who operated a government weather station and ran a school for the Indians. Mr. Jones was killed by the invaders and his wife was sent to Japan. On Kiska we had a radio weather-reporting station with 10 enlisted men. All were captured except one man who escaped to the hills, where he existed for 50 days before surrendering.

There began a strange campaign in the mists and gales of this desolate country. The Aleutians are mostly volcanic islands rising out of the sea—the tops of a range of submerged mountains believed to have formerly joined North America with Asia. Treeless, but largely grass-covered, their lower portions are tundra, that form of swamp in which a layer of sod floats on water varying from a few inches to several feet deep. Snow blankets the islands in winter and gales of tremendous force frequently pound them. In summer, they are shrouded much of the time with the kind of fog that persists even in a strong wind. Sheltered harbors are few and far between. Some anchorages that afford protection from winds in one direction are treacherous traps when the wind suddenly shifts to the opposite quarter. Cloud layers exist at different levels and between them aviators experience unpredictable wind shifts. Dead-reckoning navigation is entirely unreliable; only the most skilled instrument flyers survive. These were the conditions that governed the Aleutian campaign.*

Following their discovery of the invaders, Navy patrol planes and Army bombers began bombing the harassed Japanese whenever the weather would permit. Only about one day in three were they able to get through, but whenever possible, they made it increasingly difficult for the Japanese to establish themselves.

About 1,200 mixed combat and labor troops had been put ashore by the enemy in each of their initial landings at Kiska and Attu. Additional personnel were gradually sent in for antiaircraft and communication duties, as well as for submarine base crews, until in the end they had 2,500 men on Attu and 5,400 on Kiska. To oust them we eventually employed upward of 100,000 men and untold quanties of materials and shipping.

The intial bombings had slight effect on the Japanese, and caused them to dig in all the more. Although they attempted to establish seaplane forces at their newly occu-

---

*For the full story of the only military campaign to be fought on North American Soil in WW II read, *The Thousand Mile War* by Brian Garfield. Another volume in THE BANTAM WAR BOOK SERIES.

pied bases, they met with tremendous difficulties in Kiska's foggy harbor, where a constant ground swell seriously hampered operations. In addition, the lightly armed and unarmored seaplanes were no match for our heavy bombers and fighters. Since their tenders could not remain in the harbor on account of our frequent bombing, the Japanese attempted to operate them at some distance offshore, occasionally entering the harbor in darkness or bad weather to unload supplies or planes. The Japanese seaplanes never became a serious threat, and their carriers, after the first month, never again visited the Aleutians.

Late in the summer, our forces occupied Adak. An air strip was constructed there and was ready for use on September 13. This island, located well out in the chain, was destined to become our largest base in the theater.

Our submarines played an important part in maintaining the blockade of the islands occupied by the Japanese. The *Triton* sank an enemy destroyer, the *Nenohi*, off Agattu on July 5. Struck by one torpedo, the vessel capsized in two minutes with the loss of 200 lives. On the same day, the *Growler* sighted off Kiska Harbor three destroyers, the *Arare*, *Kasumi*, and *Shiranuhi*, which had just escorted the cruiser *Chiyoda* and a transport into the harbor with reinforcements. On account of the fog, the destroyers had anchored outside. Firing three torpedoes, the *Growler* made one hit on each of them. The *Arare* sank immediately, the bow of the *Kasumi* was broken off and hung down at an angle of 30 degrees, and the *Shiranuhi* had her hull broken amidships. Both the *Kasumi* and *Shiranuhi* received emergency repairs and got back to Japan.

In the fall, the Japanese decided to hold their Aleutian posts permanently, reinforcing them as a regular part of their outer-perimeter defense. Imperial Headquarters ordered the moving in of additional troops, the construction of defenses, and the building of airfields on Kiska and on an unnamed island adjacent to Attu. They planned to complete these tasks by February, 1943. Whatever chance they had of success was nullified by their late start. Our forces had already begun to close in on them.

Under cover of planes operating from Adak and with Navy Catalinas furnishing antisubmarine patrols, our troops occupied Amchitka on January 12, 1943, and by February 17, fighter planes were flying off a new airfield constructed there.

This base was only 65 miles from Kiska and permitted our air patrols to extend far to the westward, even to the Kurile Islands. With our domination of the air, our surface forces could now operate well to the westward to cut off the supply lines from Japan to the besieged enemy forces.

On February 19, the heavy cruiser *Indianapolis*, under the command of Rear Admiral C. H. McMorris and accompanied by two destroyers, shelled and sank the 3,100-ton Japanese supply ship *Akagane Maru*, en route to Attu loaded with a platoon of troops, stores, and materials for an air strip. As a result of this attack, the enemy decided to send their supply ships only in convoys with heavy escorts. Under this procedure, a convoy made a successful run from Paramushiro, in the Kuriles, to Attu and back early in March.

Endeavoring to repeat the performance, an enemy convoy made a contact with our forces on March 27 (East Longitude date). This encounter resulted in the naval engagement called the Battle of the Komandorskis, taking its name from the group of Russian islands located about halfway between Attu and the coast of Kamchatka.

THE BATTLE OF THE KOMANDORSKIS

Our force consisted of the heavy cruiser *Salt Lake City*, the old light cruiser *Richmond* (Admiral McMorris' flagship) and four destroyers, the *Bailey, Coghlan, Dale* and *Monaghan*. The Japanese detachment comprised the heavy cruisers *Nachi* (flagship of Vice-Admiral Moshiro Hosogaya) and *Maya;* the light cruisers *Tama* and *Abukuma;* the destroyers *Wakaba, Hatsushimo, Ikazuchi,* and *Isasuma;* the auxiliary cruiser *Asaka Maru* and the transport *Sakito Maru*.

In the twilight of the early dawn, while steaming on a northeasterly course, our ships suddenly made out the masts of vessels on the horizon to the north. Unable to determine the composition of the enemy force, but considering it to be another convoy, Admiral McMorris formed his ships in column and headed for the contact. The Japanese, on their part, had been cruising back and forth in the area to await the joining of two additional vessels and thought they were too far west for a contact with our patrols. On first sighting our ships' masts, they took them for the vessels they were expecting. Acting on this assumption, they turned eastward to head for Attu, which placed them between our force and its bases. Soon Admiral Hosogaya identified the craft as American, and determined that they were inferior in strength to his own ships.

Directing his convoy to retire to the northwest, the Japanese admiral disposed his units for battle. Both forces opened fire at 5:40 A.M. at a range of 20,000 yards. The *Richmond* was promptly straddled but fortunately received no hits.

With the clearer visibility of the growing daylight, Admiral McMorris now realized that he was greatly outnumbered and outgunned. It was a serious situation and dictated his immediate withdrawal, but the enemy was between him and his base. The only way to disengage was to turn away and head for Japan, which he promptly proceeded to do. As our column turned southwest, the *Salt Lake City* became the rear ship and thus bore the brunt of the enemy's fire.

The *Nachi* launched her seaplane, which spotted for the Japanese ships during the engagement, while we had no planes to observe our cruisers' shooting. Fire was exchanged at ranges between 16,000 and 22,000 yards without doing much damage during the first half hour. Both sides were using dye-loaded shells to assist in identifying their own salvos, and the drab sea was brilliantly marked by purple, green, and other colored splashes.

Shortly after six o'clock, the *Salt Lake City* received a hit below the water line which tore a big hole in her hull. An hour later, she received a second damaging hit. Still heading west, Admiral McMorris now ordered his destroyers to drop astern and make smoke. This move seriously hampered our own gunfire but did not affect the enemy, since they had the benefit of spotting by their seaplane. Under cover of the smoke, however, the American ships turned south to try to get around the enemy and head back for home.

Although hidden by the smoke, the *Salt Lake City* was hit twice again in rapid succession by gunfire spotted by the *Nachi*'s plane. She began to lose headway and just before nine o'clock stopped dead in the water with a flooded engine room. For a while, she lost all power and was unable even to fire her guns. The situation was desperate, the American ships facing imminent annihilation by the superior Japanese forces.

As a last resort, Admiral McMorris ordered three of his destroyers to make a torpedo attack on the pursuing ships, which were rapidly closing the range. Under a hail of Japanese gunfire in which survival appeared impossible, our leading destroyer, the *Bailey*, was hit by two eight-inch shells but fired five torpedoes at extreme range as she turned away from the murderous salvos. The other two destroyers followed her around and withdrew without launching any torpedoes.

However, the attack achieved its purpose. Apprehensive of passing through torpedo-filled water, the enemy formation turned away. They never resumed the action against the helpless American ships, but retired to Paramushiro. As in other, later actions, they failed to take advantage of the opportunity offered them to wipe out the ships they were engaging. The battle was a tactical success for the enemy, but it might be called a strategic victory for our forces, for they were still afloat and the Japanese gave up their effort to take the convoy to Attu. Our ships had had a narrow escape from complete destruction. None of the Japanese vessels was seriously damaged. Both the *Salt Lake City* and the *Bailey* were crippled by flooding, were reduced in speed, and suffered other damage. Admiral Hosogaya subsequently explained his withdrawal by stating that he feared an air attack from American airfields and that his ammunition was getting low. Both participants had been firing for over three hours, with remarkably few hits.

While establishing new bases near enemy-occupied Attu and Kiska, the Americans had been preparing an amphibious expedition to expel the Japanese. Rear Admiral T. C. Kinkaid relieved Rear Admiral Theobald in the Alaskan command early in January, 1943. Rear Admiral F. W. Rockwell, who had been at Manila during the early days of the war, was given command of the amphibious force, the troops of which consisted of units trained in the hot deserts of California for campaigning in the tropics! Major General A. E. Brown was the Army commander. The covering force consisted of the escort carrier *Nassau* and the old battleships *Pennsylvania*, *Idaho* and *Nevada*, plus transports, destroyers and auxiliaries. The expedition gathered for last-minute preparations and training at Cold Bay, Alaska, where it experienced a blinding snowstorm on May 3. However, it sailed on May 4, through fog-shrouded waters and felt its way cautiously toward Attu.

D-Day, originally set for May 7, was changed to the 9th when reconnoitering submarines reported bad weather and high surf off the island. The transports circled to the north of

Attu to await a break in the weather. Again D-Day was postponed, to the 10th. The situation was getting serious. The ships were running short of fuel and if much further delay occurred, would have to return to port for fresh supplies and start out all over again.

Finally, after a conference on the flagship, during which the fog was so thick the personnel could not see the bow from the bridge, and two destroyers were disabled by a collision, D-Day was set for the 11th. Two main landings were to be made, one at Holtz Bay, on the north coast of the rugged island, and the other at Massacre Bay, on the south.

When the ships arrived, the designated beaches were invisible in the fog, but the sea was calm. Navigation had been entirely by radar, dead reckoning and soundings. The troops clambered into their boats and headed for the inhospitable shore. They were only partially trained, poorly clothed and inadequately equipped for the task ahead.

The fog played into our hands in one respect. The Japanese, previously alerted, had decided there would be no landing in that kind of weather and had recalled their beach-defense personnel to barracks. As a result, no opposition was encountered at the water's edge.

The landings started at Holtz Bay at 2:50 in the afternoon and by nightfall, 1,000 combat troops had been put ashore, despite boats getting lost in the fog. At Massacre Bay, similar conditions were experienced and departures from the ships were an hour later. One group of boats got lost and landed several miles from its designated area. Notwithstanding these difficulties, more than 2,000 men were put ashore at Massacre Bay by the end of the day. The Holtz Bay force dug in for the night on a high ridge slightly more than two miles from the head of the bay. Patrols from Massacre Bay had advanced only one mile from the beach.

The plan had been for the two forces to push rapidly inland for a junction, thus forcing the Japanese into the eastern half of the island where they would be eliminated. But the enemy withdrew to the heights between the detachments and stubbornly held on. The soupy weather made both air support and surface ship bombardment almost impossible. Any flight operations were most hazardous. Nevertheless, the escort carrier *Nassau* flew 171 sorties, on one occasion losing four out of eight planes in crashes or collisions. The ships bombarded whenever they could see their targets. Additional troops were landed until a total of 12,000 were ashore, which included the entire reserve. The southern force was still pinned down on the 15th in front of the divide between Massacre Valley and Holtz Bay, although the northern force had been gradually inching its way ahead toward the junction. Despairing of ousting the Japanese by frontal assault, General Brown asked for reinforcements from Adak.

The fog now lifted enough to provide ceilings of 400 to 800 feet. Planes from the *Nassau* and P-38's from Amchitka were able to make badly needed air attacks on the entrenched enemy. The troops began to move forward. By now Major General Eugene Landrum had relieved General Brown. The men suffered from cold, dampness and trench foot. In the soggy tundra, their fox holes always half full of water, they were never dry. They were exhausted and miserable. Then the break came.

Under the improved air support and with the aid of ships' gunfire, they began to advance. By the morning of the 18th, contact had been established between the northern and southern landing forces. But there was still much hard fig'ing ahead.

That night the requested reinforcements from Adak arrived and the Army took charge on shore from Admiral Rockwell. The Navy ships, their ammunition and fuel exhausted, departed for their bases, leaving three destroyers to furnish shore bombardment.

On May 28, the remaining Japanese had been compressed into a strong position near Chicagof Harbor. The Americans were prepared for a final assault on this position. Then the Japanese took things into their own hands. Knowing they could receive no help, and with ammunition dwindling, they made a suicidal charge on our lines. Crazed with sake and screaming banzais, the hysterical horde rushed our positions in the early dawn and surged over our intrenchments into Massacre Valley. Many were cut down by machine-gun fire, but the survivors drove on. Killing Americans wherever they could, they slashed tents, bayoneted men sleeping in fox holes, and slaughtered the wounded in a hospital tent.

Finally the wild charge slowed down. A few individuals had managed to reach within a mile of the shore at Massacre Bay. The Americans organized a new defense line and before long the remnants of the berserk Japanese were bunching up in groups and attempting to take cover. In the end, most of them committed suicide by blowing themselves to pieces with hand grenades. The Tokyo radio reported that the Japanese sick and wounded had killed themselves beforehand.

It now became a question of mopping up the few remaining isolated enemy detachments. Of 2,500 men on the island, only 29 decided to accept life as prisoners. On June 2, 1943, Attu was declared secure. The United States had lost 550 killed, 1,100 wounded, and 1,500 put out of action by trench foot and other ailments.

With the Attu experience behind us and with more than twice as many Japanese estimated to be on Kiska, a much larger assault force was organized for the seizure of that island. Our troops numbered over 34,000, of whom 5,300 were Canadians. Improved Arctic equipment was provided. More than 100 ships were assembled, and greatly increased air support, shuttle bombing and frequent surface ship bombardments were arranged. The rocky coast of Kiska offered few landing places and these were easily defensible. Then followed one of the greatest anticlimaxes in history.

Preliminary softening up proceeded as scheduled. On August 12, the large expedition sailed from Adak. Before dawn on the 15th, the first troops reached the shore and reported no opposition. At 6:21 A.M., the assault boats of the main landing hit the beach under the thunder of a terrific barrage from the supporting ships. Still no Japanese. It was considered they must have taken to prepared positions in the hills and were waiting to counterattack. Our troops dug in at their appointed objectives. More were landed the next day. Still no sign of the enemy. Finally, at the end of the second day, when the G.I.'s reached Gertrude Cove, site of the main enemy installations, it was realized that there were no Japanese on the island. The trap had been sprung but the enemy had fled.

As early as May 21, Japanese Imperial Headquarters had decided to evacuate Kiska. A directive issued on that date stated in part, "The Kiska Garrison Force will evacuate in successive stages, chiefly by submarine, as expeditiously as possible." After losing the submarine I-9 on June 1, the I-31 on June 14, and the I-7 on June 23, while attempting to reach Kiska, the enemy abandoned this method. The I-9 was sunk by ramming by our PC-487 off Shemya Island; the I-31 by depth charges of the destroyer *Frazier*, near the coast of

Kiska. The I-7 was destroyed by gunfire from the destroyer *Monaghan* near Gertrude Cove, where it was beached.

A force of two cruisers and 10 destroyers, under cover of a heavy fog, made a successful dash into Kiska Harbor on July 29. Hugging the northern shore line, they ran in at high speed and anchored at 2:35 in the afternoon. They embarked 5,100 men in 45 minutes and departed by the same route. Outbound, the cruiser *Abukuma* sighted one of our submarines off the northwest coast. It was the only contact with our forces. Our surface patrols had been absent from station while engaged in fueling, and the fog had prevented our air searches from functioning.

Following the departure of the Japanese, the Aleutians were built up by our forces as a threat to the northern islands of Japan. Adak became our main headquarters in the area and was soon the scene of tremendous activity. Two very large airfields were built there. Harbors were developed for shelter under all wind conditions, and repair facilities, including a floating drydock, were established. Prodigious stocks of all kinds of goods were assembled to create a huge supply depot. Recreation facilities, mostly indoors on account of the climate, were constructed. They included gymnasiums and motion-picture theaters. Blocks of barracks were built for housing thousands of troops in staging an invasion force against Japan. But they were never so used, since the invasion route eventually led across the Central and South Pacific.

A Navy bomber field and an Army fighter strip were

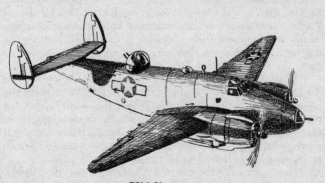

PV-1 Ventura

built at Massacre Bay, on Attu. Another bomber field was built on Shemya, just to the east. Radio aids to flying were established all along the island chain, making air operations not quite such a gamble.

From Attu, Navy PV planes, the famous Venturas, started continuous harassment of the enemy in the Kuriles. Although heavily overloaded with gasoline and bombs, they regularly took off for bombing missions on Paramushiro and vicinity. If one of their two engines cut out, it meant crashing to death. Many brave crews were lost in this manner. They had insufficient gasoline to remain long over the target. Frequently they took navigational bearings on Russian radio stations in Kamchatka and dropped their bombs through the overcast on targets reached by dead reckoning. A Russian lighthouse, kept operating during the war, was also of considerable assistance. Despite heavy losses, many of them operational, these planes kept up their hazardous work until the end of the war. In the later stages, they were joined in their attacks by Army B-24's from the Shemya field. The pilots of these planes contributed their part to the ultimate victory. This war in the storms and fogs of the Aleutians and Kuriles forced the enemy to maintain a large defensive force in his northern area, influencing the fighting to the south and hastening the final surrender.

During this period of stalemate, and while the Aleutian campaign was going on, General MacArthur was slowly building up his forces in Australia. With the war in Europe getting priority in troops, ships and equipment, the amount available for the Pacific was exasperatingly small. But the Southwest Pacific forces were not idle. After the Battle of the Coral Sea, which turned back their attempt to take Port Moresby in southern New Guinea by sea, the Japanese attempted to cross the Owen Stanley Mountains.

With Port Moresby almost defenseless, American and Australian troops were rushed there just in time to meet the enemy attack, which they repulsed on the south side of the mountain divide, only 30 miles from its destination. From this beginning, the New Guinea campaign developed. It produced heavy land fighting in the dank swamps, jungle ravines and hot, humid forests of this tropical country.

New Guinea, lying north of Australia, is the third largest island in the world. Approximately 1,500 miles long and 400 miles wide, its area is some 235,000 square miles. Blocking

MacArthur's advance toward the Philippines, New Guinea had to be occupied or neutralized. Much of its interior was unexplored and the bulk of its approximately 800,000 inhabitants were primitive, many of them head-hunters.

Late in 1942, MacArthur's forces had reached sufficient strength to turn from defending Port Moresby to counterattacking against the Japanese establishments on the north shore of the Papuan Peninsula of eastern New Guinea. This favorable ratio developed largely because the Japanese were centering their attention to the eastward on the bitter fighting for strategic Guadalcanal, in the Solomons.

No major naval engagements occurred in the New Guinea theater during its reconquest, but sea power played its part in this operation. While the stalemate period lasted, neither side had enough aircraft carriers to use in more than one area. The Japanese elected to make Guadalcanal the critical point of contact and employed their carriers in that campaign, which forced us to meet their threat with the few carriers we had left. Hence these actions had an important though indirect bearing on the New Guinea fighting. The absence of enemy carriers enabled General George Kenny's Fifth Air Force to secure local control of the sea in this vicinity, while the Solomons occupied the attention of the Japanese carriers and many of their shore-based naval air squadrons.

By the end of February, 1943, our forces had rounded the corner of the Papuan Peninsula and were in a position to begin operations against the strong Japanese positions at Salamaua and Lae. Rabaul, on New Britain, was enemy headquarters for both the Solomons and New Guinea and the base for distribution of supplies and reinforcements. An attempt to send a convoy from Rabaul to Lae early in March resulted in the engagement known as the Battle of the Bismarck Sea, which demonstrated our control of the sea in this area.

THE BATTLE OF THE BISMARCK SEA

On the afternoon of March 1, a large convoy was sighted by Army B-24 bombers patrolling north of Cape Gloucester. It consisted of eight destroyers, the *Shikiname, Ukikaze, Asakumo, Uranami, Arashio, Asashio, Shirayuki* and *Tokitsukaze;* the special service vessel *Nojima* and eight transports.

On board were 5,000 troops besides aviation gasoline and spare parts badly needed by the Lae garrison.

A tropical weather front of heavy rain and low clouds did not deter the U.S. Army and Australian bombers. Using the new tactics of masthead bombing, they swooped down on the convoy at dawn on March 2. In this form of attack, a plane at masthead height flies straight and low over its target and as it passes over, drops a bomb with a delayed-action fuse. The delay on the fuse amounts to as much as four or five seconds to permit the plane to get clear of the explosion. These tactics permit deadly accuracy, but the low approach is suicidal against ships heavily armed with antiaircraft guns.

Despite the unfavorable weather, repeated attacks against the light ships of the convoy on the first day brought excellent results. Several vessels were hit and sunk, although Japanese planes from Rabaul were furnishing air cover and vicious air fights occurred. In the afternoon, the weather closed in completely, preventing further attacks for the rest of the day.

During the night, Navy seaplanes tracked the convoy and dropped bombs intermittently, but obtained no hits. At dawn on March 3, the Japanese ships had reached an approximate position only 60 miles east of their destination. At this point the weather became more favorable for air attacks. The enemy vessels were now in a clear area, while the weather front had drifted eastward, between them and Rabaul, so that the fighters from that stronghold could not get through to

B-24

defend them. The Allied fighters and bombers, on the other hand, shuttled continuously from their New Guinea bases to Huon Gulf in attack after attack.

Navy PT boats made contacts after dark. One fired a torpedo into a damaged cargo vessel lying dead in the water, and sent it to the bottom. The next morning, Allied airplanes ended the battle by sinking the only destroyer remaining in the area.

In these attacks, 13 ships were sent to the bottom. Only four destroyers, the *Shikiname*, *Ukikaze*, *Asakumo*, and *Uranami*, managed to get back to Rabaul. The loss of men and materials was a tremendous blow to Japanese hopes of maintaining their positions in New Guinea. This decisive action stopped the free flow of Japanese reinforcements and supplies to their troops by water routes along the north shore. They were now forced to rely on barges, small craft, and submarines to provide a trickle of supplies. Even these means of transportation were ultimately to be cut off by PT boats, destroyers and air patrol.

Realizing the necessity of control of the air, the Japanese began a series of heavy air strikes by land-based aircraft on our advance positions. Although these attacks achieved some success, our air forces downed the enemy planes faster than they could be replaced.

To meet this situation, the Japanese Fourth Air Army was established at Wewak, in northern New Guinea, nearer than Rabaul to the scene of action, and this base became the center of their air operations in the western area. Their Army Air Forces were given the primary responsibility for air warfare in New Guinea while their Naval air forces continued to devote their efforts to the Solomons.

As steppingstones in their advance, the Allies landed without opposition first on Woodlark Island and Goodenough Island, then simultaneously at Kiriwina Bay and Nassau Bay on the New Guinea mainland, and finally at Dobadura. Airfields were rapidly constructed and huge supply stores established. The Fifth Air Force attained numerical and qualitative superiority over the Japanese air forces in a ratio steadily increasing until the end of the campaign.

On August 17, 1943, the Allies unleashed a heavy air offensive against Wewak. In five days, about 250 enemy aircraft were destroyed on the ground and in the air, forcing the Japanese to rely on air support from their more distant base at Hollandia. The air forces at Rabaul, to the east, could render no assistance since they were under heavy pressure in the Solomons, where Admiral Halsey's forces were now firmly established on the island of New Georgia.

With the United States Seventh Fleet furnishing naval support, our amphibious forces under the command of Rear Admiral Daniel E. Barbey left Milne Bay and Buna on September 4 for the next advance along the New Guinea coast. The following day Nadzab, principal escape outlet for the Japanese at Salamaua, was captured by airborne troops, and by the 5th our planes could operate from the airfield. On September 11, Salamaua fell, and on September 16 our forces entered Lae, which had been softened up by heavy air attacks on its pillboxes, trench defenses and gun positions. The remnants of the Japanese garrison put up only slight resistance and then fled north into the jungle. Operations against Finschhafen, near the end of Huon Peninsula, followed, and the drive rolled into that important base on October 2.

The capture of Salamaua, Lae, and Finschhafen within approximately one month, fighting over some of the most difficult terrain in the world, was a magnificent military achievement. It gave us complete control of Huon Gulf, with all its strategic advantages, and Vitiaz Strait was now available for our patrol boats to operate against enemy barge traffic between New Guinea and Rabaul. The difficult job of moving our bases of operations around the hump of the Papuan Peninsula had been achieved. Our new acquisitions cut the line of communications between Rabaul and the north New Guinea coast, and sealed the fate of that area.

This was the situation in the Southwest Pacific area as the period of stalemate came to a close. Our offensive operations in the whole Pacific Ocean were about to start moving at a greatly accelerated pace. In the summer of 1943, when our new *Essex*-type carriers appeared in the Pacific, our naval air strength was increasing by leaps and bounds. An entirely separate campaign of amphibious operations across the Central Pacific was about to begin, to be carried out simultaneously with the reconquest of that part of New Guinea still unoccupied by the forces of the Southwest Pacific.

Like the parallel campaign in the Solomons, the New Guinea campaign so far had been a sinkhole for Japanese forces, particularly their aircraft. In addition to many other air units, the enemy's Fourth Air Army, composed of the Sixth and Seventh Air Divisions, which had been moved into New Guinea between August 1 and September 20, 1943, with headquarters at Wewak, was almost completely destroyed immediately after it became operational. The attrition of their air forces in the Solomons and New Guinea was an important factor in the inability of the Japanese to hold their defense lines in the major offensive about to fall upon them.

The ineffectiveness of the enemy planes was due partly to inadequate bases, shortage of spare parts, and inability to provide maintenance equipment for aircraft and fields. These conditions resulted from our control of the sea, which prevented the Japanese from transporting necessary matériel and personnel by water. Thus many of their planes were unable to take to the air to withdraw before a threatened attack, nor could the Japanese even disperse them, so restricted were the clearings in the jungle.

In the meantime, a bitter, parallel struggle was being fought out at Guadalcanal and elsewhere in the Solomons.

8

LIMITED OFFENSIVE FOR GUADALCANAL

In the stalemate period which developed after the Battle of Midway, the main objective of our underlying strategy was the protection of our lines of communication with Australia and New Zealand. Our weakness in carriers prevented any large-scale offensive but it was vital that our route to Australia be held. Our slender resources, however, cast doubt upon our ability to hold this line.

One advantage in defending this area was that here the enemy also was at the end of a long line of communications. However, his possession of the Solomons Islands gave him bases from which planes and submarines could raise havoc with our shipping proceeding to Australia. To meet this threat, the joint Chiefs of Staff decided on a limited offensive to wrest Guadalcanal from the Japanese and prevent any further advances. There had to be a line drawn at some point and Guadalcanal was selected as that point.

The Japanese strategy to advance their defensive perimeter had received a decisive setback in the Battle of Midway. Their carrier losses there forced them to abandon their grandiose plans to extend their line clear to the Fijis, New Caledonia, and Samoa. But they had infiltrated most of the Solomons Islands in small parties and had begun to develop a major airfield on Guadalcanal. This they were determined to hold.

The First Marine Division, under Major General A. A. Vandergrift, with most of its troops stationed in New Zealand for training, was selected for this operation. Although not yet fully trained, it had received amphibious instruction and was the best available. Its second echelon sailed from the West Coast of the United States, arriving in New Zealand on July 11, 1942. The division had not expected to be ready for combat before the following January.

The Joint Chiefs of Staff originally set the landing at Tulagi and adjacent areas for August 1, 1942. Rear Admiral Richmond K. Turner, head of the War Plans Division of Naval Operations in Washington at the time of Pearl Harbor, was placed in command of the amphibious forces. In his Washington assignment, he had had a large part in the planning of the operation he was now to command.

A South Pacific Area Command had been created on May 12 and placed under Vice-Admiral Robert L. Ghormley, who replaced Vice-Admiral Herbert F. Leary. It was a subdivision of the Pacific Ocean area under Admiral Nimitz at Pearl Harbor and its western boundary was contiguous with General MacArthur's Southwest Pacific Area. This division resulted in many complaints about divided command. Admiral Ghormley was independent of General MacArthur in his over-all direction of the operations for the occupation of Tulagi and Guadalcanal.

When the second echelon of the First Marines arrived in New Zealand, their transports had to be unloaded and then reloaded for combat. It was found impossible to meet the scheduled D-Day of August 1.

Accordingly, the date was postponed until August 7. When more difficulties led to a request for another week's delay, the Joint Chiefs of Staff ordered that the August 7 date be met. The Japanese were known to be rapidly strengthening their positions, their airfield was almost ready, and it was considered essential to attack as soon as possible. As it turned out, it was a wise decision.

The American plan provided for three major task forces, the first two of which were under the command of Vice-Admiral Frank Jack Fletcher. He had been senior officer at the Battle of the Coral Sea and had also participated in the Battle of Midway. One task force was the Air Support Force under Rear Admiral Leigh Noyes, with the carriers *Saratoga*, *Enterprise* and *Wasp;* the new fast battleship *North Carolina;* five heavy cruisers, the *Minneapolis, New Orleans, Portland, San Francisco* and *Salt Lake City* (later prominent in the Aleutians); the antiaircraft cruiser *Atlanta;* and 16 destroyers. The second task force, the Amphibious Force under Turner, contained 19 transports, four destroyer-transports, and two fire support groups having a total of three heavy cruisers, one antiaircraft cruiser and six destroyers. In addition, the Amphibious Force had a screening group of three heavy cruisers and one light cruiser, among them the Australian ships *Australia, Hobart* and *Canberra*, and nine American destroyers. Also included in the Amphibious Force were five destroyer-type minesweepers. It was the largest force yet assembled for combat in the Pacific.

The third task force, operating directly under Admiral Ghormley, comprised the land-based planes and seaplanes under Rear Admiral (later Vice-Admiral) John S. McCain. Based at airfields on Efate, Noumea, Tonga Tabu, the Fijis and Samoa were a total of 287 planes—131 fighters, 34 patrol seaplanes, 25 scout planes and 97 medium, scout and heavy bombers. There aircraft included units from the United States Army, Navy and Marine Corps, as well as some from New Zealand.

Twelve transports left Wellington, New Zealand, on July 22 and rendezvoused with seven others which had sailed directly from the West Coast of the United States. They met at a point 400 miles south and east of Suva, on July 26. Here a conference of all the commanding officers was held on the *Saratoga*. At this meeting many of them received their first information of the task ahead of them and were handed their operation orders. A rehearsal was held on the island of Koro in the Fijis and on the night of July 31, the ships headed northwest for their objective.

Shortly after midnight on the morning of August 7, the darkened ships rounded the western end of Guadalcanal by the light of the setting moon. Savo Island was visible to the north and contact with Japanese patrols was expected in the strait. None were encountered. In the calm sea the ships' white wakes stretching out astern marked their tracks through the water. The Marines clutched their equipment and individually wondered what lay ahead of them. At 3 o'clock, the ships silently separated into two groups, one bound for Tulagi, proceeding north of Savo Island, and the other edging its way along the dark shore of Guadalcanal.*

The aircraft carriers, well to the eastward, launched their first flights an hour before sunrise. There was no indication the enemy was aware of the presence of the American expedition. No shots were fired, no picket boats were encountered, and no signs of the Japanese were evident. The island apparently lay sleeping as the first signs of dawn appeared in the east.

At 6:13, the silence was suddenly broken as our fire support cruisers and destroyers opened fire on the peaceful-looking beaches where our 19,546 troops were about to land. Then the dive bombers and fighter planes from our carriers dived down and bombed and strafed their designated targets. One enemy plane appeared at 6:52, as if curious to find out what was going on. It was promptly shot down by our fighters.

The boats from the transports, filled with men, reached the shores of Guadalcanal and Tulagi practically simultaneously. Stronger resistance had been expected on Guadalcanal with its half-finished airfield, but the opposite turned out to be the case. The enemy troops on the larger island fled to the hills at the first bombardment. The assault waves formed with quiet efficiency, the still-untried Marines meeting only a few scattered snipers as they moved inland. Pushing through the coconut groves near the beach, they soon reached the jungle, which was a new experience for most of them.

The jungle of Guadalcanal is of the type known as "rain forest." It is composed of giant trees of the hardwood variety mixed with solid growth of smaller kinds, dank and dark and

---

*A fine account of this campaign is The Battle for Guadalcanal by Samuel B. Griffith II. Brigadier General, USMC (Ret.) Another volume in THE BANTAM WAR BOOK SERIES.

almost impassable, with twisting vines clinging everywhere and interlacing the impenetrable mass. Strange birds and hordes of stinging insects abound and it occasionally houses large snakes of the boa constrictor family as well as lizards, rats, scorpions, centipedes and leeches.

However, it looked like a pleasant war when the Marines found large quantities of stores undamaged in the deserted Japanese bivouacs. In an abandoned enemy camp, the remnants of hastily deserted breakfasts lay on the tables. An electric power plant was taken intact, and cold-storage boxes, medicines, sake and—more to the Marines' liking—large quantities of Japanese beer was found. It looked like a pleasant war.

Over at Tulagi, across the strait, there was a different story to tell. Three major land objectives were involved; Tulagi Island, Gavutu-Tanambogo, and Florida Island. The first waves to land received scattered sniper and machine-gun fire, but found the enemy securely holed up in the many caves with which the island abounds. It took a new technique to overcome them, but the Marines blasted them out or sealed up the openings of their caves with high explosives. Many casualties were suffered in tough fighting, but by the following morning it was all over. Four hundred Japanese were buried, three were taken prisoner and 40 were estimated to have escaped to neighboring islands.

On Guadalcanal, 11,000 Marines were landed the first day. Supplies piled up on the beach faster than they could be taken away and placed in suitably dispersed dumps. One of the lessons of this operation was the necessity for better organization of the beach parties to handle the supplies and equipment after they were landed.

The troops moved cautiously through the jungles, looking for Japanese. None appeared on that first day, but the men were jittery at the prospect of an ambush. They bedded down for the night not far from the landing place. Firing at every strange noise, they got little sleep. Next morning they advanced beyond the airfield and found the Japanese camps deserted, and showing the same evidence of headlong flight. A defense perimeter was set up and the task of placing the airfield in operation was begun. The Marines named this field in honor of Major Loften R. Henderson, Marine flyer, who had died in the Battle of Midway just two months before.

The Japanese headquarters at Rabaul reacted immediately to the American invasion. The first enemy air raid, at 1:00 P.M. on the day of the landing, consisted of fighter-escorted bombers which concentrated on the shipping, ignoring the sprawling supplies laid out on the beaches. Only minor damage was inflicted. On the second day, a larger raid set afire the transport *George F. Elliott*, causing the subsequent destruction of a large quantity of much-needed stores.

As the sun set on the evening of August 8, the water off the Guadalcanal beaches was crowded with our transports and cargo ships, unloading their supplies onto the shore. Less than half of their cargo had been landed.

A difficult situation had developed. A dispatch had been received stating that our aircraft carriers were to be withdrawn because of the large and increasing number of enemy planes in the vicinity. This would leave the Marines and the unloading transports with no air cover to ward off the fury of the enemy air attacks.

A midnight conference on Admiral Turner's flagship, the *McCawley,* was attended by Rear Admiral V.A.C. Crutchley, the British admiral in command of the screening force off Savo Island, and General Vandergrift of the Marines. Turner informed Crutchley and Vandergrift that since the carriers were leaving, he planned to withdraw the transports at daylight the next morning.

In the meantime a Japanese task force of five heavy cruisers, the *Chokai, Aoba, Furataka, Kinugasa,* and *Kako;* the light cruisers *Tenryu* and *Tatsuta;* and a destroyer, were approaching from Rabaul with orders to attack and destroy our transports in the Guadalcanal-Tulagi area. Commanded by Rear Admiral Mikawa, the enemy ships had been sighted by one of our search planes at 11:30 that morning. Although promptly reported, the contact message was not received by all our ships because of confusion in its relaying.

Turner had stationed the screening force, consisting of six heavy cruisers and six destroyers, off Savo Island for the specific purpose of guarding against such an attack. The *Vincennes, Astoria* and *Quincy,* with the destroyers *Helm* and *Wilson,* were north of the island, with the cruisers *Australia, Canberra* and *Chicago* and the destroyers *Bagley* and *Patterson* to the south. The destroyers *Ralph Talbot* and *Blue* had been stationed farther out as radar pickets, the former to the north and the latter to the south.

Crutchley left the Savo Island vicinity with the *Australia* before midnight to attend the conference on the *McCawley* in the transport area. Few of our ships had received any warning of the impending action. Their crews had been at battle stations for as long as 48 hours and half of the weary men were sent to get some rest.

Hugging the south shore of Savo Island to avoid detection in the darkness, the approaching Japanese force made out the picket destroyer *Blue* heading in the opposite direction and passed astern of her only five hundred yards away. Surely, they thought, they would be seen. But no, she gave no sign of being aware of their presence. They slowed to 12 knots to reduce their white wakes, and trained all their guns on the unsuspecting vessel. Seeing no evidence of alarm, they withheld their fire and soon resumed their speed toward their larger objectives. The *Blue*'s lookouts, worn out by their long vigil, had failed to detect the enemy ships. Her radar had failed to function against the background of the land and the stage was set for a surprise attack on our unsuspecting cruisers to the eastward.

After passing the *Blue*, the oncoming enemy ships rapidly approached our southernmost cruisers. Our ships were quite visible to the Japanese in the light of flares dropped by their planes, which had been catapulted about two hours earlier, and in the distant glare of the burning transport *Elliot*. At the same time the enemy were blacked out from our lookouts against the shores of Savo Island.

The destroyer *Patterson* first sighted the enemy close aboard. She immediately gave the alarm, but it was too late. Before the prepared ships could bring their guns to bear, the *Canberra* was struck by at least 24 shells and one or two torpedoes. Within a few minutes she was enveloped in flames, her captain mortally wounded. The *Chicago* was hit by torpedoes and gunfire while attempting to locate her target and a large section of her bow was blown off. She fired a few ineffective salvos before the enemy ships disappeared in the darkness.

Without pausing, the enemy cruisers turned hard left and headed for our northern group of ships, which were puzzled by the flashes of gunfire to the south. Having become separated during the turn, the Japanese used their searchlights to identify their targets and opened fire at point-blank range. Before the American ships could get to battle stations, they were smothered by overwhelming enemy fire and torpedoes. Burning furiously, the *Quincy* and *Vincennes* sank within the hour and the *Astoria* survived only until morning. The American units managed to fire only a few salvos before their guns were silenced. One broadside struck the enemy flagship *Chokai* just abaft the bridge, damaging the operations room and destroying Mikawa's charts of the area. This salvo had an important effect later on.

After this attack, the Japanese headed northwest, away from the transport area. On the way out they shelled the other picket destroyer, the *Ralph Talbot*, which suffered heavy damage. The *Canberra* had to be sunk by our own torpedoes the next morning. The heavily damaged *Chicago* managed to reach a home port for repairs. Nearly half of the 3,500 men on the four lost cruisers were killed or missing.

As the withdrawing Japanese force approached Kavieng, the cruiser *Kako* was suddenly struck by several torpedoes and sank before she could make port. They were fired by the American submarine S-44, which had been lying in wait.

A mystery unsolved until after the war was why the enemy did not go on to our transport area and sink the helpless ships unloading there. With all five of our heavy cruisers off Savo disabled or sunk, there was nothing left to stop them except the lone *Australia*. Interviewed after the war, Japanese officers explained that the loss of the flagship's charts made navigation hazardous, while delay in assembling their formation after the action and fear of being caught by dive bombers from our carriers at daylight were additional reasons for their withdrawal. Providence had intervened in our favor. It was not to be the only time the Japanese would fail to capitalize on a golden opportunity.

The loss of this engagement was attributed by the responsible American officers to fatigue, lack of proper precautions, and confusion. The sinking of the cruisers, in addition to the withdrawal of the carriers, left the Marines on shore very much on their own. Fletcher's recommendation to withdraw the carrier task force from the operation, and its approval by Ghormley, were astounding. With the loss of four cruisers in addition to the departure of the carriers, Turner was certainly justified in ordering the half-unloaded transports away before they too were sunk. They departed at dawn on August 9, leaving the Marines on shore without either the support or the supplies which they needed.

It was a bleak outlook. In the circumstances it was

impossible for the troops to undertake any extensive mopping up of enemy remnants on the island, and it was difficult even to form a strong cordon of defense around newly acquired Henderson Field. The Japanese landed reinforcements on the northern end of the island without opposition. Almost nightly, their surface ships paraded off the Guadalcanal beaches, bombarding our Marines with impunity. Fully realizing the threat of our occupation to their position in the Solomons, the Japanese began accumulating ships and men in major force to expel us from Guadalcanal. As it turned out, all the power each nation could assemble was to be applied in the Solomons with the apparent intention of settling the entire war right there. Japan's losses in this campaign were to affect vitally the Pacific War as a whole.

THE BATTLE OF THE EASTERN SOLOMONS

On August 19, an enemy convoy of four transports, escorted by four destroyers, under the command of Admiral Tanaka, left Rabaul with reinforcements for Guadalcanal. As a covering force to the east and north of the island chain were the large carriers *Shokaku* and *Zuikaku*, veterans of the Battle of the Coral Sea; the light carrier *Ryujo;* eight battleships, including the *Hiei* and *Kirishima;* four heavy cruisers and 12 destroyers. The seaplane carrier *Chitose* was also in the general vicinity of the transports. About 100 miles east of Guadalcanal, in a position to intercept forces approaching our beachhead, the American carrier task force had resumed operations as a guard against the approach of the enemy fleet. It was not committed, however, to the task of furnishing direct air support over Guadalcanal. At this time it consisted of the carriers *Saratoga* and *Enterprise;* the battleship *North Carolina;* the heavy cruisers *Minneapolis, New Orleans* and *Portland;* the light cruiser *Atlanta,* and 10 destroyers.

Although the enemy transports were sighted on August 23 by one of our long-range patrol planes, the main covering force to the north was not discovered until the afternoon of the 24th, when the flattop *Ryujo* was sighted by a plane from the *Enterprise,* 198 miles northwest of our carriers. Shortly thereafter, the *Shokaku* and *Zuikaku* were contacted slightly farther north.

At 4:20 P.M., an attack group from the *Saratoga* swooped down on the *Ryujo* and scored 10 bomb hits. Notwithstanding the heavy antiaircraft fire put up against them, not a plane was lost, although several returned badly shot up. The enemy carrier burned fiercely and finally sank. Commander Don Felt led the *Saratoga* air group in this outstanding attack.

In the meantime, planes from the *Shokaku* and *Zuikaku* were on their way to attack our carriers. They arrived over the *Enterprise* just as she was launching a second wave of planes for another strike on the *Ryujo*. Eluding our fighters, the enemy aircraft dived out of the sun on the *North Carolina* and *Enterprise*. The volume of our antiaircraft fire, especially from the new *North Carolina,* was tremendous. Flaming planes were falling all around, but those still intact continued straight down in their dives. When they pulled out, the gallant *Enterprise* had received three direct hits and several damaging near misses. Fires raged on board, but the carrier's smoothly functioning damage-control crews eventually got them in hand. The *Enterprise* was unfit for further action although she was able to withdraw from the combat area at 24 knots. Many *Enterprise* planes, unable to locate their carrier after dark, landed at Henderson Field on Guadalcanal, where they remained for the next few weeks. By this time a Marine air group had been stationed there, and although gasoline and maintenance personnel were in critically short supply, the reinforcement was most welcome.*

During the night of August 24, the American task force retired to the south to refuel, and the Japanese covering force, their ardor dampened by the loss of the *Ryujo*, withdrew to the north. The enemy transport force, however, continued on toward Guadalcanal. Located on the 25th, at 9:35 A.M., by a Marine dive-bomber squadron from Henderson Field, the *Jintsu* was hit and damaged so severely that Tanaka transferred his flag to the destroyer *Kagero* and ordered the cruiser back to Truk for repairs. At the same time, the 9,300-ton transport *Kinryu Maru* was set on fire and had to be abandoned. About an hour later, a flight of Army B-17's from the 11th Bombardment Squadron at Espiritu Santo arrived at the scene and bombed the old destroyer *Mitsuki*, which received three hits and sank at 11:30 A.M. The *Chitose* was also damaged. With only one destroyer and two patrol

---

*For the full story of these brave fliers read, *The Cactus Air Force* by Thomas G. Miller, Jr. Another volume in THE BANTAM WAR BOOK SERIES.

boats left to rescue the many survivors now swimming in the water, the attempt to land the remaining troops on Guadalcanal was canceled and the surviving ships returned to the Shortland Islands.

In this action, the Japanese lost a carrier, an old destroyer and a transport sunk, plus 90 aircraft and pilots which they could ill afford. In addition, a seaplane carrier and a light cruiser were damaged. We lost 20 aircraft, many of whose personnel were rescued, while the *Enterprise* suffered major damage. The attrition was beginning to work in our favor.

THE BATTLE OF CAPE ESPERANCE

After the Battle of the Eastern Solomons, the new carrier *Wasp*, commanded by Captain Forrest P. Sherman, joined our forces. The *Enterprise* was first sent to Noumea for urgent repairs, and eventually back to Pearl Harbor. On August 31, while cruising northwest of Espiritu Santo, the *Saratoga* for the second time in the war was hit by a submarine torpedo and had to be ordered home again for overhauling. To take her place, the carrier *Hornet* was sent down from Pearl Harbor.

On September 15, we suffered another hard blow. The *Wasp*, while patrolling between Guadalcanal and Espiritu Santo, was hit by three torpedoes from an enemy submarine. Wrapped in flames from burning gasoline, she took a heavy list. Hopelessly afire and shaken by terrific explosions, the carrier was abandoned and her charred hulk sunk that night by torpedoes from the destroyer *Lansdowne*. At the same time, the new battleship *North Carolina*, about seven miles away, and the destroyer *O'Brien*, were also torpedoed. The *O'Brien* sank while proceeding to an advanced base, and the *North Carolina* joined the list of ships sent home for repairs.

With the *Enterprise* still under repair at Pearl Harbor, the *Hornet* was the only carrier in the area ready for duty. However, the new fast battleship *Washington* had reported to take the place vacated by the *North Carolina*.

Despite the reinforcements being steadily received by the Japanese on Guadalcanal, though in small units, our situation there had gradually improved. Additional air strips had been constructed and shore based air units considerably strengthened. On October 11, a large convoy with Army reinforcements approached Guadalcanal from the southeast.

To protect this convoy, our naval forces were disposed in three groups. One, built around the *Hornet*, was stationed southwest of the island; a second, built around the battleship *Washington*, was east of Malaita Island; the third, a cruiser force under the command of Rear Admiral Norman Scott, was south of Guadalcanal. It consisted of the heavy cruisers *San Francisco* and *Salt Lake City*, the light cruisers *Boise* and *Helena*, and five destroyers.

Early in the afternoon our planes reported an enemy cruiser and destroyer force headed for Guadalcanal in the so-called "Slot," the passage through the Solomons from Rabaul to Guadalcanal. Scott immediately proceeded with his force to Cape Esperance on the northwest tip of the island. At 10 P.M., planes were launched to search for the enemy.

The Japanese ships turned out to be three heavy cruisers and two destroyers. They were coming down to cover the landing of a detachment of troops from a transport and two destroyers, and to bombard Henderson Field.

Picking the enemy up on their radars at 10:32, our cruisers opened fire, catching them completely by surprise. The Japanese, under the command of Rear Admiral Goto, thought their own supply ships were firing on them by mistake. All of them immediately reversed course to the right except the *Kinugasa* which, through confusion, turned left. All but one were hit and Goto was mortally wounded. The heavy cruiser *Furataka* sank soon after completing the turn. The destroyer *Fubuki* was sunk before she could get around. The others fled northwestward, with the *Aoba* badly damaged and the *Kinugasa* somewhat the worse from the encounter. One of our destroyers, the *Duncan*, was caught between the lines and received fire from both sides, from which she sank the next day. Of our other ships, the *Boise* and *Farenholt* received major damage, but the *Salt Lake City* was injured only to a minor degree.

The Japanese destroyers *Murakumo* and *Natsugumo*, which returned to the scene of the action next morning to rescue survivors, were sunk by dive bombers from Henderson Field.

Although we were inflicting severe losses on the enemy, they kept on coming, stepping up the intensity of their air attacks on Henderson Field, where the situation was becoming critical. Though our air losses were much lower than theirs, we were having great difficulty in replacing our damaged and lost planes. Our surviving aircraft were battered, with pilots and ground crews on the edge of exhaustion. Our aviation gasoline supply was dangerously low when on the night of October 13 a bombing attack caught many planes on the ground and set afire one of the few remaining fuel dumps. That night and the next, enemy battleships, cruisers and destroyers lay off Savo Island and poured in shells to create chaos on the field. Only four of our planes were now fit to fly. With more Japanese landing each night, the situation was obviously reaching a climax. An American convoy arrived on the 13th and unloaded 6,000 troops of the 164th Infantry under air attack by day and naval bombardment by night.

The Japanese now had on the island a full division, heavily reinforced, and had sent down Lieutenant General Hyakutake, Commanding General of the XVIII Army, to take personal charge. During the night of October 20 and again on the night of October 24, full-scale ground attacks on our lines were turned back with heavy losses to the enemy. To support these attacks the Japanese dispatched a strong naval force from Truk. Their arrival precipitated the crucial Battle of Santa Cruz, on October 25-26.

THE BATTLE OF SANTA CRUZ

After the Battle of the Eastern Solomons on August 24, the Commander of the Japanese Second Destroyer Squadron had reported: "Gradual reinforcement of landing forces by small units subjects all of the troops involved to the danger of being destroyed piecemeal. Every effort must be made to use large units all at once." In accordance with this recommendation, plans were made for the capture of Henderson Field in a major land, sea and air operation, to be followed later by the elimination of the American remnants left on the island.

Finding the hunting so good, the Japanese assigned six more submarines to Indispensable Straits, seeking to cut our communications between Guadalcanal and Espiritu Santo. On October 20, one of them put a torpedo into the heavy cruiser *Chester* and sent her back to a navy yard. Another lay off Espiritu Santo and threw shells into the harbor at night in a nuisance raid.

The enemy had been landing about 900 men each night on Guadalcanal from the decks of destroyers and light cruisers which traveled only at night, using a chain of staging points from which they would dash in to Cape Esperance, unload, and be out of reach of our planes by daylight. This was the so-called "Tokyo Express." Their peak strength on the island had reached a total of 26,000 army troops and 3,000 special naval attack troops.

The enemy ground forces kept up frequent attacks on the air-field perimeter. In the encounters known as the Battle of the Tenaru, on August 20-21, and the Battle of the Ridge, September 12-14, they were thrown back with heavy losses. On September 18, the 7th Marines regiment arrived from assignment elsewhere to rejoin their old outfit, the First Marine Division and on October 13 we had landed the 164th Infantry Regiment of the Americal Division.

Command of the sea now belonged to neither side. Aircraft endangered both Allied and Japanese surface units during daylight. The enemy endeavored to neutralize Henderson Field by conducting nightly air attacks and naval bombardments from October 13 on. To replace our losses, we flew in all available planes from Espiritu Santo. Even so, by the 26th we had operating only 23 fighters, 16 dive bombers, and one torpedo plane, and gasoline was critically short. While the Japanese attacks were increasing in fury, gasoline had to be flown in by Marine C-47 transports assisted by the Air Force's 13th Troop Carrier Squadron. Harassed by enemy fighters in the air and artillery on the ground, each of the unarmed

C-47

transport planes carried only enough fuel to keep 12 fighters in the air one hour. The situation was all but desperate.

The date for the all-out Japanese assault on our lines had originally been set for October 21. After gaining possession of Henderson Field, they intended to stock it with planes from their carriers lying off to the north. But the strength of our ground resistance forced the enemy to postpone the main attack to the 23rd. On that day, the Fifth Marines repulsed a heavy assault which cost the Japanese over 2,000 men and 12 tanks. Again Y-Day was postponed. After another failure to break our lines on the 24th, it was put off to the 25th. On the insistence of Vice Admiral Nagumo, who warned that the Japanese naval forces would have to retire for fuel if the attack did not take place at once, the major assault was launched that day.

On October 8, Admiral Halsey had relieved Admiral Ghormley at Noumea in command of the South Pacific Area. The orders for our task force operations had already been issued and Bill Halsey's magnetic leadership was not fully felt in this area until later.

The Japanese naval task force assembled to cover this assault was their strongest since Midway. It had sortied from Truk on October 11. It consisted of four carriers, the *Junyo*, *Shokaku*, *Zuikaku* and *Zuiho;* four battleships, the *Kongo*, *Haruna*, *Hiei* and *Kirishima;* eight heavy cruisers, two light cruisers; and 28 destroyers. To oppose this armada, an American task force had been formed under the command of Admiral Kinkaid. His command was composed of the carriers *Enterprise* (repaired at Pearl Harbor since the Battle of the Eastern Solomons) and *Hornet;* the battleship *South Dakota;* the heavy cruisers *Portland*, *Northampton* and *Pensacola;* the antiaircraft cruisers *San Juan*, *San Diego* and *Juneau;* and 14 destroyers.

Under constant surveillance from Japanese submarines and aircraft, these ships skirted the northern shore of the Santa Cruz Islands looking for the enemy. On the morning of the 25th, a shore-based patrol plane spotted the enemy ships 360 miles from our carriers. Next morning at 7:17 search planes from the *Enterprise* sighted the enemy battleship striking force, and at 7:50, his carrier force. Two of the search planes promptly attacked the *Zuiho*. They scored two bomb hits, causing fires and such extensive damage to the flight deck as to render the Japanese carrier inoperative.

Air attack groups from the *Hornet* hammered their way past vicious Japanese fighters and bombed the flagship *Shokaku*. Six bombs found their mark, but the tough *Shokaku* was not to succumb at this time. *Enterprise* planes attacked the *Kongo* but made no hits. Other *Hornet* planes scored two hits on the heavy cruiser *Chikuma*.

While these attacks were being carried out, planes from the Japanese carriers were making furious attacks on the *Hornet*. Despite the determined efforts of her combat air patrol and antiaircraft gunners, the veteran of the Doolittle raid was hit by four bombs and two torpedoes and two suiciders crashed on her flight deck. Unable to steam, she continued to be hit throughout the day by planes from the undamaged *Zuikaku*. The *Northampton* took the stricken carrier in tow, but had to cast off to repel an aerial torpedo attack. Repeatedly set on fire by these successive blows, the *Hornet* was finally abandoned at 6:40 P.M. and torpedoed by American destroyers just as the oncoming Japanese ships hove in sight in the gathering darkness. The remaining American ships disappeared to the south just in time to avoid contact.

While the *Hornet* was undergoing her agony, the *Enterprise* was also fighting for her life. Planes from the *Junyo* concentrated on her and although many were shot down, two of their bombs landed aboard and started fires which ravaged her decks. In addition, one hit the *South Dakota* and one the *San Juan*. While the destroyer *Porter* was picking up the crew of one of our planes which had landed in the water, she was torpedoed by the submarine I-21 and sank shortly afterward. Another destroyer, the *Smith*, was crashed by an enemy plane. This started a fire on her forecastle which was put out by plunging her flaming bow into the high-flung wake of the speeding *South Dakota*.

Thus ended the battle of Santa Cruz. Although the enemy lost no ships, two of their carriers were damaged and again their forces withdrew northward while our ships were speeding away to the south. We had lost the *Hornet* and *Porter* and 74 planes, many of whose crews were rescued. The Japanese had lost 100 planes and suffered damage to two carriers, a heavy cruiser and two destroyers.

In the all-out assault of their ground forces on the night of October 25, the Japanese had swept to the southern edge of Henderson Field before being driven back in bitter counterattacks by the tired and desperate Marines.

The reinforcements the Japanese had brought in had been literally cut to pieces. Their commander had reported prematurely to Nagumo that Henderson Field had been captured at 11:00 P.M. As a result, at dawn the next morning, 14 fighters and a few bombers from the carriers at sea appeared over the field and circled, awaiting a signal to land. Although hampered by the recent heavy rains, eight of our fighter planes were dug out of the mud, took off, and shot them all down.

Admiral Keizo Komura, Japanese commander of the cruisers in the naval action, said after the war, "Our naval losses in the engagement were not important, but the general assault to recapture Guadalcanal failed at a time when our forces were much stronger than yours. . . . I think this was the turning point of the war in that area."

THE BATTLE OF GUADALCANAL

Doggedly the Japanese persisted in their efforts to get more men to Guadalcanal across the sea they could not command. Our own transports were now regularly landing supplies and personnel. Our First Marine Division was very tired. For almost four months, they had fought in the foul dankness of the jungle, undergoing almost incessant air attacks, day and night, and night bombardments by ships' gunfire. But now fresh American troops began to pour in. By November 12, part of the Second Marine Division had arrived, most of the Americal Division was ashore, and our strength in planes and artillery had greatly increased.

In their new attempt, the Japanese assembled 12 heavy transports in the Buin-Faisi area, with two reinforced divisions on board ready to join the battered and ragged survivors of their previous failures. This time they intended to land more heavy artillery and more of everything. Although their previous losses in carrier planes and the damage to their flattops precluded their having fleet air support, strong surface forces were provided to cover the convoy. For air protection, they relied on their shore-based planes.

They began operations with a heavy air attack on our transports unloading off Lunga Point on November 11 and 12.

Our planes from Henderson Field drove them off with severe losses, but they succeeded in damaging three transports as well as the heavy cruiser *San Francisco* and the destroyer *Buchanan*.

On the morning of November 12, our search aircraft located two enemy forces approaching Guadalcanal from the north. One contained the battleships *Hiei* and *Kirishima*, with a light cruiser and 15 destroyers, while the other, somewhat farther away, consisted of the slower transports escorted by 13 destroyers. Not located by our forces at that time was another group in the vicinity, composed of four heavy cruisers, two light cruisers and four destroyers.

Our transports had arrived escorted by a task force of the heavy cruisers *San Francisco* and *Portland*, the light cruiser *Helena*, the antiaircraft cruisers *Juneau* and *Atlanta*, and eight destroyers, all under the command of Rear Admiral Daniel J. Callaghan. Cruisers were never intended to face battleships, but the dauntless little force stood aggressively out to the vicinity of Savo Island to endeavor to turn back the approaching enemy and prevent the landing of his troops and the bombardment of our air fields.

At 1:24 on the morning of November 13 (which happened to be Friday), the first radar contact with the enemy ships was made by the *Helena*, seventh ship from the head of our formation. Callaghan was aboard the *San Francisco*, fifth in the column, which was not then equipped with radar. Rear Admiral Norman Scott, second in command, was on the *Atlanta*, which was fourth ship, behind three destroyers. Callaghan, without radar, was unable to visualize the situation; the verbal reports coming in on the voice radio were only pieces in a jigsaw puzzle. Furthermore, being in the middle of the column, he was unable to use "follow the leader" tactics.

The night was pitch dark. There was no moon and black, low-hanging clouds hid the stars. The cruisers stood on toward the enemy, the two forces now closing on each other at a terrific combined speed. Our officers did not know it, but they were meeting the Japanese detachment of two battleships, one cruiser and 15 destroyers. Suddenly they were in the middle of the enemy formation.

Illuminated by the Japanese searchlights, Callaghan gave his now famous order, "Odd ships fire to starboard, even to port." As the enemy opened fire at point-blank range, our ships maneuvered individually to fire their torpedoes, which threw our own line into confusion. Collisions between our ships became imminent and identification of friend or foe was impossible. In this turmoil, our cruisers blazed away with their guns and fought the enemy as best they could. Occasionally, in the melee, they were firing at each other.

Launching their torpedoes, the Japanese destroyers made hits on American destroyers and cruisers. However, the battleship *Hiei* received the concentrated fire of our ships and went dead in the water, out of control, hit by 85 projectiles. The destroyers *Akatsuki* and *Yudachi* were sunk in this blazing Armageddon.

At the end of the battle royal, our ships had passed clear through the enemy disposition and disappeared into the darkness beyond. Only one of them, the destroyer *Fletcher*, had escaped unscathed. The *San Francisco*'s bridge had been smashed by a salvo from the *Hiei* which killed Admiral Callaghan and Captain Cassin Young, who had won the Congressional Medal of Honor at Pearl Harbor. The *Helena*, *Atlanta* and *Juneau* had all been so badly damaged that they sank during retirement. Admiral Scott was instantly killed by an enemy salvo early in the engagement, before the *Atlanta* was gutted and sunk. The destroyers *Barton, Cushing, Laffey* and *Monssen* had also been sunk. The *Portland, San Francisco, Aaron Ward, O'Bannon* and *Sterrett* had received major injuries.

However, the enemy abandoned their intention of bombarding the shore installations and retired, as did the Japanese transports. Left behind, out of control, the *Hiei* was repeatedly bombed and torpedoed by planes from Guadalcanal the next day and was finally abandoned and scuttled by her crew shortly after sunset. In addition to the two enemy destroyers sunk during the action, four others received moderate damage.

Next night, however, the separate bombardment force mentioned above came in and shelled Henderson Field with only motor torpedo boats to oppose them. But assistance was on its way. With repair crews from the repair ship *Vestal* still aboard, the damaged *Enterprise* put to sea from Noumea to help prevent new enemy landings on Guadalcanal. At daylight on November 14, her search planes located the enemy cruisers to the westward, guarding the transports. Air-attack groups immediately took off from the carrier and from

Henderson Field. In vicious dive-bombing and torpedo-plane strikes, and with their guns blazing, they sent to the bottom the heavy cruiser *Kinugasa*, and the cruisers *Chokai* and *Isuzu* and destroyer *Michishio* were all seriously crippled. After this attack, the *Enterprise* air group landed on Guadalcanal to reinforce our planes there. They were not too welcome, since the facilities were inadequate, but this procedure permitted the *Enterprise* to remain outside the area of danger of attack by enemy planes.

At 8:30 A.M. on the 14th, search planes found the Japanese transports again heading back for Guadalcanal. Despite their reverses, the enemy continued blindly with their plan. Two *Enterprise* search planes first attacked the transports and badly damaged two of them. About 1:00 P.M., 40 Marine aircraft swooped down on the helpless ships. At 3:00 P.M., the *Enterprise* group joined in the slaughter. Eight transports were either sunk or gutted by the thousands. But the remaining four transports pushed on. During the night they were beached near Tassafaronga, where many of their personnel swam ashore, but were prevented from unloading their heavy equipment and supplies by attacks by our planes, PT boats and surface ships.

The Japanese cruiser bombardment group on November 14 again turned back toward the shores of the embattled island in support of the futile advance of their transports. Expecting this movement, Halsey ordered the new fast battleships *Washington* and *South Dakota*, assigned to the *Enterprise* task force, to proceed with four destroyers west of Savo Island to meet the threat. Arriving about midnight, November 14-15, they made contact with the enemy force, which now included the battleship *Kirishima* as well as two heavy cruisers, two light cruisers and nine destroyers. Our force was commanded by Rear Admiral (later Vice-Admiral) W. A. Lee and the Japanese by Vice-Admiral N. Kondo.

In the succeeding engagement, the enemy were taken completely by surprise, but reacted with their usual fanaticism. Our superior radar gave us a tremendous advantage, but the Japanese superiority in number of destroyers and destructiveness of torpedoes was to play its part too. Fire was opened shortly after midnight. Gun flashes, the blaze of tracers and soon, that of burning ships, illuminated the scene. A destroyer picked out the *South Dakota* with her searchlight and the huge battleship became the target of the

Kirishima's guns. The *Washington,* not illuminated, was pouring salvo after salvo of 16-inch shells into the *Kirishima.* Our destroyers mixed in the fray, engaging cruisers and destroyers with equal abandon. Before the battle was over, all but one of our heroic destroyers were at the bottom of the sea, sunk by enemy gunfire, and the lone survivor was gravely damaged.

The *South Dakota* received many hits. Most of them were in her mast structure, but her voice radio and radar were put out of commission. Unable to reach Admiral Lee by radio, she withdrew from the action to the southward. The *Washington* continued on northwestward, absolutely alone, until her commander was sure the enemy had retired and that no further targets could be found. She then turned south and rejoined the *South Dakota* the next morning.

Unnavigable and gutted by fire, the *Kirishima* was later abandoned and scuttled. The Japanese also lost one destroyer. The Americans lost three, the *Benham, Preston* and *Walke,* while the badly damaged *South Dakota* had to return to the United States for repairs.

Although the losses inflicted on the enemy in this night battleship action were not impressive, considering the power of our two modern battleships, they turned back the attack, and this was the last time the Japanese employed large units in their attempts to reinforce Guadalcanal. From then on they confined their efforts to trying to run in minor quantities of supplies and small troop detachments whose objective was limited to harassing our occupation forces. Later they were to attempt to evacuate the half-starved remnants of their ill-fated expedition.

THE BATTLE OF TASSAFARONGA

The build-up of our naval forces in the South Pacific had now reached the stage where we had replaced most of our losses in previous engagements. Alerted by an increase in shipping in the Shortlands area, noted by our air scouts, Admiral Halsey directed a cruiser task force to proceed from Espiritu Santo to the vicinity of Savo Island to intercept an expected enemy landing attempt. The force consisted of four heavy cruisers, one light cruiser and six destroyers, under the command of Rear Admiral C. H. Wright. It would seem that it was an entirely adequate force to meet the eight enemy destroyers which comprised the "Tokyo Express" that night.

Heading west through Lunga Channel, the American ships made radar contact at 11:00 P.M. with the Japanese vessels close up against the Tassafaronga shore. The destroyer *Fletcher* launched torpedoes at 11:16 and a minute later the cruisers opened fire with their guns. The night was extremely dark.

Admiral Tanaka had ordered his ships not to open fire with their guns unless necessary for defense, but to use torpedoes if attacked. This was a wise move, as it prevented disclosing the ships' positions by gun flashes. Only one destroyer, the advance picket *Takanami*, failed to carry out these instructions. She was overwhelmed by the volume of fire from our task force, and sank. The others launched their deadly torpedoes at our oncoming cruisers and then fled at high speed westward.

We learned the hard way about Japanese torpedoes. They contained fifty per cent more explosive than ours and had appreciably greater range. The enemy was highly skilled in their use and had specialized in this form of night action.

Our cruisers advanced to what they thought would be the "kill" for their targets. Unseen in the darkness, the torpedoes were approaching. Before the ships realized what was happening, two struck the *Minneapolis* so close together that the blast sounded like one explosion. Amid the smoke of fires and the spume from the sheet of water thrown up in the blast, the cruiser's entire bow section forward of her No. 1 turret was torn loose and hung down vertically, dragging through the water. Although the *Minneapolis* fired a few more salvos before she lost power, she was soon out of action.

The *New Orleans*, just astern, turned hard right to avoid the stricken *Minneapolis* and just as she did so, was herself rammed by a torpedo. Also hit forward, her magazines exploded and her entire bow was blown off as far as her No. 2 turret. Drifting along her side, the bow section tore great holes in her plating as it passed. Afterward, her crew claimed she was the only ship in the world which had rammed herself. Although critically injured, she was able to limp off toward Tulagi and was subsequently repaired.

The *Pensacola* sheered out to clear the two damaged cruisers and had proceeded only a short distance when she too received a torpedo. Her hit was in a fuel tank and fires raged aboard for hours, but she reached Tulagi for ultimate restoration to fighting trim.

The worst blow befell the *Northampton*. About the same time the *Pensacola* was hit, two torpedoes were sighted streaking in toward her port side. Before anything could be done, they struck amidships. With fires raging, and mortally hurt under water, the doomed ship began to roll over until the list increased to nearly 30 degrees and Captain Kitts ordered her abandoned. Just after 3:00 A.M., she capsized and sank. It was the end of a gallant ship with a magnificent fighting record.

The undamaged *Honolulu* searched through the area, but the enemy had escaped. As in some of our other battles, we held the field of action, but at a terrific cost. The enemy had lost one destroyer sunk to our loss of the heavy cruiser *Northampton* and three others so badly damaged that they were out of action for months.

This was the last surface-ship action in the Guadalcanal campaign, although constant air attacks were continued by Japanese planes from Bougainville and Rabaul. But our shore-based aircraft were being greatly strengthened and new landing strips were being constructed. The half-starved Japanese on the island were gradually being compressed into the northwest corner in the vicinity of Tassafaronga. The end of their resistance was not far off.

In December, General Vandergrift and his Marines were relieved by newly arrived Army units and Major General (later Lieutenant General) A. M. Patch assumed command of the island. The Marines, weary and weakened by malaria and fever, had set a modern record for length of time in combat, and in doing so they had beaten the jungle as well as Japan's toughest and most experienced troops.

Our supplies and replacements were now going through on regular schedule. We had general control of the sea around the island, but enemy air attacks were still bothersome. During the night of January 29, 1943, a newly arrived cruiser division under the command of Rear Admiral (later Vice-Admiral) R. C. Giffen was attacked south of Guadalcanal by enemy torpedo planes. One of the torpedoes plunked against the side of the heavy cruiser *Chicago*. With her engine room flooded, the cruiser was taken in tow by the *Louisville* and the division retired to the southwest. Next morning, a task force under my command, built around the *Enterprise*, was directed to meet the damaged cruiser and give her air cover while withdrawing to Espiritu Santo. Just north of Rennell Island, about 3:00 P.M., 12 enemy torpedo planes made a feint against the *Enterprise* and then swerved toward the *Chicago* which was now in tow of the tug *Navajo*. Our fighters downed all but one of the enemy planes, but not before five of them had released their torpedoes. Two of the missiles struck the previously damaged *Chicago* and one hit the escorting destroyer *Lavallette*. In a few moments, the *Chicago* rolled over and sank. It was an unlucky end for this plucky ship which had survived the battle of Savo Island five months before and had just returned to action after repairs.

Since early November, 1942, the Japanese had been evacuating their destitute and hungry troops from Guadalcanal. Under constant air attack from our fighters and dive bombers based on the island, approximately 600 enemy planes and 21 destroyer transports had been destroyed or damaged during t ese operations. The Second Marine Division had remained w th the Americal Division after the departure of the First Marines, and the Twenty-fifth Infantry Division arrived in mid-January. An enveloping movement around the concentrated enemy troops in the vicinity of Cape Esperance was started early in February. On February 8, our forces met at the end of the island to find only a few miserable stragglers and large quantities of abandoned supplies. It was the end of organized resistance. On February 9, Radio Tokyo announced that the Japanese High Command, deeming Guadalcanal of little value, had withdrawn their troops intact without interference from the badly beaten-up Americans.

Our Guadalcanal campaign had started on a shoe-string as far as naval forces to maintain command of the sea were concerned, but it had produced enormous results. Although conducted in a period of approximate equality in aircraft carrier strength, it has been considered by many to have been the turning point of the war.

An interesting sidelight on this campaign came out after the war. By late January, 1943, the Japanese had assembled approximately 50,000 troops at Rabaul, with ships and naval vessels to transport them. Although these forces were originally intended for another all-out effort to recapture Guadalcanal, the success of General MacArthur's forces in New Guinea caused their diversion to that area. En route thither in early March, many of them were sent to the bottom in the air attacks of the Battle of the Bismarck Sea.

Marines killed in action or missing on Guadalcanal totaled 1,242. The wounded numbered 2,655, not including men put out of action by sickness. Few who fought there failed to contract malaria, dengue fever, or dysentery. Not for almost a year would most of the First Marines units again be ready for combat.

To supply any sizable military force on an island requires control of the sea. More than 11,000 Marines were landed on Guadalcanal in the first two days. Against them were only 600 Japanese soldiers and 2,000 Korean laborers. There was no question at the time of the adequacy of our force to take and hold the island. But the unfortunate decision to withdraw our aircraft carriers from the area on the second day gave the command of the sea to the enemy, who unlike ourselves had air fields within range, without even a struggle. This decision forced Admiral Turner to retire his transports immediately, before they were even half unloaded, leaving the Marines short of food, ammunition, barbed wire and many other essentials. It permitted the Japanese to bring in reinforcements for their small force and gradually build it up to sizable proportions. It prolonged the struggle for Guadalcanal for months and left the issue in doubt for a long time.

In addition to minor engagements, the Guadalcanal naval campaign was characterized by a succession of naval battles—Savo Island, Eastern Solomons, Cape Esperance, Santa Cruz, Guadalcanal and Tassafaronga—that eventually restored to us control of the sea. Most of them were major engagements, and our forces were usually fighting against odds. Although aircraft carriers participated only in the battles of the Eastern Solomons and Santa Cruz, these two actions enabled us to retain a measure of sea control, hampering the Japanese efforts to send in reinforcements and supplies while leaving us free to do so. These conditions decided the issue of the campaign.

Naval losses in major combatant ships during the Guadalcanal campaign were as follows:

	United States	Japan
Battleships	0	2
Aircraft carriers	2	1
Heavy cruisers	6	2
Light cruisers	3	1
Destroyers	15	12
TOTAL	26	18

In this campaign, we gained something more than the island. We regained the initiative. After Guadalcanal, the Japanese, no longer able to choose the battleground, fought where we decided to attack. We were henceforth on the strategic offensive, and never to be stopped until we reached Tokyo. In addition, we had learned much about Japanese psychology. We found them to be brave individual fighters with a degree of fanaticism, men who apparently sought to compensate for an inferiority complex by acts of barbarism, but who also showed a great deal of stupidity. When set plans went awry, not even their highest officers seemed to be able to meet the new situation with intelligent action. The knowledge we acquired of Japanese military characteristics was one of the most valuable gains of the Guadalcanal campaign.

9

THE TIDE TURNS: FROM GUADAL-CANAL TO BOUGAINVILLE

With the securing of Guadalcanal on February 8, 1943, preparations went ahead for advancing farther up the Solomons chain. We had no supporting bases closer to Guadalcanal than Espiritu Santo, and our new outpost had no adequate harbor where ships could ride at anchor. The harbors of Tulagi and Purvis Bay, across the strait, were small and although these places had been developed as auxiliary bases, their usefulness was limited. Their rugged, hilly terrain was unsuitable for airfields or other large shore establishments, and room to expand our land-based air forces was our most pressing need.

The boundary between the South Pacific and Southwest Pacific theaters passed just west of Guadalcanal. During the Guadalcanal campaign, Admiral Nimitz had requested that General MacArthur's air forces west of the line carry out diversionary operations against Rabaul, and such operations had been conducted sporadically. However, the scale and results of the raids were not always to the liking of the naval forces to the east. Such differences were part of the penalty we paid for divided command.

Only 65 miles west of Guadalcanal, in MacArthur's territory, lay the Russell Islands. These islands, where coconut plantations had been developed, were suitable for airfields and had good, though small harbors. The Russells looked attractive as a supporting base for Guadalcanal and jumping-off-place for our next move westward. Fighter planes operating from them would be just within range of the enemy airfields on the southern end of Bougainville. So that he could undertake their occupation, Admiral Halsey obtained from the Joint Chiefs of Staff a shift of the boundary line westward to include these islands.

Led by Marines of Carlson's Raiders, a full-scale amphibious expedition landed on the Russells at dawn on February 21, 1943. There was no opposition, as the Japanese had pulled out of the Russells when they evacuated Guadalcanal. Supplies and men, including the ubiquitous "Sea Bee" construction battalions, poured in for the primary purpose of building an airfield. Mud and the continual tropical rainstorms hampered their work. The field was not finished until late May, when it proved of great value in our advance to New Georgia.

Expelled from Guadalcanal, the enemy prepared energetically for resistance farther up the line. Japanese Army air force units had arrived at Rabaul in January to make up for the heavy losses their naval air contingents had suffered in their operations against Henderson Field. In February, partially trained carrier air groups were also dispatched to this area, where constant damage was being inflicted by our increasingly powerful air forces. Operations beyond the Russells had to be approved by General MacArthur. It was an anomalous situation in which one command was conducting a campaign in the other's area, without being subject to the latter's orders.

As part of their preparations, the Japanese began building an airfield on Munda Point, in northwestern New Georgia, about 200 miles from Guadalcanal. Without cutting down the coconut palms, they graded and leveled the ground beneath them. Not until the work was almost finished did our aerial photographs begin to show the outline of a runway under the palm fronds. All at once, the trees were removed, and there was an airfield ready for use.

The new airfield was bombarded on the night of January 4, 1943, by the cruisers *Nashville*, *St. Louis* and *Helena* and the destroyers *Fletcher* and *O'Bannon*, under Rear Admiral Walden L. Ainsworth. Runways were well cratered and buildings and stores burned, but eighteen hours later planes were again taking off to attack our shipping and dispute control of the air. Repeated attacks by bombers from Henderson Field had little effect on the operations of the new airfield.

The Japanese constructed another field at Vila-Stanmore, on Kolombangara, directly across from New Georgia. Night surface forces bombarding this field on March 6 encountered and sank two Japanese destroyers, the *Minegumo* and *Murasame*.

During this period, both sides conducted frequent air operations. Our aviation units shot down many Japanese planes and the attrition was important in weakening the Japanese. However, neither bombing nor shelling accomplished much toward putting these advanced airfields out of action.

The next step planned by the South Pacific forces was the capture and occupation of New Georgia. On June 21, the Fourth Marine Raider Battalion went ashore at Segi Point, on the southeastern tip of the island, to construct a fighter strip to furnish air cover for the projected advance. On June 30, with strong naval and air support, Army troops were landed at Rendova, an adjacent island across from the airfield at Munda Point, to place Army field guns there to support the assault on New Georgia. Landings were also made in the Bairoko-Enogai area on the north coast to isolate the enemy garrison there from Munda airfield.

To support the main landing on New Georgia, Rear Admiral A. S. Merrill on June 30 steamed up the Slot with the cruisers *Montpelier*, *Denver*, *Columbia* and *Cleveland*, and the destroyers *Philip*, *Pringle* and *Saufley*, and at midnight bombarded the Buin-Shortland area of Bougainville. This was the farthest up the Slot that any of our surface ships had ventured. Two destroyers, the *Renshaw* and *Waller*, simultaneously shelled the Kolombangara plantation establishments. Then, at dawn, the troops went ashore at their assigned landing places.

That afternoon 24 enemy torpedo planes, strongly escorted by fighters, attacked our transports off Rendova. Despite a heavy antiaircraft barrage, many of them reached a position to drop their torpedoes. Admiral Turner's flagship, the *McCawley* (the ex-passenger liner *Santa Barbara*), took a torpedo hit

amidships and was seriously crippled. She remained afloat
until after dark but it was evident that she was doomed. All
personnel were removed and preparations were being made
to sink her when one of our PT boats dashed out of the
darkness and mistook her for an enemy. Here was its great
opportunity. The little vessel promptly fired three torpedoes,
all of which hit. The transport flagship sank in 30 seconds.

In the air fighting on the first day, Army, Navy and
Marine Corps fighters shot down 101 enemy planes out of
130 engaged in combat.

The landings proceeded according to schedule. In the
Bairoko-Enogai area, troops were landed on July 5 at Rice
Anchorage, where they met stubborn resistance. However,
by July 12, they had wiped out the garrison at Enogai Inlet
and cut the Japanese communications from Munda to Bairoko
Harbor. The units which landed on the eastern and southern
coasts promptly consolidated their positions and, in bitter
fighting, slowly drove forward to Munda airfield, which was
finally in our possession on August 5.

The intensity of air operations reached a greater pitch in
this campaign than in any previous period in the Solomons.
Our aircraft shot down the amazing number of 259 fighters,
60 bombers, 23 dive bombers and 16 float planes, while
providing continuous patrols over convoys and beachheads
and close air support to the advancing ground forces. Long-
range bombing planes conducted neutralizing raids on Rabaul
airfields and attacked enemy shipping, while search flights
guarded against the approach of enemy surface units. The
Japanese Army aviation units at Rabaul, which had suffered
severe losses, were finally withdrawn from combat, leaving
further air operations to the Imperial Navy.

THE FIRST BATTLE OF KULA GULF

On July 4, the night before the landing at Rice Anchorage, the cruisers *Honolulu, Helena* and *St. Louis*, with the
destroyers *Nicholas, O'Bannon, Strong* and *Chevalier,* under
Rear Admiral Ainsworth, bombarded the enemy positions at
Enogai Inlet and at Vila-Stanmore. The *Strong* was torpedoed
by a Japanese submarine unexpectedly encountered in the
area. The enemy shore batteries opened up on her with star
shells and enemy bombers got into the fray. Despite these
difficulties, 75 per cent of the *Strong's* survivors were trans-

ferred to the *Chevalier* before she sank. Others were later rescued from the water by the *Gwin*, screening the transports, but many were killed and injured by the *Strong*'s depth charges, which exploded as she went down.

Short of ammunition and fuel, the cruiser division was returning to Espiritu Santo for replenishment on the afternoon of the 5th, when Halsey radioed Ainsworth to go back up the Slot and intercept the Tokyo Express running that night from Bougainville to New Georgia with reinforcements for the Munda garrison. Racing back up their track, the cruisers arrived in Kula Gulf shortly after midnight. They could remain only until two o'clock because of their depleted fuel tanks. With 20 minutes left before they would have to depart, the radar brought the welcome news: targets approaching, distance 22,000 yards.

Two groups of enemy ships were made out on the radar screen, one of five destroyers and the other of four. Just before two o'clock our ships opened a deadly fire and two Japanese ships burst into flames. The enemy retaliated with salvos of deadly torpedoes. Three of them hit the *Helena*, under the command of Captain C. F. Cecil, and that gallant ship went down to the accompaniment of thunderous gunfire. The enemy did not wait to see the results of their attack but fled up the Slot without delivering their reinforcements. Our task force gave up the pursuit to rescue the *Helena*'s survivors. Leaving two destroyers to complete this assignment, the other ships returned to base. Many men in the water were picked up, but others found their way to Japanese-occupied Vella-Lavella Island, where friendly natives hid them from the enemy. Most of them eventually returned to our lines.

In this battle, the Japanese lost two destroyers, the *Nagatsuki* and *Niizuki*, to our loss of the *Helena*.

THE SECOND BATTLE OF KULA GULF

On the night of July 12, the Tokyo Express again attempted to run. Once more Ainsworth received orders to intercept. The British cruiser *Leander*, under Captain C. A. L. Mansbergh, RN, had replaced the *Helena*, and additional destroyers were assigned so that the task force now comprised 10 of that class, in addition to the three cruisers.

Shortly after midnight, one of our night search planes

reported an enemy force of one cruiser and six destroyers approaching our ships and only 30 miles away. The Americans now felt at home in these waters and were ready for them. Engaging on opposite courses, firing guns and torpedoes, Ainsworth ordered our units to reverse course simultaneously to prevent running past the enemy. This order was put out on the voice radio, but many of our ships failed to receive it and our line was thrown into disorder when some of the ships turned and others did not.

The *Leander* turned late, forcing the *Honolulu* to turn wide. Just at this moment, a torpedo crashed into the British cruiser, forcing her to drop out of the battle. Several enemy ships were sighted burning and apparently dead in the water. Then the *St. Louis* was hit by a tin fish and a few minutes later the flagship *Honolulu* was struck on the starboard bow and again on the stern. The second torpedo failed to explode. In addition to the cruiser, the destroyer *Gwin* had been struck while in a turn, and was afire. With the damaged ships stopped dead in the water, two other destroyers collided, receiving minor damage.

Our gunfire had been concentrated on the light cruiser *Jintsu*, which was burning brilliantly. The remaining enemy ships, after firing their torpedoes, once more fled back up the Slot and our crippled ships limped home—all but the *Gwin*. Although under air attack, she had been taken in tow, but at 9:00 A.M., she was settling fast and had to be abandoned. She was sunk by torpedoes from the *Ralph Talbot*.

After the war, it was found that the *Jintsu* had been sunk, taking down with her the admiral, his staff, the commanding officer and most of her crew.

Although these actions had been expensive to us, the enemy losses were sufficient to cause them to abandon the use of Kula Gulf and confine their operations to small ships and landing barges around Vella-Lavella and west of Kolombangara.

THE BATTLE OF VELLA GULF

Deciding it was not worth the effort to hold it, the Japanese planned to evacuate their garrison from Bairoko Harbor, on the northwest coast of New Georgia, to Kolombangara, across the water. The Vila-Stanmore garrison was being strengthened by nightly runs of the Tokyo Express, which had a relatively short distance to come from the Shortlands area to Vila. Destroyers and landing barges were used in this work. We now had motor torpedo boats to combat this traffic, and the courageous Sea Bees had reconditioned Munda airfield. Planes operating from there kept the enemy airfield at Vila under attack, as well as the fields farther on at Balle and Kahili on Bougainville.

About midnight on August 6, a task force of six destroyers under Commander Frederick Moosbrugger was prowling the waters of Vella Gulf looking for a Japanese convoy of destroyers reported coming in with reinforcements for Kolombangara. There was no moon and it was extremely dark. Soon the radar spotted four vessels standing in at high speed. Our tactics had now changed to give the enemy some of his own medicine with torpedoes. Moosbrugger's Division 12 was joined by Commander Roger Simpson's Division 15. Division 12 maneuvered across the bow of the oncoming enemy and fired 24 torpedoes, while Division 15 took position on the flank. All the aiming was done by radar.

The plan worked perfectly. The enemy ships, consisting of four destroyers, were transporting 950 troops and supplies to Vila. The destroyers *Hagikaze*, *Arashi* and *Kawakaze* were hit by our torpedoes before they were aware of our presence. The American destroyers opened up with gunfire just as the torpedoes hit and the three enemy ships quickly disappeared beneath the surface, while the *Shigure*, heavily damaged, fled to the north. Our ships were not touched. It was a perfect night action. This action caused the Japanese to decide to withdraw their garrison from Kolombangara rather than let it wither on the vine, since it little threatened our further advance. Our next operation then assumed the character of attempting to prevent this evacuation.

THE FIRST BATTLE OF VELLA-LAVELLA

At this time, the first of the by-passing operations which were to become more frequent from then on was undertaken. With the fate of Kolombangara settled, it was decided to leap-frog to Vella-Lavella, farther to the west. A group of our officers had landed there secretly on July 21, and without being discovered, reconnoitered the island for days. They reported it lightly held and suitable for airfield development. On August 15, a week after the Battle of Vella Gulf,

troops were landed at Barakoma on the southeastern tip of
Vella-Lavella. There was little ground opposition, although
the landing was only 90 miles from Kahili, the largest Japanese
air base in the Solomons. During the day, four enemy bomber attacks were beaten off by fighter cover from our newly
acquired field at Munda. By 3:30 P.M. the Sea Bees had
begun constructing a new airstrip on a new island.

Just after midnight two days later, four of our destroyers,
under Captain T. J. Ryan, were sweeping the area north of
Vella-Lavella when they encountered four enemy destroyers
under Rear Admiral M. Ijuin. They were escorting 17 landing
barges, two auxiliary subchasers, four shipboard landing craft,
and three armed Diatsu boats, some of them loaded with
personnel to strengthen the forces on Vella-Lavella, while
others were empty and intended for use in the evacuation of
Kolombangara.

Under a full moon, the calm sea was nearly as bright as
day, and surprise played no part in the action. The smaller
Japanese landing craft were in plain sight, with the destroyers
somewhat farther away as enemy planes appeared and dropped
flares over our destroyers, together with a stick of bombs
which barely missed the *Nicholas* by 100 yards.

Captain Ryan ignored the barges to get at the enemy
destroyers beyond. Fire was opened by both sides at about
14,000 yards, and the Japanese destroyers reversed course
and headed northwest at high speed. This maneuver was
intended to draw our ships into the path of torpedoes fired as
the enemy made their turn, but Captain Ryan accepted the
challenge and pursued. He was lucky, as none of our destroyers was hit, although several torpedoes passed dangerously
close.

The Japanese destroyer *Isokazi* received minor damage
from gunfire, but the enemy ships made good their escape
and our task force returned to devote its attention to the
barges. These small craft were now pretty well scattered and
difficult to locate. Five were sunk, but the ones intended for
the evacuation, escaped without, however, effecting their
purpose. Others managed to unload personnel on Vella-Lavella.

On August 25, 1943, our troops on New Georgia had
finally captured Bairoko Harbor, which had held out tenaciously
for eight weeks. Vella-Lavella was considered secure on September 3, but mopping up continued until October 7, when
New Zealand troops who had relieved the Americans closed

in and wiped out the enemy remnants at dawn. On September 27, the new airfield at Barakoma on Vella-Lavella had become fully operational. Pinched between American airfields at Munda and Barakoma, Kolombangara was now completely useless to the enemy. Constantly attacked by our planes, the personnel remaining, estimated at 10,000, faced a slow death by starvation.

After the fall of Bairoko Harbor, our troops crossed over, on August 27, to the island of Arundel, on the north side of the strait, and to other small islands adjoining. These landings gave us full control of this area and further tightened the Kolombangara blockade. Although Japanese troops from there had infiltrated across to oppose our forces on Arundel, they were completely eliminated by September 21.

The efforts of the enemy to evacuate Kolombangara depended largely upon barges, which by night crept slowly along the reefs and by day hid in the small inlets, concealed by jungle growth and camouflage. Our PT boats, now based in large numbers in the New Georgia area, performed brilliantly in disrupting this traffic. These small vessels had many a thrilling night action in which they were shelled by shore batteries and attacked by night-flying aircraft. Many Japanese barges and personnel were destroyed by the fast-moving mosquito craft.

THE SECOND BATTLE OF VILLA-LAVELLA

On the moonless night of October 6, it had been estimated that the enemy would attempt to run the blockade with a large number of barges and destroyers to complete their withdrawal from Kolombangara. Their tactics for several weeks had been to feint with their destroyers from the Shortlands area in order to distract our destroyers from the barge traffic. This method had some success, as our destroyers were inclined to seek the larger targets and leave the smaller craft to the PT boats. On the evening of the 6th, intelligence indicated a strong possibility that enemy destroyers would again be in the area.

A task group consisting of the *Selfridge, Chevalier* and *O'Bannon* under Captain Frank R. Walker, was combing the waters north of Vella-Lavella. To reinforce them, Rear Admiral (later Vice-Admiral) Theodore S. Wilkinson, who had relieved Admiral Turner as Commander of Amphibious Forces,

South Pacific, on July 15, ordered Commander Harold O. Larsen to join them with the *Ralph Talbot*, *Taylor* and *Lavallette*.

Later in the afternoon one of our air groups which had been pounding the enemy airfield at Kahili reported that they had seen four destroyers or light cruisers heading south. Japanese planes had been snooping Captain Walker's division, in spite of his efforts to throw them off by dodging in and out of rain squalls. About 10:30 P.M., Walker's division made radar contact with two groups of enemy ships about 10 miles away. They were nine destroyers under the command of Rear Admiral Ijuin, who had also been in command during the action on August 17-18. Outnumbering the ships three to one, the Japanese decided to engage, although three of their destroyers were acting as transports and carried boats for evacuation purposes. Walker boldly dashed in to attack. As the enemy were in two sections, he headed for the larger one, hoping Larsen's detachment would arrive in time to engage the other. Our destroyers turned to fire torpedoes and then opened up with their guns. One of the targets, the large *Yugumo*, burst into flames from a torpedo hit and blew up five minutes later in a violent explosion.

Shortly after opening fire, the *Chevalier*, second ship in our line, was hit by an enemy torpedo which blew off the entire bow forward of the bridge. Out of control, she was rammed by the *O'Bannon*, coming up astern at full speed. The collision flooded the *Chevalier*'s after engine room and left her without power. The leading destroyer *Selfridge*, continuing on against the enemy and blasting away with her guns, was soon afterward struck by two torpedoes which sheared off her bow and left her a wreck as far aft as the bridge.

This was the end of the battle. Having fired their torpedoes, the Japanese were only too anxious to get away. They had been pounded by our aggressive tactics so many times that their offensive psychology had now changed to hit and run, avoiding decisive action with our forces at all costs. The *Chevalier* had to be sunk when it became apparent that she could not remain afloat to be towed back to Tulagi. The *Selfridge* and the *O'Bannon* reached port and were repaired to fight again.

Larsen's destroyers, which arrived after the action was over, searched for enemy barges, but none were found.

Under cover of the battle, most of the enemy soldiers left on Vella-Lavella had made good their escape to Bougainville. How many of the Japanese garrison on Kolombangara escaped will never be known. After the war, we found that most of the enemy records had been destroyed, and exact information could not be ascertained. We know that many loaded barges were sunk during the evacuation, with heavy loss of life. When our reconnaissance parties landed there early in October, they found large quantities of abandoned equipment and a few half-starved Japanese who promptly disappeared into the jungle. Most of these miserable creatures, surrounded by hostile natives, probably survived for a few weeks or months, only to leave their bones in the forests or hills of the faraway tropical island.

With the evacuation of the Japanese from Vella-Lavella and Kolombangara, the campaign for the Central Solomons was now complete. The next step was the island of Bougainville, 130 miles long and averaging 30 miles wide. Near its northwestern tip, and across a narrow strait, was Buka Island. Approximately 35,000 Japanese were estimated to be concentrated at various places on the big island and its adjacent smaller ones, and they had had ample time to prepare its defense.

Around the southeastern end of Bougainville, the Shortland Islands formed a sheltered water area which comprised an excellent anchorage. Most of these islands had been strongly fortified. Airfields had been constructed on the island of Ballale, at Kahili and Kara near the southeastern end of Bougainville, at Kieta on its northeastern coast, at Bonis on its northwestern tip, and on Buka across the strait. The terrain consisted of a central mountain range rising to several thousand feet, impenetrable jungle with few trails, and dismal swamps along the shore line. It was a tough nut to crack.

At the beginning of the Solomons campaign, our ultimate objective had always been Rabaul. This city was the Japanese headquarters for the whole southern area. The metropolis of the area, it had been the seat of government for the Solomons, and had an excellent harbor. Its capture seemed essential. Talk in the officers' clubs built on our newly acquired bases had always been prefaced with "When we get to Rabaul...." But to get to Rabaul, we had to have airfields on Bougainville in order to bring it under round-the-clock air attack with fighter protection for the bombers.

The task of seizing sufficient real estate on Bougainville for airfields was assigned to the First Marine Amphibious Corps, under General Vandergrift. It consisted of the Third Marine Division, Major General A. H. Turnage; Thirty-Seventh (Army) Infantry Division, Major General Robert S. Beightler; Marine Raider Regiment, Lieutenant Colonel Alan Shapley; Second Marine Parachute Battalion, Lieutenant Colonel V. H. Krulak; Third Marine Defense Battalion, Lieutenant Colonel E. H. Forney; and Eighth New Zealand Brigade Group, Brigadier R. A. Row. Major General Roy S. Geiger was to relieve General Vandergrift nine days after the landing, when the latter returned to the United States to become Commandant of the Marine Corps.

As a diversion to the main landing, the Treasury Islands, about 30 miles south of the Shortlands, were occupied on October 27, 1943, by the New Zealand Brigade, reinforced with some United States elements. These islands would protect our communications. As a feint, the Marine Parachute Battalion was landed by boat on the island of Choiseul, to the northeast. Both these expeditions met opposition and the Treasury Islands were not secured until November 12. The forces on Choiseul, having accomplished their purpose, skillfully withdrew to rejoin the main expedition against Bougainville on the night of November 3-4.

Empress Augusta Bay, near the middle of the western coast of Bougainville and adjacent to Cape Torokina, was selected as the landing point. It was far enough from the enemy concentrations to prevent strong counterattacks from developing until after we had secured a beachhead, and the ground, although swampy, seemed suitable for airfield construction.

D-Day for the Bougainville landing was set for November 1. For three weeks, heavy preparatory air attacks pounded the island's airfields and the stronghold of Rabaul. From Munda, Vella-Lavella, and eastern New Guinea came a relentless, round-the-clock succession of planes. Total sorties in October amounted to 3,259, and resulted in the destruction of 290 enemy aircraft besides extensive damage to ground installations.

During the night of October 31-November 1, Admiral ("Tip") Merrill's Task Force, comprising the cruisers *Columbia, Montpelier, Cleveland* and *Denver,* with the destroyers *Charles Ausburne, Dyson, Claxton, Spence, Thatcher, Con-*

verse, *Foote* and *Stanly*, bombarded the airfields at Buka and Bonis. Then Merrill raced back to the Shortlands to shell that area in the first daylight surface-ship bombardment in the Solomons. During the bombardment, Merrill's ships were protected by the fighter cover provided for the landing.

At the time, I was in command of a carrier task force consisting of the carriers *Saratoga* and *Princeton;* the antiaircraft cruisers *San Diego* and *San Juan;* and the destroyers *Lardner, Farenbolt, Woodworth, Buchanan, Landsdowne, Grayson, Sterett, Stack, Wilson* and *Edwards*. For the assault on Bougainville, we were assigned the task of striking the Buka-Bonis airfields during the landing operations on November 1 and 2. It would be the first time carriers had operated within range of the strong enemy bases at Rabaul and Kavieng.

We on the carriers had begun to think we would never get any action. All the previous assignments had gone to the shore-based air. Admiral Halsey had told me that he had to hold us for use against the Japanese fleet in case it came down from Truk to interfere with our Guadalcanal and New Georgia operations. We were now to have our opportunity.

With smiles on their faces, the alert young pilots took off from our carrier decks over a glassy sea and proceeded with their work of destruction. During the two days, they destroyed or damaged 33 enemy planes, nine cargo ships, eight barges and three smaller ships, and so damaged the fields as to render them unusable during the period of the landings at Empress Augusta Bay. Only three of our pilots and four crewmen were lost. Radio Tokyo broadcast the usual bombastic claim of sinking one large and one small carrier—which indicated, however, that they knew the exact composition of my task force.

On November 1, when the Marines went ashore, they met determined opposition from 300 Japanese strongly entrenched along the water's edge. The number was not great, but that many men can make it exceedingly difficult for any force to get ashore. This was not the only obstacle. In one section, the leathernecks encountered an extremely high surf and a very steep beach which caused some 70 boats to capsize and dump their occupants and cargoes into the sea. In another area, they found the jungle so dense and the swamps so deep that advance seemed almost impossible. Other jungles which the Marines had experienced were tame by com-

parison. Nevertheless, they got ashore, but by the third day
the perimeter had moved inland only 1,500 yards.

THE BATTLE OF EMPRESS AUGUSTA BAY

After bombarding the Shortland Islands on November 1,
Merrill's task force was standing by to the northwest of the
landing area to guard against interference by surface ships.
During the forenoon, reconnaissance planes reported an enemy cruiser force approaching from Rabaul. Merrill's four
cruisers were the only ones available to protect the transports
and landing craft, other cruisers previously assigned to the
South Pacific having now been withdrawn for operations in
the Central Pacific.

The Japanese force, under Rear Admiral S. Omori,
consisted of three heavy cruisers, the *Myoko, Haguro* and
Agano; the light cruiser *Sendai;* and six destroyers. They had
orders to make a night attack on our invasion forces. In
fighting strength they slightly outweighed Merrill's ships
since the heavy cruisers carried 8-inch guns, whereas those of
our cruisers were only of 6-inch caliber.

Merrill made radar contact with the approaching enemy
ships at 2:27 A.M., November 2. The night was dark, with an
overcast sky and occasional rain squalls, as the two forces
closed the range with no visual indication of each other's
presence. Merrill realized that his job was to turn the enemy
away without too much damage to his own ships, since his
force constituted the only surface protection available in the
South Pacific.

The Japanese vessels were disposed in three groups, and
the initial contact had been made with the northern one,
consisting of the *Sendai* and three destroyers. The heavy
cruisers were in separate detachments the *Myoko* and *Haguro*
in the center and the *Agano* on the right flank with the three
remaining destroyers. The American ships were in column
heading south across the enemy track. This picture of the
situation gradually unfolded on the radar screen in flag plot
on Merrill's flagship.

Captain Arleigh Burke's destroyer division increased speed
and on radar bearings loosed a flock of torpedoes for the
northern group. Merrill had intended to wait until these
torpedoes reached their targets before opening fire, but his

radar plot showed the enemy ships changing course during the torpedo run, so that they would miss. The order to commence firing was then given at 2:49 A.M. and the enemy promptly replied.

The ensuing gun action lasted for an hour. At first, the northern group were the targets, but in the later phases the enemy center and southern groups were also engaged. Soon after opening fire, Commander B. L. Austin's destroyer division went in to fire torpedoes.

In the ensuing melee, our cruisers reversed course several times, steaming generally in a north and south direction. The Japanese fired torpedoes too, but the action was primarily a gunfire engagement, with our cruisers keeping out of torpedo range of the enemy destroyers. We had learned the deadly effectiveness of these weapons.

The enemy's gunfire was quite accurate and the Denver, Columbia and Cleveland were repeatedly straddled by enemy salvos. At 3:20 A.M., the Denver received three 8 inch hits which caused her to take on water and turn out of formation for a few minutes. To throw off the enemy's fire, the Admiral ordered the cruisers to make smoke, and behind this screen they made evasive maneuvers. The Japanese commander reported afterward that he had had difficulty in locating our ships, although star shells and aircraft flares were repeatedly used. Our superior radar permitted our ships to fire accurately through the smoke.

Early in the action, the Sendai, leading the northern group, had come to a stop under the terrific punishment of our gunfire. Soon afterward she exploded with a tremendous flash that brilliantly illuminated the surrounding darkness. The destroyers Samidare and Shiratsuyu, accompanying her, collided while maneuvering to avoid the onslaught of torpedoes and gunfire and both retired from action, the Shiratsuyu seriously damaged. On our side, the destroyer Foote was struck by a Japanese torpedo which completely disabled her, and the Spence, in addition to the Denver, was hit by the enemy's guns.

At this stage, Omori decided to break off the action and retire to Rabaul. He gave as his reasons the poor illumination, the unknown composition of our force, damage to his ships from collision, and the fear of being within range of American dive bombers at daylight. Upon arrival at Rabaul he was immediately relieved of his command for failure to destroy the invading transport force.

In this action the Japanese lost the light cruiser *Sendai* and the destroyer *Hatsukaze*, while the heavy cruisers *Myoko* and *Haguro* and the destroyer *Shiratsuyu* were severely damaged. On our side, the *Denver* and *Spence* were damaged by gunfire and the *Foote* by a torpedo. The latter was taken in tow by the *Claxton* and eventually reached port for repairs.

After daylight, while retiring eastward for fuel and much-needed rest, Merrill's force was attacked by between 60 and 70 Japanese dive bombers and horizontal bombers protected by fighters. With only four P-38's for air cover, they had to rely for defense mainly on antiaircraft fire and evasive maneuvers. The action lasted only seven minutes, but the air was full of bursting shrapnel and flaming planes. In the welter of gunfire and turning, twisting ships, it was impossible to determine how many planes were shot down, but they were conservatively estimated at 25. Our ships suffered no damage, except to the *Montpelier*'s catapult, which was demolished.

By nightfall of November 2, the beachhead at Empress Augusta Bay had been firmly established. Construction of airstrips and an advance naval base was immediately begun. Despite swampy ground, two fighter strips and one bomber strip were shortly in operation. A barbed-wire defensive line was set up, but no immediate effort to advance was made, since our purpose was only to seize ground for the necessary airfields. Later, when the Japanese finally concentrated to attack our lines, sharp fighting was experienced. The last of these major clashes occurred on December 12-18, in an action at "Hellzapoppin" Ridge where the Marines eliminated a strongly held enemy position which threatened our defenses.

THE FIRST CARRIER AIR RAID ON RABAUL

My carrier task force had retired for fuel after the Buka-Bonis raids on November 1 and 2, when we received information that a new force of Japanese cruisers and destroyers had arrived at Rabaul. This was a decided menace to our amphibious operations at Empress Augusta Bay. On November 4, I received a dispatch from Admiral Halsey to launch an all-out strike on this shipping on November 5, with cruisers and destroyers as priority targets. We were directed to launch the attack from north of the Solomon Islands. On receiving the message, we had just completed fueling northwest of Rennell Island, south of the Solomons. To reach the assigned position we had to proceed all night at maximum formation speed of 27 knots. Arriving at the launching position just before daylight, we found the weather to the westward ideal for air operations, with a number of near-by rain squalls to give us some protection.

The plan was to attack with every plane we had, including all our fighters. To guard us against enemy air attack while our planes were away, fighter planes from Munda were to come out to give us cover. These land-based Navy planes, their pilots trained for carrier landings, would land on our decks and be refueled, thus assuring continuous fighter protection.

The *Saratoga* and *Princeton* air groups were launched and left on their mission with Commander Henry Howard Caldwell heading the combined air groups and Commander Joseph C. ("Jumping Joe") Clifton, the escorting fighters. Our attack group consisted of approximately 50 bombing and torpedo planes and 55 fighters. They accomplished a marvelous job. Arriving over Rabaul, they found about 100 hostile fighters in the air waiting to receive them. As they circled inland so as to make their dives toward the open sea, to facilitate their getaway, our own fighters formed a close protective screen around the bombers and torpedo planes. The Japanese vainly searched for an opening. When in position, our attack planes pushed over in the beautiful precision of a coordinated attack. The fighters went down with their charges protecting them all the way.

The scene below was beautiful, with the circular bay surrounded by towering mountains, and with a smoking conical volcano near the harbor entrance. The town of Rabaul nestled against the hills on the northeast sector of the bay, and the water was covered with ships. Besides seven heavy cruisers, three light cruisers, two destroyer leaders and 12 destroyers, there were scores of merchantmen and auxiliaries.

As the planes dived from the cloudless sky, all hell broke loose below. Every ship in the harbor opened up with all its guns. In addition, there seemed to be thousands of these weapons lining the shore. At this moment, the enemy fighters made their attack. Our dive bombers and torpedo planes were not to be diverted. Our fighters peeled off to engage the menacing enemy planes and the air was full of vicious combat. It was magnificent teamwork.

After dropping their bombs and torpedoes, the attacking planes pulled out to rendezvous off Cape St. George for the return flight to our carriers. Only seven failed to join up at the rendezvous. The purpose of this attack was to damage the enemy force as a whole so that it would be unable to attack our transports off Bougainville, which had only the protection of Admiral Merrill's four light cruisers. Information obtained from Japan after the war showed that the heavy cruisers *Maya*, *Atago*, *Mogami* and *Takao*, the light cruisers *Agano* and *Noshiro* and the destroyers *Fujinami* and *Wakatsuki* were severely damaged in this attack. In addition, our pilots estimated that 25 enemy planes were certainly shot down, plus another 25 probables, for the loss of seven of our planes. The following message was received from General H. H. Arnold, head of the Army Air Forces:

> The Army Air Forces congratulate the Navy for the magnificent day attacks by carrier force aircraft on Japanese warships in Rabaul Harbor November 5th. Your fliers have established a record for damage done per bomb and torpedo that all other airmen will find difficult to equal. Please extend my congratulations to all concerned.

Admiral Halsey came aboard my flagship, the *Saratoga*, at Espiritu Santo after the attack to personally thank all hands "from the bottom of my heart for the recent operations of this task force, particularly on November 5th." He stated that their success was "primarily responsible for saving the critical situation in the campaign for the Solomons Islands." A message was also received from General MacArthur extending his sincere congratulations for the accomplishments of the task force and stating, "Every officer and man engaged deserves commendation."

Following this attack, all the enemy cruisers returned to Truk, from whence some of them had to go all the way back to Japan for repairs. The plan to attack our forces off Empress Augusta Bay was abandoned, and enemy surface ships in force never appeared again in the Solomons area.

THE SECOND CARRIER STRIKE ON RABAUL

After the Rabaul strike on November 5, we returned to Espiritu Santo for fueling and fresh bombs and torpedoes. We were joined there by a newly formed carrier task force consisting of the recently completed *Essex* and *Bunker Hill* and the new light carrier *Independence*, with screening vessels, under the command of Rear Admiral A. E. Montgomery. Admiral Halsey directed another coordinated air attack on shipping in Rabaul Harbor to be executed on November 11 by the two carrier task forces, plus the heavy bombers of the shore-based air command in the Solomons. My task force launched again from a point north of the islands, and Montgomery's from the south. We struck at 8:30 A.M., Montgomery at 9:30, and the shore-based bombers immediately thereafter, in order to prevent interference between air groups at the target. As before, fighters from our Solomons bases furnished us air cover while our planes were away.

In this attack, the weather was unfavorable. Low clouds over the harbor made it impossible to conduct a satisfactory dive-bombing attack. My planes reported damage to a light cruiser and three destroyers sighted through a hole in the clouds. Reports obtained after the war showed one destroyer, the *Suzunami*, sunk near the harbor entrance, while the heavy cruiser *Agamo*, the light cruiser *Yubari*, and the destroyers *Urakaze*, *Nagamami* and *Umikaze* received minor damage.

The enemy reacted to this strike with a heavy air attack on Montgomery's force south of the islands. Possibly they located it by following its planes back from Rabaul. The enemy planes numbered about 120, all from the Rabaul vicinity. In a wild turmoil of gunfire, attacking planes, dogfights and near misses, it was estimated that over half of the attacking planes were shot down. None of Montgomery's ships were damaged. My group was not attacked and retired without incident.

Following these actions, the Japanese efforts to resist our advance were confined to air raids against our supply shipping. They received large aircraft replacements about this time and made 869 sorties during November, although many of them were by fighters in defense of Rabaul. They succeeded in sinking one high-speed transport off Cape Torokina and in damaging several other vessels. By the end of November, our shore-based aircraft, both from the Solomons and from New Guinea, had so hammered their airfields on New Britain, and had shot down so many of their planes, that their air forces were reduced to impotence and never again became a serious threat in the Solomons. They were limited to occasional night raids of little effectiveness.

THE BATTLE OF CAPE ST. GEORGE

One more surface action was to occur in the Solomons area. Our destroyers were now patrolling the waters between Bougainville and Rabaul for the purpose of preventing the enemy from reinforcing or supplying his sealed-off troops on Bougainville.

On the night of November 24-25, five of our destroyers, under Captain Arleigh Burke, cruising between Buka and New Ireland in St. George's Channel, encountered five Japanese destroyers engaged in transferring some 700 troops from Buka to Rabaul. Our ships vigorously attacked and pursued the enemy to within 60 miles of Rabaul. Three of the Japanese destroyers were sunk and one damaged, without injury of any kind to our forces. Following this action, the enemy undertook no more surface operations in the Solomons.

CARRIER AIR RAIDS ON KAVIENG

Following the naval actions during the occupation of Bougainville, I commanded a new carrier task group which carried out a series of air raids on Kavieng, at the northern extremity of New Ireland, between Rabaul and Truk. These raids were for the purpose of supporting the Marines' landing at Cape Gloucester, at the western end of New Britain. They demonstrated the completeness with which we controlled the sea in that area, although at the time we did not fully appreciate how complete our sway actually was.

After our second Rabaul strike, my task force had proceeded to the Central Pacific area, where we had participated in the capture of Tarawa, in the Gilbert Islands, furnishing air cover to the landing forces. (The Gilberts campaign will be discussed in Chapter XI.) On the way north, we had conducted a strike on the small island of Nauru, from which the Japanese obtained phosphates and sugar, and where they had an airfield used by reconnaissance planes. We dropped 90 tons of bombs, thoroughly pounding the airfield and leaving the runways pitted and hangars burning. Two enemy fighters were shot down and three or four medium bombers left in flames on the ground.

At the conclusion of the Tarawa operation the carrier task forces of the Pacific Fleet were reorganized. In this shift, I was transferred from the *Saratoga* to the new carrier *Bunker Hill* and was assigned, in addition, the new light carrier *Monterey* and the destroyers *Bradford, Brown, Cowell, Bell, Charrette* and *Connor*. With this force, I returned to the South Pacific after the capture of Tarawa to serve temporarily under Admiral Halsey.

Arriving at the familiar anchorage at Espiritu Santo, we soon received orders for an air attack on the Kavieng area at dawn on Christmas Day, 1943. In order of priority, our assigned targets were combatant ships, merchant ships and airfield installations. We had little idea of what to expect in this operation, but we knew it was another thrust into waters which had hitherto belonged to the enemy, and that we would be within range of enemy airfields capable of operating hundreds of planes. This time we were without the protection of our old associates, the antiaircraft cruisers *San Diego* and *San Juan*. Our screen was very weak, consisting of only the six destroyers.

After fueling on December 23, the task group proceeded at high speed to a point 150 miles northeast of Kavieng. The weather at the launching point was fair, with broken, fleecy white clouds and unlimited ceiling and visibility, and with prevailing northwest monsoon winds.

Launched at dawn on Christmas Day, the air groups met no air opposition over Kavieng, where they found no large combatant ships. Against heavy ack-ack from shore and ships, they sank a medium-sized merchantman and three barges and damaged several others. Although no worth-while targets were present, valuable photographs of the Japanese installations were obtained.

The location of our task force was not long unknown to the enemy. At 7:20 A.M. the combat air patrol intercepted and shot down a four-engine patrol plane 30 miles from our disposition. Again, in the afternoon, two Betty snoopers made contact, both of which were shot down. At dusk we were subjected to repeated attacks by an estimated 18 to 30

Bettys carrying torpedoes. These planes, using flares and coming in two or three at a time, attacked until 8:30 P.M., when we managed to throw them off by making smoke and by radical, simultaneous changes of course.

During the evening our antiaircraft fire shot down three of the enemy planes. We accomplished our withdrawal without receiving any damage.

While returning to Espiritu Santo, we suddenly received orders from Halsey to fuel at sea from tankers and make another attack on Kavieng on the morning of January 1, 1944, with cruisers as first-priority targets. During the run to our launching point, the *Charrette* suffered an engineering casu-

"Betty"

alty which reduced our destroyer screen to five. Arriving in position, we proceeded to make our search and attack as a celebration of New Year's Day. After these Christmas and New Year's strikes (followed later by attacks on Saipan and Tinian on Washington's Birthday), the *Bunker Hill's* crew called her "Holiday Inn." The attack group located two cruisers and two destroyers about five miles west of the harbor. Our planes were opposed by 30 Japanese fighters and intense ack-ack, while the ships attempted to dodge our bombs and torpedoes by radical evasive maneuvers. The enemy fighters dropped spectacular phosphorous bombs and attacked from above as the bombers started their dives. Our fighters shot down 14 enemy planes and listed 12 more probables. We lost two fighters and one dive bomber, with minor damage to 15 others. Reports obtained from Japan after the war were to the effect that the light cruiser *Noshiro* and two destroyers had been damaged.

While retiring from this attack, the task force was intercepted by two enemy fighter planes, evidently scouts. One was shot down by our combat air patrol but the other escaped into a cloud. Another snooper picked us up about an hour later. From these contacts, we expected a dusk torpedo-plane attack, and we were not disappointed. From 7:41 P.M. until 9:30, numerous bogeys were on the radar screen. The enemy planes were milling around, trying to find us. By radical changes of course, we evaded them, no planes getting within 15 miles of our disposition.

But we were not yet finished with attacks on Kavieng. Once more, after fueling at sea, we received orders to attack on January 4. We were beginning to feel at home in this "Indian Country" between Truk and Rabaul, but with two of our destroyers out during part of this attack we also felt rather naked. The protection of the antiaircraft guns of the array of battleships, cruisers and 12 to 15 destroyers which were normally part of a fast carrier task force would have been very welcome in case of large-scale air attack.

A surprising aspect of the lack of these ships in our disposition was that Vice-Admiral W. A. Lee was stationed with a fast battleship task force about 150 miles east of us while we were in the "hot area" around Kavieng. His mission was to come to our support in case we got into trouble or if strong surface forces appeared on the scene. Located by

Japanese search planes, Admiral Lee was concerned about having to take an attack without air cover. We, for our part, would have liked to have had his ships and their antiaircraft guns in our disposition in case we were attacked. As it was, we were in an area the farthest yet advanced into enemy waters with the weakest screen ever assigned to large aircraft carriers.

On this third attack on Kavieng, only one medium-sized merchantman and several small vessels were found in the harbor, and two destroyers in the channel to the west. The air group attacked the two destroyers, mistaking them for cruisers, and were opposed by 10 to 20 enemy fighters. The latter were reluctant to engage, probably because of their heavy losses in the previous attack. Two of the enemy aircraft were shot down.

Since this was our third such strike, we fully expected heavy air attacks from the enemy. Occasional bogeys spotted us during the day. At 1:30 P.M. the radar picked up a group of enemy planes 90 miles away, approaching from the direction of Truk. Here, we thought, was the major attack we had been expecting. Additional fighters were hurriedly launched and defense disposition assumed. Because of broken clouds, the combat air patrol failed to intercept, and at 2 P.M. enemy planes were in plain sight only 15 miles away. Much to our surprise, they failed to attack and withdrew to the west. Our fighter planes, coached by the *Monterey*'s radar, took up the pursuit. At a distance of 70 miles, they made contact and found the enemy formation consisted of one four-engine plane and six fighters. In a short fight the entire enemy formation was shot down. "Splash one!" "Splash two!" "Oh hell, splash the whole formation," came over the voice radio in rapid succession. At first we thought the escorted four-engine bomber was probably carrying a high-ranking Japanese officer. Later the incompetent tactics of the group led us to believe that the fighters were manned by untrained pilots and were replacements being ferried to Rabaul from Truk, with the big bomber as their navigator and mother ship.

This ended our Kavieng strikes. It was the fifteenth air raid we had made in a period of nine weeks. These actions had extended from Rabaul and Buka in the Solomons to the Gilberts, far to the eastward and north of the equator. During our Kavieng strikes, we had obtained valuable photographs of

Emirau Island, about 45 miles north of New Hanover, where our amphibious forces were to land shortly thereafter.

These strikes also ended our carrier operations in the Solomons area. The new technique of by-passing indicated that the capture of Rabaul was unnecessary and that it could be sealed off and neutralized. Admiral Halsey's amphibious troops soon afterward occupied Green Island and Emirau, still farther to the northwest. These landings were made without opposition and were followed immediately by the construction of airfields. Rabaul and Kavieng were now completely surrounded, and our troops were spared the losses which would have been involved in their seizure. The forces of the South Pacific were now joined with those of General MacArthur of the Southwest Pacific on the road to Tokyo.

The Solomons campaign, started on a shoestring, had developed into one of the most decisive of the war. Our line of communications had stretched 6,000 miles across the Pacific. The losses suffered by the enemy in this campaign had a vital effect upon their eventual loss of the war. Particularly important was the destruction of planes and pilots. Determined to settle the issue in the Solomons, the Japanese had poured in aircraft reinforcements from both their naval carrier organizations and from their Army air forces. They were never able to recover from the terrible losses suffered in the fighting in the Solomons area. After this campaign, the average quality of the Japanese pilots we met in succeeding operations steadily deteriorated. The tide had turned.

10

THE RISING TIDE

In June, 1943, the new aircraft carrier *Essex*, prototype of the class destined to rule the Pacific, arrived at Pearl Harbor. The event was historic; it marked the beginning of a new period in the war against Japan. A month later, the light carrier *Independence*, constructed on a hull originally designed as a cruiser, put in her appearance at the Hawaiian base. Additional ships of these types arrived at the rate of almost one a month until, by the end of the war, a total of 16 of the *Essex* type and nine of the *Independence* class were operating against the enemy. In addition, 53 escort-type carriers were completed and participated in the fighting in the Pacific. Our supremacy in aircraft carriers became so great that the entire character of the war changed from an approximate stalemate to an overwhelming rolling offensive by the American forces. As Pearl Harbor initiated a period of defeat and as the Battle of Midway symbolized the phase of stalemate, the fall of 1943, with the capture by the American forces of Tarawa, in the Gilbert Islands, was the beginning of the eclipse of the Rising Sun of Japan.

Blockade had always been a major part of our grant strategy for defeating Japan. For her very existence, let alone her ability to carry on a war, Japan was dependent upon imports. Most essential of these imports was food, for Japan produced only a fraction of the amount necessary for her teeming population, which had reached nearly 65 millions. Next in importance were petroleum products—fuel oils for ships and industries and gasoline for motor vehicles and planes. Only a trickle of oil was available within Japan's own Empire, but it was estimated that she had accumulated a two years' supply before she started the war. She was also deficient initially in metals of all kinds, and in rubber, wool, cotton and other essential commodities.

Japan's lightning conquest of the Dutch East Indies, Malaya, Borneo and the Philippines, however, necessitated a radical change in the blockade concept. Her new possessions assured her of ample supplies of petroleum, rubber, rice, tin and many other staples. Close blockade of so vast an area was manifestly impracticable. There was one way, however, to reduce her ability to transport these products to her home islands, and that was to attack her shipping by means of submarines.

Six hours after the attack on Pearl Harbor, an order to "execute unrestricted air and submarine warfare against Japan" was received by the Commander in Chief of the Pacific Fleet from the Chief of Naval Operations. Our submariners had not expected such a directive. They had been trained for orthodox methods of waging war, confined mainly to attacks against enemy combatant ships. Their officers had been taught that submarine warfare was limited by treaty restrictions and that submarine captains who violated these rules were subject to being hunted down and captured or sunk as pirates. The established international law required that submarines, in attacks on merchant vessels, could not sink a ship without having first placed its passengers, crew and ship's papers in a place of safety. Japan's flouting of international law and obligations, as in her sneak attack on Pearl Harbor, and the unrestricted submarine campaigns being waged in the Atlantic by her ally, Germany, led to the issuance of the unrestricted-warfare orders to our submariners.

With the receipt of these orders, our submarines went to sea to sink everything that floated and carried a Japanese flag—merchant shipping as well as men of war. At the start, there were 14 submarines based at Pearl Harbor and 29 with the Asiatic Fleet in the Philippines. The history of their activities is one of daring, courage, hardships and heroic achievements. The "silent service" received little publicity, but it contributed magnificently to the war effort as a whole and furnished many examples of heroism.

After the fall of the Dutch East Indies, the submarines of the Asiatic Fleet were based at Freemantle, in southwest Australia. By the end of 1942 they were being credited with sinking an average of 15 ships per month in the Southwest Pacific. Others, based at Pearl Harbor, patrolled off the coast of Japan. Submarine operations reached a peak in 1944, when 492 ships, totaling 2,387,780 tons, were sunk or destroyed by submarine torpedo and gun attacks.

Important though these submarine sinkings were, our grand strategy continued to contemplate closing in on the home island of Japan for the purpose of establishing a tight blockade by surface ships and planes as well as by undersea vessels. But the planners were now beginning to believe that blockade alone would not cause the Japanese to give in. Such a process, they feared, might last indefinitely.

Even though Japan could be closely blockaded to the east and south, it was estimated that we could never halt all traffic from the mainland across the Yellow Sea and the narrow Tsushima Strait. Holding Manchukuo and Korea, the Japanese could not easily be starved out. The view was now taking root that to end the war within a reasonable time, a landing on the main islands of Japan would be necessary.

To assist in maintaining a close blockade, it was essential

to keep China in the war so as to maintain pressure on Japan from the mainland. This was one important motive behind the stationing in China of the American combat air force under Major General Claire L. Chennault. Supplies for Chennault's force as well as for Chiang Kai-shek's troops were being flown in over the Hump from India, although it required Herculean efforts to transport a modicum of the needed commodities. A plan for eventually seizing a port on the China coast for the direct supply of these forces was contemplated for some future date if the situation developed favorably.

Until this point in the war both nations had been weak in aircraft carriers. The profound importance of this new type of warship was now fully appreciated and it was realized that carriers were vital for control of the open sea. Without them, shore-based aircraft of both sides had fought for local control in limited areas adjacent to their bases. In the Southwest Pacific, General MacArthur's forces had gradually advanced along the coast of New Guinea with the support of our shore-based Army Air Force. Similar progress was made in the Aleutians, but there the enemy's air power never became a serious contender and our aviation was supreme from the start, obstructed only by the weather.

In the Solomons, the initial point of contact with the enemy, Guadalcanal, was too far from our nearest shore bases to receive adequate air support from them, and the carriers of both sides were therefore injected into the early fighting. After the sinking of the *Ryujo*, the *Hornet* and the *Wasp*, both sides became reluctant to commit their carriers to all-out battle and the rest of the campaign was fought largely by land-based planes until our flattops resumed the offensive during the Bougainville occupation, near the end of the Solomons operation.

Production of carrier aircraft and training of pilots kept pace with the increase in carrier strength. During the summer of 1943 our Grumman F4F Wildcat fighter planes were superseded by F6F Hellcats, also made by Grumman, and by F4U Corsairs, manufactured by Curtiss-Wright. The Hellcats had a top speed of 370 miles per hour and the Corsairs 390. These planes were heavier and faster than the contemporary Japanese fighter types, but owing to their weight were still not so maneuverable. They carried six 50-caliber machine guns in their wings, as well as rockets under the wings. Some were later fitted with 20-millimeter cannon. They were well protected by armor and self-sealing gasoline tanks. Our pilots were quite enthusiastic about their performance.

However capable its planes, a flattop is not much use without trained men to fly them. The Japanese found this out after the Coral Sea and Midway battles, in which they lost the cream of their trained aviators and found themselves without adequate replacements, or even a program for producing them. In contrast, our Naval Bureau of Aeronautics, under Rear Admiral J. H. Towers, as early as 1940 had the foresight to start a training program to produce 30,000 pilots a year, and half of our stepped-up production of aircraft at that time had been devoted to producing training planes.

Grumman F6F "Hellcat"

When our new carriers began arriving on the scene in 1943, we had two fully trained air groups ready for each carrier, each group alternating in the combat zone to prevent either one from becoming stale through combat fatigue. Rarely were our pilots sent into combat with less than 18 months of training or 500 hours in the air. On the other hand, the bulk of the Japanese airmen encountered by our pilots from this time on were vastly inferior in skill. Many had less than 100 flying hours' experience when they were sent into action. Not only had Japan made a late start in her training program, but the ravages of our submarines had created a shortage of gasoline in the Empire which seriously hampered her efforts to provide a new supply of skilled aviators.

In addition to the great increase in our naval air strength, we had produced enormous quantities of amphibious landing craft. Five Marine Divisions and several Army Divisions had been trained in amphibious warfare and were ready to land as shock troops in overseas expeditions. Greatly increased numbers of cruisers and destroyers were available, as well as the cargo ships and transports for carrying supplies and men to our overseas forces.

With the men and materials available, the grand strategy of the Pacific War entered a new phase. No longer would it be necessary to limit our fighting to near-by objectives under the protection of shore-based air forces. Under the cover of the planes from our armada of carriers, we would be free to choose points of attack anywhere in the Pacific. The flattops formed the Fast Carrier Task Force, commanded by Rear Admiral (later Admiral) Marc A. Mitscher, which was to drive westward across the Central Pacific. Our offensive would no longer be confined to island-hopping campaigns, slowly and painfully building up each conquest as a steppingstone to the next one. The scope of action possible under our carrier supremacy was boundless, and the vision of our planners could be given full play. We could choose our objectives at will. The release of the sea power inherent in our carriers and the full exercise of control of the ocean, with all that this meant to military operations, was at hand. The initiative had passed to the United States and Japan could only guess where the next attack would come.

The Japanese fleet at this time was still largely intact. In addition to the *Ryujo*, two battleships, the *Hiyei* and *Kirishima*, had been sunk in the Solomons fighting, and the Japanese had suffered considerable losses in cruisers and destroyers. They had increased their carrier strength to 24, however, and had 10 battleships remaining in commission, including the giant *Yamato* and *Musashi* with large numbers of cruisers and destroyers still intact. Their greatest weakness lay in the critical shortage of trained carrier pilots.

Considering these circumstances, the Joint Chiefs of Staff in Washington decided on a direct move across the Central Pacific with the initial purpose of liberating the Philippines. It would join there with the forces of the Southwest Pacific, which were slowly moving northward. When completed, this campaign would have the advantage of eliminating the roundabout line of communications via the South Pacific, a great saving in shipping. While the Pacific Fleet took the direct route, General MacArthur's forces would continue their campaign along the coast of New Guinea and would approach the Philippines from the south. Only such islands in the Central Pacific area as were needed for fleet operating bases and for neutralizing adjacent enemy airfields would be occupied by our forces. The Americans would put on seven-league boots and boldly strike long distances across the sea, keeping the enemy guessing as to where the next blow would fall. Exploiting our command of the sea was to be the basic feature of this campaign. Under these circumstances, the top command was logically assigned to Admiral Chester W. Nimitz, Commander in Chief of the Pacific Fleet.

This decision of the Joint Chiefs was destined to result in two major naval battles, in addition to many carrier strikes on shore installations, and to produce amphibious warfare on a scale never before achieved in history. These naval battles were to result in the complete annihilation of the Japanese Navy as a fighting force. They will be described in the succeeding chapters.

11

THE GILBERTS AND MARSHALLS

The character of the islands in the Central Pacific was quite different from that of the Solomons and New Guinea. These were small coral islands scattered over thousands of miles of ocean, each rising only a few feet above the surface of the sea. In most cases, outlying coral reefs made access to the beaches difficult. In contrast to the islands south of the equator, there was little vegetation that could be classed as jungle, and what did exist consisted usually of a few wind-swept coconut palms clinging precariously to the meager soil. Few of the islands had any water, and all fresh water had to be brought in, distilled from sea water with apparatus brought from distant bases, or even obtained by catching rain water. Fresh water was the key to existence in these islands and provisions for obtaining it ranked in priority ahead of even food and ammunition. The hot sun beat cruelly down on troops who had the misfortune to be stationed there, and the blinding glare of the white coral sand was almost unendurable. Fortunately, cooling sea breezes somewhat tempered the heat and tropical showers occasionally relieved the monotony of the endless sunny days.

Ships of the newly formed Fast Carrier Task Force in the Central Pacific made air strikes on Marcus, in August, 1943, on Tarawa and Makin during September, and on Wake in October. These raids were for the purpose of giving combat training to the newly joined carriers and their air groups, as well as to soften up Japanese installations and to keep the enemy guessing as to where our next full-scale attack would be delivered. The raids took a heavy toll of enemy planes in the air and on the ground, with little loss on our side.

American plans called for initial landings on Tarawa and Makin, in the Gilbert group, on November 20, 1943. Beginning November 13, shore-based aircraft from Funafuti and other near-by bases commenced heavy day and night attacks on all Japanese positions in the Gilberts. The plan to take Tarawa was premised on the necessity of having a shore air base within striking distance of the Marshall Islands, our first major objective. It was a necessary preliminary to the larger operations to follow.

Tarawa atoll was heavily fortified and garrisoned by about 3,500 Japanese troops on Betio, the principal island in the group. It was ringed by a solid bottom of coral from 500 to 1,000 yards off shore, sprinkled with sharp jagged rocky formations which the Japanese had used in conjunction with artificial hindrances, including mines and barbed wire, to form obstacles to landing forces and on which they had ranged in many guns, from 8-inch mortars to machine guns. Betio was only two and a half miles long and less than half a mile wide. It was honeycombed with fixed enemy gun positions.

The Japanese commander boasted that a million men could not take Betio by assault in a hundred years. After intense aerial bombing and ship-gunfire bombardment, our amphibious troops landed on Tarawa and Makin on the morning of November 20. On Makin, the 27th United States Army Division brought ashore 6,500 troops during the assault. They overcame determined resistance by the garrison of 800 men. By nightfall of the second day they had completely secured the island with total casualties of only 186 men.

Tarawa proved one of the toughest nuts our Marines had to crack during the whole war. Our previous information as to the depth of water over the reef proved considerably in error. The task went to the veteran Second Marine Division under Major General Julian C. Smith. This outfit had fought at Guadalcanal. They were to learn that the capture of a small coral island required an entirely different fighting technique. Despite heavy preparatory shelling, our assault boats were ripped by heavy enemy mortar and machine gun fire. The first three waves got ashore without serious losses and were pinned down to a narrow beachhead. The boats of the fourth wave grounded on the reef hundreds of yards from shore. Then began the terrible carnage associated with the name of Tarawa. Under the murderous fire, the men with their heavy equipment jumped out of the boats into water up to their necks and attempted to wade ashore. Many of them drowned and many others were killed by the withering fire. Of the 15,000 combat Marines employed during the assault and the ensuing two and a half days of hand-to-hand fighting required to eliminate the garrison, 20 per cent were casualties.

The principal mistake in this landing was in the time element between the lifting of the gunfire barrage from the beaches and the arrival of the first assault boats. Preliminary strafing, bombing and bombardment put the enemy into their holes but did not keep them there. We learned at Tarawa that a predetermined time schedule for lifting the barrage could not be kept, due to currents and other sea conditions that might delay the landing boats. The fire had to be controlled by on-the-spot observers acd continued just ahead of the troops.

To furnish air-combat patrol over Tarawa, my task force had returned from the South Pacific. With the *Saratoga* as flagship, we maneuvered about 60 miles east of the island, our fighter planes guarding the transports off shore and the Marines on the beaches. Few Japanese planes came down by daylight from their bases in the Marshalls, but at night we received many air attacks.

On November 27, the carrier task forces were reorganized and I shifted my flag to the new flattop *Bunker Hill*, sister ship of the *Essex*. We continued our assigned task. The light carrier *Monterey*, also brand new, was attached to us, together with the modern fast battleships *Alabama*, *South Dakota* and *Washington*, and the destroyers *Izard*, *Charrette*, *Connor*, *Burns*, *Lang*, *Stack* and *Wilson*. Our antiaircraft gunners shot down many enemy planes during this period, but our ships received no damage. We also had several contacts with submarines which were driven off without loss.

On the night of November 20, a small force of 78 Marines landed on Apamama Island from the American submarine *Nautilus*, although she was attacked by mistake and damaged by depth charges from one of our destroyers during the operation. The island was found to be undefended except by a small group of lookouts. Apamama was soon secured, although we suffered five casualties in wiping out the 20 men stationed there.

During these operations, the light carrier *Independence*, in another task group, received a torpedo hit during a night air attack which forced her withdrawal from action for repairs. In addition, the escort carrier *Liscome Bay* was torpedoed by an enemy submarine just before daylight. She was soon a mass of flames and went down with heavy loss of life, including Rear Admiral Henry M. Mullinnix, Commander of the Escort Carrier Group. This gallant officer had shortly before been my flag captain in the *Saratoga* and had only recently been promoted to Rear Admiral.

Although the cost of taking the Gilberts was high, possession of these bases was essential to our further operations in the Marshalls. We had learned many lessons in the new kind of amphibious warfare which we were to experience in our westward progress. We were now ready to proceed with our more ambitious undertakings in the heavily defended Marshalls. By the end of December, we had four new airfields operating in the Gilberts area, three of them suitable for heavy bombers. Land-based aircraft maintained increasing pressure on Japanese bases in the Marshalls and on Wake, Nauru and Kusaie. Although the Japanese sent in numerous air reinforcements to their garrisons in the Marshalls, our aviators dominated the situation and had shot down approximately 100 enemy planes by January 1, 1944.

The Marshalls chain extends 650 miles from Mille Is-

Nautilus

land, on the southeast, to Eniwetok, on the northwest. Located just short of halfway between Hawaii and the Philippines, and north of Tarawa, acquired at such heavy cost two months earlier, the Marshalls were captured from Germany by the Japanese in World War I. In 1920, the League of Nations mandated them to Japan, specifying that the Japanese were not to fortify them. They had nevertheless been fortified in every possible way as a bastion in the outer Japanese defense perimeter. Some 24,000 troops garrisoned six of the most important islands, Mille, Wotje, Maloelap, Kwajalein, Jaluit and Eniwetok, where excellent airfields had been built.

Though the Japanese decided not to commit their fleet to defending the Marshalls, they attempted to reinforce their garrisons on islands likely to be attacked. They expected landings at Jaluit, Mille or Wotje, one Japanese staff officer stated after the war. Few thought we would strike at Kwajalein, in the very heart of the Marshalls.

While preparations were going on for the next advance to the Marshalls, my own task force again returned to the South Pacific. On the way south, we made another attack on Nauru. The battleships conducted a bombardment with their heavy guns, in addition to the intense bombing by our planes. During this return visit to Admiral Halsey's domain, we conducted air strikes against Kavieng on December 25, January 1, and January 4, as previously described. On January 19, we left Espiritu Santo to return to the Central Pacific for the Marshall's assault.

At Funafuti, we were joined by the new battleships *Iowa* and *New Jersey*, which had just arrived from the Atlantic. The new light carrier *Cowpens* was also added to my task force. On January 28, we struck Kwajalein in devastating attacks for the purpose of neutralizing the air strip. No enemy fighters were encountered and we made a shambles of the field. Two enemy planes were shot down over the island. After this operation, we proceeded to Eniwetok and at daylight the following morning, launched attacks on that base. This strike was to prevent Eniwetok's being used as a threat to the landings which had already begun in the Marshalls. It was the farthest west in the Central Pacific area that any of our forces had yet penetrated. For three days we pounded the atoll, and at the end the pilots reported difficulty in finding any worthwhile targets. Everything above ground had been obliterated and the island looked like a desert waste.

Under the new policy of by-passing, it was planned to capture Majuro Atoll and Kwajalein, and later Eniwetok. Jaluit, Mille, Maloelap and Wotje were to be neutralized. Preliminary preparations consisted of heavy carrier strikes against all six of the fortified atolls. Majuro had a fine anchorage in its lagoon, and its fringing islands afforded ample space for airfields and for the necessary shore establishments for an advanced naval base. It was well located in the middle of the Marshalls group, and intelligence indicated that it was not occupied in any force by the Japanese.

The amphibious forces under the command of Rear Admiral (later Admiral) Richmond K. Turner consisted of 297 ships carrying 84,000 troops. The assault forces included the Fourth Marine Division and the Seventh Army Division, under the over-all command of Major General Holland M. Smith of the Marine Corps. Task Force 58, the Fast Carrier Force, under the over-all command of Rear Admiral Marc A. Mitscher, was divided into four task groups. These were commanded respectively by Rear Admirals J. W. Reeves, Jr., A. E. Montgomery, S. P. Ginder and myself.

In the preliminary air strikes, practically every enemy plane in the Marshalls was destroyed. Ground installations were reduced to mounds of rubble; hardly a tree was left standing and those remaining were completely stripped of their foliage by the terrific bombardment. Over half the Japanese garrison of 8,600 troops on Kwajalein atoll were killed before the first American troops reached the shore. The survivors were shell-shocked and deafened by the terrific bombardment they had experienced.

On February 1, 1944, the troops landed at Majuro and on Kwajalein. There was no opposition on Majuro, and immediately the Sea Bees were busy constructing airfields and other shore establishments.

On Kwajalein, despite the tremendous preliminary bombardment, determined resistance was encountered. This lagoon is the largest in the world. The principal installations were located on the adjacent islands of Roi and Namur, at its northern end, and on Kwajalein Island at the southern end. The lagoon stretched for 30 miles between those islands. The Marines were assigned the task of taking Roi and Namur and the Army troops the job of occupying Kwajalein. There was little opposition to the initial landing. By the afternoon of February 3, Roi and Namur were secured, but Kwajalein was not finally mopped up until the afternoon of February 5. In characteristic fashion, the desperate Japanese had hidden in shell holes and heaps of rubble, from whence they emerged in suicidal attacks until they were finally wiped out. Of the 42,000 assault troops landed, 368 had been killed and 1,148 wounded. Except for 437 dazed prisoners, the Japanese garrison was completely annihilated.

On the last day of the attacks by my task group on Eniwetok, we had the misfortune to lose the Commander of the *Bunker Hill's* torpedo squadron, Lieutenant Commander Frank M. Whittaker, and the distinguished newspaper columnist, Raymond Clapper, in a mid-air collision of two planes over the lagoon, off Engebi. Mr. Clapper had been aboard the *Bunker Hill* to witness our operations. He had asked permission to make a flight over the target in one of our attack planes for the purpose of comparing our bombing methods with those used by the Army Air Force in Italy. I assigned him to fly with Whittaker, who was one of our best and most experienced pilots. In rendezvousing after the attack, while other planes were forming up behind him, Whittaker suddenly dived out of formation, perhaps to go back over the island to show Mr. Clapper the effects of the bombing. In doing so, he collided with another plane which was joining up. Both planes plummeted to the water in flames. There were no survivors. Everyone in our task group, as well as millions elsewhere, was saddened by this unfortunate occurrence.

In view of the successful results of our attacks on Eniwetok Atoll, I felt that little opposition would be found by landing forces there and recommended that its occupation be expedited before the enemy had time to recuperate. As a result of this recommendation, troops which had been assigned in reserve for the Kwajalein operation, and which were not needed there, were sent on to capture Eniwetok. Two regimental combat teams, the 22nd Marines under Colonel J. T. Walker, and the 106th Infantry under Colonel R. G. Ayers, U. S. A., were used. On February 18, the Marines landed on Engebi Island, and although extremely heavy fighting developed as the Japanese emerged from their fox holes, the island was secured before nightfall. On the 20th, Eniwetok Island was taken by the Army, aided by the Marines, and on the 22nd Parry Island fell. Captured documents indicated that this island contained the headquarters of Major General Nishida,

Commanding General of the First Seaborne Brigade. So much rubble had been created by the heavy aerial bombing and gunfire that definite confirmation of this could not be obtained, nor was the body of the General himself ever identified.

We had no need for any additional bases in the Marshall Islands, and remaining positions were left to be neutralized by local forces. The first bastions of the outer-perimeter defenses of the Japanese Empire had fallen.

Immediately after the taking of Kwajalein, the Fast Carrier Task Force assembled in Majuro Atoll for fueling, replenishing ammunition, and conferences on the next operation. This was to be a carrier strike against the reputedly mighty fortress of Truk, sometimes called the Gibralter of the Pacific. It would be the first strike ever made on that stronghold. We hoped to catch there a large portion of the Japanese fleet. The operation would also serve to cover the landings at Eniwetok, some 600 miles east and north of Truk. Three of the four carrier task groups, those commanded by Admiral Reeves, Admiral Montgomery, and myself, participated in the expedition, which was under the over-all command of Admiral Spruance, with his flag on the battleship *New Jersey*. Altogether we had five large and four light carriers, six fast battleships, five heavy cruisers, three light cruisers, two antiaircraft cruisers and 29 destroyers. On February 12, with everything shipshape, the powerful striking force got under way from the Majuro lagoon and fanning out over the ocean, bore westward for Truk. Hopes were high for striking a crippling blow at the power of Japan by knocking out much of her remaining naval strength.

A reconnaissance plane from the South Pacific, however, had flown over Truk at high altitude a few days before our arrival at that island bastion. It had given the alarm. By the time our first attack groups arrived, the Japanese fleet, with few exceptions, had departed for safer waters. No enemy planes appeared on our radars as we proceeded without detection to a point 94 miles northeast of Dublon Island in the Truk Atoll. Here the first strike was delivered at daylight on February 16. Taken completely by surprise, many enemy aircraft were still on the ground and most of them were destroyed. Vice-Admiral Kobayashi, the atoll commander, had committed a costly blunder. He had held the base at full alert for two weeks immediately after our attack on Kwajalein, but on February 15 he had assumed that the danger was past and ordered most of the planes grounded, defueled and disarmed. Our planes struck the next morning. After this raid, Kobayashi was promptly recalled to Japan.

In the two-day raid, 129 enemy planes were shot down in the air, 82 destroyed on the ground, and 70 damaged. In addition, several cruisers, a number of destroyers, and many merchant ships and tankers were sunk or heavily damaged.

One of the incidents of this attack was the circling of Truk by a detachment consisting of the new battleships *New Jersey* and *Iowa*, the cruisers *Minneapolis* and *New Orleans* and the destroyers *Izard*, *Charrette*, *Burns* and *Bradford*, under the personal command of Admiral Spruance. About noon, this detachment left the carrier dispositions to ring the Truk archipelago in order to head off and destroy any enemy ships crippled by the air attacks which might be attempting to escape. However, this expedition accomplished little and only complicated the attacks by the carrier planes. We were ordered to maintain fighter cover over this group at all times, which involved a wasteful use of planes.

Just north of the Truk lagoon, Spruance's unit sighted an enemy cruiser which had been damaged by our aircraft. Standing by it, and probably rescuing survivors, were a cruiser and a destroyer. Our fighter planes patrolling overhead reported that when the undamaged cruiser sighted the masts of our battleships coming over the horizon, she immediately put on a burst of speed and disappeared to the westward. Had our battleships not scared her away, we would have had an opportunity to finish her off on our next air strike.

When our approaching ships opened fire on the damaged cruiser and destroyer, the Japanese responded by launching torpedoes. Our covering planes sighted them and reported them by radio, our ships turning away just in time to avoid being hit. One torpedo passed a few feet from the bow of the *Iowa* and the captain of the *New Orleans* stated that the timely warning given by our aircraft enabled him to maneuver just in time and thereby "escape from what would have otherwise been at least one sure hit." Had any of our ships been torpedoed so close to strong enemy bases and so far from our own repair ports, it might have resulted in their total loss.

After sinking this cruiser and destroyer by gunfire, the group proceeded to the westward of Truk Atoll. They were naturally apprehensive of attack by enemy planes, and when one of our own SBD's, perhaps damaged, approached, the nervous gun crews opened fire and shot it down in flames.

The fighter cover we were providing for this detachment was due to be relieved at five in the afternoon. The relieving planes, however, were delayed in finding the ships, and Spruance retained the first group until almost night. They were from the light carrier *Cowpens* and had never made night landings on a carrier before. About 8:30 P.M., when it was pitch dark, with numerous enemy snooper planes about and a neighboring task group being attacked by torpedo planes, a group of friendly planes suddenly appeared on our radar. They were our long-overdue fighters. Relieved at their safe return, but unsure of their ability to land at night, and in imminent danger of attack, we turned into the wind to take them aboard. The chart showed that a coral reef, only 15 miles away and invisible in the darkness, was directly in our path. Despite the hazard of enemy planes in the vicinity, we turned on our landing lights and the planes landed safely on the *Cowpens*, the last one just as we reached the point where we had to turn away on account of the indicated reef.

We were under minor attack during the rest of the night, but my task group was not damaged. The *Intrepid*, in another group, received a torpedo hit in the stern which damaged her steering gear, and she was forced to retire to Pearl Harbor.

Air attacks on Truk continued for two days. They so wrecked that overrated "Gibraltar" that it was no longer a serious menace to our advancing forces. Upon withdrawing from these operations, we rendezvoused with our tankers to the north of Eniwetok, and after refueling, again headed west for a smash at the enemy air bases on the islands of Saipan and Tinian in the Mariana Islands, north of Guam and far to the northwest of Truk. It was a bold operation, and one which was little expected by the Japanese. It was conducted by only two carrier task groups, those commanded by Admiral Montgomery and myself, under the over-all command of Admiral Mitscher. This raid took us within 1,500 miles of Tokyo.

At 2:01 P.M. on February 21, while running in for the launching position for this attack, a low-flying "Betty" (two-engined Japanese bomber) was sighted 20 miles northwest of the force. This plane escaped and reported the position of our advancing carriers. We were then 420 miles due east of

Saipan. Admiral Mitscher radioed the force that we had been sighted and stated that it would be a finish fight. It was the first time in our many raids that enemy search planes had detected us on the day before a scheduled attack. We expected heavy air attacks during the rest of our approach.

We were not disappointed. At 9:13 that night, the first bogey appeared on our radar screen, and from then until dawn the next morning we were under constant attack. The Japanese planes were dropping many flares and hunting us by the white streaks of our wakes. We soon realized that their planes had no radar. Knowing the location of the enemy planes as shown by our own radar, we were able to avoid many of their largest attacks by making radical maneuvers in the darkness, with no lights showing. We withheld our short-range machine-gun fire, which depended on tracers for aiming, unless the attacking aircraft could be sighted visually. We freely used our 5-inch guns, which had flashless powder and proximity fuses and did not use tracers that gave away the positions of our ships. Thanks to radar fire control, our screen shot down three or four planes during the night. In this game of hide and seek in the night, we had difficulty making good our desired course to the westward, but at daylight we were at the prescribed launching point, ready for business. Montgomery's group had a similar experience but used tracer ammunition, which attracted more attackers. Consequently they shot down a bigger bag of enemy planes than we did.

Just before dawn, when we could start launching our air groups for the attack, the radar showed a large flight of enemy planes only 20 miles away and apparently trying to locate us for attack. It was a critical moment, since with all our planes gassed and armed on deck, we were extremely vulnerable. A single Zero strafing our decks could start fires among the closely packed aircraft that would completely put our carriers out of action, if not resulting in their sinking. In the faint light of dawn, while we were making high speed into the wind to launch our planes, our brilliant white wakes would be easily visible to attacking planes, and while launching aircraft, we would not be free to maneuver. Furthermore, we would be much more clearly visible to the enemy planes than they to us. Our gunners would have a hard time seeing them.

Taking advantage of a small rain squall between us and the oncoming aircraft, we quickly catapulted a group of fighters from the *Cowpens* which a few minutes later intercepted the enemy planes and "splashed" them all. This ended a period of critical suspense. We soon had all our strike groups in the air, headed toward Saipan and Tinian, and our defensive combat patrol overhead.

When our planes arrived over Tinian they ran into low clouds through which they had to dive to make their attacks. Moderate air opposition was encountered and 11 Japanese fighters were shot down. During the day four enemy bombers were splashed in the vicinity of the task group.

On the ground, much to our surprise, many Japanese aircraft were found lined up on their runways. Why they were not in the air, after full warning of our approach, we have never known. It seems likely that these were new planes being ferried to the Marshalls and that qualified pilots for them were not available at Tinian. In any event, they were a rich target and our planes destroyed all of the 69 planes on the ground as well as pitting the runway with bomb craters.

One fighter group from the *Bunker Hill*, under Commander Sam Silber, was en route to Tinian above an overcast containing numerous rain squalls. After flying the proper distance, Silber went down through the clouds to take a look. He soon sighted an island, with an airfield on it, which he took to be Tinian. The group shot down four planes in the air and destroyed seven more on the field. On their way back to the carrier, they refigured their navigation and to their surprise discovered that they had attacked the island of Guam by mistake. This was the first sight of Guam our forces had had since its fall at the beginning of the war. We had not known that the Japanese had constructed an airfield on Orote Point, so the information Sam Silber brought back was invaluable. He received no censure for attacking the wrong target.

These raids ended the campaign for the Marshall Islands. The work of developing our newly acquired bases on Kwajalein, Eniwetok, and Majuro went on apace in preparation for our next advance, to the Marianas.

The Japanese were well aware of the seriousness of the breach in their outer defenses. They believed that holding the next line in the Marianas was vital to the security of the Empire. It was impossible for them to be strong everywhere, however, and they were uncertain as to our next point of attack. Their fleet moved to Tawi Tawi in the Sulu archipelago of the southern Philippines to be ready to strike either to the eastward, toward the Marianas, or south toward Hollandia. They planned to shift their shore-based planes in either direction when our major attack appeared to be definitely committed.

Operations thus far had bridged 2,000 miles of open water between the Hawaiian Islands and the nearest Japanese positions in the Central Pacific. From this time on, our amphibious operations could be conducted with shorter distances between the points of attack and our nearest bases. While our positions in the Marshalls were being consolidated, preparations went forward for the capture of Saipan, Tinian and Guam.

12

SEVEN-LEAGUE BOOTS

THE FIRST BATTLE OF THE PHILIPPINE SEA—SAIPAN, TINIAN, GUAM

Following the capture of the new bases in the Marshalls, the Fast Carrier Task Force (Task Force 58) was loaned to General MacArthur to cover the longest thrust of his forces yet taken along the northern New Guinea coast. With the carrier planes assuring control of the air, the amphibious forces of the Southwest Pacific jumped 400 miles from the Huon Peninsula, at the northeast corner of New Guinea, to Hollandia, by-passing and isolating upward of 56,000 Japanese troops at Wewak and various other points along the way. With the Army's Fifth Air Force pounding the enemy air bases from Wewak to Wakde, 80,000 men were landed on April 22, 1944, at Hollandia and at Aitape, 75 miles to the east. The Aitape landing was covered by jeep carriers newly assigned to the Seventh Fleet under Admiral Kinkaid.

This was the first time in the long series of operations by the Southwest Pacific forces that carriers had been used to furnish the close air support. It was also the largest operation yet undertaken in that area. So negligible was the enemy's air reaction that the fast carriers were released by MacArthur on April 23 to return to the Central Pacific.

Here troops were being readied for the capture of Saipan,

Tinian and Guam, 1,500 miles west of the Marshalls. The distances involved testified to the tremendous power now in the hands of our Pacific Fleet, spearheaded by the new aircraft carriers.

Definite decision had been made to by-pass Truk. Because of its outlying reef, its capture would be difficult, and the mountainous terrain of its central group of islands made them unsuitable for the development of airfields. On both these counts, the taking of Truk was not worth the effort, especially as it could easily be neutralized from other bases.

Our swift conquest of the Marshalls had seriously alarmed the Japanese High Command. They realized that the inner defenses of the Empire were threatened and they began pouring troops, equipment and supplies into the Marianas and western Carolines as rapidly as possible. They were at a loss to foretell where our next objective would be. Their plans called for concentrating their shore-based aircraft wherever our attack developed. When our carrier task force appeared off Hollandia, they mistakenly assumed that we were committed to that line of approach only and failed to realize that the main blow was coming across the Central Pacific.

The Japanese fleet was divided between the Singapore area and the home waters of Japan for continued training. Its Commander in Chief, Admiral Koga, was awaiting developments at Palau aboard his flagship, the *Musashi*. The carriers and their new air groups were in home waters, where training was proceeding, except for Carrier Division One, which was sent to Singapore. It remained there until May 15, when it moved up to Tawi Tawi to join the rest of the fleet. Its air groups had been almost completely wiped out by our carrier air strikes on Rabaul the previous November.

Admiral Koga announced his decision to hold the Marianas-Palaus line until death, in the conviction that once this inner defense line was broken, there could be no further hope for Japan. He had decided that if the attack were in the north, he would command from Saipan and if in the south, he would base at Davao, in the Philippines.

At dawn on March 30, just before the Hollandia landings, Task Force 58 made a devastating strike on Palau. This strike lasted two days and was for the purpose of destroying enemy naval ships and air forces there and of mining the entrance channels to close them to ships using or attempting to use that base. Supplementary attacks were also made on Yap, Ulithi and Woleai. When the two days were over, many enemy planes had been destroyed in the air or on the ground and, in addition, two destroyers, four escort vessels and 20 merchant vessels and tankers had been sunk, amounting to a total of 104,000 tons. Approximately 150 enemy aircraft were destroyed, against United States combat losses of 25 planes.

When Admiral Koga found that our task force had moved westward after this attack, and when transports were sighted proceeding toward Hollandia, it was decided that the main landing was going to be in western New Guinea. Accordingly most of the fighter planes in the Marianas were moved to Palau and the planes of the carriers at Tawi Tawi were ordered to Davao. The latter, although their pilots were not sufficiently trained for effective use from carriers, could be used from land bases. Admiral Koga himself took off from Palau on the evening of March 31 in a four-engine flying boat, bound for Davao. Another plane carried the bulk of his staff. Both these planes encountered a severe bad-weather area between Palau and Mindanao. The one carrying the staff circled the storm to the north and then crashed in an attempted night landing near Cebu. Admiral Koga's Chief of Staff was one of the few survivors. The other plane, with Koga on board, was never heard from after entering the bad-weather area. It was a severe blow to the Japanese. Admiral Toyoda succeeded Admiral Koga but it was not until May 3 that he actually assumed command. To have a new Commander in Chief and an almost entirely new staff take over just as critical operations were about to begin was a tremendous handicap.

Threatened on a long front which extended from western New Guinea through the southern Philippines and Palau to the Marianas, the Japanese strength at any one point was wholly incapable of seriously opposing the overwhelming forces the Americans could now bring to bear wherever they chose to strike. Japanese lines of communication with their forward areas were highly insecure under the constant attacks of our submarines and air forces, and their land-based air strength was being continually reduced by the attacks of both our land-based and carrier aircraft. Japan's only hope of repelling our advance lay in employing the mobility of their fleet, in concentration with their shore-based aviation, in a coordinated attack on our approaching forces. This was their intention under what they called the "A" Plan.

Saipan, the largest island in the Marianas, is approximately 12 miles long by five and a half miles wide and contains a land area of 81 square miles. It is of coral-volcanic origin, which produces rather rugged terrain with sharp ridges, fissure-like valleys, and many natural vaults and caves. The highest elevation, Mount Tapotchau, rises 1,554 feet in nearly the geometric center of the island, from which foothills and ridges lead off in several directions. Near the southern end of the island was the main airfield, Aslito, and near the northern end a smaller air strip was in process of construction.

The American troops assembled for the capture of Saipan comprised the largest force to operate in the Pacific up to this time. It consisted of the Third and Fifth Amphibious Corps, including three Marine divisions and one Marine brigade, all of them reinforced, and two Army infantry divisions, likewise reinforced, besides corps and miscellaneous supporting troops. The assault forces were divided into two groups, the northern group to attack Saipan and Tinian and the southern group to attack Guam. Lieutenant General Holland M. Smith was in command of the troops as a whole and in addition had command of the northern group; Major General Roy S. Geiger was in command of the southern group. The troops assigned to the northern operation comprised the Fifth Amphibious Corps, which totaled more than 77,000 men.

D-Day for the Saipan landing was set for June 15. Task Force 58, which had returned from Hollandia, departed from Majuro on June 6 and in the afternoon of June 11 launched air strikes against Saipan, Tinian, and Guam. The force was undetected during its approach and devastating attacks by fighter planes and dive bombers swept down on the unsuspecting enemy to carry out their work of destruction. On this and the three following days, a total of 147 Japanese planes were destroyed. They represented approximately one-third of the estimated total Japanese air strength in the Marianas. Our carriers suffered the loss of 11 fighters, the pilots of five of which were subsequently rescued. Complete control of the air in the vicinity of Saipan was thus attained. In addition to the destruction of aircraft, enemy airfields were rendered temporarily unusable, coastal defense and antiaircraft gun positions were destroyed, and many ships were sunk. The enemy air opposition was of very limited effectiveness. Two carrier task groups went north on June 13 and on June 15 and 16 struck the enemy air installations at Iwo Jima and Chichi Jima, only 600 miles from Japan. They destroyed over 100 planes parked on these fields as well as about 30 to 40 fighters encountered in the air and left the area in a poor condition for staging planes into the Marianas.

Heavy strikes from the carriers, delivered by 160 bombers and 72 strafing planes, hit Saipan just ahead of the leading wave of boats on June 15, as the troops went ashore promptly at the designated hour. In 30 minutes, approximately 8,000 troops were landed on the southwestern shore of the island. The Japanese reacted vigorously, although not fully prepared for our landing. In spite of the enormous weight of our naval gunfire and air strikes, enemy artillery, mortar and antiboat gunfire made the Saipan landing a grim and bloody business. The invasion became a toe-to-toe slugging match which continued throughout the first two days. The Japanese were confident and had an exceptional quantity of heavy artillery and tanks. The garrison consisted of nearly 30,000 seasoned troops and the terrain features were all in their favor.

In the heavy fighting which developed at the beachhead, some of the assault units sustained 35 percent casualties by one o'clock. By nightfall the beachhead line had been pushed inland only to a depth of about 1,500 yards. The Japanese still held dominating heights in front of the Marine positions. They still had plenty of artillery and heavy mortars. Some of our units were out of direct contact with the units on their flanks, and strong counterattacks were anticipated during the night.

All afternoon unengaged Japanese troops could be seen holding ceremonies in the town of Garipan, midway up the west coast. They were observed conducting parades and gathered around for patriotic speeches and much flag waving. About 8:00 P.M., from that direction, tanks and infantry, clanking and clattering, moved down the shore road in platoon columns making enough din to alarm troops far less alert than our Marines. Our own tanks and mobile artillery converged on the threatened point. At this moment, the Japanese decided to stop for a few more patriotic speeches before beginning the attack. While this was going on, our naval vessels lying off shore began to pour point-blank gunfire into the assembly. The Japanese attack was completely broken up before ever reaching the Marine lines. A later attempt was made in the early dawn, but was beaten off after hand-to-hand fighting.

There was heavy fighting at other points, and all night long the atmosphere reverberated with the roar of heavy guns as the scene was sporadically lit up by our flares. The second day was a continuation of the dogged slugging match, with our forces gradually pushing their way farther inland. Casualties for these two days amounted to over 3,500 men. By the evening of the fourth day, our lines had reached the eastern shore and were in a position for a sweep northward across the entire width of the island.

While this intense fighting was going on ashore, the Japanese fleet, which had been based at Tawi Tawi in the southern Philippines, awaiting definite determination of the point at which our main assault would be made, moved out to the Philippine Sea to participate in the defensive operation. This movement produced a major naval engagement which was to be known as the First Battle of the Philippine Sea.

THE FIRST BATTLE OF THE PHILIPPINE SEA

Admiral Toyoda, the new Commander of the Japanese Combined Fleet, had received instructions from Imperial Headquarters to prepare the fleet and shore-based air forces for decisive action by the end of May. He was told that these forces should be committed only under conditions and in an area favorable to exerting maximum strength. The Japanese now had a healthy respect for the power of our aircraft carriers. In taking command, Toyoda stated to his forces: "The war is drawing close to the lines vital to our national defense. The issue of our national existence is unprecedentedly serious, and unprecedented opportunity exists for deciding who shall be victorious and who defeated." The issue would soon be known.

The Japanese fleet now consisted of nine carriers, five battleships, including the enormous *Yamato* and *Musashi*, 11 cruisers and 30 destroyers. The American forces comprising Task Force 58 included seven *Essex*-type carriers, eight light carriers, seven fast battleships, 13 cruisers and 58 destroyers. In addition, there were 14 escort carriers, seven old battleships, 12 cruisers and 122 destroyers and destroyer escorts, giving close support to the landing operations on Saipan. As in the earlier battles of the Coral Sea and Midway, the first action in the Philippine Sea was to be fought entirely by airplanes except for our submarines *Cavalla* and *Albacore*, which were to play a most prominent part.

Task Force 58 carried approximately 1,000 aircraft, and in addition we had 764 land-based planes of combat type in the advanced area for scouting and neutralization of enemy bases. It is estimated that the Japanese carriers had 450 planes, and their shore bases in the vicinity disposed about 600 more. Many of the latter, however, had been destroyed in the air or on the ground before the battle began.

Leaving Tawi Tawi on June 13, 1944, the Japanese fleet shifted its base to Guimaras, in the central Philippines. After the war, they gave as the reason for this move the lack of air defense and an airfield for training at Tawi Tawi. The shift may also have been influenced by the activities of our submarine *Harder*, which sank three enemy destroyers and crippled two others in five days off that port and gave the Japanese the impression that they were facing a heavy concentration of submarines in the vicinity. It was beyond their comprehension that all these attacks had been made by one submarine.

With the report of our air attacks on Saipan, the Japanese fleet paused at Guimaras only long enough to refuel, and at 6:00 P.M. on June 14 sortied through San Bernardino Strait into the open waters of the Philippine Sea. This move was promptly reported by the American submarine *Flying Fish*, on patrol in that vicinity. Admiral Raymond A. Spruance, in command of the Fifth Fleet and all the Marianas operations, and Admiral Marc A. Mitscher, commanding Task Force 58, immediately took steps to meet the enemy's threat. Spruance was embarked in the heavy cruiser *Indianapolis*, with the task force, and was in general charge during the battle.

The Japanese plan was to keep their carriers outside the range of our carrier planes, but to send their own planes to attack our carriers and then to have them land on Guam and other bases in the vicinity, for refueling and rearming before returning to their parent ships. By this means, they could make shuttle attacks on our fleet without exposing their own vessels to attack by our carrier planes.

On June 18, Admiral Spruance separated our battleships from the carriers and formed them into an independent task force stationed 15 miles west of his carriers, except for one group of the latter which was designated as the battle-line carrier group and assigned the duty of furnishing air cover for the battleships. This plan apparently visualized a surface engagement between battleships and contemplated the primary role of carrier planes as protecting the battlewagons so that the latter could annihilate the enemy with their turret guns. The idea of the supremacy of battleships was hard to kill.

A submarine contact report on June 18 gave the position of the enemy well to the westward. Mitscher appreciated that the developing situation would permit the Japanese carriers to launch their planes from beyond our counterattack range by having them land on Guam and adjacent airfields for refueling.

He reported to Spruance that he proposed to head west at high speed during the night to insure having the enemy flattops within range of our planes at daylight, and thus avoid giving them the advantage of using the islands as unsinkable carriers. Spruance disapproved this proposal in what quickly became famous among aviators as the "end run" message. He directed Mitscher to head east during the night and concluded his message with the words, "Beware of an end run." It indicated that Spruance still was thinking in terms of a surface action. He did not grasp the tremendous power of our air weapons or their ability to strike in any direction to the limit of their fuel supply. There were no "ends" in aerial warfare.

This critical decision rendered it inevitable that our forces would receive tremendous air attacks the next day, with no chance of striking back at the enemy ships. It resulted in the escape of the bulk of the Japanese fleet to fight another day, when it might have been completely destroyed.

The morning of June 19th found the enemy ships about 400 miles west of our forces, which were now approximately 60 miles northwest of Guam. In the early dawn, the Japanese carriers launched their planes, which began arriving in the vicinity of our vessels shortly after daylight. The first radar report revealed the presence of many planes in the vicinity of Guam, and shortly thereafter fighters from the *Belleau Wood*, patrolling there, radioed for help and stated that strong air forces were taking off from Agana Field on that island.

Reinforced fighter groups were dispatched from our carriers to meet these attacks, and until 10 o'clock the air was thick with dogfights and aerial combat. Thirty-five enemy planes went down for the loss of each one of ours. Then the battle shifted to the vicinity of the task force.

At 10 o'clock, the *Alabama* reported a large bogey 125 miles away at 24,000 feet altitude or higher, and closing in. Mitscher immediately ordered additional fighters into the air and the return of fighters over Guam. Soon our carrier decks were cleared of planes and the stage was set for what the pilots were later to call the "Marianas Turkey Shoot." They intercepted the enemy 60 miles from the fleet and found 50 to 70 Japanese dive bombers and torpedo planes. In a running fight, most of the Japanese were shot down, but a few got through to make their attacks against the fire of our ships' antiaircraft guns. These desperate remnants, singly and in small groups, managed to hit the *South Dakota* with a small bomb, to crash one plane into the side of the *Indiana*, and to score a near miss on the *Minneapolis*.

Ships' gunfire shot down nine more planes and the attack group was virtually annihilated. Few planes were left to land on Guam or any other island for refueling. But there were still additional groups from the enemy carriers on their way, determined to do their best for the Emperor.

An hour later our radar screens showed another large bogey approaching from the westward. Intercepted by our fighters, it was found to contain 60 to 70 planes of fighter, bomber and torpedo types. Furious air combat resulted in the destruction of all but a few enemy planes before reaching attack position. The *Bunker Hill* and *Wasp* each received near misses. Three planes were shot down by antiaircraft fire. No appreciable damage was suffered by any of our ships.

Until two o'clock in the afternoon, sporadic attacks by small groups of planes continued. Periodically our carriers turned into the wind to land and reservice their fighters. Air battles occurred at distances from two to 60 miles from the fleet, but the worst was over. However, all hands remained tense at their battle stations, ready for whatever the Japanese could throw into the fight.

Before the first attack on our fleet, our bombers and torpedo planes had been launched simply to get them off our carrier decks, so that they would not present an additional hazard and interfere with the launching and landing of fighters. They were directed to hit the airfields on Guam and Rota so as to hamper the enemy's use of these bases. Although

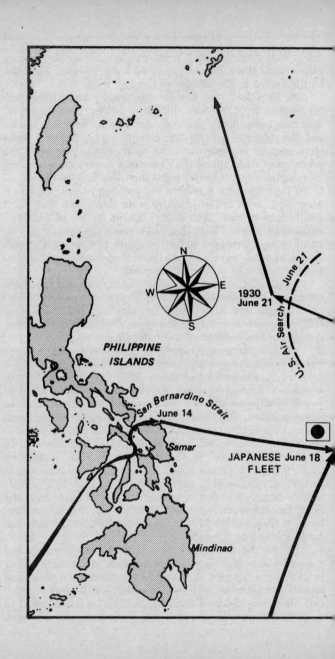

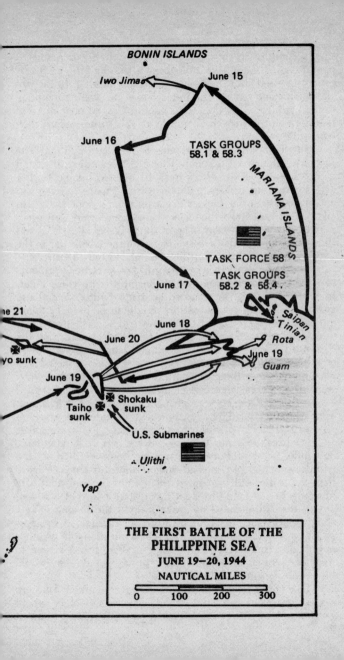

BONIN ISLANDS

Iwo Jima — June 15

June 16

TASK GROUPS
58.1 & 58.3

MARIANA ISLANDS

TASK FORCE 58

June 17

TASK GROUPS
58.2 & 58.4

June 18

Saipan
Tinian

June 20

Rota

ne 21

June 19
Guam

yo sunk

June 19

Shokaku
sunk

Taiho
sunk

U.S. Submarines

Ulithi

Yap

THE FIRST BATTLE OF THE PHILIPPINE SEA
JUNE 19–20, 1944
NAUTICAL MILES

| 0 | 100 | 200 | 300 |

they accomplished considerable damage, the fields remained operational. It is difficult to damage a landing strip so that it cannot be used after the bomb craters are filled in. In the late afternoon came reports that numerous planes were attempting to land at Guam and Rota. Our fighters dashed once more to this area and destroyed 75 planes of this group before they were able to land.

This completed the last stage of the day's fighting. The Japanese offensive was spent. That night, snoopers remained in the vicinity of our forces until 10 o'clock, but no further action occurred. Evidence obtained from Japan after the war established their day's losses in carrier planes alone as 297. In addition, at least 100 of their shore-based planes were destroyed, making a total for the day of approximately 400 aircraft. It was the greatest single day's loss of planes in the entire war in the Pacific. Our own losses on this day totaled only 18 aircraft.

Because of Spruance's disapproval of Mitscher's proposal to head west to close the enemy during the previous night, the role of our carriers had so far been limited to defense against the Japanese air assaults. Nightfall of June 19 found our ships farther to the east than they had been that morning, as a result of the frequent courses they had made during the day into the easterly wind to land and launch aircraft.

In a belated effort to get closer to the enemy Task Force 58, after landing their last patrols of the day, headed westward at 23 knots. One carrier group, comprising the *Essex, Cowpens* and *Langley*, was left behind to cover the Marianas area. The force heading west, however, included six large and six small carriers—plenty of strength for the job in prospect.

Daybreak of June 20 found this fast carrier striking force 300 miles west of Rota. The enemy, however, had started withdrawing the previous afternoon, and a distance of more than 275 miles still separated them from our position. The morning search failed to sight them, and a second was sent out in the afternoon. This group located the fleeing enemy ships at a distance of 310 miles from our carriers. It was now so late in the day, however, that it was questionable whether our planes could reach the Japanese vessels and return to their carriers on their fuel supply. In any event, they would be unable to get back before dark.

Few of our pilots were qualified in making night landings on carriers. On the other hand, the enemy ships might escape unless they were attacked immediately. A difficult decision confronted Admiral Mitscher. He determined to send off the strike.

Two hundred and sixteen planes were launched at 4:30 P.M. for this long perilous, over-water flight. At the end of it, they could not be certain of locating the enemy, and they faced the probability of running out of gas before they could return. In addition, the problem of locating our carriers and landing in the dark was an entirely unfamiliar one to many of the pilots. It was a grim prospect.

They arrived in the vicinity of the Japanese ships just at sunset. The enemy were in three groups. One of our attack units located their tankers and, despairing of finding the carriers in the waning light, proceeded to attack. They sank two of the oilers and damaged another. The other planes found their primary target, the carriers, with their escorting battleships, cruisers and destroyers. Against the opposition of about 35 enemy fighters and through heavy antiaircraft fire, they dived down on the targets in the gathering dusk. In spite of their magnificent effort, they succeeded only in damaging, not sinking, five carriers, one battleship and one cruiser. According to Japanese reports, one damaged carrier, the *Hiyo*, succumbed to a submarine's torpedo a short time later. Our planes shot down 22 enemy fighters and we lost 20 in the melee.

Then our pilots turned into the strong east headwind for the long trek back to their carriers, with swiftly emptying gas tanks. From the midway point, planes started going down in the darkness into the black water beneath them, out of gas. Others managed to reach the vicinity of our task force, only to be forced to land in the sea while waiting their turn to go aboard the carriers. Locating and rescuing the survivors of these crashes was extremely difficult during darkness, and most of those who managed to inflate and get into their rubber boats or life jackets had to wait for daylight to be picked up. Subsequent reports stated that 77 per cent of the pilots who landed in the water were recovered.

The scene was spectacular. Mitscher had ordered searchlights turned on to help guide the returning planes, despite the danger of such illumination in the vicinity of enemy planes and submarines. A plain-language message was broadcast to our planes to land on any carrier they found, without waiting to locate their own.

Blinded by the unfamiliar blaze of lights, and inexperienced in night landings, some pilots attempted to land on cruisers and battleships, which, of course, had no flight decks. Others failed to take wave-offs on the carriers and landed on top of planes just ahead of them or crashed into the barriers. Many men who had survived the air battle were killed on the flight decks in this confusion of landing. Altogether, 80 planes were lost by water landings or crashes on the carriers. After accounting for those rescued from the water the next day, flight personnel killed or missing totaled 38.

It is now necessary to go back to the preceding morning, when our task force was busy fighting off the Japanese air attacks. At this time, two of our submarines, the *Albacore* and the *Cavalla*, were on patrol near the area in which the Japanese fleet was conducting its flight operations.

At 8:10 A.M., the *Albacore* had the thrill of getting an enormous enemy carrier in the cross wire of its periscope. It was the brand-new 40,000-ton *Taiho*. From a salvo of torpedoes, only one hit was obtained. Although not immediately effective, it was enough. As on the *Lexington*, in the Battle of the Coral Sea, accumulated gasoline vapor exploded with tremendous force at 2:32 P.M., resulting in raging fires, and the huge carrier finally sank at 6:28 that night. It was the first time she had gone to sea.

Meanwhile, the *Cavalla* maneuvered to within torpedo range of the *Shokaku* at 11:20 the same morning. "When I raised my periscope at this time," her commander wrote in his report, "the picture was too good to be true. I could see four ships, a large carrier with two cruisers ahead on the port bow and a destroyer about 1,000 yards on the starboard beam." The submarine fired six torpedoes. Four of them found their mark and exploded against the side of the tough veteran of the attack on Pearl Harbor, the Coral Sea battle, and other engagements with our forces.

From the *Cavalla* later came the urgent dispatch: "Hit *Shokaku* class carrier with three out of six torpedoes . . . accompanied by two *Atago* class cruisers, three destroyers, possibly more . . . received 105 depth charges during three hours period . . . supersonic gear out, hull induction flooded, no other serious trouble. Sure we can handle it. Heard four terrific explosions in direction of attack 2½ hours after attack. Believe that baby sank." The belief was correct, the carrier was the *Shokaku* and she did sink.

When the *Taiho* was abandoned Admiral Ozawa, the

Japanese force commander, had shifted his flag to the *Shokaku*. Now he was again forced to transfer to a new flagship, first to the cruiser *Haguro* and next day to the *Zuikaku*, the only remaining large carrier.

The sinking of these two vitally important ships by our submarines was the most serious damage, aside from the wholesale destruction of their planes, inflicted on the enemy fleet in the entire battle. It added to the difficulties of the Japanese air groups returning from their attacks on our fleet, and the disruption of communications kept Ozawa from directing the operations or knowing the exact situation in regard to his planes. Many of them, so far as he knew, might have landed safely on the island bases. The only information he had while on the *Haguro* was that his remaining planes numbered less than 100 and that the first day's attack had not gone as scheduled. He decided to retire westward to reorganize and to recall his planes from the island bases.

Thinking he was out of range of our planes and estimating that our fleet had been damaged at least as badly as his own by the previous day's air attacks, Ozawa paused on the afternoon of June 20 to refuel his ships and to take stock of the situation. At this time he received the astounding news that our carriers, still in great strength, were heading west and rapidly approaching his position.

Upon receipt of this startling information, Ozawa hastily broke off fueling and the Japanese fleet turned westward at maximum speed to avoid the prospective engagement which might mean the loss of his remaining ships. Although our planes managed that afternoon, as reported above, to get in the one sunset attack which resulted in such grievous losses of our planes on their night return to the carriers, the Japanese fleet was out of range the next morning, and no further action occurred. The enemy had been defeated in their effort to stop our invasion of the Marianas, but they had escaped with most of their ships still afloat.

The principal reason for this Japanese defeat was the amazing ineptitude of their poorly trained aviators, and by contrast, the superb fighting efficiency of ours. Our carrier aviators were the best pilots in the world. By contrast, the Japanese airmen in this battle were mere novices. One enemy flying squadron went into action with only six months' training, another with two, and a third with three. A Japanese report states that many of their flyers could barely handle monoplanes, and their maneuvering was extremely poor. The pilots of one reconnaissance squadron had had no more than 100 hours of flying experience and no practice in radio transmission or reception. Under these conditions, it was not surprising that our men shot them down in the over-all ratio of 20 to 1 in the "Marianas Turkey Shoot." Because of our aggressive action in pushing so rapidly across the Pacific, the Japanese were continuously kept off balance and were unable to prepare for the next attack. They were losing aviators much faster than they could train them.

Back on Saipan on June 19, the troops had completed their realignment for the drive northward, and the advance began. The ground contained many coral-limestone caves

Flame Thrower

formed when volcanic forces created the island. Finding these caves difficult to take, the assault troops pushed relentlessly on, leaving them to be mopped up by the reserve with flame throwers and demolition charges.

When the 27th Division failed to keep pace with the two Marine divisions on its flanks, Lieutenant General Holland M. Smith, of the Marine Corps, commanding the amphibious forces, arbitrarily relieved Major General Ralph Smith, U. S. Army, the division commander. Under Major General Sanford Jarman, U. S. Army, who succeeded to the command, the 27th Division rectified its tactical position and continued successfully against the Japanese until the end of the campaign.

On June 26, a novel incident occurred. During the night a large group of Japanese who had been cut off and penned up in the southeastern tip of the island broke out of the trap and started hell-bent for the airfield, where our planes were now freely operating. The Japanese were well organized and had adopted the slogan, "Seven lives to repay our country." Each man was apparently expected to kill seven Americans before going to join his ancestors. Their further objective was to do as much damage as possible to our planes and equipment on the airfield and then get through to their own lines in the north.

Just how many started out on the fantastic venture was not determined. More than 500 bodies were counted the next morning, and some may have got through to their own lines or to the protection of the jungle. On the whole, this suicidal attack was singularly unsuccessful. The Japanese failed to inflict more than about seven casualties on our forces. They reached the edge of the airfield, where they destroyed one parked plane and damaged two others before being driven off by an enraged crowd of Sea Bees and aviation ground personnel. The survivors made off toward the north, where they encountered a regiment of Marines, then in reserve. Here the remnants were wiped out, the infuriated Marines blasting stragglers out of bushes and fox holes until well into the morning.

After minor advances, on July 2 the whole line pushed forward. The town of Garapan, although mostly reduced to rubble, was occupied and substantial advances were made all along the line against diminishing opposition. On the 3rd, Tanapag Harbor was taken and on the 4th, the enemy seaplane base and the important dock area in that vicinity were occupied. By these maneuvers, the Japanese were concentrated along the northwestern shore.

In this extremity, the enemy made one more strenuous attempt to break out of their position. General Saito, in supreme command on the island, realized that the extravagant promises from the homeland of naval and air relief would not be lived up to. Brought up under the code of *Bushido*, he had set forth his thoughts in a last message to his troops:

"The barbarous attack of the enemy is being continued. . . . We are dying without avail under the violent shelling and bombing. Whether we attack or whether we stay where we are, there is only death. However, in death there is life. We must utilize this opportunity to exalt the Japanese manhood. I will advance with those who remain to deliver still another blow to the American devils, and leave my bones on Saipan as a bulwark of the Pacific."

Saito planned a banzai charge of all the remaining troops he had left. His communications were so thoroughly disrupted that he had to rely upon runners to get out his orders. All personnel still able to walk were to rendezvous at a designated spot near the village of Makunsho by the night of July 6. Some of the runners fell into American hands and our people were well aware of what was brewing. All hands were alerted accordingly, although the exact time of the charge and the direction it would take were unknown.

Saito's closing words were: "I advance to seek out the enemy. Follow me." But he did not intend this to be taken literally. Having issued his message, the old general sat down to the most sumptuous meal his attendants could prepare from their depleted food supply. After various ceremonies he walked to the mouth of the cave which served as his headquarters, bade farewell to his staff, and seated himself cross-legged, facing in the direction of the Emperor's palace. A ceremonial dagger was handed to him and he went through the motions of drawing his own blood. The instant blood flowed, his aide, acting upon previously given orders, shot him in the right temple. The Marines subsequently recovered his body and buried it with military honors.

Admiral Nagumo, the other high-ranking officer marooned on the island, is believed to have followed a similar procedure in his own quarters at about the same time. It was he who had commanded the task force which attacked Pearl Harbor at the beginning of the war, and the Japanese carrier striking force in the attempt to capture Midway which had resulted in the sinking of four of his flattops.

About 4 o'clock on the morning of July 8, the enemy troops started southward on their final charge. About 3,000 men participated. Moving down a narrow-guage railway near the shore, they scattered the American outposts and slammed head on into the forces waiting for them. They succeeded in breaking through; there was no stopping that many men whose only thought was to kill and be killed. Dawn revealed a chaotic situation. Savage fighting was swirling around a dozen isolated American pockets of resistance. The main body of Japanese drove relentlessly on.

Observers in the hills then saw a strange thing. Behind the enemy formation moved an almost unbelievable procession; the sick and wounded from the hospitals had come forth to die; swathed in bandages, some on crutches, they moved along, some of them carrying bayonets lashed to long poles as their only weapons, many with no weapons of any kind. It was discovered afterward that some 300 patients too weak to move had been killed in the hospital by their own people.

Our artillerymen, stationed with their 105's about 1,000 yards behind the infantry positions, were furiously shelling the spearhead of the banzai column. Soon they lowered their sights to point-blank range. Still the Japanese came on. Many died as our artillery fired straight into the advancing mob. The survivors kept coming. After removing the firing blocks to make the guns useless, the Marines fell back, fighting as infantry when the enemy overran their emplacements.

But the end was not far off. Men from other units, including clerks, messmen, and communications personnel, hurried to their comrades' aid with rifles, carbines and machine guns to join in the slaughter. Rushing in over the heap 1 bodies of enemy dead, they recaptured the guns and again turned them on the Japanese. The greatest of all banzai charges was over.

The rest of the day was spent in mopping up the remnants. At nightfall there remained only two pockets of remaining enemy resistance, pinned against the shore, and these were cleaned up the next day.

The carnage had been terrific, and to bury the great number of enemy dead took several days. One observer described our exhausted soldiers lying down to sleep amid rotting corpses because there was no spot in the area unencumbered with them.

After this charge, the campaign was soon over. Spreading northward against trifling resistance, the Marines encountered a handful of Japanese who had missed the banzai charge for some reason, and these were killed in their fox holes. Others fled to the edge of the cliff at the north end of the island. There many died by their own hands.

Hundreds of civilians had fled before our advance and had taken refuge on the northern shore. Here occurred an orgy of self-destruction. Mothers and fathers stabbed, strangled or shot their hysterical children; some hurled them into the sea and leaped in after them in plain view of our troops who were on the cliffs or clambering down to the beach. Battle-hardened veterans of the campaigns in the Pacific turned sick at the sight.

Pleas for surrender were largely ignored. These poor people had been told that the Americans would torture and kill them and had been urged to destroy themselves rather than surrender. When a few of them showed an inclination to give themselves up, they were shot down by Japanese soldiers in their midst. One soldier was seen to shoot, one by one, a group of about 15 civilians, mostly women and children, and to end the performance by blowing himself up with a hand grenade.

Although some thousands of armed Japanese still lurked in the jungles, hills and caves, the island was formally declared secure at 4:15 P.M. on the afternoon of July 9. During the ensuing weeks Japanese were hunted out and killed, when they refused to surrender, frequently at the rate of more than 100 a day. The American casualties in taking the island amounted to 3,143 killed, 13,208 wounded, and 335 missing. The Japanese losses were 23,811 dead, 1,810 military prisoners, and 14,735 civilian prisoners who were interned in stockades. The number of civilian dead could not be estimated.

Although in our original plan we had visualized a landing on Guam three days after the landing on Saipan, both operations to proceed simultaneously, the strong resistance encountered on Saipan had necessitated using the troops intended for Guam as a reserve for this attack. After the securing of Saipan, the forces were reorganized and the Guam

landing was set for July 21. Other forces were assigned the task
of capturing Tinian in a shore-to-shore movement from Saipan
across the channel, which was less than three miles wide.

The initial landing on Tinian was ordered for July 24.
Slightly smaller than Saipan, this island was entirely different
in its topography. Most of the land was level and planted to
sugar cane. There were, we knew, many excellent roads and a
narrow-gauge railroad. Much of the coast line consisted of
cliffs where it would be impossible to land boats to secure a
beachhead. Japanese troops on Tinian totaled between 9,000
to 10,000, and they were generally better armed than those
on Saipan. In addition, they had, of course, been forewarned
of the impending attack.

During darkness on July 10 and 11, reconnaissance
parties went ashore undiscovered by the Japanese to investigate the possible landing places. They found on the northwest coast two narrow beaches defended with only a few
mines, obstructions and other weak defense installations. The
Japanese apparently expected the landings to be made on the
other side.

The Second and Fourth Marine Divisions and the Army's
27th Infantry Division landed just before 8 o'clock on the
morning of July 24, on the selected beaches. They were
supported by naval gunfire, artillery emplaced on the south
coast of Saipan, and air strikes both from the aircraft carriers
and from our newly acquired airfields on Saipan.

The Japanese counterattacked furiously, but were so
thoroughly smashed that by the morning of the second day
their Tinian garrison had ceased to exist as an organized
command. Mopping up sporadic resistance, our troops moved
down the island until on July 31 they reached Tinian town. As
usual a number of Japanese remained in isolated pockets or
lurked in the caves or among the boulders and thickets of the
final low ridge in the center of the island. Again the troops
were treated to the spectacle of the civilians hurling their
children over the cliffs and leaping after them. Leaflets
urging surrender and promising good treatment were dropped
into the area, but many persisted in the useless self-slaughter.

On Tinian the bodies of 6,050 Japanese army and navy
personnel were counted in addition to those they themselves
had buried, and there were 255 prisoners. Interned in the
stockade were 13,262 civilians. The action had cost our troops
290 killed, 1,515 wounded, and 24 missing. It was the price

paid for an island which was to become a great air base for B-29 bombing attacks on the home islands of Japan.

After the fall of the Marshalls and our air strikes on Truk, the Japanese had rushed men, guns and fortification materials to Guam. The garrison numbered about 18,500 troops, including the 29th Division, from the famous Manchurian Army, and a naval contingent of about 5,500. The island is of volcanic origin, rugged and broken, and fringed with coral. The interior is a high tableland, eroded into numerous gullies and rock outcroppings. The highest mountain rises only a little over 1,100 feet, and the northern half of the island is almost entirely blanketed with low, dense jungle, but lacking the large trees characteristic of the rain forest of New Guinea and the Solomons. The island is roughly shaped like a peanut. On the west side, at the narrow waist, lies Agana, with Apra Harbor a short distance below it. Just to the south is the long Orote Peninsula, site of the principal airfield.

B-29

The Guam operation was assigned to the Third Amphibious Corps commanded by Major General (later Lieutenant General) Roy S. Geiger. The corps comprised the Third Marine Division, First Marine Provisional Brigade, 77th Army Division, and 9th and 14th Defense Battalions, in addition to Corps artillery and special troops. The postponement of the operation on account of the difficulties on Saipan necessitated these troops' remaining on their overcrowded transports, in the heat of the tropics, for 48 to 52 days. Food deteriorated and cigarettes had to be rationed. Nearly everyone suffered from heat rash. When the time finally came to land on the hostile shores of Guam, the prospect of leaving those uncomfortable ships was a welcome one.

Fourteen days of naval shelling and coordinated air strikes preceded the Guam landing. At 8:30 A.M., July 21, the troops went ashore on schedule. One force hit the beaches a mile below Agana, the other just south of Orote Peninsula. Surprisingly light opposition was encountered near Agana, but resistance stiffened as the men tried to push inland. The Orote landing had as its objective the main airfield.

Both landings faced high ground on which the Japanese were strongly intrenched. Orote Peninsula gave the enemy a strong flanking position for enfilading fire against our beachhead there.

The Third Marines, below Agano, had the enemy looking down their throats from Chonito Cliff, which had to be occupied before progress inland could be made. During the first four days, the troops battled their way inch by inch against dogged opposition, suffering heavy casualties. Finally, on the morning of July 26, they broke the opposition when a strong Japanese counterattack failed.

This attack was an extraordinary performance. It consisted of banzai charges, infiltration and sharp thrusts through the gulleys at separated units, and was marked by courage, hysteria, fanaticism and stupidity. Heavily supported by artillery, mortars acd tanks, the personnel were fortified for their mission with whiskey and saki. Shortly after midnight, heavy artillery and mortar fire began to fall on the Marines' front lines. The main Japanese attack began about 4 A.M. The enemy came on in great force and suffered terrible casualties, but by sheer weight and impact they overran the thinly held front lines. Strange to say, their advance was finally halted, by, of all things, the division hospital. Here the walking wounded turned out in pajamas and underwear, grabbing up grenades, rifles or whatever weapons they were able to find. The more seriously wounded fired from their hospital beds at the Japanese intruders. Sixteen Japanese were killed in and around the surgery tent. The enemy's charge was spent at this point, where daylight trapped them. The hard-hit Marines now gathered all the makeshift reserves that could be found: engineers, service troops, cooks, bakers, messmen, and clerks. The force which had attacked the hospital was effectively liquidated by two companies of pioneers and large miscellaneous units. Stragglers and small groups in caves and ravines were being dug out for days afterward.

Near Orote Peninsula, the Japanese reaction to the landing was immediate and violent. Shortly after dark on the first day, they began swarming out of their caves on Alifan Ridge, dominating this area, and three strong counterattacks developed between 2:30 and 4 A.M. Jabbering and yelling in characteristic fashion, the first wave of enemy infantry was massed behind six tanks and guns mounted on trucks, making a terrific clanking and rattling that could be heard above the chatter of small arms and cough of mortars which preceded the advance. Soon a couple of our own tanks lumbered up from the rear, knocked out the enemy tanks, and went to work on the infantry. The Japanese morale wilted under this fire and those who could slunk off behind the ridge. Another assault came down the ridge and there was hot, close fighting in the flare-lit darkness. Breaking through the perimeter and rolling on toward the artillery, this attack was finally stopped by the artillerymen with rifles, grenades and tommy-guns. At dawn, three enemy officers and 66 soldiers were discovered on a knoll only 50 yards from a regimental command post. A hurriedly assembled patrol of 25 men liquidated them with a loss of only six wounded. By nine A.M., our lines had been reformed and the troops were again moving forward.

On the afternoon of July 24, the shore of Apra Harbor was reached, sealing off Orote Peninsula. The trapped Japanese made a determined effort to break out the next night, picking an assembly point at the edge of a heavily wooded mangrove swamp near our lines. The Marines could clearly hear their preparations, which seemed to consist mainly in absorbing all the intoxicants in the immediate area; there were yells, shrieks, laughter and the shattering of empty bottles, which sounded more like a New Year's Eve celebration than a deadly assault. At five minutes before midnight, the enemy boiled out of the swamp and started across the open ground. Just at this moment, our artillery opened fire which landed squarely in the surging mass. This charge never made contact with our lines. The survivors fled back into the swamp where the artillery continued to pound them.

Despite the failure of these enemy charges, the conquest of Orote Peninsula proved a slow and costly business. The entire area had been converted into a great fortification which had to be taken by frontal assault. Nevertheless, our advance moved steadily up the peninsula, supported by air strikes, naval gunfire and artillery. The airfield was captured on July 29 and that afternoon the peninsula was declared officially secure, although several days were to pass before the last miserable straggler was blasted out. The Marines here had lost 279 killed, 1,525 wounded and 152 missing. They buried 3,372 Japanese on that mangled stretch of jungle coral; only four surrendered.

The two landing forces merged to form one beachhead line on July 29. After the joining of our forces, the two divisions joined for a sweep up the island abreast, the Third Marines on the left and the 77th Division on the right. The assault units started off at 6:30 on the morning of July 31, moving down off the high ground into dense scrub jungle which plagued them throughout the drive. The advance proceeded against light to moderate opposition. The Japanese were never able to mass troops for major resistance. Enemy tanks were encountered at odd times, singly and in small groups, sometimes with and sometimes without infantry support. The wide areas between our columns enabled many Japanese to take cover and hide out in the jungle. Organized resistance ended on August 10, 20 days after the landings, when the drive reached the northern cliffs and eliminated the last of the Japanese units on the shore below.

The recapture of Guam had cost us a total of 9,111 casualties: 1,919 killed, 7,122 wounded, and 70 missing. Enemy losses amounted to 17,300 killed and 485 prisoners, although many more Japanese hiding in the jungle were liquidated during the months that followed.

Between June 15 and August 10, the Central Pacific Forces under Admiral Nimitz had taken three large islands in the Japanese inner defense line and had fought a major sea battle with the Japanese fleet. Concurrently, the Southwest

Pacific Forces under General MacArthur had advanced to the western extremity of New Guinea. These tremendous operations placed the American forces in a position which threatened the Japanese ability to continue the war. The fall of Saipan produced the resignation of the Tojo Cabinet which had been in power in Japan since before Pearl Harbor. General Tojo, the one man most responsible for Japan's entry into the war, stated: "Japan has come to face an unprecedentedly great national crisis."

Our carrier striking forces roamed the sea wherever they chose, bringing death and destruction to the Japanese. Our submarines, cruising in Empire waters, were continually whittling down the fleet of merchant ships Japan so vitally needed for bringing in the food and oil necessary for her existence. Although a long war was still envisioned in Washington, the Americans in the combat area sensed that the end was approaching. The stage was now nearly set for the return of our forces to the Philippines. General MacArthur had promised, "I shall return." Before that promise could be fulfilled, however, another preliminary operation remained to be undertaken. This was the occupation of the Palaus.

Japanese Medium Tank

13

THE PALAUS

While our amphibious forces were fighting for Saipan, Tinian and Guam, Army heavy bombers from Eniwetok pounded Truk, and Marshalls-based planes continued the bombing of the by-passed Japanese islands in the Marshalls. Antiaircraft fire continued to rise although 7,200 tons of bombs were dropped on Mille, Wotje, Maloelap and Jaluit between January and July of 1944.

Airfields rapidly took form on our newly acquired bases in the Marianas. By the end of July, Isely Field on Saipan, with its 6,000-foot runway, was capable of handling 150 aircraft. This runway was being extended to 12,000 feet to accommodate the huge B-29's which were being assembled in plants at home for the bombing of Japan.

Our Fast Carrier Task Force made strikes on Yap, Ulithi, Fais, Ngulu and Sorol, primarily to obtain photographic coverage of those islands. They encountered no airborne opposition, but destroyed a few grounded planes, damaged numerous small vessels, and inflicted considerable damage on ground installations. In addition, some of the Fast Carrier Task Groups attacked Palau, over which the planes met intense antiaircraft fire. A fair number of enemy aircraft were destroyed and a number of shipping targets were blown up and sunk.

With the new strategic situation following our advance to the central Carolines, the directives of our naval forces in the Central Pacific were broadened to include the following: "To gain and maintain control of the eastern approaches to the Philippines-Formosa-China Coast area." It was further specified that our forces should "maintain and extend unremitting military pressure against Japan. Apply maximum attrition to enemy air, ground and naval forces by all possible means in all areas."

The operations in the three months from July through September, 1944, involved every major command in the area and extended over the entire Central and Western Pacific. The forces being used on these missions comprised nearly 800 vessels, 1,600 aircraft and an estimated 250,000 personnel of all branches of the armed forces.

In order to close the gap between the forces of the Southwest Pacific and those of the Central Pacific, it was originally planned to occupy three additional bases, the Palaus, Yap and Ulithi. The Japanese troops in the Palaus were estimated at 38,000, with 10,000 additional on Yap. Ulithi was estimated to be very lightly defended, if at all.

As part of the covering operations for the occupation of the Palaus and Ulithi, the fast carrier groups conducted a series of raids on the Philippines which were to have a profound effect upon subsequent operations. These will be described in the next chapter. As regards the landing on the Palaus, it is sufficient to state that these carrier raids prevented any interference with that operation by the Japanese Navy or the enemy Philippine-based air forces.

The Palau Islands lie at the western extremity of the long Caroline chain, which runs east and west across the Pacific a few degrees above the equator. Their total area encompasses 190 square miles. They were a key position in the Japanese defensive system and had received priority in development even over the Marianas. They are only 530 miles from the southern Philippines, roughly a little over halfway from Guam to Mindanao. They were too far distant from any of our newly acquired bases to be effectively neutralized by land-based planes, and would be a menace to our lines of communication when we landed in the Philippines. They already cut across our direct line to the MacArthur forces, by this time installed on the island of Morotai, just south of Mindanao. Their capture was necessary for the security of any further advance.

The Palaus are of the same volcanic-coral character as other islands we had captured in the Central Pacific, and their coral-limestone ridges contain the characteristic caves. In many cases the Japanese had improved on nature by installing in these caves elaborate lighting and ventilating systems, wooden decks, stairs, telephones and radios.

Babelthuap was the largest island of the group, and contained the principal town and harbor. A naval base was located at Koror, close by. At the southern end of the chain was the small island of Peleliu, with an extreme length of only about six miles and a maximum width of some two miles. Level, low-lying, Peleliu was mostly cleared save for a dense mangrove swamp. It had an airfield constructed by the Japanese. Seven miles to the southwest was the smaller island of Angaur, only two and a half miles long and less than two miles wide at its broadest point. It was estimated that the capture of Peleliu and Angaur would be all that was necessary to obtain complete domination of the group and the use of the necessary airfield.

At the northeast end of the Palau group was the excellent anchorage of Kossol Roads, formed by outlying small islands and a coral reef, and large enough to contain several hundred ships. Its disadvantage was that it was in plain sight of the Japanese on Koror, who could observe the goings and comings of any ships using its facilities. I anchored there with my task group several times before Ulithi became available later as a fleet anchorage.

The troops on Peleliu were of the best quality in the Japanese Army, most of them veterans of the crack Kwantung Army from Manchuria. It had been estimated that they numbered slightly more than 10,000, but we later found that the garrison was considerably stronger. The defense system consisted of positions in depth covering practically every position of tactical importance, and was centered around a strong entrenchment in the ridges north of the airfield.

The First Marine Division and the 81st Infantry Division were assigned to assault this base. Major General William H. Rupertus commanded the Marines and Major General Paul J. Mueller the Army division, both of which were units of Major General Roy S. Geiger's Third Amphibious Corps. The 81st Division, staged and trained in the Hawaiian area, was as yet untried in combat; the Marines had prepared for the assault in the Russell Islands.

Although the issue was never in doubt, the capture of Peleliu involved some of the bitterest fighting that took place in the entire Pacific. Direct air support for the landing was furnished by a group of escort carriers which was later augmented first by one, and then by two fast carrier groups. Behind smoke screens laid to hide the reef and black-out enemy information posts on the high ground north of the airfield, and with dive bombers and fighter planes darting in and out, strafing enemy positions, dropping bombs, and launching rockets, the Marines went ashore on the morning of September 15. Resistance was moderate to heavy and several amphibious craft were hit by enemy fire and set on fire as they grounded on the outlying reef.

Pounded by enemy fire which caught them in enfilade, the first wave suffered severe casualties as they landed on a beach heavily mined and defended by pillboxes dug into the coral, with roofs of reinforced concrete which blended so well with the natural terrain that they could not be recognized until practically stepped upon. Later waves crossed the reef amid the wreckage of the gear and vehicles of the preceding one; shells still fell among them and some were hit, but they managed to get ashore to reinforce the troops clinging to a narrow beachhead. By sunset they held a line approximately 3,000 yards long, with an average depth of about 500 yards. Just to the north was the heavily defended elevation which became famous under the name of "Bloody-Nose Ridge."

On the afternoon of the landing, the enemy counterattacked with vigor and determination, covered by a preliminary artillery and mortar barrage and supported by tanks. By this time, however, 30 of our own Sherman tanks had safely crossed the reef and were lined up ready to receive the Japanese. The action did not last long. Between the bazookas and antitank guns of the infantry and the heavy guns of our Shermans, the enemy were thoroughly cut to pieces. Their troops riding the tanks vanished as their vehicles were blasted by our guns. With this action, the Japanese tanks ceased to be a factor in the battle for the island.

Enemy counterattacks continued during the first night, with wholesale infiltration. These assaults were made with all the vigor and ferocity of the characteristic banzai charges. But they were no match for the experienced Marines. Our lines held and our advance was resumed the next morning. That day the Fifth Marines Regiment drove to the opposite shore and seized the entire airfield. In the south the Seventh Marines completed their move to the eastern shore, and by nightfall of the second day they had secured all this end of the island except two narrow-necked points at the southern extremity.

The next phase was for our lines to swing to the north and assault "Bloody-Nose Ridge." The precipitous slopes of this elevation were topped with weird spires and pinnacles and honeycombed with a system of caves which exploited

the terrain with devilish ingenuity and formed the strongest
position the Marines had yet been called upon to take. In the
rocky tangle, the troops measured their advances in yards or
feet, and slugged it out for over a week. By September 23,
the attacking units had suffered 60 per cent casualties. Gradually
the enemy position was whittled down. At 4:00 P.M. on the
23rd, the Army's 321st Infantry relieved the First Marines
and took over the job of isolating the enemy ensconced in this
strongly defended area. By September 26, they had driven a
wedge across the high ground and secured a dominating hill,
and by evening of the next day they had sealed off the
Japanese in the cave defense system from reinforcement from
the north or from any escape in that direction.

In the meantime, other troops had driven to the north
and were in position on the shore directly opposite the small
island of Ngesebus, connected with Peleliu by a causeway.
On September 28, the Fifth Marines in a shore-to-shore
operation stormed across the shallow reef and occupied
Ngesebus and its smaller neighbor, Kongauru, linked with
Ngesebus by another causeway.

By September 30, for all practical purposes, the Peleliu
campaign was over. We held the airfield and all of the island
we wanted to use. The Japanese still resisted on "Bloody-
Nose Ridge," where, since they would not surrender, they
had to be exterminated—a long and bloody business.

When it became clear that the First Marines could
handle the situation on Peleliu, the 81st Division was released to seize Angaur, seven miles to the southwest. Two
regimental combat teams landed there on September 17.
There were only about 1,000 Japanese troops on this island.
Serious resistance was encountered on high ground, but that
area was isolated and Angaur was declared secure on September 20. The Japanese isolated in the pocket held out in
caves until October 15.

On September 21, a third regiment of the 81st Division,
which had not been required on Agnaur, left Peleliu under
strong escort to seize Ulithi, approximately 345 miles away to
the northeast. The atoll was taken over on September 23. Its
lagoon, some 20 miles long and about eight miles wide,
provided one of the finest anchorages in the entire Pacific.
The small islands on its fringing reef, however, offered but
scant room for shore installations, which were necessarily
scattered and limited. Minor ship repairs could be effected

there. One island was used for a small airfield, and another, Mog Mog, for a recreation area. The assemblage of ships anchored in the Ulithi Lagoon was an impressive sight as I took my task group in on October 2. During the next few months, this anchorage was frequently occupied by as many as 600 ships—aircraft carriers, battleships, cruisers, destroyers, amphibious landing craft, scores of merchant ships, floating drydocks, and auxiliaries of every description.

The assault phase on Peleliu was officially declared over on October 12, but casualties were still being experienced by troops fighting on the ridges. Many Japanese were still holding out in their caves and a number of them did not give up until well after the end of the war.

The Japanese garrisons on Babelthuap and Koror, to the north, were neutralized by frequent air attacks during the rest of the campaign. No attempt was made to dig them out. They could not interfere with our use of the Peleliu and Angaur airfields. Our lines of communication were secure, and the way was now open for the coming assault on the Philippines and the move north to Japan. Although we made no great use of the Palaus, their possession by the Japanese could have resulted in considerable interference with our future operations.

While our original plan had called for the occupation of Yap as well as Ulithi, the success of our carrier strikes on the Philippines, to be described in the next chapter, made this unnecessary. Beyond occasional air raids, Yap was left alone, and the troops scheduled for that operation were diverted to take part in our return to the Philippines.

14

SWEEPING THE SEAS: THE CARRIERS CLOSE IN

On September 13, 1944, Admiral William F. Halsey, now commander of the Third Fleet in the Central Pacific, sent a dispatch to Admiral Chester W. Nimitz at Pearl Harbor. Nimitz approved it and passed it along to President Roosevelt, who was then meeting with Prime Minister Churchill and the Joint Chiefs of Staff at Quebec. Upon the concurrence of General MacArthur, commander in the Southwest Pacific theater, Halsey's proposal was approved by the war leaders. This decision, reflecting the shift of power in the Pacific, involved important changes in our schedule of operations.

Halsey's dispatch recommended by-passing Yap, putting the ground forces thereby released at the disposal of General MacArthur, and landing on Leyte, in the eastern Philippines, at the earliest possible date. He had also recommended abandoning our operations to seize the Palaus, but it was now considered too late to halt the campaign there, which was already under way. The attack on Yap, however, was held in abeyance. Our landing on Leyte had been scheduled for December 20. The Quebec conferees now advanced that date to October 20, a change in over-all time schedule which shortened the war by two months or more. A plan to invade the Philippines initially through Mindanao was now abandoned.

Halsey's recommendation was immediately based upon the results of the first carrier strike against the Japanese-occupied Philippines. This operation was carried out from September 9 to 12 by three out of the four groups of the Fast Carrier Task Force. Intelligence gained in the course of the strike, and the virtual elimination by our planes of air opposition, gave evidence of the weakness of the Japanese in the Leyte area.

Our ships in the Central and Southwest Pacific were now organized as two fleets. The Seventh Fleet, under Vice-Admiral Thomas C. Kinkaid, was attached to the forces of General MacArthur. It comprised amphibious forces, older battleships, and all the escort or "jeep" carriers. The Third Fleet, under Admiral Halsey, consisted of the fast carriers and new battleships, with their many attendant cruisers and destroyers. The entire striking force of the Third Fleet was organized as Task Force 38 under the command of Vice-Admiral Marc A. Mitscher, and was further subdivided into four task groups, commanded respectively by the late Vice-Admiral John S. McCain, Rear Admiral Gerald F. Bogan, Rear Admiral Ralph E. Davidson, and myself. Halsey's flag-ship, the *New Jersey*, was attached to Bogan's group. Mitscher had his flag on the new carrier *Lexington*, in mine.

It should perhaps be mentioned that following the air strikes on Truk and the Marianas in February, I had been detached from combat duty and assigned to the Pacific Coast as Fleet Air Commander there. My absence from the fighting area lasted only until July. On Aguust 16, I took a task force consisting of the carriers *Enterprise, Intrepid* and *Independence*, with four destroyers, from Pearl Harbor to Eniwetok, now an American operating base, where Admiral Halsey ordered me to the carrier *Essex* as Commander of Task Group 38.3. Besides the *Essex*, the group comprised the carriers *Lexington, Langley* and *Princeton;* the fast battleships *Washington, Massachusetts, Indiana, Alabama* and *South Dakota;* the cruisers *Sante Fe, Birmingham, Mobile* and *Reno;* and 18 destroyers.

We sortied from Eniwetok on August 29 to support the Palaus invasion, and on September 6, 7 and 8 my task group, in company with Groups 38.1 and 38.2, carried out strikes against Peleliu. These strikes inaugurated the use of napalm, jellied gasoline dropped in belly tanks. On hitting the ground, the substance set up an intense fire over an area of 30 or 40 yards. It was deadly to both personnel and matériel. We lost several planes to antiaircraft fire, but there was no air opposition. Our cruisers and destroyers also bombarded the shore installations and started many fires. Damaged or destroyed were 25 to 30 barges—the only surface craft in evidence—radio buildings, fuel dumps and barracks. Following this, the three fast carrier groups turned over the air cover for the Palaus landings to Fast Carrier Group 38.4, strengthened by a group of 10 escort carriers, and departed for the initial carrier strikes against the Philippines.

Dawn of September 9 found us 60 miles east of Mindanao. Hundreds of planes took off from the carrier decks and swooped down on the island like locusts. All Japanese airfields and installations thereon were heavily pounded. Mindanao, with a land mass about equal to the state of Indiana, contained nine major air bases and a number of subsidiary strips, and we had expected that it would be defended vigorously by planes. Yet, surprisingly few Japanese planes were found either in the air or on the fields. All were quickly destroyed. Altogether about 58 enemy planes were obliterated, most of them burned on the ground.

Planes of my group during the day spotted a convoy of about 40 small merchant vessels proceeding southward, close along the east central coast of Mindanao. They were carrying badly needed supplies to the Japanese forces on the island. The fighters roared in with guns blazing and sank eight of them outright, leaving 10 or 12 more burning and sinking. Two cruisers and four destroyers were sent in to finish the job. They found the remnants of the convoy just off shore and made short work of sinking them with their guns. Some prisoners were picked up out of the water.

The strikes against Mindanao were continued on September 10, but little enemy shipping and few planes were found. The runways of the airfields were of turf, and it was felt that little useful damage could be accomplished by bombing. The pilots reported hardly any suitable targets available, and before noon the task force retired to the eastward for fuel.

When the weakness of the enemy reaction on Mindanao was discovered, Admiral Halsey decided to probe farther north. On September 12 we were back in Philippine waters for what was designated the first Visayas strike. The three task groups were each assigned separate areas in the central Philippines. My group was given the mission of destroying enemy aircraft, shipping, aircraft facilities, and ground installations on the islands of Cebu, Negros and Bohol. For three days we sent in hordes of planes. Our first sweep encountered many Japanese planes in the air over Cebu and reported shooting down 40 to 50. It also attacked more than 100 enemy aircraft on the ground. Without air opposition, subsequent attacks concentrated on large ships found in Cebu Harbor and extensive oil tanks on near-by Mactan Island. In these three days of strikes, the whole force destroyed over 300 Japanese planes and burned 13 large merchant ships, 20 smaller ones, and 35 sampans or barges. We had lost few planes by comparison, my group's losses consisting of 10 planes, three of them in operational accidents, and 10 men.

After refueling, Task Force 38 boldly came back to the Philippines for a strike on Manila, still farther along on the road to Japan, and the focus of the Japanese occupation three and a half years before. On September 21, the carriers arrived at the launching point 157 miles from Manila and just east of the island of Luzon. One carrier group was assigned to destroy enemy aircraft and installations in the Manila and Batangas area, another had a similar mission in the vicinity of Clark Field, and the third was assigned to destroy shipping in Manila Bay. Manila, with its docks, installations, shipping, and near-by major airfields, was one of the most important targets outside the Empire, and it was estimated to be defended by over 500 aircraft.

Over Manila many enemy planes were encountered and most of them were shot down in fierce fighting. After the first sweep, only a few enemy planes remained to dispute the control of the air over the city and its environs. Although the Japanese aviators were unable to cope with our fighters or prevent their attacks, our pilots reported that the antiaircraft fire was very intense.

Relentlessly diving on their targets, the carrier air groups in two days of attacks destroyed over 300 planes and sank a huge amount of shipping, including three destroyers, three tankers and 20 freighters, with major damage to many more. Planes from my group alone claimed 63 enemy planes shot down and 112 more destroyed on the ground. The terrible devastation was a demonstration to the Japanese of the fury our carriers could loose. The total score for the two days of strikes on Manila and other points in Luzon was 405 planes destroyed or damaged, 103 ships sunk or damaged, several airfields gutted, while Manila Harbor was left littered with wrecked vessels. Our losses had been only 15 planes and about a dozen men.

After again fueling from tankers to the eastward on September 23, Task Force 38 was once more back in the Central Philippines. Coron Bay, in the western part of this region, was an excellent anchorage, and we believed the Japanese were using this port to shelter their shipping, on the assumption that it was too far across the Philippines for our air attacks to reach. It was estimated that many vessels had taken refuge there.

As soon as fueling was completed, Task Force 38 started a high-speed run for a launching point off San Bernardino Strait, which was reached at dawn of the 24th. Coron Bay was still 350 miles away, but was brought within range of our Hellcat fighter planes by having them carry extra gasoline tanks under their wings. In addition to its regular armament, each plane was fitted with a 500-pound bomb with a four to five second delay fuse. They were to drop these bombs from masthead height, at the same time strafing with their six .50-caliber machine guns.

In addition, the task group sent off strikes against airfields, installations, and shipping at Cebu. Another group was assigned similar targets on northwest Negros and Panay.

Winging their way across the full expanse of the Central Philippines, with the sparkling sea and the tropical islands beneath them, the fighter planes arrived at Coron Bay, where the Japanese considered themselves entirely secure. There 17 to 20 large merchant ships and tankers were swinging peacefully at anchor, oblivious of the coming attack. Wasting no time, the planes swooped down at full throttle, so low that they barely skimmed over the ships' masts. Many hits were observed. One tanker exploded and sank immediately, and other ships were left burning. When the attack was over, 19 tankers, transports and merchant ships had been sunk, as well as four destroyers and 11 small craft. A number of enemy planes had been engaged in air combat, and 36 of them were shot down in flames. The strikes which had been dispatched to Cebu and Masbate destroyed additional shipping and damaged docks, buildings and other installations.

Near Masbate Island, a *Princeton* fighter pilot, Ensign O. L. Scott, was forced down and made a landing in the water, where other planes saw friendly natives pick him up.

Kingfisher (OS2U-2)

We sent with the next strike a Kingfisher seaplane which landed on the water. The pilot hailed the natives on the beach. In a few minutes, the downed aviator was ferried out to the plane, scrambled aboard into its rear seat, and was on his way back to his carrier. Many similar rescues were to be made in succeeding months.

Upon completion of the second Visayas strike, the Task Force withdrew to replenish its ammunition, fuel and provisions and get a little rest from the month's strenuous activities. One group remained at sea to cover the Palaus, and the others retired to Manus, Saipan, and Kossol Roads. My group went to the Kossol anchorage, where we were within sight of the Japanese on the northern islands of the Palaus. On October 2, we shifted to the more comfortable and private base at Ulithi.

The Task Force left Ulithi on October 6 for another precedent-shattering strike. Bound for the Nansei Shoto area just south of the main islands of Japan, our carriers were bringing the war home to the enemy with a vengeance. Having smashed Japan's air strength in the Philippines, where nearly 3,000 wrecked planes had been counted on the various fields, we now undertook to knock out the air bases from which reinforcements could be sent to that area while our troops were landing in Leyte Gulf. Moving in behind a typhoon which grounded enemy reconnaissance planes, we arrived off Okinawa at daylight of October 10. The mighty armada of carriers launched their planes to strike all enemy targets along a 300-mile arc from Amami O Shima on the north to Myako Jima on the south. Again the Japanese were caught napping. No airborne opposition was encountered, but as usual the planes had a great deal of flak to penetrate. Once more they wrought havoc and destruction. Ninety-three enemy planes were destroyed, 87 vessels were sunk, ammunition and fuel storage at Naha on Okinawa was left blazing and exploding, and numerous air facilities were demolished. None of our ships was damaged.

Next day we fueled from tankers within range of Luzon and at the same time sent fighter sweeps against bases on that island. Upon their completion, we headed in for a raid on the Japanese-occupied island of Formosa, off the China coast. From October 12 to 16, there occurred the greatest battle of the war up to that date between ships and shore-based air.

The Japanese on Formosa had been alerted by the Nansei Shoto attack and were ready for us. They made the mistake, however, of initially using their planes defensively over their air bases instead of striking at our vulnerable carriers.

When our pilots arrived over Formosa they found many enemy planes in the air waiting to engage them in combat. The Japanese had rushed air reinforcements from the homeland to the threatened area on a lavish scale, and had even sent in their partially trained carrier air groups in the hope of striking a crushing blow. Our planes engaged aggressively and the sky was full of aerial dogfights. The incursion into one of their strongest areas had provoked the Japanese into fighting back with all they had.

Our plan of attack had contemplated continuing the action for only two days, but at dusk on the second day the heavy cruiser *Canberra*, in Admiral McCain's group, was torpedoed by enemy planes and left dead in the water. A difficult decision faced Admiral Halsey. Should he abandon and sink the wounded ship and continue the retirement, or should he try to save her? He decided to endeavor to tow her home, even though the attempt meant undergoing heavy air attacks. The *Wichita*, another heavy cruiser, maneuvered alongside in the darkness and took the *Canberra* in tow. She could creep along at only four knots. The enemy attacks continued and at 9 P.M. the heavy cruiser *Houston* was also torpedoed. Her engine room flooded, she also had to be taken in tow.

Radio Tokyo opened up with a broadcast claim that their intrepid flyers had almost annihilated the American fleet. The Japanese surface fleet, Tokyo added, had sortied from the Inland Sea to destroy the remnants of Admiral Halsey's ships. This gave Halsey an idea. It seemed a heaven-sent opportunity to entice the main Japanese fleet from its harbors and then blow it out of the water. The two damaged ships were immediately organized, with escorting cruisers and destroyers, as "Crippled Division Number One." It was unofficially called the "Bait Division." Radio deception was used to create the impression that the fleet had been seriously damaged, in the hope of drawing the Japanese within range of our planes and battleships. As part of the plan, the carrier groups renewed their strikes on Formosa and continued them for two more days. "The Third Fleet's sunken and damaged ships," Admiral Halsey radioed to Admiral Nimitz, "have been salvaged and are retiring at high speed toward the enemy."

Torpedo planes and bombers continued to attack our ships during the next two days, and many of them were shot down. The *Houston* was hit by another torpedo, but remained afloat. She and the *Canberra* had been taken in tow by ocean-going tugs, but their progress was still disappointingly slow. But the attacking planes had viewed the great number of carriers and surface ships still capable of action. The Japanese fleet, which had emerged from the Inland Sea, thought better of its mission of destruction and discreetly returned to safer waters. The damaged cruisers, after weathering a typhoon, eventually reached Ulithi safely and lived to fight again.

In the four days of the Battle of Formosa, we had destroyed over 680 Japanese planes and had sunk 140 vessels and damaged 248 others; our losses were 95 planes, and two cruisers damaged. Many of our downed flyers had been recovered. The Japanese plane losses were to play an important part in their inability to repel our landings at Leyte, which occurred a few days later, and in the Battle for Leyte Gulf.

About 5 P.M. on October 14, my task group had recovered its planes and was heading eastward to refuel. Suddenly the radar picked up a large group of bogeys approaching and the Combat Air Patrol was vectored out to engage them. Although many of the attacking planes were shot down, our visual lookouts a few minutes later sighted 12 to 15 hostile aircraft closing our formation at high speed, and at such low altitude that they had successfully avoided radar detection. Amidst the furious barking of our antiaircraft guns, they made their runs upon the carriers and heavy ships in our disposition. Making radical evasive turns, and with the sky black with flak, the ships narrowly avoided several torpedo hits. In this melee, 25 enemy planes were destroyed by ships' gunfire and by our combat air patrol. One plane shot down by the light antiaircraft cruiser *Reno* crashed on her fantail and started a fire, but without causing serious damage.

The Fast Carrier Task Force now consisted of eight large *Essex*-type carriers, eight light carriers of the *Independence* class, seven fast battleships, four heavy cruisers, seven light cruisers, three antiaircraft cruisers, and 60 destroyers. This force was entirely independent of the older battleships, escort carriers, cruisers, and destroyers assigned to the Seventh Fleet and to the Amphibious Forces. Our control of the sea now had been pushed out from Pearl Harbor, where the war began, to the coast of Japan and to the Philippines. The fast carriers could go with impunity anywhere they pleased in the entire Pacific. Capable of putting more than 1,000 planes into the air from its carrier decks, this powerful striking force dominated the sea everywhere within range of its planes. Its main offensive weapon was aircraft, but the wealth of antiaircraft guns mounted on its surface ships added considerably to its defensive strength.

Since August 31, the force had conducted raids on the Bonins, Mindanao, the Visayas (twice), Luzon and Manila, the Palau Islands, Okinawa, the Nansei Shoto, and the island of Formosa. Its airplane sorties numbered well up into the thousands. These operations were carried out approximately 6,000 miles from our mainland bases. The succession of devastating strikes had continuously kept the Japanese off balance. Of particular importance was their continuing loss of pilots. It takes at least a year of strenuous training and large amounts of aviation gasoline to produce an aviator ready for combat. With the accelerated pace of our air attacks, the constant drain upon Japan's qualified aviators, and the increasing shortage of aviation gasoline in the Empire, the Japanese were never able to train sufficient qualified pilots to man their carrier air groups or even to supply their shore-based aviation units. The war had penetrated at last to their inner core of defense.

The raids by the flattops had made possible the imminent invasion of the Philippines. They had not only probed the weakness of the defenses, but they had also broken the back of Japanese aviation units stationed in those islands and at the supporting bases along the line of communications to the Empire. The carrier task force represented the most powerful offensive naval weapon the world had yet known.

The invasion of the Philippines, however, was to produce one more great naval battle. The Japanese planned to exploit the main gunnery strength of their fleet, which had never been tried in combat under cover of their land-based air forces.

LEYTE AND THE BATTLE FOR LEYTE GULF

General MacArthur had promised the Filipinos he would return. The time had now come to redeem that promise. Aside from the moral obligation to do so, the reoccupation of the Philippines would sever completely Japan's communications with the rich area of the Dutch East Indies, from which she had to obtain oil, foodstuffs, rubber, tin and other supplies necessary to continue the war.

During the two and a half years following the surrender of Corregidor, communications with the Filipino guerrillas had been constantly maintained by radio and by American submarines. Surfacing off designated beaches at night, these vessels furnished ammunition, guns, portable radios and other necessities to the patriots. From the guerrillas we had received valuable information as to conditions in the Philippines. What was of even greater importance, a friendly population awaited our return.

These rich islands, embracing an area of over 114,000 square miles and some 13 millions of people, presented a terrain different from any other over which our advancing forces had thus far fought. The climate, generally speaking, is tropical, with heavy rainfall. From the air, the land looks beautiful and lush, much of it forest-covered but with large areas devoted to farming and pasturage. Many of the islands are mountainous, with numerous volcanoes, but also with fertile plains and valleys, spotted with rivers and lakes. It was a paradise compared to the rain forest and dense jungle of the Solomons and New Guinea, or the barren coral atolls of the Central Pacific.

The reoccupation of the Philippines was the culmination of the long campaign of General MacArthur's forces of the Southwest Pacific. Save for several Marine air groups used for close support of the ground troops, and two battalions of jungle-wise Marine artillery, the ground operations were strictly a United States Army affair. The Seventh Fleet, under MacArthur's direct control, conducted the amphibious phases, bringing the troops in, furnishing the covering fire for the landings, and providing air support from its jeep carriers. The Third Fleet, operating directly under Nimitz and not under MacArthur's authority, was to "cover and support" the invasion, but its main job was to guard against interference by the Japanese fleet.

MacArthur assigned the primary ground force role to Lieutenant General Walter Krueger's Sixth Army. In addition, he had available as area reserve the XXIV Corps, totaling some 50,250 men; garrison forces amounting to 20,000 men; and the 77th Division, all furnished for this campaign from Admiral Nimitz' Central Pacific forces.

The Seventh Fleet, under Kinkaid, consisted of four groups of transports with associated escort, landing, control and mine craft; a fire-support group of six old battleships, four heavy cruisers, four light cruisers and numerous destroyers; a support group of 18 escort carriers with their screening vessels; and miscellaneous service units. Admiral Halsey's Third Fleet consisted of the four groups of the Fast Carrier Task Force (Task Force 38). It included 12 fast carriers and six modern fast battleships with their numerous screening cruisers and destroyers.

Although Halsey conferred with MacArthur and Kinkaid at Hollandia for three days late in September regarding coordination between the two fleets, the fact that they were not under unified naval command later had serious results.

On the morning of October 17, 1944, an advance party of our invading fleet appeared off Leyte Gulf and landed troops on the small islets at its mouth to secure the entrance. Nine minutes later Admiral Toyoda from his headquarters in Tokyo, sent out a radio message alerting his forces for the operation designated as "Sho No. 1," the defense of the Philippines. Far to the east and southeast, converging on Leyte, huge convoys of ships were steaming on a carefully arranged schedule bringing the Americans back to the Philippines.

For the succeeding three days, mine-sweeping and underwater demolition teams conducted their hazardous operations off the selected landing beaches. At the same time, battleships, cruisers and destroyers bombarded the coastal defenses and the escort carriers flew off their planes for bombing and strafing of enemy units on the ground.

On the morning of October 20 came a final blasting of the landing beaches with heavy guns, rocket fire and aerial bombardment. Then the barrage was shifted inland and troops of the Sixth Army went ashore at two points on the east coast. Despite their previous losses, Japanese planes soon arrived and struck savagely at the ships lying offshore. The light cruiser *Honolulu* was hit by an airborne torpedo and a tug and an LCI were sunk. Of ominous portent, the Australian cruiser *Australia* was struck and heavily damaged by a Japanese suicide plane. Japanese pilots had flown into Allied ships before, but always as a last resort, their planes already damaged. The pilot who crashed the *Australia* was the first of the new *kamikaze* or Special Attack Corps dedicated to sacrificing their lives by diving their bomb-laden planes directly onto the decks or sides of their targets.

The Japanese troops in the Philippines were commanded by General Tomoyuki Yamashita, conqueror of Malaya and one of Japan's ablest field commanders. Realizing the vital necessity of holding the Philippines if Japan was to continue the war, Yamashita decided to make Leyte the decisive point of the campaign. He began pouring reinforcements from Luzon and other islands onto Leyte in an effort to wipe out our beachhead.

In addition to fighting the Japanese, the American forces had to contend with the torrential rains which began to fall soon after the first landings. Furthermore, we soon discovered that the character of the soil on Leyte was unsuitable for landing fields. Even if a hard surface was constructed, it sank into the mud as soon as a heavy rain occurred. Army planes had been scheduled to support the troops from fields on Leyte, beginning two or three weeks after the landings, but because of the unsatisfactory landing fields, planes from both the jeep carriers of the Seventh Fleet and fast carriers of the Third Fleet were required for a much longer period than had been anticipated. In the end, Marine aviation was brought in to furnish the air support.

The dramatic moment had now arrived for the Japanese to commit their entire fleet to the defense of the Philippines. Although still not fully ready, their Navy had to be committed to action now if it was to be used at all. Its entrance precipitated one of the greatest naval engagements in history.

This last great naval battle of the Pacific war was fought on October 24-25, 1944, and was originally called, by its participants, the Second Battle of the Philippine Sea. Later Admiral Nimitz designated it as the Battle for Leyte Gulf and directed the use of this name in all official correspondence. The change was unfortunate, for the original name much better describes the battle and more fully indicates its broad consequences. The battle area extended 600 miles from north to south and several hundred miles from east to west. The principal actions took place in the Philippine Sea, far outside of Leyte Gulf, and virtually eliminated the Japanese Navy as a factor in the war. This result was more important than the immediate effect of the battle on the ground fighting around Leyte Gulf or elsewhere in the Philippines, since it opened the door for a possible invasion of Japan itself.

It was now four months since the invasion of Saipan, when in the First Battle of the Philippine Sea the Japanese fleet had lost three carriers and most of its partially trained carrier pilots. Immediately the enemy had begun to reorganize and train a new supply of aviators for another naval battle. They were in the midst of this task when our unexpected landings on Leyte upset their schedule.

Because of extreme shortage of fuel, both gasoline and oil, in the Empire, the majority of the Japanese surface ships had been sent for their training to the Singapore area. The carriers, however, had to be held in Japan to await the graduation of new pilots and the completion of replacement aircraft. In addition, considerable navy-yard work was necessary to repair the damage these ships had suffered.

This weakness in carriers forced the Japanese to adopt a plan making maximum use of the gun strength of their surface ships, which had not been directly engaged with our fleet since the Solomons campaign in the fall of 1942. Accordingly, they decided that their battleships and cruisers, approaching from the south, would fight their way through to the landing beaches off Leyte, where they would destroy our invasion shipping, while at the same time their carrier force, with whatever pilots and planes could be made ready, would emerge from home waters and act as a decoy to lure our Fast Carrier Task Force away from the intended decisive scene of action.

At the last minute, one light and two heavy cruisers and

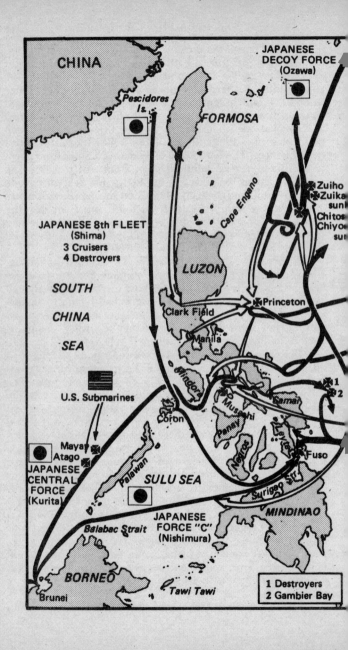

CHINA

Pescidores Is.

JAPANESE
DECOY FORCE
(Ozawa)

FORMOSA

✕ Zuiho
✕ Zuika sunk
Chitose
Chiyoe sunk

Cape Engano

JAPANESE 8th FLEET
(Shima)
3 Cruisers
4 Destroyers

LUZON

SOUTH

CHINA

SEA

Clark Field

✕ Princeton

Manila

U.S. Submarines

Mindoro

✕1
✕2

Samar

Masbate

Coron

Panay

Leyte

✕ Fuso

Mayay
Atago ✕
JAPANESE
CENTRAL
FORCE
(Kurita)

Negros

Palawan

SULU SEA

Surigao Str.

JAPANESE
FORCE "C"
(Nishimura)

MINDINAO

Balabac Strait

BORNEO

Brunei

Tawi Tawi

1 Destroyers
2 Gambier Bay

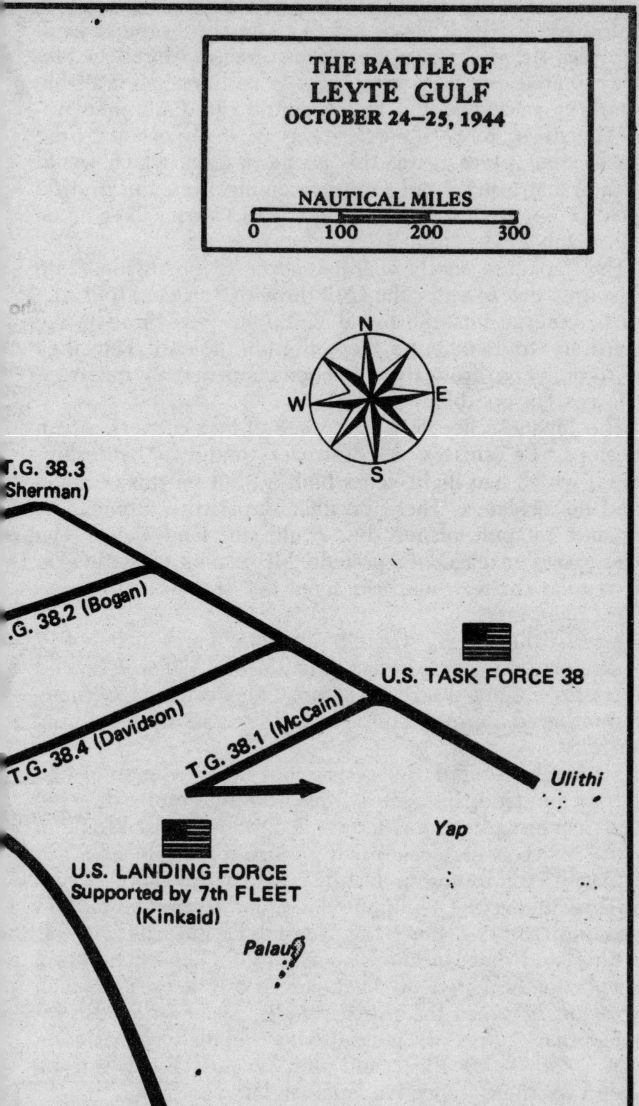

THE BATTLE OF
LEYTE GULF
OCTOBER 24–25, 1944

NAUTICAL MILES
0   100   200   300

N
W   E
S

T.G. 38.3
(Sherman)

T.G. 38.2 (Bogan)

T.G. 38.4 (Davidson)

T.G. 38.1 (McCain)

U.S. TASK FORCE 38

Ulithi

Yap

U.S. LANDING FORCE
Supported by 7th FLEET
(Kinkaid)

Palau

four destroyers which happened to be in the Formosa area, under Vice-Admiral Kiyohide Shima, were ordered to join the forces attacking from the south. In addition, all available submarines were directed to concentrate in Philippine waters. The decoy force of carriers was most important to the Japanese plan, since it was this northern force which would give their battleships and cruisers coming from the south a chance to escape destruction by our Fast Carrier Task Force and to reach Leyte Gulf.

The Japanese southern forces were to be divided into two groups, one to enter the Gulf through Surigao Strait, the other to emerge into the broad Philippine Sea through San Bernardino Strait and enter the Gulf from the east. Thus they were to converge from two directions and destroy our invasion forces "in one blow."

The Japanese fleet was composed of four carriers, seven battleships, 19 cruisers, 33 destroyers and two battleship-carriers, which had flight decks built aft but on this occasion carried no airplanes. These peculiar ships were intended to carry and catapult planes, but could not land them. The Japanese had managed to provide 116 planes to station on their regular carriers, and had about 600 shore-based planes in the Luzon area.

Against this enemy strength, our total forces included 12 fast carriers, 18 escort carriers, 12 battleships, 20 cruisers and 104 destroyers and destroyer escorts. Our carrier-based aircraft numbered approximately 1,280. It was an overwhelming superiority.

Although Admiral Halsey was not under General MacArthur's command, his orders from Admiral Nimitz directed him to "cover and support forces of the Southwest Pacific in order to assist in the seizure and occupation of objectives in the Central Philippines, to destroy enemy naval and air forces in or threatening the Philippine area, and to protect air and sea communications along the Central Pacific axis." It was also stipulated that "in case opportunity for destruction of a major portion of the enemy fleet offer or can be created, such destruction becomes the primary task." Halsey was also instructed that "necessary measures for detailed coordination between the Third Fleet and the Seventh Fleet will be arranged by their respective commanders."

Third Fleet plans provided for the separation from Task Force 38, upon command, of all the battleships, plus one carrier group for air cover, and their formation into a separate command which would be designated as Task Force 34. This was conceived as a surface fighting unit and was to come into being if occasion arose for a battle-line engagement. It showed an instinctive feeling still prevalent that a gun engagement between battle lines might be expected as a part of naval combat.

The eve of this historic battle found the officers and men of Task Force 38 in need of rest to restore them to full combat efficiency after their two months of grueling strikes against the enemy from Okinawa to the Philippines. Unlike other battles in the Pacific, no previous radio interception had given any inkling of enemy intentions. On the night of October 22, therefore, Admiral McCain's group had been ordered back to Ulithi for rest and replenishment, and Admiral Davison's group was scheduled to go back for the same purpose on the 24th.

The three carrier groups remaining after McCain's departure fueled 280 miles to the eastward of the Philippines on October 23 and then headed back to their operating stations about 75 miles off the coast, with 125 miles between groups. My command was the farthest north and was off Cape Engano, on the northeastern tip of the island of Luzon.

The jeep carriers of the Seventh Fleet were about 50 miles off Leyte Gulf, furnishing their scheduled air cover to the troops on shore. The battleships of this fleet, the *Mississippi*, *Maryland*, *West Virginia*, *Tennessee*, *California* and *Pennsylvania* (all except the *Mississippi* had been salvaged after the attack on Pearl Harbor), were inside Leyte Gulf giving fire support to the troops along the beach. They had been loaded principally with shore-bombardment ammunition as distinguished from armor-piercing shells intended for use against warships.

In the early morning of October 23, shortly after midnight, came the report that two of our submarines stationed off Palawan, the *Darter* and *Dace*, had sighted the Japanese fleet heading north for Leyte Gulf. It was the first contact of the battle. The two "pig boats" had made out, on the 22nd, what they thought in the darkness were three cruisers, but they lost them and during the remainder of that day, found nothing else.

Then, on the 23rd, came the crucial sighting when the two submarines made contact with a much larger force. This time it was the main fleet from Singapore, consisting of five battleships, 12 cruisers and 15 destroyers, commanded by Vice-Admiral Takeo Kurita. This will hereafter be called the Central Force. These enemy ships were proceeding up Palawan Passage, bound for Leyte Gulf via the Sibuyan Sea and San Bernardino Strait. Another detachment, under Vice-Admiral Shoji Nishimura, had been left behind at Brunei Bay in Borneo to proceed independently to Leyte Gulf via the Sulu Sea and Surigao Strait. This will be called the Southern Force.

Nishimura's division slipped into the Sulu Sea between Borneo and Palawan while our submarines were preoccupied with the main fleet, and was undetected until sighted by planes from the *Enterprise,* of Task Force 38, on the morning of October 24. It contained two 30,000-ton battleships, the *Fuso* and *Yamashiro,* the heavy cruiser *Mogami,* and four destroyers. Although 26 *Enterprise* search planes joined up to attack this force, they inflicted only minor damage.

The large Central Force was sighted by a search plane from the *Cabot* entering the Sibuyan Sea and heading for San Bernardino Strait. It had also previously been reported by the submarine *Guitarro* near Mindoro.

Later in the morning of the 24th, another search plane sighted Shima's seven ships coming down from Formosa, and heading southeast across the Sulu Sea. Our high command assumed this to be Nishimura's southern force, sighted earlier, because it was composed of the same number of ships. The discrepancy between the two heavy cruisers, one light cruiser and four destroyers of Shima's force, and Nishimura's two battleships, one heavy cruiser and four destroyers, was not observed. Shima's detachment was not attacked prior to its entry that night into Surigao Strait, nor was Nishimura's after the first ineffective attack of the *Enterprise* search planes.

Upon receipt of the submarine and search-plane contact reports, the commanders of the Seventh and Third Fleets took independent action to meet the separated detachments of the oncoming Japanese armada. Admiral Kinkaid was unaware that two different groups, Nishimura's and Shima's, were approaching to enter the gulf through Surigao Strait, the southern gateway, but believed he had to deal with only one. Admiral Halsey ordered the attacks of the Third Fleet's fast carrier planes to be made on Kurita's Central Force in the Sibuyan Sea, to the north, and disregarded the enemy ships approaching Surigao Strait from the south. He assumed they would be taken care of by Admiral Kinkaid's Seventh Fleet.

This division of tasks, undertaken without prior arrangement by the two fleet commanders, set the stage for a surface engagement in Surigao Strait that night. It resulted in the old battleships' having the rare opportunity of engaging the Southern Force of the Japanese fleet with their big guns.

There can be little doubt that had sufficient air attacks been diverted against these groups, they would never have reached the Strait. However, Kinkaid considered that he had plenty of strength to take care of them without calling on his aviators or the Third Fleet, while Halsey continued to direct all his efforts against the Central Force.

The *Darter* and *Dace,* in contact with the Central Force shortly after midnight on the morning of the 23rd, decided that their scouting role was more important than an attack during the darkness, and waited until daylight in order to identify the ships encountered. Using their radar, they took position ahead of the two enemy columns and proceeded along with them like two unseen pilot vessels leading the way. They estimated the force to consist of 11 heavy ships.

At dawn, the submarines submerged and took positions for a coordinated attack. The *Darter* struck first, taking the port column, and fired 10 torpedoes at the leading ship. The submariners counted five explosions, then swung hard left and fired their stern tubes at the second warship in line. Four hits were estimated. Then the *Darter* quickly went down deep to avoid depth charges.

Through the periscope of the *Dace,* her commander saw two cruisers burning as a result of the *Darter* attack. He fired six "fish" at the third ship in the starboard column, obtaining four hits before enemy destroyers forced him to dive deeply.

It was established after the war that four of the *Darter's* torpedoes sank the heavy cruiser *Atago,* Kurita's flagship. The heavy cruiser *Takao* took two hits from the same source and was badly damaged, while the *Dace's* attack sent the cruiser *Maya* to the bottom. These submarines had struck the first blows, but the crippled fleet continued toward its rendezvous with destiny in Leyte Gulf.

The sinking of the *Atago* forced Kurita to shift to another flagship amidst the confusion of a critical situation. With half of his staff communications personnel killed, he transferred first to the destroyer *Kishinami* and later in the afternoon to the super-battleship *Yamato*.

Surfacing three hours after their attack, the *Darter* and *Dace* sighted the damaged *Takao* retiring toward Brunei. While pursuing the *Takao* during the night, the *Darter* ran aground on Bombay Shoal and was unable to get off. Responding to a radio message from her sister ship, the *Dace* rescued the entire crew, then destroyed the grounded submarine by gunfire and torpedoes.

Arriving on their stations east of the Philippines at 6:00 A.M., October 24, the three carrier groups of Task Force 38 sent out a search for the enemy force reported by our submarines. The pilots found the Central Force threading its way through the Sibuyan Sea along the approach route to San Bernardino Strait. They were thrilled by the sight of the new super-battleships *Yamato* and *Musashi* in the enemy disposition as they flashed their report to Admiral Halsey. The presence of the huge battleships was gratifying news, but where were the enemy carriers? It seemed inconceivable that the Japanese would send the *Yamato* and *Musashi* to attack without the support of their carriers, and the latter should be somewhere within the area of operations.

Admiral Halsey decided to use all of his air strength to stop this Central Force from reaching San Bernardino Strait. Our fleet could not enter the Strait because the narrow waters would prevent the carriers from launching and landing aircraft and because of the danger from enemy mines. The air attack had to be launched from the open sea east of the Philippines and the planes had to cross the island barrier to reach their targets.

The weather over the Sibuyan Sea was generally fair, with occasional fleecy white clouds racing along before the fresh easterly winds. The turquoise sea below was interspersed with tropical isles covered with green, and at intervals mountain peaks rose to a height of 8,000 feet. The scene hardly suggested the bitter battle about to be fought in its environs.

All of the carrier groups were hampered by the excessive strength sent out on the initial search. Each search team had been composed of four bomber scouts and four fighters. As their search sectors scattered them over a wide area, these planes were unavailable for a strike immediately after the contact was made. My group, in addition to the search, had been directed to send a 20-plane fighter sweep against the Manila airfields, which further reduced the number of planes we had available for attack.

Admiral Bogan's group got off the first strike, which included planes from the *Intrepid* and *Cabot*. They sighted the enemy ships at 10:20 A.M. and took position on opposite sides of them for a coordinated attack by 19 fighters, 12 dive bombers, and 13 torpedo planes.

Against a terrific barrage of antiaircraft fire, including the novelty of salvos from the enemy battleships' turret guns, the attack went in. No enemy fighters rose to defend the hard-pressed enemy ships, but two torpedo planes were shot up so badly that they had to make water landings. A fighter plane disappeared in flames. But the returning airmen estimated they had obtained two torpedo hits on a *Yamato*-class battle-ship and two on a cruiser. In addition, bomb hits were believed to have been scored on two ships of the *Kongo* and *Yamato* classes.

A second strike from the *Intrepid* reached the enemy at 12:45. By this time, the Japanese fleet had advanced 30 miles farther along its route to the Strait. It was still intact and belched forth an inferno of flak against its attackers. This air group hit one of the *Yamato* class ships with three torpedoes and two 1,000-pound bombs. Another bomb hit the *Nagato*. But the Japanese were yet to receive our most intense air attacks.

Task Group 38.3, under my command and farthest to the north, had been shadowed throughout the night by enemy snooper planes during our approach to the coast of Luzon. Night fighters had kept most of them at some distance from the disposition, and one had been "splashed" at 2:27 A.M. At six o'clock, there were still five on the radar screen. The enemy apparently had full information of the location of my group, if not of the others.

There were a number of medium-sized rain squalls in our vicinity that morning, with intervals of clear weather. They did not hamper flying particularly, but offered some cover to the ships if one happened to be close by when an air attack came in. Aside from the squalls, the sky overhead was partially veiled by broken white clouds at about 2,000 feet.

When the report from the *Intrepid's* search planes reached us about 8 A.M., we immediately prepared to launch our strike on the force in the Sibuyan Sea. Before we could get it off, our radars showed a large group of Japanese planes heading our way from the west. Soon another large group was detected behind the first. A few minutes later, a third one, even larger than the others, was seen on the screen 60 miles southwest of us. All were closing. It was evident that we were about to receive heavy attacks. The planes were coming from the direction of Luzon, which did not yet imply enemy carriers in our vicinity. So many of our fighter planes were now away on the search to the westward and on the Manila sweep that we had too few left both to defend our force against the impending attack and to escort the attack group to the Sibuyan Sea. I decided to postpone sending off the strike until after the incoming attacks were settled. We hastily launched—"scrambled" is the Navy term—all our available fighters to meet the oncoming threat. As soon as the planes were off, we headed into one of the near-by rain squalls for cover, like soldiers going into their fox holes. Throughout the day we played hide and seek in these squalls. They proved very helpful in avoiding the attacking planes.

Commander David McCampbell, the *Essex* Air Group commander, leading a division of seven Hellcats, was first to make contact with the enemy aircraft. His planes met a group of about 60 and dived into them in spite of the disparity in numbers. Unable to contend with these tactics, the enemy scattered. Even their fighters seemed more concerned with defending themselves than with protecting the bombers and torpedo planes they were supposed to guard. A general melee resulted, with fighting spread out over a wide area between small groups of planes. McCampbell, one of the world's greatest aces and a marvelous shot, knocked down nine Japanese aircraft himself, an all-time record. His wing man got six and the remaining pilots nine for a total of 24 by the planes of the *Essex*. Other fighter groups, too, made spectacular records: the *Princeton*'s planes reported 34 enemy aircraft destroyed; the new *Lexington*, 13, and the *Langley*, five. It was a field day. Such a bag of Japanese planes had not been accomplished since the "Marianas Turkey Shoot" the previous June. All the enemy types encountered were carrier planes, but they were operating from the bases on Luzon. None survived long enough to reach position to attack our carriers.

Finally, at 9:39 A.M., when the radar screen showed no

hostile aircraft within 50 miles of our disposition, we emerged from the rain squall and headed into the wind to take aboard our fighters which were low in ammunition and gasoline. The operation was almost completed when suddenly a lone Japanese bomber was sighted diving out of a low cloud toward the *Princeton*. Although immediately taken under fire, it dropped its bomb squarely on her flight deck. A *Langley* fighter shot it down as it streaked away. This hit caused me no great immediate concern, as I felt the *Princeton* was much too tough a ship for one hit by a 500-pound bomb to cause any very serious damage. Soon, however, a serious fire broke out on her hangar desk, where planes armed with torpedoes had been parked while we launched our fighters to repel the attack. Flames and smoke could be seen coming out of the openings in the side of the *Princeton*. Suddenly a tremendous explosion occurred, leaving a column of smoke towering several hundred feet into the air. The fire had set off one or more of the torpedoes on the hangar deck. This catastrophe blew up the flight deck and spread the fire the full length of the ship, amid the places loaded with gasoline, ammunition and torpedoes. Desperately fighting the fire, the wounded carrier dropped out of formation and the antiaircraft cruiser *Reno* and three destroyers were ordered to stand by to protect her against air attack and to assist with the fire.

Our remaining carriers sent off the strike against the Japanese Central Force in the Sibuyan Sea about 11:00 A.M. The largest attack of the day in that area, it was executed by 32 torpedo planes, 16 fighters and 20 dive bombers. They reached their targets at 1:30 P.M. and through the same hell of antiaircraft fire, drove home their attack. The fliers estimated that they had scored three torpedo hits on one *Yamato*-class battleship, one or more bomb hits on another, four torpedo hits on a *Nagato*-class battleship, and additional hits on five cruisers and several destroyers. The intensity of the flak prevented our pilots from determining the precise damage caused by these hits.

While my task group was launching a second strike to the Sibuyan Sea, radar contact was made at 12:45 with a new group of enemy planes bearing down on us from the northeast, and 105 miles distant. The contact at last indicated the whereabouts of the enemy carriers whose location had been a matter of such concern. We had been preparing for a search to the north and northeast, but with a heavy attack coming in, we could not now spare the fighters required for that job. While the enemy planes were still some distance away, we got off the strike to the westward, but we had to scramble all the remaining fighters to ward off this new threat. Meeting the incoming attack 45 miles from our formation, our aggressive pilots, in furious dogfights, sent most of the Japanese flaming into the sea.

While this was going on, another large group was reported coming in 40 miles behind the first. More fighters were sent off. They intercepted the second raid barely 25 miles away. Several of these planes evaded our fighters and dived on our carriers. By twisting and turning, in violent maneuvers, and pouring out a stream of lead from every gun that would bear, all of our ships avoided being hit. Three *kamikazes* plummeted into the sea like flaming torches. Despite their suicide tactics, they had not succeeded in crashing into their targets. The raid was soon over. Our planes and antiaircraft guns had shot down a total of 167 planes in less than six hours.

At 2:05 P.M., we sent off scout bombers for the search to the north. They went out unaccompanied, since all our fighters required reservicing after the hectic fight. At 4:40 P.M., the scouts discovered the Japanese carrier forces only 190 miles distant to the north. It was too late in the day to send off an attack, but at last the enemy carriers had appeared on the scene and we knew where they were.

While the *Princeton* had been trying to extinguish her fires, we maneuvered in her general vicinity to give her what protection we could. The cruiser *Birmingham* and a fourth destroyer also had been sent to her assistance. While the *Birmingham* lay alongside like a fire tug, with her hoses laid across and pouring water into the blazing ship, an after magazine on the *Princeton* exploded and showered the *Birmingham* with fragments. About 255 men on the upper decks of the cruiser were killed. Many more, including her captain, were wounded.

The *Princeton* was now a blazing hulk that would handicap us in our prospective engagement the next morning with the enemy carriers to the north. Admiral Mitscher directed me, after all personnel were removed, to have her sunk. Much as I hated to give up this gallant ship, it was the wisest thing to do. She was sent to the bottom just after dark by torpedoes from the *Reno*.

While the planes of our three task groups had been

attacking the enemy's Central Force moving across the Sibuyan Sea, and while my group was receiving the bitter air attacks of both the enemy carriers to the north and the shore-based planes from Luzon, Nishimura's Southern Force, as well as Shima's Fifth Fleet, were proceeding undisturbed across the Sulu Sea for Surigao Strait. Although Admiral Kinkaid of the Seventh Fleet believed that only one force was approaching from the south, the gunpower of the ships assembled to meet it was far superior to that of the enemy, even had the two Japanese forces been combined. Considering that the Third Fleet would take care of the Central Force heading for San Bernardino Strait, Kinkaid made no preparation to guard that end of the line. This was a consequence of the divided command and of our failure to fix definite areas of responsibility.

The Japanese had difficulties of the same sort, but worse. Vice-Admiral Shima, coming down from Formosa, had orders to cooperate with Nishimura's detachment of the Singapore force, which was attacking Leyte from the south. He learned only at the last minute that Nishimura was to precede him through Surigao Strait.

Senior in rank to Kurita, commander of the forces from Singapore, Shima was not under the latter's authority. Their common superior was Admiral Toyoda in Tokyo. No communications passed between Shima and Nishimura. Neither made the slightest effort to coordinate the operations of their two forces. It was a typically Japanese "face-saving" procedure.

Admiral Kinkaid had placed Rear Admiral Jesse B. Oldendorf, with his flag on the *Louisville,* in command of the ships defending Surigao Strait. This force consisted of the old battleships *West Virginia, Maryland, Mississippi, Tennessee, California* and *Pennsylvania,* under the command of Rear Admiral George L. Weyler; eight cruisers, 26 destroyers, and 39 PT boats. The last, under Commander Selman S. Bowling, were stationed at the southern end of the Strait.

Surigao Strait, which connects the Mindanao Sea, north of the island of that name, with Leyte Gulf, is about 30 miles long. About 12 miles wide at its southern end, it broadens to about 25 miles when it enters Leyte Gulf. Strong currents flow through its narrow portion.

Preparations were made for a night action. The plan drawn up by Admiral Oldendorf provided for our battleships to line up across the Strait near its northern end, our cruisers and destroyers taking stations on the flanks, somewhat advanced toward the enemy's direction of approach. The PT boats were to attack, as opportunity offered, at the southern end of the passage.

Loaded primarily with shore-bombardment ammunition, our battleships and cruisers had too few armor-piercing shells on board for a prolonged engagement with ships. The approach of the Japanese formation up the Strait, however, offered an ideal situation for a destroyer torpedo attack.

Unaware of the overwhelming force awaiting him, Nishimura approached the Strait at 10 P.M. He encountered the PT boats first and under star-shell and searchlight illumination, repelled their attacks by heavy salvos of gunfire. The small PT boats fired numerous torpedoes and made heroic efforts, but obtained no hits.

The enemy ships forged steadily up the Strait. At 2:15 A.M., the *Louisville's* radar picked up the advance units 25 miles away. Captain J. G. Coward's destroyers, in our van, opened the main attack about 3 o'clock by firing a total of 47 torpedoes at the approaching vessels. Numerous explosions were heard in the vicinity of the targets.

From then on the fight became a massacre. Destroyers from the flanks charged in and fired their flocks of tin fish. The night was lit up with tracers and the swift flashes of gunfire, and star shells overhead illuminated patches of the scene like spotlights on a stage. Searchlights stabbed through the darkness, attempting to hold their beams on their elusive targets, as the Japanese ships delivered a terrific fire from their guns.

Although thrown into confusion, the Japanese fleet staggered on. Suddenly the battleship *Yamashiro*, Nishimura's flagship, blew up and sank. Explosions presumably occurred in her magazines as a result of torpedo hits. Nishimura was heard to announce on the voice radio: "We have received a torpedo attack. You are to proceed and to attack all ships." That was the last ever heard from him. Thereafter, command devolved upon the captain of the *Fuso*. He issued no orders, but continued blindly northward to his doom.

At this point the destroyers on our right flank, under Captain K. M. McManes, advanced to contribute their part to the blows that were falling on the enemy. Skillfully passing Coward's division, which was retiring from its attack, McManes' craft swung around and fired their torpedoes. The enemy replied with salvos of 5-inch and 8-inch projectiles, as well as torpedoes of their own. Using smoke screens and making evasive changes of course, the attacking destroyers miraculously escaped being hit. Firing their guns at any targets within range, they saw bright orange flashes and heard the thunder of torpedoes detonating against their targets. In the welter of gunfire, smoke screens, star shells, flares and searchlights, and with ships dashing madly about at full speed, the exact sequence of events on the Japanese ships can never be known. McManes' torpedoes probably sank two destroyers and damaged the heavy cruiser *Mogami*.

The strongest destroyer attack was still to come. It was delivered by the destroyers of our left flank, under Captain Roland N. Smoot, beginning at 3:37 A.M. when Admiral Oldendorf issued the order, "Launch attack; get the big boys." As these small ships went in at full speed, our cruisers opened fire at a range of 15,600 yards from the nearest enemy ship, and then our battleships joined in at 21,000 yards. The Japanese formation by now had been reduced to only four ships; the *Fuso*, *Mogami* and two destroyers. Under a storm of salvos from our battleships and cruisers, and probably hit by torpedoes from Smoot's destroyers, the *Fuso* sank at 4:18. The *Mogami* was flaming brilliantly. At this point, realizing the hopelessness of proceeding farther, she and the two remaining destroyers turned away and attempted to retire down the Strait.

Smoot's ships were now between our own battle line and the enemy. It had been feared that in the confusion some of our ships might mistake them for Japanese. And so it happened. The last one in column, the *Grant*, was smothered by shells from both sides. Taking eleven hits from our cruisers and nine from the enemy, she was a shambles. Dead in the water, with no headway, on fire, and in danger of sinking, the helpless ship suffered 129 casualties.

Learning at 4:10 that our destroyers were under the fire of our own guns, Oldendorf immediately gave the order to cease firing. By chance, the enemy stopped firing at the same moment, and the battle area suddenly became comparatively dark and silent. When ordered to resume firing ten minutes later, none of our ships could find any targets. The battered and burning *Mogami* was out of range, steaming south with two destroyers, one also afire, but the other undamaged. Two battleships and two destroyers of this force had been sunk.

Of our battleships, the *West Virginia* had fired 16 salvos, the *Tennessee*, 13; the *California*, nine; and the *Maryland*, six. The *Mississippi* and *Pennsylvania* fired only one salvo each to unload their guns after "Cease firing" had been given.

In spite of our overwhelming force, in the strongest position known to naval tactics—the crossed T—the three remaining Japanese ships disengaged and escaped down the Strait. Oldendorf felt that if his ships pursued, they might be mistaken for the enemy and fired on by our PT boats somewhere to the southward, as well as risking torpedoes from Japanese destroyers lurking in the darkness.

But at this time, unknown to Oldendorf, another force, the three cruisers and four destroyers of Shima's Fifth Fleet, were advancing up the Strait. Although he failed to communicate with Nishimura, Shima planned to enter the Strait at 3 A.M. to give support to the preceding ships. He arrived only in time to witness the retreat of the remnants.

Aware that fighting was going on at the upper end of the Strait, Shima had two of his destroyers screening ahead. PT boat No. 137 fired a torpedo at one of these destroyers, missing her but hitting the light cruiser *Abukuma*, farther away. With her radio room flooded, and other damage, the cruiser was slowed to 10 knots.

Shima went on with the rest of his ships. At 3:45, he sighted burning vessels on both sides of the channel. Soon afterward, his detachment entered an area filled with smoke. About 4:20 their radar spotted a group of American ships and the enemy vessels fired torpedoes in that direction up the Strait. Two of these were sighted and reported by one of our destroyers, which caused our battle line to turn away, as the British ships had turned from a threat of German torpedoes in the Battle of Jutland.

Just then, the *Nachi*, leading the enemy column, sighted a large, burning ship close aboard. It was the battered *Mogami*, retiring at slow speed. Unable to maneuver, she rammed the *Nachi* and left her shipping tons of water through a gaping hole in her side. Shima then decided to retire down the Strait and all efforts to enter Leyte Gulf from the south came to an end.

Oldendorf cautiously followed in pursuit. His flagship regained radar contact with the enemy ships, but most of them were out of range. Two burning ships were in sight, one of them probably the *Mogami* and the other a destroyer, and they were taken under fire at 5:24. Despite her damage, the

Mogami was now making 17 knots. After inflicting further damage upon her, Oldendorf abandoned the chase at 5:39 and our cruisers turned back toward the Gulf.

A half hour later, now in full daylight, our cruisers again reversed course and went back down the Strait looking for cripples. They located the damaged destroyer *Asaguma* and sank her by gunfire at 7:21. Five or six columns of smoke could be seen over the horizon to the south.

At this point in the action, the air was called in after all, when Admiral Oldendorf suggested to Admiral Kinkaid that planes from the jeep carriers operating off Samar be assigned the job of finishing off the cripples. Unaware that shortly thereafter they would themselves be facing annihilation, the baby flattops were given the assignment.

In two air attacks, planes from these carriers sank the *Mogami*, which had withstood such an incredible amount of punishment, while their parent carriers, owing to subsequent developments, were fighting for their lives off Samar. The light cruiser *Abukuma*, of Shima's force, which had limped away, was overtaken next day and sunk by Army B-24 bombers.

The remaining ships of Shima's Fifth Fleet, the cruisers *Nachi* and *Ashigura* and four destroyers, escaped to the westward. Of Nishimura's force, only the destroyer *Shigure* avoided destruction. With astounding and dramatic events about to occur off the eastern entrance to Leyte Gulf, Oldendorf's eight cruisers were near the southern end of the Strait but the six old battleships were still in the Gulf, near its northern end.

At dawn on October 25, the small escort carriers, in three groups to the east of Leyte Gulf, launched their scheduled patrols for the day's missions. These included combat and antisubmarine patrols around their own ships, support and spotting tasks for the troops on shore, and the attack on the cripples left by Oldendorf's force south of Surigao Strait. There was never a thought that Halsey's powerful Third Fleet had not stopped the enemy's Central Force, reported the previous day as heading for San Bernardino Strait.

The sea was calm, with a gentle breeze of about ten knots from the northeast, and broken white clouds floated slowly overhead. Visibility was good, except for a few scattered tropical rain squalls in the vicinity. The ships were in their usual circular formation, with the escorts screening the carriers in the center.

Suddenly, at 6:45 A.M., one of the patrolling planes overhead made the astonishing report that he had sighted the Japanese fleet and was under fire. It was unbelievable. There must be some mistake. But soon the lookouts on the bridges of the northernmost group of carriers saw for themselves the pagodalike masts of the Japanese battleships slowly coming over the horizon. The situation was appalling. With no guns worth mentioning, the small ships faced imminent and complete destruction.

By some slip-up, unknown to them, the enemy's Central Force, reported in the Sibuyan Sea the day before, had passed through San Bernardino Strait and was now here in sight, bearing down on the escort carriers. Rear Admiral C.A.F. Sprague, in command of the northern group, ordered all planes launched and took an easterly course at full speed, 16 knots, in a hopeless effort to escape. It was like a tortoise trying to run away from a hare.

Within ten minutes came the first salvo from the giant battleship *Yamato*. She had opened up with her 18.1 inch guns at a range of 15 miles. Within a few minutes, straddles were dropping around the *White Plains*, which had just started flying off her aircraft. Shells exploding underwater close aboard were shaking the little carrier violently, but she continued launching her planes and started making heavy black funnel smoke. Considering this an indication that she was done for, the Japanese ships shifted fire to the adjacent *Saint Lo*.

As the new target, in turn, was being bracketed, Sprague ordered the escort vessels to make a smoke screen which, with the help of funnel smoke from the carriers themselves, effectively concealed the apparently doomed ships for the moment.

At this time, Sprague broadcast an urgent appeal for help and reported the situation. Kinkaid read this message on his flagship, the command ship *Wasatch*, in Leyte Gulf at 7:24, and it was also picked up by the Third Fleet, far to the north off Luzon. Halsey could do nothing about it. He was 500 miles away engaging the decoy force. The Seventh Fleet's cruisers were at the south end of Surigao Strait, 50 miles from the jeep carriers, but its slow battleships were in the Gulf and might have been available to go to Sprague's relief.

Of Kurita's original Central Force of five battleships, 12 cruisers and 15 destroyers, the giant battleship *Musashi*,

sister ship of the *Yamato*, and two cruisers had been sunk by
our carrier and submarine attacks the previous day. Two other
cruisers and several destroyers had been badly damaged and
sent back. The force was not the fresh fighting unit it had
been when it started from Brunei Bay. The *Yamato* and
Nagato had been damaged by bomb hits, but their fighting
efficiency and speed were not seriously affected. The force
bearing down on the jeep carriers was thus composed of four
battleships, eight cruisers and 10 destroyers, still a very
formidable force, but one which Oldendorf's six battleships,
eight cruisers and 26 destroyers were capable of handling had
they been in the right position.

Oldendorf was ordered to assemble three battleships,
the *Tennessee*, *California* and *Pennsylvania*; five cruisers and
18 destroyers at the eastern entrance to the Gulf. The
battleships were reported to be short of ammunition, but the
amount fired in the previous night's engagement would not
seem to substantiate this report.

The predicament facing the jeep carriers had been caused
by the failure of the Seventh Fleet to realize that the Third
Fleet had left San Bernardino Strait unguarded when it
proceeded north. Consequently, Kinkaid had not sent out any
search in that direction at daylight. In the emergency which
now faced Sprague's group, there was no hope of immediate
outside assistance and annihilation was staring them straight
in the face.

Kurita's Chief of Staff said after the war that the contact
with our carriers was as much a surprise to them as it was to
us. They thought they had run into a fast carrier group of the
Third Fleet and that it included battleships and cruisers. For
this reason, they were slow in pushing home their attack.
They deployed to fight a decisive action. If they won, they
intended to go into Leyte Gulf, destroy our transports, and
retire through Surigao Strait.

This deliberation was a godsend to our small ships.
Momentarily covered by a smoke screen, the carriers had the
good luck to run into a near-by rain squall which gave them
some additional protection. Salvos continued to drop around
them, but the enemy's accuracy was poor in the reduced
visibility. Kurita sent a division of heavy cruisers around the
flank to get to windward of the carriers while the battleships
bore down relentlessly from astern.

Sprague now ordered his seven screening vessels to

make a torpedo attack. Three destroyers and four small destroyer escorts then fought one of the most daring and sanguinary actions of the war. Maneuvering at high speed, in and out of smoke screens and rain squalls, firing their guns at battleships and cruisers at ranges as low as 6,000 yards, the courageous bantams launched their torpedoes in a turmoil of gunfire and battle smoke. Forcing the enemy to maneuver to avoid torpedoes, and obtaining a hit on the heavy cruiser *Kumano,* which had to withdraw from the battle, they succeeded in delaying for an appreciable time the enemy advance.

It was a miracle that any of the small vessels survived. The destroyers *Hoel* and *Johnston* and the destroyer escort *Samuel B. Roberts* were sunk, and the remainder suffered grievous casualties. Kinkaid afterward reported this attack as "one of the most gallant and heroic acts of the war."

In the meantime, the designated cruisers gradually crept around the northern flank until they were abeam of the carriers. They maintained a grueling fire on the American flattops, which replied with their "peashooters." Each was equipped with a single 5-inch gun. All of the carriers were hit. The *Gambier Bay,* nearest to the enemy, finally went dead in the water and drifted astern in the path of the oncoming Japanese. Shortly afterward, under continuous salvos, she capsized and sank, with one enemy cruiser firing on her from a range of 2,000 yards.

In the meantime, planes from all the escort carriers, including those farther south, were being launched and sent off for attacks on the enemy. One division of bombers scored nine hits on a heavy cruiser, which later blew up and sank. Torpedo hits were made on at least two others. Other planes attacked with rockets and small bombs and strafed the bridges of the enemy. Planes without bombs or torpedoes made dummy runs in an attempt to bluff the Japanese into turning away. Every unit was doing its utmost to save the carriers from being pounded by the enemy guns.

While this engagement was going on, Japanese suicide planes from Philippine shore bases attacked the southern group of jeep carriers, under another Sprague, Rear Admiral Thomas L. Sprague. The *Santee* and *Suwanee* were both hit and badly damaged, and in addition the *Santee* was struck by a torpedo from an enemy submarine.

About 9:25 A.M., just as the wiping out of our northern group of escort carriers seemed a question of minutes only, an amazing thing happened. The Japanese fleet reversed course and quickly steamed away. It was almost unbelievable. Admiral C. A. F. Sprague, in his report, gave credit to "the definite partiality of Almighty God." It was like a last-minute reprieve from a death sentence, though the Americans were unable at the moment to determine whether it was a permanent release or only a delay in the execution.

They were not entirely clear of punishment by the enemy. At 10:49, while licking their wounds and recovering aircraft, they were suddenly attacked by six suicide "Zeke" fighters. The *Saint Lo*, hit and racked by internal explosions, sank at 11:00 o'clock. The *White Plains* and *Kalinin Bay* also were hit and set on fire, and another *kamikaze* missed the *Kitkun Bay* by 50 yards ten minutes later. But this episode concluded the attacks for the day on this fighting group of escort carriers. The *White Plains* and *Kalinin Bay* eventually put their fires out. It was a miracle that any of them were still afloat after the day's ordeal.

Kurita's forces, after their incredible withdrawal, milled around for two hours just north of the general vicinity of the engagement. They neither headed for San Bernardino Strait nor did they proceed toward Leyte Gulf, where they had been directed to sink our transports. They were "taking account of the situation," so they reported after the war. Those of our small carriers which were still undamaged continued pounding them with air attacks by all the planes they could muster.

Far to the east, and proceeding to Ulithi for rest and replenishment when the battle opened, was Admiral McCain's group of the Fast Carrier Task Force. On the night of October 24, these vessels had been recalled. On the morning of the 25th, they had been given orders to search to the westward for the purpose of joining in the Third Fleet's attacks on Ozawa's decoy force.

However, when Halsey received Kinkaid's frantic and urgent request for assistance off Samar, McCain was directed to steam at maximum speed in that direction and to launch air strikes on Kurita's Central Force as soon as he was within extreme range. These strikes arrived over their targets at 1:10 P.M. and 3:00 P.M. Both inflicted additional damage, but neither succeeded in sinking any ships. By this time, the enemy were heading away from Leyte Gulf.

In the jeep-carrier attacks, Kurita had lost three cruisers

sunk, and other ships had been severely damaged. The psychological effect of being continuously under air attack for two days, coupled with the progressive sinking of his ships, probably influenced his thinking and affected his decision to withdraw instead of attacking our transports in Leyte Gulf and retiring through Surigao Strait as planned.

Most of the credit for repelling Kurita's Central Force rightfully belongs to the air squadrons of the jeep carriers and to the determined and heroic torpedo attack of the tiny escort vessels of their northern group. Their courage, perseverance, and willingness to accept hopeless chances will live long in naval tradition.

When Kurita was interviewed after the war, he was unable to explain satisfactorily why he had turned back just when he had our small carriers at his mercy. He had headed north, he said, "to join Admiral Ozawa" and "to seek out the enemy." In other words, after Ozawa had succeeded in his decoy mission of luring the Third Fleet away from the Gulf, Kurita was going north to attack the force which had been drawn away so as to permit the accomplishment of his mission! Clearly this does not make sense. Kurita further stated that he had felt he could not be effective inside the Gulf, and also that he wanted to be inside San Bernardino Strait by nightfall. Adding it all up, it seems that he was confused in his thinking, was apprehensive of further air attacks, and went north with the hazy idea he might save face by doing some damage to part of Admiral Halsey's fleet before retiring through the Strait that night. After undergoing heavy air attacks for two days and losing one of the world's most powerful battleships, the *Musashi*, in addition to six cruisers, and with many of his ships crippled, Kurita's decision to withdraw is understandable only as a breakdown of morale. His lack of information concerning the happenings up north, the fate of Nishimura's ships, or the location of our forces, all undoubtedly contributed to his inability to reason logically. He showed himself a pitifully incompetent commander at the end of two days of intense fighting in which his ships had suffered tremendous losses.

A pathetic aftermath of the battle was the plight of the survivors of our sunken ships off Samar. The men from the *Gambier Bay*, the *Saint Lo*, the *Johnston*, *Hoel* and *Roberts*, were left in the water, hanging onto rafts, nets, and wreckage, suffering from thirst, sunburn, and attacks by sharks, for two days before rescue ships arrived to take them on board. This failure was a disgrace to the Seventh Fleet authorities charged with responsibility for the rescue of personnel. Many died from thirst, wounds and exhaustion. Two men were known to have perished from the attacks of sharks. Those still alive were picked up on the morning of October 27 by subchasers and LCI's from Leyte Gulf.

We will now go back to the Third Fleet in the north, off Cape Engano on Luzon, where my scouts located the Japanese Carrier Force late in the afternoon of October 24. Throughout that day, the carriers of Task Force 38 had concentrated their attacks on Kurita's Central Force in the Sibuyan Sea. Exact damage accomplished was unknown, but there were reports that one *Yamato*-class battleship (the *Musashi*) had been sunk and all the other battleships badly hit; that one cruiser had capsized, and that bomb and torpedo hits had been scored on three additional cruisers. When last sighted, the force was heading westward, away from San Bernardino Strait. It was estimated to be incapable of pushing on to its rendezvous in Leyte Gulf to attack our transports. The aviators' reports of damage were subsequently proved to have been overly optimistic.

On the other hand, the enemy carrier group, just reported to the north, had not yet been attacked. Carriers had come to be considered, in naval warfare, the most dangerous and powerful ships afloat. Halsey decided that this new enemy contingent constituted the greatest menace to the landings then going on. To meet it, he concentrated all three of our Fast Carrier Task Groups to the north and left San Bernardino Strait unguarded, although realizing that it was at least partially a Third Fleet responsibility.

During the night of October 24, Task Force 34, the surface ship fighting organization, was formed ahead of the carriers to be ready for a gunnery action. It comprised the six fast battleships, seven cruisers and 18 destroyers. These ships were separated from the carrier groups, which weakened our antiaircraft screens, but no enemy air attacks developed that day.

At earliest dawn of the 25th, all our carriers launched planes. Scouts were sent off to locate the enemy, while the air-strike groups were directed to proceed north for 50 miles and there wait for contact reports of the Japanese ships.

At 7:35, the scouts located the enemy 140 miles north

northeast of my group. From then on, continuous air strikes shuttled back and forth to deliver a stream of bombs and torpedoes against the all but helpless Japanese force of four carriers, two battleships with flight decks aft, three cruisers and 10 destroyers. Our first attack centered on the light carrier *Chiyoda*. She was hit by many bombs and several torpedoes. Commander David McCampbell, *Essex* air-group commander, saw her blow up and sink. Another carrier of the same class was left on fire and dead in the water. From a succession of strikes, a rain of bombs was falling on the two flight-deck battleships, the large carrier *Zuikaku*, the small carrier and the accompanying cruisers. Torpedoes dropped from the planes streaked through the water to find their targets.

Ozawa's group had accomplished its mission of luring the Third Fleet away from Leyte Gulf, and had succeeded in this task far beyond their expectations. Here were all the ships of Task Force 38 almost 500 miles north of the landing beaches, leaving Kurita with a clear track to accomplish his mission. In attaining this result, the enemy had expected to lose most, if not all, of their decoy vessels. "The main mission," Ozawa said after the war, "was all sacrifice."

About 16 fighter planes, all that remained of the 116 with which he had started out, rose to oppose the first strikes of my group. Our fighters quickly shot them down, and for the rest of the day only intense antiaircraft fire hampered our pilots in their work of destruction. We lost 10 planes from this cause during the day. The weather was ideal. We made all the speed we could to close with the enemy, as it was my intention to get within sight contact and permit the carrier crews actually to witness the attacks by our planes and see the enemy ships sink beneath the waters.

Then, about 8:25, came the astounding message from the Seventh Fleet that Kurita's Central Force had appeared off Leyte Gulf despite its pounding of the day before, and at that moment was threatening to wipe out our jeep carriers.

Admiral Halsey states in his memoirs that he was surprised at Kinkaid's dispatch requesting assistance, since it was not his job to protect the Seventh Fleet, but to strike on the offensive, as he was now doing, against a force which threatened the whole Pacific strategy. Close at hand was a powerful enemy detachment which his combined forces were in the process of annihilating.

Throughout the morning, frantic messages continued to come in from Kinkaid, appealing for assistance to prevent the disaster that seemed to face the ships in Leyte Gulf. Finally a message was received from Admiral Nimitz at Pearl Harbor, inquiring, "Where is Task Force 34?"

Although these ships could not possibly reach the scene before daylight the following morning, they were ordered at 11:15 A.M. to reverse course and race back in a futile gesture to help the units off Samar. Just when they had the crippled ships of Ozawa's northern force almost within range of their guns, it was a bitter blow to the battleship officers to be turned away from this rare chance to engage heavy combatant ships. This action caused the Second Battle of the Philippine Sea to be called facetiously in some circles "The Battle of Bull's Run."

Admiral Bogan's carrier group was directed to go south with the battleships. Davison's group, with my own, continued to pound the Japanese carrier force. From the time of our initial contact, the enemy had been steaming to the north, drawing us farther from Leyte. In the bright sunshine, with unlimited visibility, we gradually lessened the distance to our targets until, toward the end of the afternoon, we could see the smoke of one of their burning carriers on the horizon.

Early in the afternoon the large carrier *Zuikaku* received her death blow. She was the last survivor of the enemy carriers that had attacked Pearl Harbor. Hit by many bombs and torpedoes, on fire and pouring forth smoke, she rolled over and with an enormous battle flag flying, sank at 2:30 P.M.

A half hour later, the *Zuiho*, already heavily damaged, took more bombs and torpedoes and disappeared beneath the waves. Far to the south, the *Chitose*, the only carrier left, lay dead in the water, deserted by her escorts and awaiting her end by whatever means came along. She was the ship whose smoke was seen from my task group about 4 P.M.

When our battleships had turned south, four cruisers and eight destroyers from Task Force 34 were directed to return to my task group. I proposed to Admiral Mitscher that they go north and attack the fleeing ships after dark. With his concurrence, I sent them four additional destroyers under Commander Carlton R. Todd. Contrary to my expectations, however, they delayed to sink the already helpless *Chitose* by gunfire, and as a result were able to overtake only a crippled destroyer, which they sank about 8 P.M.

Of the original 17 vessels comprising Ozawa's force, nine had now been sunk. The escaping remainder, straggling over a distance of 45 miles, were speeding northward for the safety of the Inland Sea. They had accomplished their mission of luring our Third Fleet away from Leyte Gulf but they still had to run the gauntlet of two of our submarine "wolf packs" lying in wait for them along their track.

The *Halibut*, in the first group of submarines, fired torpedoes in the darkness at what was thought to be a battleship, but no hits were obtained. The *Pintado*, in the second group, had better luck. Three of her torpedoes struck the light cruiser *Tama*, which went down in flames and shaken by violent explosions. The remaining seven ships of Ozawa's depleted force eventually arrived back in Japan.

Task Force 34, with Halsey embarked in the *New Jersey*, was delayed in its dash southward by the necessity of refueling the destroyers from the battleships. Halsey then took the two fastest battleships, the *New Jersey* and *Iowa;* three cruisers, the *Vincennes, Miami* and *Biloxi;* and eight destroyers, and advanced at 28 knots toward the entrance to San Bernardino Strait. They missed an interception with Admiral Kurita's escaping Central Force at that point by about two hours.

Along the coast of Samar, however, they encountered in the darkness the destroyer *Nowake*. Unknown to the Americans, she was loaded down with survivors from the heavy cruiser *Chikuma*. Under a hail of gunfire that lasted nearly 45 minutes, she went down in a tremendous explosion at 1:35 A.M.

At dawn the next morning, October 26, McCain's group, which had been speeding to the scene from the eastward, joined with Bogan's group off San Bernardino Strait, and air strikes again went across the Philippines against the remaining ships of the Central Force, hurrying southward to escape destruction. They were almost out of range, but planes from six carriers reached them at 8:30 A.M. In spite of cloud cover and still heavy flak, the planes went in and punished the fleeing ships with additional bombs and torpedo hits. A second strike, which confined itself to stragglers, sank the light cruiser *Noshiro* and blew the bow off a destroyer that later was grounded and left a wreck. A third strike located and destroyed off the coast of Panay a large landing ship which had brought reinforcements to the enemy troops on Leyte.

The sturdy jeep carriers off Samar received another *kamikaze* attack that morning, in which the *Suwanee* was hit, with resulting fires which caused many casualties. While this was going on, planes from this group discovered a Japanese detachment of one cruiser and four or five destroyers west of Leyte. They also had landed more troops for the enemy ground forces on that island and were retiring to the westward. In deadly attacks, planes from our small carriers sank the light cruiser *Kinu* and the destroyer *Uranami*.

This action marked the end of the Second Battle of the Philippine Sea. From that time on the Japanese Navy no longer existed as a fighting organization. In size of forces engaged, in extent of area over which the contestants fought, and in decisiveness of results, the action will go down in history as one of the greatest naval battles of all time.

Admiral Halsey's decision which left San Bernardino Strait unguarded will be discussed by critics for the next hundred years. It was made after full consideration of the situation and, in Halsey's own words, "offered the best possibility of surprise and destruction of the enemy carrier forces... [which] would mean much to future operations." The main factor which permitted the unexpected appearance of the Central Force off Samar was our divided command. Halsey stated afterward that the fact that our naval power was not coordinated under a single authority was an invitation which disaster nearly accepted.

Although many have assumed that Admiral Kinkaid had insufficient strength to handle the situation which arose, there is little doubt that had he carried out proper security measures by making an aerial reconnaissance at dawn in the direction of San Bernardino Strait, he had sufficient force to have prevented the arrival of Kurita's ships off Samar, let alone their entry into Leyte Gulf. The old battleships under Admiral Oldendorf's command have been represented as being short of ammunition, but this is difficult to reconcile with the few salvos fired in the battle in Surigao Strait the night before. Even with the reduced number of armor-piercing projectiles carried in their magazines for this operation, they must have had sufficient strength to repel the battered ships of Kurita's Central Force. In addition, the air forces from the jeep carriers alone, if organized and directed for that purpose, could have driven back the enemy's attempt to penetrate the Gulf.

The Japanese conduct of the battle was defective in many respects. Cooperation between their naval forces and their shore-based air was completely lacking. Reconnaissance of our dispositions was scanty, and exchange of information between the four widely separated forces as to their respective situations was practically nil.

Kurita's failure to carry through with his task, when fate had given him the great opportunity toward which the whole enemy plan had been directed, cost him the possibility of winning a success which might well have prolonged the war.

16

MASTERS OF THE PACIFIC

The destruction of so much of the enemy fighting strength in the Second Battle of the Philippine Sea ushered in a new phase of the Pacific War. Altogether, that action saw the loss by the Japanese of three battleships, including the monstrous *Musashi*, four aircraft carriers, six heavy cruisers, five light cruisers, and nine destroyers. It was the greatest loss of combat ships in modern history, 50 per cent greater than the combined British and German losses in the Battle of Jutland in World War I. Many additional ships were so badly damaged that they would never fight again. Furthermore, Japan's supply of fuel oil was so short that there was only enough to operate a few ships as a last resort. These conditions put an end to any hope of future large-scale operations by the Japanese Navy.

The ships which escaped to the south could neither replenish their ammunition nor obtain satisfactory repairs away from their home bases. Consequently, those able to move were recalled to Japan.

Following the battle, Task Force 38 remained off the eastern coasts of the Philippines until it was evident that no further interference by the Japanese fleet was probable. My task group and McCain's were sent back to Ulithi for rest and replenishment; Davison's and Bogan's were kept off Samar and Luzon to continue furnishing air support to shore operations. The Japanese *kamikaze* campaign had just begun. Although the Army Air Force had taken over responsibility for direct air support of the Leyte operations, Admiral Kinkaid had requested the Third Fleet to stand by. He was not satisfied with the air cover General Kenney was able to give the Seventh Fleet, and he could not provide his own after the sinking or damaging of so many of his escort carriers in the battle off Samar.

As a result of their long weeks of action, the Third Fleet personnel were suffering from combat fatigue. An increasing number of pilots were unfit for further fighting and the normal level of operational accidents was rising. All echelons were weary.

On October 29, a large flight of *kamikaze* planes struck at Bogan's group, which included Halsey's flagship, the *New Jersey*. Although the alert fighter patrols shot down 21 of them and the ship's antiaircraft got another, one managed to break through and crashed into the *Intrepid*, Bogan's flagship. The next day another group attacked Davison's carriers and hit the *Franklin* and *Belleau Wood*, killing 158 men and destroying 45 planes. On November 1, they shifted their attack to Kinkaid's destroyers in Leyte Gulf, sinking one and damaging five. The enemy's "Special Attack Corps" was taking a serious toll.

My task group, now comprising the *Essex*, *Ticonderoga*, *Lexington* and *Langley*, plus four battleships, two cruisers, and 16 destroyers, had arrived at Ulithi on October 30 for ammunition, provisions and minor repairs. We were then directed to proceed to the recently acquired naval base at Manus, in the Admiralty Islands, to complete replenishment and repairs. We sailed from Ulithi on November 1 and steamed south, looking forward to a restful period at Manus.

Another dispatch from Halsey, however, ordered us to reverse course and proceed immediately toward a point off the Philippines. The change in plans was caused by erroneous reports of strong enemy forces steaming in the general direction of Leyte. MacArthur had also requested additional strikes from the fast carriers on the enemy airfields in the

Luzon area. We joined up with Task Groups 38.1 and 38.2 and again headed west to strike Manila in accordance with this request.

About 11:30 on the night of November 3, the three task groups were steaming along in the bright moonlight, through smooth seas. Everything was quiet and normal. The radar gave no warning of any enemy units in the vicinity. I was in my emergency cabin off the bridge of the Essex when suddenly I felt a heavy explosion close aboard. Almost immediately the light cruiser Reno, just ahead of the Essex, reported having been hit by a mine or torpedo. Her fuel oil tanks were punctured and two compartments were open to the sea. Smoke poured out of her port quarter as she lost steering control and reported she could make only 12 knots.

It was evident that the Reno was badly hurt. I directed her return to Ulithi with an escort of three destroyers. The story of her trip is an epic in itself. Threatening to capsize and founder at any moment, she was eventually brought into port after passing through the edges of a typhoon. It was finally decided that a Japanese submarine had fired two torpedoes at long range from outside our screen, and that one had exploded against the Reno while the other had just missed the Essex and detonated at the end of its run, close aboard.

In two days of destructive fighter sweeps and bomber attacks on November 5 and 6, the planes of the task force devastated 14 different airfields on Luzon and in the Manila Bay area. A total of 729 enemy aircraft were destroyed; a score or more of cruisers, destroyers and merchant ships in Manila Harbor were sent to the bottom, and others were severely damaged. The heavy cruiser Nachi, Admiral Shima's flagship in the Second Battle of the Philippine Sea, was sunk as she was leaving the harbor. The actions against the airfields were immediately reflected in a lessening of the number of kamikazes over Leyte.

Enemy planes met by our fighters over Manila were reluctant to engage in combat. Many of them hid in high cloud cover, avoiding action except to dive on small numbers of our planes strafing the airfields. Even with the advantage of altitude and numbers, they were content to make one pass and then withdraw.

Over our task group, a small number of enemy "banzai

boys" appeared. It was reported that the Japanese flyers wore green and yellow silk suits to indicate their suicide mission. Seven or eight of these planes got through our patrols and attacked our ships. Four were shot down by antiaircraft fire. At 1:39 P.M., one crashed in flames on the bridge of the *Lexington*. About the same time, another dived on the *Ticonderoga*, narrowly missing her as it plunged into the sea. the *Lexington*'s battle efficiency was not greatly affected, but she had 41 officers and men killed and 126 seriously injured.

On November 7, 1944, Halsey and McCain departed for Ulithi with Task Group 38.2 and left me in command of the Fast Carrier Task Force off the Philippines. Task Group 38.4 had joined when 38.2 left. Shortly after midnight on November 10, I received a dispatch from Halsey stating that an enemy force of four battleships, three heavy cruisers, three light cruisers and three destroyers was reported in Balabac Straits between Borneo and Palawan, heading for Leyte Gulf.

Plowing through heavy seas at 26 knots, we arrived at launching position shortly after dawn. Search planes were sent out and all three task groups prepared to launch full air groups for strikes. Our searchers found no enemy battle forces, but they sighted a large convoy approaching Ormoc Bay, on the west coast of Leyte. There were four transports, three large and one medium-sized, five destroyers and a destroyer escort. All of them except three destroyers were sent to Davy Jones's locker. Of the remaining destroyers, one was left awash, one had its bow blown off, and the other was badly crippled. All these ships were loaded with Japanese troops bound for Leyte. None arrived there. An estimated 18 aggressive Japanese fighters were downed over the convoy, for a loss of 11 of our planes, mainly to antiaircraft fire.

On November 13 and 14, strikes on Manila were conducted in the familiar pattern, except that my policy was to mass all available planes in concentrated attacks instead of sending them off in smaller groups, designated as "deckloads," the method used by Mitscher and McCain. We dropped 290 tons of bombs, and fired 37 torpedoes and 267 rockets. At least one cruiser, five destroyers, a floating drydock, 15 large cargo ships, one repair barge and many small craft were sunk or damaged. Forty enemy planes were shot down in the air or destroyed on the ground. Four piers, many warehouses in the Manila dock area, the runway at Nichols Field, a five-car ammunition train, and other installations in the bay area were smashed. Large fires were left burning in the dock area and the Cavite Navy Yard.

McCain, with Task Group 38.1, rejoined the task force at midnight, November 13-14, and took over from me. Admirals Nimitz, Halsey and McCain signaled congratulations for the work of the task force while under my command. On completion of the Manila strikes, my task group was detached and set course for Ulithi for a much needed rest.

Our stay at Ulithi was more eventful than we had anticipated. A few minutes past 6 A.M. on November 20, I was awakened with a report that enemy midget submarines were inside the great lagoon, which was crowded with hundreds of our ships. The tanker *Mississinewa*, moored near the entrance, had been torpedoed and was burning furiously. The cruiser *Mobile* sighted a periscope and opened fire, whereupon the raider submerged. Outside the entrance, a midget was rammed and sunk by one of our destroyers.

I ordered all destroyers to get under way immediately to form an inner-harbor patrol around all heavy ships. Outside, one of the destroyers located another midget with her underwater sound devices, depth-charged it and brought it to the surface. Patrolling aircraft bombed and sank the surfaced submarine before we could call them off. Near the *Mobile*, the destroyer escorts *Rall* and *Holloran* dropped charges on a suspicious swirl in the water. The bodies of two Japanese rose to the surface, amid debris. Apparently unconscious from the effect of the depth bombs, they sank again before we could reach them.

No further contacts occurred, but all that day and the next night we felt that we were sitting on a powder keg which might go off at any time. Far from enjoying a rest period, we felt we might be safer in the open sea.

Shortly after midnight on the morning of November 21, the American submarine *Sea-Lion*, patrolling hundreds of miles to the westward of Ulithi in the northern approaches to Formosa Straits, picked up on her radar a large force of ships at extreme range. It was the remnants of the Japanese fleet on their way back to Japan from the south after the Second Battle of the Philippine Sea.

The sea was calm and there was no moon. The *Sea-Lion* approached on the surface. From her conning tower were discerned the shapes of two battleships, two cruisers and three destroyers. Reaching firing position undetected, the *Sea-Lion* loosed six torpedoes at one of the battleships and three at the other. Out of the night came three explosions as torpedoes hit the first target, then another on the second.

The *Sea-Lion* put on full speed to the westward. Her crew heard a long series of depth-charge explosions as the enemy escorts industriously hunted her on the opposite side of the formation. Suddenly, one of the stricken battleships blew up, in a tremendous explosion, and disappeared beneath the surface. It was the last of the *Kongo*, a survivor of the battle off Samar. She was the only enemy battleship ever sunk by a United States submarine.

Back at Ulithi, Task Group 38.3 completed its replenishment, and on November 22, we sailed to resume operations off the Philippines. November 25 found us resuming our strikes on the northern part of Luzon, as far down as Manila; while the other task groups covered the area to the south. Our pilots brought back the usual reports: a heavy cruiser sunk in Santa Cruz; a large freighter sunk in San Fernando Harbor and another left burning furiously; two large merchant ships torpedoed and both left beached and useless; seven planes shot down in the air and 50 others strafed or burned on the ground at Clark Field.

In the afternoon, we were again attacked by a considerable number of *kamikazes*. One enemy plane crashed on the flight deck of the *Essex*, my flagship, where it burst into intense flames. Nine of our men were killed, six were missing and 44 wounded. A torpedo plane was burned, my cabin was set on fire, and there was other damage. The *Essex* continued flight operations without interruption.

In the meantime, the other task groups were undergoing similar attacks. The *Hancock*, *Intrepid* and *Cabot* were all hit by suicide planes. The *Intrepid* suffered worst. Wrapped in flames, with blazing gasoline running down her sides, she was rocked by explosions and hidden by black smoke rising high into the air. Despite this condition, she kept position in the formation and Admiral Bogan, whose flag was on board, retained his control of the task group except for a half hour during which his communications were disrupted. But the tough *Intrepid* suffered such severe damage that she had to return to Pearl Harbor for repairs.

In spite of the losses and damage inflicted by the *kamikazes*, we had to continue our operations off the Philippines until the shore-based air could take over the job. Admiral Halsey finally withdrew the entire carrier Task Force to Ulithi, where we were permitted to remain for seven days.

Meanwhile, the ground forces on Leyte had pushed ahead in heavy fighting. Early in December, destroyers of the Seventh Fleet passed down through Surigao Strait and around to the western side of Leyte to attack enemy shipping in Ormoc Bay. Shortly afterward, MacArthur sent additional amphibious forces to land in that area, and the Japanese troops were then squeezed into the northwest end of the island. Not until December 26 was Leyte finally declared secure. In the fighting on this island, the cream of the Japanese army in the Philippines had been committed and ground to pieces.

On December 15, even before Leyte was secured, MacArthur's forces, by-passing the many strongly held islands in the central Philippines, landed on Mindoro, just south of Japanese-occupied Luzon, thereby gaining an airfield within easy reach of the heart of the island. During the approach, the enemy attacked with upward of 150 planes, many of them suiciders, seriously damaging the cruiser *Nashville* and the destroyer *Haraden*. But the fast carrier raids on Luzon, going on at the same time, and the effective air cover furnished by the jeep carriers, limited our losses during the landing to two LST's, at a cost to the Japanese of 100 *kamikazes*. Ten days later, two enemy cruisers and six destroyers coming up from Singapore conducted a brief night bombardment of the beachhead. They were attacked by our planes newly installed on Mindoro, which sank one destroyer and damaged other ships, at a cost to us of 21 aircraft. The enemy vessels retired at high speed. This was the last effort of surface ships to attack our forces in the Philippines.

To cover the advance of the amphibious forces to Mindoro, the Third Fleet was assigned the mission of neutralizing all airfields in Luzon. The mighty armada sortied from Ulithi on December 11. The Task Force had been reorganized into three groups. New methods of protection against suicide attacks had been devised, but at the cost of reducing the number of fighter planes available for offensive operations against the enemy. Under the new procedure, a continuous blanket of fighters was kept over the entire Luzon area, and night planes were sent out on heckling missions during darkness to deny the enemy the use of their bases at night.

During the three days of operations beginning December 14, 62 enemy planes were shot down in the air and 208 were destroyed on the ground; 16 ships were sunk and 37 were damaged; and the usual damage was inflicted on enemy fuel and ammunition dumps, warehouses, hangars, truck convoys, and locomotives.

At nightfall on December 16, Task Force 38 withdrew to fuel from tankers to the eastward. Our plans were to return to Luzon on the 19th. But at this fueling rendezvous, we were to encounter an enemy of another kind. We ran into one of the destructive typhoons for which the western Pacific is notorious.

Weather reporting in this area was sketchy. No advance warning had been received when it became clear that a typhoon was moving upon us. The three task groups, with their assembled tankers and service ships, covered an expanse of many square miles. Throughout the area, the wind and sea increased, making fueling operations increasingly difficult. Finally, they had to be discontinued entirely. Admiral Halsey directed a fleet course which offered hope of avoiding the center of the storm. But as we changed course, so did the typhoon; it seemed to be maliciously chasing us.

It is an awesome experience to be in or near the center of a typhoon. The mountainous seas rose to unbelievable heights. The rain poured down in sheets, reducing visibility to a few yards. The 75-mile wind, its velocity rising in gusts up to 120 miles an hour, tore many aircraft from their moorings on the flight decks of the carriers and blew them away like autumn leaves. It was impossible to stand up on the open deck against the pressure of the wind. The ships were tossed like toys and rolled as much as 40 degrees on a side. Planes got adrift on the hangar decks of the carriers *Monterey*, *Cowpens*, and *San Jacinto* and there was bedlam as they plunged like battering rams from side to side. Friction or broken electrical connections soon resulted in dangerous fires and the excessive motion of the ships made fire fighting extremely difficult. Nineteen aircraft mounted on catapults were blown overboard. A total of 146 planes were lost and many ships suffered widespread damage.

But the most tragic fate befell the destroyers *Hull*, *Spence* and *Monaghan*. These light vessels actually rolled over so far that they capsized and sank. Their loss of life was enormous. Although hundreds of ships of the fleet surrounded the sinking destroyers, rescue of those who managed to get off them and into the water was impossible in the existing weather. Ships could not even be seen at a distance of 100 yards, and the tremendous seas made the launching of small boats impossible.

As soon as the weather moderated, a three-day search was instituted for survivors of the sunken ships. It was the most intensive in naval history. Every ship and plane took part, and every inch of the area in which survivors might be found was covered. Twenty-four men from the *Spence* were picked up, 44 from the *Hull* but only six from the *Monaghan*. That any had survived in the raging sea seemed a miracle.

After this experience, new strikes on the Philippines were set for December 21, but again the weather became too foul for flight operations. Now the fleet could stay at sea no longer and on the morning of December 21, it returned to Ulithi, where we spent our Christmas.

Our next operations were in support of the landings of MacArthur's forces at Lingayen Gulf, on the island of Luzon, the same spot where the Japanese had gone ashore more than three years previously. The first landing at Lingayen was scheduled for January 9, 1945. On December 30, we got under way from Ulithi. Our assignment was to take us far into the South China Sea, and for the first time we were to strike the enemy on the coast of China.

Our first carrier strikes were directed against Formosa and Okinawa, in order to prevent the enemy from staging aircraft from the Empire through those bases to attack our amphibious forces. Despite the withdrawal of our damaged carriers, the three task groups included seven large and four light carriers, six fast battleships, seven heavy and six light cruisers, and 48 destroyers. There was also a night carrier group which included one large and one light carrier, their pilots all especially trained for night operations, which required the highest skill and determination.

On the morning of January 3, the task force arrived off Formosa. The target area included the northern and central part of the island, and we were directed to conduct fighter sweeps on the southern Nansei Shoto Islands, between Formosa and Okinawa. The strikes went off, but bad weather prevented many planes from reaching their objectives. Moderate air opposition was encountered over Formosa. One group of 12 *Ticonderoga* fighters, over the northern section, met 15 enemy fighters. They shot down 12 and drove off the rest, losing one plane.

Next day, an effort was made to continue the attacks, but zero ceiling and visibility throughout most of the area forced cancellation of operations. In the two days' attacks, the enemy lost 111 planes and 16 ships sunk, and considerable damage had been inflicted on ground installations. The weather had been miserable, but American losses were relatively small. They amounted to 17 planes.

In spite of the destruction which we had previously accomplished, the desperate Japanese had been able to assemble enough *kamikazes* in the Philippines to make serious attacks on the Seventh Fleet bombardment and mine-sweeping units on their way to Lingayen Gulf. Among the casualties were the escort carriers *Ommaney Bay*, *Manila Bay* and *Kitkun Bay*, the former sunk and the latter two severely damaged, as were the cruisers, *Louisville* and *Australia* and the fast mine sweepers *Long*, *Hovey* and *Palmer*.

Since our land-based aircraft could not keep all the Luzon airfields neutralized, MacArthur requested Task Force 38 to return on January 6 and 7 for a final strike. We were dogged by bad weather during both days, but by careful searching for dispersed and concealed planes, our fliers destroyed a total of 75 on the ground. On January 7, Admiral Halsey sent this dispatch to the task force:

> Luzon is now a bloody battleground. The enemy is fighting to the death to stop our expeditionary forces and to kill embarked American soldiers. Many ships have been hard hit in the past few days. Every undestroyed enemy plane is potential death to many of our comrades. This is the time for great effort and great determination. Give it your best and God bless you.

On January 9, we went north and again hit Formosa hard. Much of the island was veiled by clouds and fog, with northeasterly gales, but considerable damage was inflicted on enemy installations.

That was the day of the landing on the shore of Lingayen Gulf. There was little resistance on the beaches. The enemy withdrew to the mountains on either side of the central Luzon plain, leaving open the route to Manila. As disembarkation proceeded, the Army pushed southward toward the capital. Hailed everywhere by enthusiastic Filipinos, our forces freed thousands of emaciated prisoners from the Japanese stockades.

Admiral Halsey had long entertained a desire to take the Fast Carrier Force into the South China Sea. Intelligence indicated the presence of a number of enemy warships in that area; the flightdeck battleships *Ise* and *Hyuga*, which had escaped us in the Second Battle of the Philippine Sea, were specifically reported to be in Camranh Bay, in Indo-China. Admiral King in Washington had refused permission for an expedition into those waters until after the Lingayen landing. Now, at last, the time had arrived for the thrust into the heart of Japan's ill-gotten southern empire.

Immediately after our last Formosa strikes on January 9 we headed south to pass through the Bashi Channel under cover of darkness. The chain of islands running down from Formosa to the northern end of Luzon left limited room for maneuvering. At one point, we passed only 80 miles from the enemy air base at Koshun. Our radar showed a stream of plane traffic between Luzon and Formosa, which seemed to indicate that the Japanese were evacuating important personnel from the Philippines. These were natural targets for our night fighters, which splashed three large transport planes.

The first objective of our China Sea venture ("Plan Gratitude") was the concentration of enemy shipping at Camranh Bay. Many Japanese airfields encircled the area, and it was important for us to avoid discovery to prevent their shipping from taking alarm and seeking refuge at Singapore, which was beyond our reach at this time due to fuel considerations.

Inside the South China Sea we found low haze, rough seas, and winds of just under gale force. Captain Jasper T. Acuff had followed us into the area with a tanker force from which we were to fuel on the 11th. The tankers had very little protection, and had they been sunk before we could obtain fuel from them, it would have been a catastrophe. Fortunately, all went well and after obtaining our oil without discovery, we began our run toward Camranh Bay.

Shortly after dawn on January 12, we launched our strikes. Task Force 38 by this time was a veteran outfit and its tremendous power was operating like clockwork. Although no warships were found in Camranh Bay, our planes located a convoy of 11 ships near Cap St. Jacques, just to the north, and sank them all. Other convoys along the coast and in other ports were smashed, and docks, air installations and fuel dumps up and down the whole area were heavily pounded. It was later verified that 41 ships, totaling 127,000 tons, were sunk and 28 more, totaling 70,000 tons, damaged. Many of the latter were swept ashore and wrecked by a monsoon which came up as we departed. The captured French cruiser *Lamotte-Picquet* was sunk at Saïgon and the Japanese light cruiser *Nashii* at sea. As Admiral Halsey has written in his memoirs, "It was a strongly worded notice that control of the South China Sea had changed hands."

Fueling from our tankers next day was made difficult and hazardous by a northeasterly gale and high, choppy seas. About half the ships succeeded in fueling, and although several men were washed overboard, all were recovered. A typhoon was raging to the south of us and we maneuvered around the South China Sea to avoid the path of its center. On January 14, we completed fueling and prepared to strike enemy shipping and installations on the Japanese-held China coast, in the vicinity of Swatow and Amoy.

Before hitting the China coast, we put in another blow at Formosa from the northern part of the South China Sea, on January 15. This measure was for the purpose of keeping that area neutralized as far as possible as a base of operations against our troops on Luzon. Again foul weather hampered operations, but many ships were destroyed in the Pescadores Islands. Warehouses, hangars, factories, locomotives, repair shops, drydock and dock facilities and many grounded aircraft were hit and destroyed.

That night the task force proceeded to a launching point for the strikes on the China Coast. Our planes took off for their targets in the morning. The area to be covered stretched northward from the island of Hainan as far as Amoy, across Taiwan Strait from Formosa. Worth-while targets were difficult to find, but numerous small ships were sunk or damaged and some air opposition was encountered. Over Hong Kong, the planes met the most terrific antiaircraft fire ever experienced in carrier strikes. It was described by one observer as varying "from intense to unbelievable." In these operations, 26 enemy aircraft were destroyed in the air and 21 on the ground. We lost 30 planes in combat and 31 from operational hazards. This was one of the few occasions in the war in which our plane losses exceeded those of the enemy. We had succeeded in sinking 12 ships, in addition to luggers and barges, and in damaging 27 others.

After fueling under difficult weather conditions on January 17, 18 and 19, we headed north to leave the South China Sea. The Tokyo radio had been describing Task Force 38 as "bottled up in the South China Sea." But on the night of January 20, we passed through Balintang Channel, north of Luzon, and into the Pacific without enemy opposition. As we approached that route, our radar again began to pick up enemy air traffic evacuating key personnel from the Philippines to Formosa. Our fighter patrols busily downed 12 planes, mostly twin-engine jobs, engaged in this transport service.

New strikes on Formosa on January 21 were a repetition of the previous ones. The usual attacks were made on airfields, ground installations and shipping, but the pilots were beginning to complain of a lack of worth-while targets.

About noon, small groups of *kamikazes* appeared. Identification was difficult with so many of our planes returning at the same time. Suddenly a single-engine plane glided out of the sun and dropped a small bomb on the light carrier *Langley*. Only negligible damage was accomplished, but within two minutes another enemy plane appeared out of the clouds and crashed onto the *Ticonderoga's* flight deck. The carrier was soon wrapped in flames and smoke from raging fires. Shortly afterward a *kamikaze* roared against her island structure. Later that afternoon, the destroyer *Maddox* was also hit and four men were killed. The *Ticonderoga* lost 140 men and was so severely damaged that she had to be sent back for repairs.

Strikes were continued next day, but the principal aim this time was to photograph Okinawa in preparation for the coming landings there. With 80 per cent coverage obtained in this photographic assignment, the task force retired to Ulithi to prepare for the immediately impending assault on Iwo Jima. In its operations in waters hitherto regarded as ruled by the Japanese, the fast carriers had succeeded in dealing heavy blows to enemy air forces and ground installations all the way from Okinawa to Borneo and Indo-China.

In the Philippines campaign, MacArthur's forces made a secondary landing near Subic Bay on Luzon on January 29-30, and still another south of Manila on January 31 to cut off the city in that direction. The advance elements from the

Lingayen forces entered its northern outskirts on February 4, against little resistance. It looked as though the city would fall easily, but such was not to be the case. The Japanese defenders fell back sullenly across the Pasig River, blowing up bridges, and set themselves up for a defense to the death. It took nearly three weeks of bitter, house-to-house fighting to eliminate them. During the process, the greater part of the beautiful city of Manila, which the carrier strikes had largely spared, was laid in ruins.

Following the capture of Manila, our forces spread out to occupy the rest of the Philippines, greatly aided by Filipino guerrillas, who turned out in ever-increasing numbers. By mid-April, Panay, Cebu, and Negros had been taken and on March 10, General MacArthur invaded Mindanao. A second landing was made on this large island on April 19, and its capital city, Davao, fell on May 21. Although pockets of enemy resistance continued to hold out in the mountains of Luzon, in the jungles of Mindanao, and in other isolated spots, the Philippine campaign was considered over and MacArthur declared the Philippines liberated on July 9, 1945.

The Marine Aviation groups won high accolades from the Army commanders for their work in this campaign. These groups were ordered to the Philippines on Halsey's suggestion about November 25, when the Army's close air defense for Leyte had been insufficient to stop the *kamikazes* or fully to protect our troops and shipping. Marine Air Group 12 composed of four fighter squadrons of F-4U's (Corsairs) arrived at Leyte in mid-December and gave close support to the ground fighting there. On January 9, they participated in providing air cover for the Lingayen landings. Later they were joined by Marine Air Groups 14, 24 and 32. Flying the little Douglas Dauntless dive bombers, which though considered obsolescent were still the work horses of the air war in the Pacific, they furnished flank security to the Army's First Cavalry Division, under Major General Verne D. Mudge, in its advance to Manila. General Mudge stated shortly after entering Manila on February 4:

> On our drive to Manila, I depended solely on the Marines to protect my left flank from the air against possible Japanese counterattacks. The job they turned in speaks for itself. We are here.

I can say without reservation that the Marine dive bomber outfits are one of the most flexible I have seen in this war. They will try anything and, from my experience with them, I have found that anything they try usually pans out.

The dive bombers of the First Marine Air Wing have kept the enemy on the run. They have kept him under ground and enabled troops to move with fewer casualties and with greater speed. I cannot say enough in praise of these dive-bomber pilots and their gunners....

The Marine Flying Artillery, as the dive bombers came to be called, literally cut a way for the infantry through Belete Pass, on the drive to Baguio, the Philippines' summer capital; they supported the guerrillas on Negros, Mindanao, and other islands, and they assisted in the occupation of Jolo and Mindanao. As a result of their work, the Marine aviation units were presented with a large commemorative plaque inscribed, "In Appreciation—Forty-First Infantry Division."

The liberation of the Philippines was a campaign which reflected great credit on General MacArthur, the Sixth Army under General Kreuger, and the intense and loyal fighters among the Filipino guerrillas. The strikes of the aircraft

Vought F-4U "Corsair"

carriers were an important factor in the amphibious operations, and it is beyond doubt that the invasion of the Philippines could not have been accomplished without their support and air coverage. It is pertinent to comment that the control of the sea rested entirely with the planes of the carriers.

17

IWO JIMA

Upon the return of Task Force 38 to Uilithi on January 26, 1945, Admiral Halsey was relieved by Admiral Raymond A. Spruance. The Third Fleet then became the Fifth Fleet and the Fast Carrier Task Force again became Task Force 58. Vice-Admiral McCain was relieved as Task Force Commander by Vice-Admiral Marc A. Mitscher. The fleet was reorganized somewhat for the coming operations, but its general composition remained the same. The Fast Carrier Task Force in this respect was the opposite of the "Pony Express" of early frontier days, when riders dashed across the plains at breakneck speed, picking up fresh ponies every few miles. In our case, it was not the ponies, but the drivers who were changed after each operation. We not only had to keep going at full speed, but each change of command brought a fresh fleet commander determined to outdo his predecessor and to get the utmost out of his forces.

Beginning in November, 1944, Army B-29 Superfortresses based on Saipan had started bombing the Tokyo area of Japan. The development of Saipan as a major base for these planes had been a tremendous undertaking. It required more than 60,000 men to service the heavy bombers, which entailed the construction of additional barracks and the provision of great quantities of supplies. Furthermore, exceedingly long runways had to be constructed of extra-thick cement to withstand the landing shock of the heavy B-29's. These planes were the only ones capable of making the round trip from Saipan to Tokyo, but in order to do so their bomb loads had to be reduced from a possible ten to approximately three tons. Fighter planes could not accompany them and they had to depend on their own guns for protection from enemy interceptors.

The Navy had been rather cool to this project, primarily on account of the enormous logistics involved and the great tonnage of ships required exclusively for its supplies. The Navy felt that the value of horizontal bombing, and its ability to hit pin-point targets, would not justify the tremendous effort required. Nevertheless, the Joint Chiefs of Staff in Washington approved the setting up of an independent strategic bombing force under the direct command of General H. H. Arnold, head of the Army Air Force in Washington. The Twentieth Air Force was thus not under the command or subject to the control of either of the theater commanders, General MacArthur of the Southwest Pacific or Fleet Admiral Nimitz of the Pacific Ocean area.

Previous experience in the war had demonstrated that high-altitude bombing required the dropping of an enormous number of bombs to accomplish worth-while damage. It was known as "saturation" or "pattern" bombing. Our bombing tables in use in the Pacific showed that it required 3,000 tons of bombs from high-altitude, horizontal bombers to accomplish the same amount of damage to a specific target as 300 tons from the more accurate dive bombers of our carriers.

Directly across the route from Saipan to Japan were the enemy bases on the Volcano and Bonin Islands, the former including the island of Iwo Jima. These islands were able to warn Tokyo of the approaching bombers and to send up interceptor planes to engage them in combat as they passed over. It was apparent that the elimination of these enemy activities and the possession of a base of our own in the area would be of great value to the B-29 operations, as well as facilitating future amphibious campaigns planned against Okinawa and Kyushu. In our hands, such a base would provide an emergency landing field for damaged bombers returning from Japan and would enable fighters to accompany them to Tokyo for protection. In addition, its availability as a base for big bombers would permit their carrying heavier bomb loads.

Iwo Jima has been called the "Inevitable Island." It had to be taken. It was 660 nautical miles from Tokyo and 700 from Saipan. It contained two large airfields with a third under construction. The Japanese Army garrison numbered nearly 23,000 men, most of them first-class troops, and in addition there were 7,000 Navy ground troops, who were overlooked by our early intelligence.

Six miles long, with a maximum width of about two and a half miles, the terrain of Iwo Jima was like nothing the Americans had ever experienced before. It is the projection above water of a partially cooled-off volcano. In spots, sulphurous volcanic smoke belches up through the crevices or steams from the ground itself. Mount Suribachi rises 566 feet at the island's southern end to dominate its entire area. In the center is a broad tableland which accommodated the two completed airfields. Toward the northern end, the ground is more hilly, some of the eminences rising to 400 feet, with interspersed gullies and ravines strewn with haphazard volcanic rock. The smell of sulphur smoke permeates the atmosphere.

Lieutenant General Tadamichi Kuribayashi, the Japanese commander, had all the men and weapons he could accommodate on the small island. Considered one of Japan's most capable strategists, he had plenty of time to prepare for defense and had used it to good purpose. Tunnels between positions hundreds of yards apart were dug clear under the airfields, and they were complete with electric lights and linked with all sectors by an elaborate communications system. On the cliff faces were caves with reinforced walls four to eight feet thick, from which artillery could fire through armor-plate doors or barely visible openings. Prepared defense positions existed everywhere, and the Japanese had good reason for believing the island impregnable.

The plan to occupy Iwo Jima was intimately connected with the next objective, Okinawa. The target date for Iwo Jima was set for February 19, 1945, and its capture had to be effected expeditiously in order to release shipping and naval forces for the Okinawa campaign, which was tentatively set for April 1. Preliminary air bombing of Iwo Jima and neighboring Chici Jima was carried out by shore-based aircraft from the Marianas, and carrier air raids were conducted against the home islands of Japan to prevent interference by planes from there with the landing operations. In addition, the carriers were to provide direct air support during the landing.

Task Force 58 sortied from Ulithi on February 10, en

route for Tokyo. This operation was one to which we had eagerly looked forward from the time of the attack on Pearl Harbor. Except for the spectacular Doolittle raid from the carriers *Hornet* and *Enterprise* in April, 1942, and the sporadic B-29 raids from Saipan during the previous two months, Tokyo had not experienced intense aerial bombing. The war was now to be brought home fully to the Japanese people.

The task force arrived at its launching position only 130 miles southeast of Tokyo at 7:30 on the morning of February 16. As our planes swept in from the sea over Tokyo and Yokohama, the ground was covered by a light fall of snow, and thick weather over the target area hampered the operations. It was a strange experience to all officers and men of the task force. After fighting so long in the tropics here we were off Tokyo at last, and we were amazed at the lack of determined air opposition. No Japanese aircraft came within 20 miles of our disposition and our planes roamed at will over the enemy's territory seeking their targets. The snow-covered ground and the snow-laden clouds made determination of landmarks haphazard and identification of assigned targets troublesome.

In spite of these difficulties, the strikes were continued for two days. Flying at times through zero-zero weather, our pilots destroyed many enemy planes in the air and strafed and burned others on the ground. They left burning hangars, smoking shipping, blasted buildings and wrecked installations. A strike against the Nakajima Airplane Plant caused heavy damage, but so much smoke poured out that accurate assessment was difficult. One of our fighters relentlessly pursued a Japanese Tony pursuit plane and shot it down flaming into the streets of suburban Tokyo from an altitude of only 2,000 feet. If the Japanese people had believed their government's propaganda that they were winning the war, all Tokyo now had evidence to the contrary.

One beautifully coordinated air strike from my task group pinpointed fifty 500-pound bombs, plus 42 rockets, into the Nakajima Tama Engine Plant. The crews had the satisfaction of observing a conflagration with smoke rising to 3,000 feet as they withdrew. Although intense flak was put up in defense of this important plant, not a single pilot or air crewman was lost. My task group alone estimated upwards of 167 enemy planes damaged or destroyed in the air and on the ground. The two days' operations demonstrated our carriers' strength and the lowly state to which the Japanese air force had sunk. They emphasized that the Rising Sun was setting.

After retiring from Tokyo on the afternoon of February 17, the task force proceeded to the vicinity of Iwo Jima. On the morning of February 19, our planes struck enemy strong points at the ends of the landing beaches and strafed the beaches themselves ten minutes before the assault waves went ashore. During the day we continued to attack inland targets, chiefly gun emplacements inaccessible to naval gunfire.

The task of capturing Iwo Jima had been assigned to the Fifth Amphibious Corps under Major General Harry Schmidt, who operated under the overall command of Lieutenant General Holland M. Smith. The Fifth Corps consisted of the veteran Fourth Marine Division under Major General Clifton B. Cates, the Third Marine Division under Major General Graves B. Erskine, and a new division, the Fifth Marines, under Major General Keller E. Rockey. The selected landing beaches were each approximately two miles long, one on the southern, the other on the western side of the island. Both faced the open sea, with no reefs to reduce the surf. On account of the prevailing wind, the initial landing was made on the eastern shore. Eventually both beaches were used for unloading operations, as the wind shifted, making one or the other a lee shore.

The first assault waves hit the beach at 9:03 A.M., and seven battalions were soon ashore. Only scattered small-arms fire and an occasional mortar shell had fallen into the area. It was small evidence of the difficulties to come. The assault troops found themselves plodding through loose volcanic ash which tugged at their feet like quicksand. The Amphtracks were unable to get traction to scale a small bluff rising from five to eighteen feet close to the shore. Just at this moment, the well-placed enemy artillery and mortars opened up. They had been carefully ranged in beforehand for this particular purpose. Under the accurate fire, the troops burrowed into the loose sand for such cover as they could contrive.

For several hours during the late morning and early afternoon, the Japanese fire was so deadly accurate that practically no landing craft were able to get ashore through the inferno of shelling. But during the uninterrupted first hour, the Marines had managed to bring ashore everything that was essential for the time being. They had landed tanks and bulldozers and sufficient airfield matting to provide traction in the worst places. They had also landed enough artillery to take care of the situation. By dusk of the first day, the Marines had overrun the lower end of Airfield No. 1, and had reached the western shore. But they had suffered heavy casualties.

During the night the lines were illuminated almost continuously by flares. But no general counterattack developed, although several sharp enemy thrusts had to be beaten off, as well as repeated infiltration attempts all along the line.

Shortly after dark, enemy planes appeared off shore in the vicinity of the task force, under a bright moon and occasional broken clouds. By means of high-speed evasive maneuvers and smoke screens, the enemy attacks were evaded without damage.

On the second day, Marine Units drove south against Mount Suribachi, while others fought their way to the north. On the lower slopes of Suribachi, the progress was painfully slow.

Mount Suribachi provided a fine observation post from which the Japanese could observe every movement of the invaders. It was connected by underground cables with the hills to the north, so that it could control the fire from any point on the island. Every Marine felt that the Japanese were looking down his throat and realized that the height must be taken at the earliest possible moment. For four days they fought for this hill. Its base was not secured until the third day after the landing, and on the fourth day, the Marines pushed along both shores to surround it. Early on the morning of the fifth day a 40-man patrol made the summit at 10:35. There they planted a small Stars and Stripes, but a symbolic flag raising occurred three hours later, when it was decided to send up another flag large enough to be seen all over the island. An Associated Press photographer, Joe Rosenthal, took the famous picture of this ceremony which was one of the outstanding pictures of the war.

Simultaneously with the assault on Suribachi, the drive to the north was also begun. There the Marines were facing an outer edge of the deep defense belt where the Japanese had chosen to make their main resistance. In four days of savage fighting, we measured our gains in scant yards. The volume of fire the Japanese were able to deliver was far greater than had ever been encountered before.

On the morning of D plus 5 day, the troops drove

squarely into the main Japanese lines. Using grenades, demo-
litions, flame throwers, bazookas, bayonets, knives, rifle butts
and fists, they surged forward. It was a clean break-through,
but the enemy were still strongly dug in in the hills to the
north.

One hill in particular, called Hill 382, became known as
the "meat grinder." It was the center of desperate fighting
and units reached the summit only to be pinned down and
cut off from support by other prepared positions so disposed
as to subject it to heavy fire from every single angle. The
grim struggle for this hill lasted for a week. Finally on March
4, the Marines gained the summit and stayed there. In this
assault, one Marine company was virtually wiped out.

On other sections of the line, similar fighting was going
on. When one position had been taken with tremendous
casualties, the process had to be repeated for succeeding
advances.

On March 9, our troops finally broke through to Iwo
Jima's northeastern shore. That night, the holed-up Japanese

Bazooka

broke out of their prepared positions in a strong counterattack. By the light of flares hanging over the battlefield they could be seen creeping, running, and dodging forward among bursting shells and heavy machine-gun fire. In hand-to-hand combat, the Marines held their ground. When dawn arrived, the enemy infiltrators were scattered and bogged down in hopeless positions. Although they had penetrated for a depth of nearly a mile, they had accomplished nothing of tactical importance. The rest of the action on the island consisted of mopping up, but that process was more difficult and deadly than it had been anywhere else in the Pacific. Not until March 26 was Iwo Jima declared secured.

The Marines lost 5,324 killed in taking Iwo, and suffered 16,000 wounded. It was the most costly and unattractive piece of real estate in the entire Pacific. Never in history have Americans engaged in more desperate and obstinate fighting.*

While the Marines were engaged in this bitter contest on shore, the Fast Carrier Task Force was maneuvering close to the island and sending in air strikes, bombing, rocketing and strafing assigned targets to assist the ground troops. With no air opposition and little flak, it was a matter of trying to get at the well-protected Japanese in their caves. Occasional strikes were sent to bomb the neighboring islands of Chichi Jima and Haha Jima, where there were small airfields from which the enemy might operate. At night, hostile planes would appear in the area, probably having come down from Tokyo. Evasive maneuvers, night fighters, and antiaircraft fire prevented them from accomplishing any damage to the ships of Task Force 58, but the *Saratoga* and the smaller carriers assigned to the amphibious forces were not so fortunate. About 7:45 P.M. on February 21, the *Lunga Point* was hit by a suicide torpedo bomber which exploded just prior to impact, skidded across the flight deck, and plunged into the sea on the opposite side. In spite of the resulting fire, she was able to continue operations on schedule the next morning.

About five minutes after the *Lunga Point* was hit, a suicide plane crashed into the *Bismarck Sea* near her after elevator, and almost immediately afterward another dived into the deck just forward of the elevator. Huge fires ensued, and explosion after explosion followed as the flames set off her

---

*For the full account of this great battle, read *Iwo Jima* by Richard Newcomb in THE BANTAM WAR BOOK SERIES.

antiaircraft ammunition. Then two large explosions occurred deep within the ship. Wrapped in flames, she was ordered abandoned and sank two hours later.

The *Saratoga* was operating as a night carrier, furnishing night fighters for interception of enemy planes appearing in the area. Just at dusk, she was attacked by a group of *kamikazes*. Four of them smashed into her flight deck and a fifth exploded against her hull. Burning planes littered the deck and there were 110 killed and 180 wounded. Heavily damaged, the veteran carrier had to be sent back to the United States for repairs.

In an attempt to disrupt the Japanese air attacks coming from Tokyo, Task Force 58 struck another blow at the enemy capital on February 25, in coordination with more than 200 B-29's from Saipan. Despite unfavorable weather, both in the vicinity of the Task Force and over the target, with visibility from medium to poor, planes took off the pitching flight decks on their mission. The enemy opposition was only halfhearted and Japanese planes which were not shot down seemed glad to withdraw from the scene of hostilities as swiftly and unceremoniously as possible. Even here, over their own capital, the enemy were notably inferior to our naval aviators in aggressiveness, tactics, and determination.

Notwithstanding the severe antiaircraft fire over the metropolitan area, the Ota and Koisumi aircraft plants were heavily damaged and radar factories, aircraft hangars, and two trains were wrecked. At least 158 enemy planes were destroyed and five small vessels sunk. We lost nine fighter planes in combat over the targets, but it was remarkable that no enemy planes came out to attack our task force at sea. This attack on Tokyo by carrier planes was coordinated for the first time with a group of over 200 B-29's of the 20th Air Force from Saipan.

Heavy seas the following day necessitated cancellation of a projected strike on Nagoya and the force withdrew to rendezvous with the tankers for fueling.

On March 1, the task force made a strike on Okinawa and at the same time took additional photographs for the coming assault on that island. The planes accomplished their usual pattern of devastation, which was now almost routine. No enemy aircraft interfered with them as one destroyer was hit in Naha Harbor and left smoking, and many small craft were destroyed or damaged. Numerous planes were strafed and burned on the ground, and the photo-mapping mission was successfully completed.

One plane from the *Bunker Hill*, Lieut. A.C. Simkuna, U.S.M.C. pilot, was shot up by antiaircraft fire and was forced down about five miles offshore. Two seaplanes from the *South Dakota*, escorted by two fighters from the *Essex*, were immediately dispatched to the rescue. Our control of the air was demonstrated when these planes landed on the water within a few miles of the enemy shore, picked up Lieutenant Simkuna and returned him to his ship in good condition the same day. This kind of teamwork played a large part in maintaining the wonderful morale of our aviators.

Following this mission, the task force returned to Ulithi for rest, relaxation and replenishment. Although the organized resistance on Iwo Jima did not end until March 25, Airfield No. 1 came into use by our light planes on March 1, and a B-29 in a strike against Tokyo made a successful forced landing there on March 3. By March 6, fighter planes began to be based on Iwo Jima, and three days later they relieved the carrier aircraft of close support of the troops. Airfield No. 2 became operational on March 16.

The jeep carriers which had been giving close support to the assault troops flew over 8,800 sorties between February 16 and March 11. They received high commendation for their destruction of enemy coast defense, antiaircraft and machine-gun positions, mortars, rocket launchers, tanks, pillboxes, supplies and troop concentrations. In addition, they conducted hunter-killer attacks on enemy submarines and were credited with one possible sinking and damage to three other submersibles.

The importance of Iwo Jima in the Pacific war was not reflected by its small size and forbidding terrain. It gave us an air base only 660 miles from Tokyo and enabled the air attacks by the Marianas-based B-29's to be materially intensified. Our possession of it lifted the morale of the B-29 crews and saved the lives of many men who would have been shot down over Japan had there been no fighter cover, or lost at sea had Iwo Jima not been available for emergency landings. The lives saved in the next few months through these factors alone exceeded the number lost in the capture itself.

Fleet Admiral Ernest J. King has stated that American history offers no finer example of courage, ardor and efficiency than that of our gallant Marines and the supporting naval units in this exceptionally difficult enterprise. It was a striking illustration of effective teamwork among our land, sea and air forces. The way was now set for our assault on Okinawa.

18

OKINAWA AND THE FLEET THAT CAME TO STAY

With the fall of Iwo Jima, and with the Philippines campaign approaching its end, the time had come for the seizure of a base close to the Japanese homeland. This was considered essential before an attack on the main islands could be undertaken.

Okinawa, lying at the southern end of the Nansei Shoto, was selected by Admiral Nimitz as the most desirable location for this base. This long, narrow island of the Ryukyu group, southwest of Japan, lies in a latitude just outside of the tropics. About 500 square miles in area, it is 70 miles long and five to seven miles wide. Its terrain contains many hills but also plenty of level space for airfields. The climate is generally pleasant, although the island is known as the "typhoon crossroads." Most of the typhoons which traverse the western Pacific pass either directly over it or close by. On the east coast, however, is a large harbor suitable for the anchorage of hundreds of ships. This haven was called Nakagusuku Wan by the Japanese, but soon after we took the island, it was renamed Buckner Bay in honor of Lieutenant General Simon Bolivar Buckner, Commander of the Tenth Army, who was killed in the final phases of the campaign.

The capture of Okinawa was to be the largest amphibious operation yet undertaken in the Pacific. Although the Normandy landing in the Atlantic exceeded it in size, it could not compare with it from the standpoint of the length of the communication lines or the logistic problems involved. Okinawa contained five airfields and was defended by approximately 140,000 Japanese, well armed and well equipped. Its capture would require the participation of more than 548,000 men of

the Army, Navy and Marine Corps, and the naval forces
employed would amount to 318 combatant vessels and 1,139
auxiliary ships, exclusive of landing craft.

Only 350 miles frgm Kyushu, southernmost of the main
Japanese islands, Okinawa supported a civilian population of
about 445,000, most of them belonging to a primitive people,
neither Chinese or Japanese, who had inhabited the island
prior to Japanese occupation. The Okinawans were simple in
nature, far from warlike, and not particularly devoted to their
Japanese rulers. The Japanese looked down upon them as an
inferior race, but they were valuable to their alien masters as
laborers and tillers of the soil. When I visited the island, I
was impressed with its delightful climate, the beautiful scenery of its rolling hills, the abundance of trees, and the
friendliness of the natives. However, many of the evergreen
trees were dwarfed and distorted in their growth, showing
the effect of the tremendous typhoon winds. It was a matter
of comment that nature in Okinawa was something like the
Japanese militarist mentality, stunted and twisted in its
development.

The operations for the capture of Okinawa, which went
on simultaneously with the latter part of the occupation of the
Philippines, were under the jurisdiction of Admiral Nimitz,
who assigned the command to Admiral Spruance, Commander of the Fifth Fleet. The Joint Expeditionary Force, consisting
of the Amphibious Forces and all elements directly engaged
in the landings, was under Vice-Admiral (later Admiral)
Richmond K. Turner. General Buckner's expeditionary troops
were organized as the Tenth Army, and comprised two corps:
the III Amphibious Corps, under Major General Roy S.
Geiger, USMC, composed of the First and Sixth Marine
Divisions; and the XXIV Army Corps under Lieutenant General John R. Hodge, USA, which included the Seventh and
Ninety-sixth Infantry Divisions. The 27th and 77th Infantry
Divisions functioned later as components of the XXIV Corps
but did not participate in the opening phases of the campaign. The Fast Carrier Force under Admiral Mitscher was
assigned the task of supporting the operation and furnishing
air support for the landings as well as for the subsequent
fighting on shore. In addition, there was a British carrier
force, Vice-Admiral H.B. Rawlings, RN; a Logistics Supply
Group, under Rear Admiral D.B. Beary, consisting of tankers
and cargo vessels which serviced the fleet close to the combat

area; an Amphibious Support Force, under Rear Admiral (now Admiral) W.H.P. Blandy, comprising escort carriers, minesweepers, underwater demolition teams, and the gunnery ships assigned to bombardment missions; and the Gunfire and Covering Force, under Rear Admiral M. L. Deyo, consisting of the old battleships and other gunnery vessels.

Prior to the main landing, the islands of the Kerama Retto group, 20 miles to the southwest, were seized in order to establish there a supply and repair base for the hundreds of small craft used in the campaign, and for seaplane operations. In addition, the small island of Keise Shima, about 10 miles from the landing beaches and only five and a half miles from Naha, capital city of Okinawa, was to be occupied. On this spot, Army artillery could be placed to command the entire southern end of the larger island. The whole preliminary operation embraced mine-sweeping on a scale never before undertaken; the clearing of obstructions in the shallow water off the landing beaches by those men of iron nerves, the underwater demolition teams; and intensive bombardment of the enemy's shore defenses by air and naval forces.

The magnitude of this amphibious assault is shown by the fact that cargo and troops were loaded and embarked in ships on the west coast of the United States, in the Hawaiian Islands, the Southwestern Pacific, the Marshalls, the Carolines and Leyte. After loading, the huge force assembled at Ulithi, Guadalcanal, Saipan and Leyte, where they rehearsed their various roles. They sailed for their objectives in more than 1,200 ships, and arrived off Okinawa without interference from the enemy.

On March 26, 1945, when Kerama Retto and Keise Shima were occupied, nets were immediately laid to protect the anchorages against hostile submarines; the seaplane base was established; and tankers, ammunition ships and repair vessels were brought into the harbor to begin their work of supplying and repairing ships engaged in the occupation. Due to the hundreds of *kamikaze* attacks which soon developed, this base played an important part in maintaining our forces thousands of miles from their home ports.

At 8:30 on the morning of April 1, 1945, after seven days of intense ship and air bombardment, the assault waves of the Tenth Army left their line of departure and through a smoke screen swarmed across the reef in Amphtracks, the unique water and land craft developed especially for such amphibious operations. They landed on the beach just south of Yontan Airfield, located about halfway up the western coast. Strong resistance had been expected, but strange to say, no serious opposition developed either during the landing or immediately afterward. By 12:30, both Yontan and Kadena Airfields had been captured with only light losses, the former almost intact, with many operational enemy planes still on its runways or in its revetments. Before dark, approximately 50,000 troops were on shore and had gained a beachhead 4,000 to 5,000 yards in depth.

The ease with which the initial landing had been accomplished was astonishing. It gave no indication of the tough, bitter fighting which was to develop later. The Japanese had learned much from our previous assaults; on this island, there would be little tactical blundering, no expenditure of their strength in useless missions, and none of the unnecessary dying-for-the-sake-of-dying which had marked so many of their previous campaigns. Before Okinawa was ours, our troops were to experience many weeks of deadly combat.

Although the Japanese had not planned to defend Yontan Airfield, they had intended to destroy the planes and make the field unserviceable. This task had been assigned to a special unit composed of second-rate troops and Okinawa conscripts, but they had proved so low in morale, and were so inadequately armed, that under the pre-landing bombardment, they had taken hastily to their heels without remaining to accomplish their work of destruction. This was a lucky break.

It was soon found that the Japanese had withdrawn most of their forces into the southernmost part of the island and had established their defenses in great depth on terrain admirably suited for the purpose. Here they had constructed blockhouses, pillboxes and caves, all strongly protected by barbed wire and minefields in great profusion. They took every advantage of the ground and were unsparing in their use of artillery.

Four divisions of our troops had landed abreast on the beaches on the western side of the island, just south of the narrow Isikawa Isthmus. They proceeded rapidly across the island to the east shore, and on April 4 the entire Yontan-Kadena segment was in our possession. The plan was for the

XXIV Corps to seize all of the island to the south and the Marine III Amphibious Corps, all the territory to the north.

The Marines pushed rapidly northward, not pausing to mop up the isolated enemy groups ensconced in caves or other places of concealment. Leaving these nests to their reserves, they pressed on and by April 8 had passed the neck of the rugged Motobu Peninsula. One regiment was deployed across the base of this peninsula to seal it off from the rest of the island. Other columns continued their advance against increasingly difficult terrain. The action then developed into a slow, deadly slugging match. Finally, a break-through on the western sector was achieved on April 17, and after that it became a matter of mopping up isolated groups of the enemy.

Motobu Peninsula, which had been sealed off, was secured by April 22, when all organized resistance in the northern two-thirds of the island ceased. Its reduction was a story of ousting the enemy with rifles, hand grenades and flame throwers. Many enemy detachments were burned out or sealed underground by closing the entrances of the caves.

Three and one half miles west of Motubu lay the island of Ie Shima, about seven square miles in area and containing a large airfield. It was garrisoned by a Japanese battalion. Ie Shima would be a valuable fighter base for intercepting the many enemy planes coming down from Japan to attack our ships. Accordingly, on April 16, the 77th Division made a landing on the western end of the island, which was secured on the 21st against spotty resistance. During these operations, the famous war correspondent, Ernie Pyle, was killed by an enemy shell. He was buried there by the soldiers who loved him so well.

In the Army advance to the south, the troops encountered the main strength of the enemy defense. Between April 4 and May 26, an advance of only about four miles was made. On April 11 our forces took a heavy pounding from the greatest and best coordinated concentration of Japanese artillery yet encountered in the Pacific. Two additional airfields had been taken, Yonabaru on the east and Machinato on the west, but there were no signs that the Japanese resistance was weakening. By this time, the troops were badly in need of rest and on April 30, the First Marine Division relieved the 27th Division. At the same time, the 77th Division, from Ie Shima, relieved the 96th Division in the center. It was apparent, however, that the entire line needed strengthening. The whole western sector was reassigned on May 7 to the Marine III Amphibious Corps, which had completed its conquest of the northern part of the island on April 27. This left the XXIV Corps of the Army concentrated on the eastern end of the line.

The hard core of the Japanese defenses extended in an arc across the usually pleasant Okinawa hills from Naha, on the west coast, through ancient Shuri to the village of Yonabaru on the east. In front of them were strong outlying positions about two miles in depth, which were manned solidly by dug-in Japanese. In two weeks of slow, bitterly contested action, every ridge and hill, every cave and pillbox, had to be taken by assault.

During this period, planes of my task group were called upon for an operation which illustrates the difficulty of the fighting on shore. Army troops were being held up by a cave on the reverse slope of a hill whose summit was occupied by our troops. Our lines were only 50 yards from the cave, but it was impossible to seal it off or hurl hand grenades into it from the top. Attempts to take it by assault had resulted in some 300 casualties. In this dilemma, the sector commander asked our planes to land a bomb in the entrance of the cave with our troops only 50 yards away.

The pilots assigned this mission landed at Yontan Airfield for special briefing and to examine photographs of the locality. The Army was willing to accept the hazard of our bombs landing within their lines, for even if that happened, their casualties would be fewer than those they had suffered in vainly assaulting the position frontally.

After a rehearsal run, the bombers dived and released their bombs at hardly more than hilltop altitude. The mouth of the cave was covered with bursts and our troops on the summit promptly scrambled down the hillside as the planes left the area. Radio reports from the ground officers stated that the accuracy of the bombing had been striking. Only one bomb had dropped within our lines, and fortunately it was a dud. The position which had held up the advance for days was taken with scarcely a casualty. The Army commander reported that the planes had given him the "acme" of ground support.

The relentless pressure of our troops was gradually wear-

ing down the Japanese morale. The enemy were physically
weary and could look for neither relief nor rest periods. Our
forces advanced until all of the town of Shuri was in our hands
except the ancient castle, with its rugged masonry walls, on
the crest of the hill. Unexpectedly discovering an open
approach, the Marines overcame the weakened defenders
and, on May 29, hoisted the flag over that formidable citadel.
Its capture ended the most bitter and protracted fighting of
the land campaign.

With the collapse of the Naha-Shuri-Yonabaru line, the
enemy's resistance crumbled in the central eastern portion of
the defenses and the American troops, hampered by mud and
by cold, driving rain, advanced against scattered snipers.
Embarked in landing craft at Naha, elements of the Sixth
Marine Division proceeded along the coast and landed behind the enemy on the outer end of Oroku Peninsula. By
nightfall of June 4, most of Naha Airfield was in our hands.

The main advance down the center of the island, on June
9, met a new line of resistance. On Kunisi Ridge, stretching
almost completely across the southern end of the island, the
Japanese had prepared for their last stand a second defensive
position almost as formidable as the previous one. It consisted
of entrenchments on the ridge, which were further protected
by the river flowing along its base.

The attack on this new position started on June 18. The
Marines on the right made a good advance against weakening
enemy resistance. The Army units on the left, however,
found progress slower.

General Buckner took this occasion to visit the front to
observe conditions. He was visiting a command post on a hill
which afforded an excellent view of the forward lines. Although the Japanese artillery had been quiescent and no
shells had fallen on the position all morning, a single gun
opened up with a few rounds. The first shell killed General
Buckner, leaving others in the vicinity untouched. Upon his
death, the late Lieutenant General Roy S. Geiger, of the
Marines, succeeded to the command of the expeditionary
troops. This was by far the largest combined force of Army
and Marine units ever commanded by a Marine. Geiger was
an outstanding aviator, equally at home commanding air or
ground forces. He had followed General A.A. Vandergrift in
command of the I Marine Amphibious Corps in the Solomons

on November 10, 1943, and had been in command at the capture of Guam. Geiger was later relieved by General Joseph W. Stilwell.

By dark on June 21, the Army and Marine units, in hand-to-hand fighting, assisted by flame throwers and tanks, wiped out the last organized Japanese in their caves and fox holes, and organized resistance on the island was declared to have ended. The campaign had lasted 82 days.

While the fighting on land was going on, the Navy was conducting an operation of unparalleled magnitude at sea. It was our job to protect the thousands of ships of the invasion forces against air attack originating in the home islands of Japan, as well as to furnish direct air support to the troops on shore.

Both the fast carriers and the escort carriers participated in this assignment. In accomplishing its mission, the American fleet was to suffer the heaviest punishment it had ever taken. The fast carriers, stationed just east of Okinawa, made frequent devastating strikes on Kyushu and on islands between Kyushu and Okinawa. The jeep carriers assisted in giving air support to the troops and made strikes on the islands to the south, toward Formosa. With most of their fleet immobilized, the Japanese centered their efforts in *kamikaze* attacks on the armada of shipping concentrated in the invasion area. They hoped to use their remaining planes, which still numbered in the thousands, to wipe out our ships, leaving the troops on shore marooned without supplies.

We had experienced Japanese suicide attacks before, but they had never approached in magnitude the effort put out in defense of Okinawa. Many of the enemy pilots had little experience, but the planes came down incessantly, day after day. No coordination was evident as each plane individually sought to crash itself with its lethal cargo against an American ship. Inexperienced in navigation, the pilots generally followed the chain of islands as landmarks to reach Okinawa. Fortunately the fast carriers were approximately 60 miles off this track. Nevertheless, hardly a day passed without their being subjected to numerous attacks by *kamikazes* as well as by aircraft using conventional methods.

The Fast Carrier Task Force was now divided into four main groups commanded by Rear Admirals J.J. Clark, R.E. Davison, A. W. Radford, and myself. There was also a fifth group, equipped exclusively with night fighters and night torpedo planes, under Rear Admiral M.B. Gardner. This detachment included only one carrier, the *Enterprise*, which at this time furnished the planes for night operations. The carriers employed in day operations included the *Hornet*, *Bennington*, *Wasp*, *Franklin*, *Hancock*, *Essex*, *Bunker Hill*, *Yorktown* and *Intrepid*, in addition to the light carriers *Belleau Wood*, *San Jacinto*, *Bataan*, *Cabot*, *Independence* and *Langley*. Included in the carrier task force were eight fast battleships, the two new cruisers *Hawaii* and *Guam*, 14 other heavy and light cruisers, and 64 destroyers.

The Okinawa campaign was inaugurated by a fast carrier strike on the Kyushu-Inland Sea area on March 18 and 19. Detected by Japanese snooper planes during its approach, the task force had to fight off a large predawn air attack in which the *Intrepid* and *Enterprise* received bomb hits but suffered only minor damage and continued to operate.

Approximately 45 airfields were involved, many of which were found to be covered with planes. Although the Japanese lacked trained aviators, they had no shortage of aircraft. Scores of fighters were in the air when our planes arrived. The intense air opposition produced many sharp aerial engagements, but our bombing and strafing attacks reduced to ashes virtually all the buildings on the airfields and damaged or destroyed 275 planes on the ground. Our fighters shot down 102 enemy planes on the first day.

Photographs taken on the 18th revealed many enemy combatant ships concentrated at Kure and Kobe, naval bases on the Inland Sea. We did not know it at the time, but many of the vessels were inoperative and had sought refuge in those waters after the Second Battle of the Philippine Sea. Admiral Mitscher decided to send our strikes on the second day against these ships instead of continuing to hit the already seriously crippled airfields. Again the planes thundered down the carrier flight decks for the second day of attacks. Murderous antiaircraft fire was encountered, but an enemy battleship, a hybrid battleship-carrier, five carriers, a heavy cruiser and a light cruiser were all hit and severely damaged. Although many of them were probably unfit for sea, these attacks were insurance against any further activity by the Japanese fleet.

While the attacks were going on, numerous enemy planes appeared over the task force and attempted to retaliate against our carriers. Our combat air patrols and antiaircraft guns downed many of them, but my flagship, the *Essex*, was narrowly missed twice by dive bombers. One plane barely cleared the flight deck and splashed close aboard on the port bow while the other, hit by flak in its dive, landed close on the port beam a half hour later.

Other carriers were not so fortunate. The *Yorktown* sustained minor damage from glancing bomb hits, the *Wasp* received a direct hit, the *Enterprise* took a bomb in her forward elevator, and the *Franklin* received two bombs squarely on her flight deck which started a series of devastating explosions and fires. The *Yorktown*, *Enterprise*, and *Wasp* were able to continue in action, but the *Franklin* was grievously crippled. Burning furiously, thousands of gallons of aviation gasoline gushed from ruptured supply lines. Planes on both hangar and flight decks caught fire and their exploding bombs, rockets and machine-gun ammunition added to the uproar. Admiral Davison, whose flag was on board, transferred to another carrier to direct his task group. Captain Leslie E. Gehres, commander of the *Franklin*, was determined to save his ship and refused to give up. For three hours, the violent explosions continued, with the ship dead in the water and unable to steam. Finally, late in the day, the explosions became less frequent and the cruiser *Pittsburgh* took the carrier in tow. During the night, the fires burned themselves out and the engineers were able to go below and restart the engines. The *Franklin* ultimately returned to the Brooklyn Navy Yard for a major repair job. Of her crew of approximately 3,000 officers and men, 832 had been killed and 270 wounded. Her return to port under her own power was an exploit that testified to her crew's determination, stamina and courage.

In addition to the enemy ships damaged at Kure and Kobe, the second day's strikes destroyed 97 more planes in the air and 225 on the ground. The task force then retired to rendezvous with the tankers for fuel. While we were withdrawing, a large group of bogeys was detected about 100 miles away. Extra fighters were scrambled, and within a few minutes 150 Hellcats were in the air and away to intercept them. They found 32 two-engined Bettys and 16 single-engined fighters. In a short wild melee, all the Japanese planes were shot down, with the loss of only two of our Hellcats. Underneath the fuselage of each enemy bomber, our fliers noticed a small, peculiar pair of wings. These were subsequently discovered to be rocket-propelled flying bombs, each manned by a suicide pilot. They were intended to be launched from their mother plane close to their targets, and it was estimated that they could attain a speed of over 500 miles an hour. Our boys called these new weapons *"baka"* bombs, from the Japanese word for "fool." Although the enemy failed to launch any of them in this attack, ships in the Okinawa area were hit later by similar missiles. On the whole, however, they achieved no great success.

On March 23 and 24, the task force returned to Okinawa for the pre-invasion attacks and for late photographic coverage of the landing beaches for the invasion forces, then under way for their initial landing.

My task group, with that of Admiral Radford, returned to Kyushu on March 29 for another strike on the enemy fleet units previously sighted in those waters. Our search planes were unable to locate the ships under their camouflage, and the bombs were dropped on airfields along the coast. The destruction of warehouses, hangars, barracks and grounded airplanes was getting to be a familiar story. In addition, numerous small ships, fishing boats and sampans were sunk.

Mitsubishi G4M2 and Baka Rocket Bomb

During these operations, Lieut. (j.g.) Ronald Lee Somerville, a dive-bomber pilot from the *Hancock*, made a forced landing in Kagoshima Bay as a result of an operational accident. His position was hazardous. He was in the middle of the bay, 15 miles from its mouth, with many enemy airfields only a short distance away. Two seaplanes were immediately catapulted from the *Astoria* and dispatched to his rescue with an escort of 24 fighters. On the way in, the group was intercepted by a squadron of aggressive Japanese fighters and a vicious aerial fight followed. Five enemy fighters were splashed, and when the battle ended the air had been cleared of all opposition. One of our fighter pilots, Ensign David Kelleher, from the *Cabot*, was shot down but was able to parachute and was in the water near Somerville. The two seaplanes swooped into the bay, landed, and picked up both men not more than two miles off the beach of a major enemy airfield. Upon taking them aboard, they gunned their engines and took off under the protection of our fighters. Within an hour they had returned the two downed pilots to their ships.

During the day the force was under almost continuous attack by enemy planes, but so tight was our fighter defense that only one was able to get through. It dropped a bomb at the *Cabot*, but missed, and the plane was shot down on its way out. Many other enemy planes were splashed by our fighters before reaching bombing positions.

The enemy's all-out air effort began on April 5 and was coordinated with a major counterattack by their ground forces on Okinawa. The air battles reached their highest intensity on April 6. That day ships and planes of my task group alone destroyed 105 air-borne enemy planes and an additional 17 on the ground.

In the late afternoon of the 6th, a message from two of our submarines stated that they had sighted Japanese fleet units, including at least one battleship, heading south for Okinawa along the east coast of Kyushu. All other missions were halted while our search planes went out next morning to verify this contact. If the report was correct, it would mean another chance at the surface ships of the dwindling Japanese Navy. At 8:15 A.M., we were thrilled by a flash from our search planes that they had sighted an enemy force consisting of a large battleship, one or two cruisers, and seven or eight destroyers. The battleship was the gigantic *Yamato*, sister ship of the *Musashi*, which had been sunk by our planes a little over four months before in the Sibuyan Sea. The *Yamato* was bound for one last suicide effort against our forces off Okinawa.

The weather in the vicinity of the *Yamato* was poor, with ceiling at 3,000 feet, visibility five to eight miles, and occasional rain squalls. Nevertheless, the search planes remained in contact and kept us continuously informed of her position, course and speed. Mitscher directed my group and Clark's to make coordinated attacks, to be followed one hour later by one from Radford's group. Armed with heavy bombs and torpedoes, the planes took off.

Just after noon they arrived at the scene of action. The weather had worsened, but regardless of the heavy, recurrent rain squalls, they concentrated their attacks on the huge battleship.

Vice-Admiral Ito of the Imperial Japanese Navy, commander of the enemy force, had his flag aboard the *Yamato*. She was accompanied by the light cruiser *Yahagi* and eight destroyers. With considerable difficulty the Japanese had scraped up the 2,500 tons of fuel oil necessary for this operation. After the war, Admiral Toyoda, their naval Commander in Chief, said that additional units of the Second Fleet had been prevented from participation by lack of fuel. Although they felt there was not a 50-50 chance of success, the enemy commanders reasoned that nothing would be gained by keeping the ships idle in home waters, and that their mission was in keeping with the traditions and honor of the Japanese Navy.

Boring in against a tremendous volume of antiaircraft fire, including projectiles from the mammoth 18.1-inch turret guns of the *Yamato*, the first attacks landed two heavy bombs on the battleship's deck and punctured her port side with one torpedo. In addition, the cruiser *Yahagi* was hit and stopped, and the destroyer *Hamakaze* was sunk. Other destroyers were damaged by strafing. About an hour later, the third air group attacked. In a few moments, the *Yamato* was hit by three additional bombs and nine torpedoes. Dead in the water and mortally wounded, the stricken ship blew up, capsized, and sank at 2:23 P.M. She and her sister ship, the *Musashi*, were the largest battleships ever constructed. It was learned after the war that in addition to displacing over 72,000 tons, she had embraced all the latest improvements known to the shipbuilders' art.

The *Yahagi*, repeatedly hit by bombs and torpedoes, sank at 2:05. Three destroyers were also sunk. Only the three surviving destroyers returned to their base at Sasebo. Of a total of 386 aircraft participating in these attacks, our losses were four dive bombers, three torpedo planes and three fighters, all to antiaircraft fire.

This action was one more example of the dominance of air power in fighting at sea, of aircraft sinking a battleship of the most modern type without the help of surface vessels. After the action, our battleships off Okinawa sent us a facetious message, sorrowfully regretting that we had deprived them of a chance for a little target practice.

While our planes were attacking the *Yamato*, enemy aircraft were giving us attention in the launching area. Two suicide planes dived on the *Essex* and were shot down in flames. Another plummeted at the *Hancock* and crashed squarely on her flight deck. Twenty-eight men were killed and 52 wounded, with some 15 missing. The *Hancock* had a 20-foot hole in her flight deck, while her forward elevator was buckled and both catapults were out of commission. These damages prevented further flight operations. Although heavy fires broke out, they were under control in about an hour and the ship was able to land her returning strike planes about 4:15. She remained with the task group temporarily but was sent home for repairs the next morning.

Day after day, we continued our operations off Okinawa, furnishing air patrols over the ground forces and withdrawing about 100 miles to the eastward to refuel from our tankers when necessary. Minor enemy attacks were a matter of daily occurrence, but not until April 11 did large groups again appear. The attack started shortly after noon. By 2:35, the air was full of antiaircraft fire and enemy planes were being splashed right and left. The destroyer *Kidd*, in a radar patrol line about 40 miles from the task force, was hard hit by a suicide plane. The *Enterprise* had two men blown overboard as the result of a near miss. Soon afterward, a *kamikaze* was splashed just off the starboard bow of the *Essex*. Then a bomb landed close aboard her port quarter, shaking the ship as violently as if she had struck a mine. At 3:15, the destroyer *Bullard*, also on picket duty, was hit by a suicide plane. At

3:30, the *Enterprise* received another near miss. Attacks continued until well after dark. We destroyed 11 enemy planes by ships' gunfire alone during the day.

On Friday, April 13, we received word of the death of President Franklin D. Roosevelt. In the midst of the fighting, we were unable to spend much time considering what effect this tragic event would have on the war.

Another big day was April 16. We sent fighter sweeps north to Kanoya, where 30 enemy planes were shot down. In addition, six bogeys were destroyed in the vicinity of the force. One came in from the direction of the sunset and was shot down just off the *Bunker Hill*. The *Intrepid* was hit and damaged again by a *kamikaze*.

Our daily routine followed very much the same pattern. Each night small groups of enemy planes appeared on our radar screen and endeavored to penetrate our defenses. Night fighters were launched to intercept them. Usually the attackers were shot down before they got within 30 miles of our disposition. Those that evaded the night fighters were bagged by the antiaircraft fire.

By day, larger groups of enemy planes approached and were intercepted by our fighters. Individual planes continued poorly coordinated attempts to make suicide crashes against our carriers. My log of the time contains numerous entries such as "Bomb missed the *Bunker Hill*, going into the water astern of her," "Suicide plane shot down by ship's gunfire," "Enemy plane narrowly missed *Bataan*, diving low over flight deck and plunging into water close aboard on her port beam."

Each day our planes carried out their patrols over the ground forces fighting on Okinawa and performed missions assigned by the Air Commander on the island. One of their principal tasks was intercepting and destroying *kamikaze* planes attempting to attack our transports and shipping which thronged the waters off the landing beaches.

The *Bunker Hill* was hit by two *kamikaze* planes on May 11. Somehow they had managed to escape our radar detection and were first sighted diving on the veteran carrier at 10:12 A.M. Heavy fires raged on board for over four hours before they were finally brought under control. It was a sad occasion when we had to detach this carrier and send her home for repairs. She had been the flagship of Admiral Mitscher, who was transferred by destroyer from the *Bunker Hill* to the *Enterprise*.

On May 13 and 14, my task group, together with that of Rear Admiral Clark, made another strike, our third, on the Kyushu airfields. Despite the many devastating attacks on their bases, the Japanese somehow were able to continue sending planes on their desperate missions. By 10:30 A.M. on the 13th, a total of 20 enemy planes had been shot down within or near our disposition. During these two days off Kyushu, 118 enemy planes were destroyed and 11,000 tons of enemy shipping sunk or damaged.

On May 11 the *Enterprise* was again hit by a suicide plane. This time she was damaged so badly that she in turn had to go back for repairs. Thirteen of her planes were destroyed by the explosion and resulting fire, and 13 men were killed and 32 wounded. The fires were soon extinguished, but the carrier could no longer operate her planes. Once more Mitscher had to transfer with his staff to another ship, this time to the *Randolph*.

Halsey relieved Spruance on May 28 as Fleet Commander, and about the same time, McCain relieved Mitscher. Task Force 58 then again became Task Force 38. On May 28, my task group was directed to proceed to Leyte Gulf for rest and relaxation. We arrived there holding a new Navy record of 79 days at sea, during 52 of which we had engaged in combat with the enemy. It had been a period of intense strain and the *kamikaze* planes which were continuously in our midst had made the assignment a tough one.

During the Okinawa campaign, the British carrier force, consisting of four carriers, two battleships, four light cruisers and 11 destroyers, had been stationed south of Okinawa to support the operation by sending air strikes against the Japanese air bases in Sakashima Gunto and Formosa. This British force operated from March 26 to April 20, and again from May 3 to May 25. During its absence, our jeep carriers took over its combat assignments. It was not equipped to stay at sea as long as the American forces and had to withdraw more frequently to replenish supplies, which were usually obtained at Manus. Although all the British carriers were hit by suicide planes, thanks to their armored flight decks none was put out of action.

Another sweep was made over the Kyushu bases on June 2 and 3, but there were few enemy planes either in the air or on the ground. On June 8, Kanoya Airfield, the enemy's principal Kyushu base, was hit again, but only a small flight of enemy planes took off to contest our control of the air. They were soon shot down, and the Japanese ability to strike in force from his Kyushu bases appeared to be definitely ended.

The major *kamikaze* attacks were made on our forces off Okinawa during the period April 6 to June 22. The total suicide sorties by the enemy amounted to 1,900, while planes using orthodox methods of attack made many more, Japanese naval aircraft alone reporting 3,700 sorties of the regular kind.

Admiral Halsey recommended about that time that Marine Air Group 14, stationed in the Philippines, be brought forward to operate from our Okinawa air bases and take over with the Army Air Force whatever air-support missions were still required. Upon its arrival, the entire Fast Carrier Task Force was withdrawn to Leyte Gulf to prepare for the next operation.

For nearly three months, the fast carriers had operated in and near the Okinawa area, supporting the ground forces engaged in the occupation of this important base. Ashore, the American losses were 7,213 killed and missing and 31,081 wounded. Afloat the cost was also high: 4,907 killed and missing, 4,824 wounded. During the course of the campaign, 36 of our vessels had been sunk and 368 damaged, most of them as a result of air action.

Twelve of our destroyers had been sunk; and major repairs were required by 10 battleships, 13 carriers, five cruisers, and 67 destroyers. Our air losses amounted to 763 planes. The fact that we could take these losses without their affecting the continuance of our oparations indicates the enormous size to which our naval forces had grown.

The cost to the Japanese was greater still. On Okinawa, approximately 131,000 men were killed and 7,400 captured. At sea, 16 of their combatant ships had been sunk and four damaged; and in the air and on the ground more than 7,800 enemy aircraft had been destroyed.

By the conquest of Okinawa, the American forces had acquired a major base, with numerous airfield sites and fleet anchorages, within 350 miles of the southern main island of Japan. A tremendous program of development, involving enlargement and new construction of air, ground and naval facilities, was immediately undertaken preparatory to the projected invasion of Japan itself.

The supremacy of carriers in control of the sea had

previously been shown in actions between ships. At Okinawa, they proved their ability to stand up against landbased aircraft and to maintain that control up to the enemy shores. When they took their stations in the limited waters around the Japanese islands, it was no sneak attack, no hit-and-run affair. Their presence was no secret, and they invited the enemy's air force to come and attack them. They took everything a major air power could throw at them and still retained control of the air. They were the fleet that came to stay.

19

BOMBING JAPAN

At Leyte Gulf, I was notified that I was to relieve Admiral Mitscher as Commander of the Fast Carrier Task Force. With mixed feelings, I turned over the command of Task Group 38.3 to Rear Admiral G. F. Bogan, on the *Essex*, my flagship in so many engagements, and took a plane from our new Naval Air Station at Samar for 30 days' leave at home. I spent a night as the house guest of Admiral Nimitz at Guam. Then I continued via Kwajalein, Johnson Island, Pearl Harbor and Oakland, arriving back in San Diego on June 22 and later flying to Washington to confer with Fleet Admiral King and Secretary of the Navy James Forrestal.

It was apparent that the war was in its final stages. Admiral Nimitz informed me during my conference at Guam that our next objective was to be the Japanese main island of Kyushu. The job of the fast carriers in this operation would be the same as at Okinawa, giving the landing forces air support and protecting our ships against probably stepped-up *kamikaze* attacks.

In the meantime, Admiral Halsey's Third Fleet had gone on the rampage in further strikes on the home islands of Japan, to keep up the pressure while preparations were being made for the invasion scheduled for the following November. With little opposition, Halsey's men raided the coasts of Japan from one end to the other.

Realizing that our next move would be an invasion of their main islands, the Japanese adopted a policy of conserving their strength for this eventuality. They elaborately dispersed and camouflaged their remaining aircraft, making it exceedingly difficult to locate and destroy them on the ground. They canceled all search operations, so that our fast carriers were able to strike wherever and whenever they wished, achieving complete tactical surprise. Supplementing the air strikes, our battleships and cruisers carried out surface bombardment of industrial targets on the eastern coast of Japan, while destroyers conducted antishipping sweeps of coastal waters. The Japanese Navy, as well as their land-based air force, was completely impotent. Our control of the air and sea was supreme, around the shores of Japan as well as over the entire area of the Pacific Ocean.

On July 10, the fast carriers under McCain struck again at airfields and industrial plants in the Tokyo area. Seventy-two enemy planes were destroyed on the ground and damage was inflicted on other targets. Although no attempt was made to conceal the location of the fleet, no planes came out to attack it and few rose to defend the Japanese capital. Halsey then moved his armada farther north for strikes against Hokkaido and northern Honshu.

With monotonous regularity, the planes flew off for their objectives on July 14 and 15. Again extensive damage was inflicted on aircraft and airfield installations. Surface units went in close enough to shore to conduct gunfire bombardments of Kamaishi in northern Honshu and Muroran in Hokkaido. To accomplish the latter, the ships had to approach through an arm of the sea which was landlocked on three sides—a three-hour trip each way, in plain sight of land. Halsey expected that the Japanese would surely use this opportunity for an air attack; but no planes came out. The enemy's only reaction to the surface ships was a desultory antiaircraft fire against their spotting planes.

The carrier aircraft, in these two attacks, destroyed 140 ships and small craft totaling 71,000 tons, shot up 38 planes and wrecked 84 locomotives. In addition, they set on fire and gutted 20 city blocks in the town of Kushiro.

Much of Japan's coal and iron came from mines on Hokkaido, from whence they had to be transferred to the main island of Honshu on train ferries. In their two days' strikes, the planes sank six of these ferries, seriously disrupting the enemy's transport of raw materials to their industrial plants.

On July 18 the carriers made another strike on Tokyo with results similar to the first. Then on the 24th and 25th came a knockout strike on the crippled remnants of the Japanese Navy moored in the Inland Sea around the Kure Naval Base. Whereas the Navy was incapable of operating as a cohesive force, many fleet units were still afloat. In concentrated attacks, our planes inflicted additional damage on 22 naval vessels, including six major ships, totaling 258,000 tons.

The units in the Kure anchorage included the flight-deck battleships *Ise* and *Hyuga* and the regular battleship *Haruna;* the carriers *Amagi, Katsuragi* and *Ryujo;* and the cruisers *Tone, Aoba, Oyodo, Iwate, Izumo* and *Settsu.* In this attack the *Ise* received ten direct hits and many near misses; her commanding officer and all personnel in the vicinity of the bridge were killed, and she settled by the bow and took considerable water. The *Hyuga* also took ten direct hits and was so badly flooded that she grounded shortly after the attack. The battleship *Haruna* received such severe damage that she filled with water and settled on the bottom. The aircraft carrier *Amagi* was hit with both rockets and bombs which caused heavy damage to the flight and hangar decks and flooded one of her engine rooms as well as four boiler rooms. The carrier *Katsuragi* received only one hit but was rendered unfit for aircraft oparations by damage to her flight and hangar decks. The carrier *Ryujo* had been badly damaged in the attack on March 19, and after temporary repairs in the navy yard was moved to a new mooring and cleverly camouflaged. She was not discovered or attacked on July 24. The heavy cruisers *Tone* and *Aoba* were hit by numerous bombs and settled on the bottom. The light cruiser *Oyodo*, flagship of the Commander in Chief of the Combined Fleet, was so severely pounded that she capsized before settling in the mud. Similar fates were dealt out to the old cruisers *Iwate, Izumo* and *Settsu.*

Not satisfied with the destruction inflicted on the 24th, Halsey brought his force back on the 28th to resume the action. "By sunset that evening," he reports in his memoirs, "the Japanese Navy had ceased to exist." Little had been left of the enemy's ships after the previous attacks, but the Americans were determined to destroy the Japanese fleet completely. Halsey gave three reasons: first, for the sake of our national morale, in retaliation for Pearl Harbor; second, on account of the Russians, in case the war continued and we had to establish a supply line to Vladivostok; and, third, to prevent the Japanese from using the existence of part of their fleet as a bargaining point at the peace table.

After the final fast carrier strikes on Kure on July 28, the planes hit Tokyo and Nagoya again on July 30. On August 9 and 10, they again raided Hokkaido and northern Honshu. Tokyo received its last strikes of the war on August 13 and 15. In conjunction with these air attacks, surface ships conducted gun bombardments of coastal targets at Omura, Shiono Misaki, Hamamatsu and Shimizu, all on southern Honshu, and whereas these bombardments by our surface ships inflicted some damage on industrial plants in urban areas, their principal effect was on Japanese morale. They brought home to the Japanese people that the sacred soil of Japan was not immune to our attacks and that, contrary to the statements of their leaders, the war was not going successfully. The aviators who participated in flights over the areas bombarded by surface ships' gunfire felt that the ships' guns accomplished little actual damage, and that the aircraft required to give them cover might better have been employed in direct attacks on the enemy. Nevertheless, they undoubtedly had some effect on morale and encouraged our battleship sailors to feel that they were not merely bystanders.

In addition to the attacks by carrier aircraft, shore-based planes from the Marianas and Okinawa, including Navy patrol planes, as well as B-29's, conducted extensive bombing missions against the Japanese homeland. They accomplished widespread destruction of land targets and burned much of Tokyo, Yokohama, and other cities. However, information obtained from Japan after the war established the fact that the vital destruction of the Japanese fleet was accomplished entirely by carrier planes.

One activity of the B-29's during the last three or four months of the war was the mining of the waters of the Inland Sea and the principal harbors of Japan. The mines dropped were of the so-called "unsweepable" type. They were exploded by the pressure in the water generated by the passage of ships overhead. Shimonoseki Strait, one of the exits of the Inland Sea between Honshu and Kyushu, was so thickly sown with these mines that many ships attempting its passage were sunk and it had to be closed to traffic. The whole Inland Sea was planted with thousands of them. Their removal was a tremendous problem at the end of hostilities.

Working in conjunction with our Third Fleet in its last raids on Japan was the fast carrier force of the British Pacific Fleet, commanded by Vice-Admiral Rawlings. This force consisted of 28 ships: four aircraft carriers, one battleship, six light cruisers and 17 destroyers. Rawlings reported to Halsey and operated in conjunction with him, but retained tactical control of his group. Under this plan, he could not be given direct orders by the American commander, but was informed of Halsey's directions to Task Force 38, which were considered as suggestions to be followed by the British. The agreement originally had provided that the British would take care of their own logistics, but when the need arose, they were fueled from our tankers at the same time as our forces. They participated with our carriers in the strikes on Japan, except for the attack on the Japanese fleet at Kure. Halsey assigned the British an alternate target, Osaka, which offered no warships of primary importance. His motive, he later stated in his book, was to "forestall a possible postwar claim by Britain that she had delivered even a part of the final blow that demolished the Japanese fleet."

The climax of this period of bombing Japan came on August 6. A lone B-29 from Saipan dropped a bomb on Hiroshima, a city on the southern coast of Honshu with a prewar population of over 300,000. It was not an ordinary bomb. American scientists had unlocked the secret of the atom, and for the first time in history, an atomic bomb had been used in warfare. It hit its target with unimaginable force and shocked the world by the awesome power of the atomic fission. Subsequent reconnaissance photos showed that more than four square miles, or 60 per cent of the city's built-up area, had been totally destroyed. Three days later a similar bomb was dropped on the city of Nagasaki.

After the surrender of Japan, I visited both Hiroshima and Nagasaki and inspected the damage inflicted by these bombs. The central part of Hiroshima was a desert of utter destruction. The surface of the ground was a litter of bits of broken glass and minute pieces of metal which covered the area like sand. Not even the former location of streets and buildings could be distinguished. One modern steel and concrete building, near the outer limits of the bomb's destructive power, was still standing, but its windows had all been blasted out and the inside was completely gutted by fire. A three-way concrete bridge which had been the point of aim for the bomb was still intact, but on its surface were printed the blurred outlines of shadows of people and vehicles that had been crossing it at the instant of the explosion. These shadows had been left on the surface, as on a photographic negative, by the radiation rays of the bomb.

The effect produced by the atomic bombs was threefold. First, they created a tremendous pressure or concussion wave which knocked down buildings and other objects as in a normal explosion, but with much greater violence. Second, they sent out an instantaneous heat wave in which temperatures reached thousands of degrees Fahrenheit and caused the spontaneous combustion of inflammable objects. Third, they emitted the deadly gamma rays which caused death by radiation and rendered radioactive materials with which they came in contact. The bomb at Hiroshima is estimated to have killed between 70,000 and 80,000 people outright and to have inflicted terrible injuries on more than 100,000 others.

Destruction in Nagasaki was similar to that in Hiroshima, but here the area under the bomb was cupped in a small valley surrounded by hills. Buildings in this locality were completely destroyed, but the land configuration apparently limited the effect of the bomb's explosion. The casualties, though heavy, were less than in Hiroshima, amounting to about 40,000 killed and 60,000 injured. Buildings on hill-tops away from the center of the explosion were destroyed, whereas similar structures in the valleys, protected by the hills from the direct line to the bomb, remained undamaged.

The profound influence of the atomic bomb on world politics and on the destiny of mankind cannot yet be fully appraised. Many of us who were fighting in the Pacific felt that the use of this terrible weapon was unnecessary. The Japanese at that time were a defeated people, and we had achieved this victory by orthodox methods of warfare. The ability of our naval and air forces to proceed up and down the coast of Japan, attacking at will, was evidence of Japan's helplessness. Unknown to us at the time, moreover, was the fact that Japanese authorities had been attempting for several months to establish a channel of surrender. In my opinion, the status of the war did not justify the use of this incredibly destructive missile. America's moral position in the world today would be better if we had not employed this super-weapon of wholesale destruction.

On the day before the second atomic bomb was dropped on Nagasaki, the Soviet Government declared war on Japan and sent its army across the Siberian border into Manchuria. The Japanese forces there were a mere shell of what they had formerly been. Long since, their best units had been transferred to other areas where they had been shattered by our amphibious forces. The close of the war was fast approaching and the collapse of Japanese resistance was close at hand.

The entry of Russia into the Japanese war was unwelcome to many American fighting men in the Pacific. We had brought Japan to her knees, and American forces had accomplished this result practically singlehanded. We acknowledged the assistance of New Zealand and Australia, and to a lesser extent, of Great Britain, but the control of the Pacific Ocean was won primarily by the United States Navy, and the conquests on the ground had been principally accomplished by American troops. The winning of air control over the Pacific by the Navy's carriers constituted a revolutionary chapter in naval warfare. We resented the entry of Russia, which gave her grounds to claim part of the credit for the defeat of Japan and to demand a seat at the peace table. We considered that she was entitled to neither.

It has been claimed that the dropping of the atomic bomb and Russia's entry into the war hastened the end of hostilities by giving the Japanese leaders the opportunity to surrender unconditionally and still save face, rather than continue a suicidal defense until the last Japanese was killed. But Admiral Toyoda, Commander in Chief of the Japanese fleet, stated afterward: "I do not think it would be accurate to look upon the atomic bomb and the entry and participation of Soviet Russia as direct causes of the termination of the war, but I think that those two factors did enable us to bring the war to a termination without creating too great chaos in Japan."

On August 10, the Japanese, through the Swiss Government, stated that they were willing to accept the Allied surrender ultimatum issued at Potsdam on July 26, provided they could keep their Emperor. On the 11th came the news that Secretary of State James F. Byrnes, speaking for the Allied powers, had accepted the Japanese surrender provided that the Supreme Allied Commander ruled Japan through the authority of the Emperor. Nevertheless, the Third Fleet and Task Force 38 continued their attacks. Negotiations were continuing, but no orders for ceasing hostilities had been issued.

At one o'clock on the morning of August 13, Admiral Halsey received a dispatch from Admiral Nimitz directing him to cancel the day's strikes and to proceed with caution toward Tokyo. It seems that the ends of all wars produce their premature armistice instructions. This first dispatch to cease hostilities was followed shortly by one canceling it. That day a strike on Tokyo was made in which 254 Japanese planes were destroyed on the ground and 19 others shot down near the task force.

On August 14, the task force withdrew to fuel. With all hands tense for further news of the surrender, nothing came through. Plans were therefore made to strike Tokyo again on the 15th. Vice-Admiral McCain signaled his force: "Our orders to strike indicate that the enemy may have dropped an unacceptable joker into the surrender terms. This war could last many months longer. We cannot afford to relax. Now is the time to pour it on. Show this to all pilots."

On the morning of August 15, the first strikes were launched at 4:15 A.M. and hit their targets two hours later. The second wave took off for its mission of destruction and was within five minutes of its objectives when the anticipated message from the Commander in Chief of the Pacific Fleet came through. It said: "Air attack will be suspended. Acknowledge." The planes about to loose their bombs and rockets over the Japanese capital were recalled by radio and those poised on the flight decks were informed that their flights were canceled. It was the long-expected moment, the end of the fighting in the Pacific.

The end of the fighting? Practically, but not quite. The torpedo and bombing planes were stowed below on the hangar decks, but the fighter planes were kept on deck and a strong combat air patrol was maintained overhead. Admiral Halsey ordered the fighters "to investigate and shoot down all snoopers—not vindictively, but in a friendly sort of way." At 10:55 A.M., August 15, 1945, the Third Fleet received the following message from the Commander in Chief at Guam:

"Offensive operations against Japanese forces will cease at once. Continue searches and patrols. Maintain defensive and internal security measures at highest level. Beware of treachery."

It was well that Halsey had taken precautions. Half an hour later, a Japanese bomber was sighted diving on the fleet. It was promptly shot down by a plane of the combat patrol whose pilot reported, "Tallyho, one bandit diving," and shortly afterward, "Splash one Judy." By the end of the day, a total of eight enemy planes attempting to attack the fleet had been shot down. All were endeavoring to hit their targets in the *kamikaze* fashion. They were thought at the time to be individuals who refused to accept the surrender orders. Admiral Halsey stated later that in his opinion they were simply units which had not been informed that the war was over, which was quite possible in view of the chaotic condition of Japan's damaged communications.

Admiral Halsey addressed the assembled ships over the voice radio at one o'clock in the afternoon. As part of his talk, the adored and dynamic leader of the Third Fleet said: "Now

Yokosuka D4Y2, Suisei "Judy"

that the fighting has ended, there must be no letdown. There must be watchful waiting. Victory is not the end, but the beginning. We must establish peace—a firm, a just and enduring peace."

Although the fighting stopped on August 15, the formal surrender was not to come until over two weeks later. In the interval, the Third Fleet organized landing parties of blue-jackets and Marines to take over key positions on shore. The end, when it came, had been so unexpected that no organization had yet been set up to occupy the important ports to be taken over. General MacArthur was appointed Supreme Commander for the Allied Powers in the Pacific, but the troops for the occupation were at Okinawa or the Philippines, and it would take time to get them embarked and transported to Japan.

Another task of the fleet during this period of waiting was the dispatch of relief flights to our prisoners of war. The Japanese were instructed to put up markers at all prisoner camps and to remove all restraint over the Allied personnel confined in them. But this did not provide our men with food, cigarettes or other comforts. Our carrier planes were sent all over Japan as "P.W." signs blossomed out in many different places. Wherever they did, planes were immediately sent to drop medicine, food, candy, cigarettes, toilet articles, etc. Many a pilot had a lump in his throat as he witnessed from the air the joyful demonstrations of the men on the ground as they gathered in the dropped supplies. Many of the prisoners were gaunt and weak from abuse and starvation.

These errands of mercy went on continually until after the occupation landings, when the prisoners could be rescued. Every corner of Japan was searched out to find outlying and hidden camps where our people had been confined. It was a work cheerfully and eagerly undertaken by the carrier pilots, who felt that but for the grace of God, they might have been down there among the prisoners instead of flying the planes overhead.

20

THE SURRENDER AT TOKYO

On August 13, in the closing days of the war, I took a plane to return to the combat area after my visit to the United States. I spent a night at Guam, where Admiral Nimitz told me he had just received a directive from President Truman to occupy the port of Dairen, near the former Japanese base at Port Arthur in southern Manchuria, before the Russians got there. He further commented that this seizure might cause trouble with the Russians. I never heard any more of this project, and presume it was later canceled. In the end, Dairen was occupied by Russia when her troops invaded Manchuria and Northern Korea. It is interesting to speculate on what would have happened had the United States taken this strategic Chinese port ahead of the Russians. It might have changed entirely the situation which developed in China after the war.

After flying to Iwo Jima, where the tragedy of war was brought home by the sight of the Marine cemeteries, with their row after row of white crosses, I embarked on the destroyer *Benham* and the next morning reported to Admiral Halsey off the coast of Japan. I hoisted my flag on the new carrier *Lexington*, named for the ship I had commanded when it was lost in the Battle of the Coral Sea over three years before. The fighting had stopped by this time and we were waiting for the formal surrender and occupation. Bluejacket and Marine landing forces were being organized and assembled on transports and small ships, ready for the moment when they would land and take possession of Japanese ports.

I received the impression, from the orders being issued, that the carriers were going to be kept at sea indefinitely, while the battleships, cruisers, destroyers and other types were immediately to enter Tokyo Bay and other Japanese harbors. I sent a message to Admiral Halsey recommending that all carriers, as soon as conditions permitted, base in Japanese ports for the benefit of the morale of the men who had played such a prominent part in winning the war. I further pointed out that this would ease the problems of logistics and replenishment, and that the show of the carrier force in Japanese waters would be beneficial to the control of the conquered people.

This recommendation was not approved, and the bulk of the aircraft carriers were denied the privilege of entering the enemy harbor with the victorious forces prior to the surrender ceremony.

In the meantime, Japanese emissaries had been flown to Manila to receive instructions in regard to the details of the surrender. The first occupation force was to consist of the Eleventh Airborne Division, which was to be flown in by air transport planes and land at the airfield at Atsugi, near Tokyo. The Navy was to occupy the naval base at Yokosuka, near the entrance to Tokyo Bay. Finally General MacArthur, who had been named Supreme Commander for the Allied Powers, would arrive by plane and proceed to the battleship *Missouri*, at anchor off Yokohama, where the surrender document would be signed. The Navy was also to station a line of destroyers between Manila and Japan to act as guards for the planes flying in the troops.

We went through two moderate typhoons on August 25 and 26 which necessitated postponing the occupation plans for 48 hours. The operation of transporting the Eleventh Airborne Division, it was estimated, would take five or six days, and the ceremony for the official signing of the surrender was set for September 2.

Although Navy planes were engaged in daily flights over Japan on their missions of parachuting supplies for the war prisoners, General MacArthur had issued instructions that they were not to land in Japan except in case of necessity. When the first Army planes landed at Atsugi on August 28, they were surprised to find a large sign painted on the Japanese hangars, "Welcome to the U.S. Army from the Third Fleet." The Navy pilots making "forced" landings had beaten the Army in the race to get into Japan. Later it developed that the Navy boys were making so many landings at Atsugi Airport that orders were issued directing that disciplinary action be taken in cases where investigation disclosed that no real emergency had forced them down. It was stated that Navy planes making "forced" landings were arriving in such numbers as to congest the facilities!

An amusing incident occurred on August 29—a squabble over receiving the surrender of the Japanese submarine I-400. In accordance with the surrender terms, all enemy submarines were to surface and surrender to the nearest Allied ship. The I-400 complied with these instructions and surrendered to the destroyer *Blue,* attached to one of the carrier task groups, which put a prize crew on board and received the sword of the Japanese captain. In the meantime, a prize crew from one of our submarine tenders was sent out to bring the captured vessel into port. The new crew was under a commander who was senior to the commanding officer of the *Blue.* Upon his arrival, he ordered the captain of the *Blue* to return the sword to the Japanese commander and made the enemy captain surrender all over again. At this second ceremony, cameras were placed for taking pictures for posterity, showing the new officer receiving the surrender. He then departed with the enemy's sword in his possession. This was hotly protested by the carrier task group commander. Which officer finally retained possession of the submarine commander's sword I never found out.

General MacArthur arrived by plane at Atsugi Airport on August 30 and set up his headquarters at the Grand Hotel in Yokohama. Admiral Halsey hoisted his flag at the ex-Japanese Naval Base at Yokosuka, and on September 1, sent out a message authorizing Admiral McCain, Commander of Task Force 38, to bring all flag officers who could be spared to the surrender ceremony set for the next day on the *Missouri.* The eleventh-hour message made no provision for transportation from the carrier task forces still cruising around at sea. I made arrangements to go in by plane from the *Lexington.*

The weather was none too good as we catapulted from the carrier deck just at dawn. With low clouds and a ceiling of 700 feet, we flew close to the water and soon sighted the green shores of Japan, the landscape of terraced hills dotted with pagoda-like houses. As we neared Tokyo Bay, we sighted a convoy of about 40 transports, part of Vice-Admiral T. S. Wilkinson's Third Amphibious Corps, entering the bay.

The Yokosuka airfield was marked by many wrecks of Japanese planes which had been burned and destroyed by our air strikes. As I got out of the plane, I was met by the new American commander of the field, and his assistant. These officers turned out to be Captain H. S. Duckworth, who had been my air officer on the *Lexington* in the Battle of the Coral Sea, and Commander Noel Gaylor, one of our leading fighter pilots in that action. It was a heartwarming experience to meet these former shipmates who had started the war with me on the *Lexington*, almost four years before, on my first landing on Japanese soil at the end of the fighting.

I proceeded at once by boat to the *Missouri*, anchored off the naval station, where I was met by Admiral Halsey. Much activity was going on in preparation for the ceremony. Dozens of high-ranking officers of all nationalities, Americans, British, Russians, Chinese, French, Canadians, Australians, Dutch and New Zealanders, were coming aboard for the historic occasion. In his cabin, Admiral Halsey confided to me that I would be ordered soon after the surrender to take a task force through the Panama Canal to New York City to celebrate Navy Day, October 27.

On the half deck overlooking the forecastle, just outside Admiral Halsey's cabin, there was a crew's mess table covered with a green cloth. Outboard of the deck itself and overhanging the water was a temporary platform built to accommodate 40 or 50 camera and newsreel men. The weather was cool, with high overcast, and by now the sun was occasionally trying to break through.

Among the many distinguished American officers present were General Jonathan D. Wainwright, Admiral Richmond K. Turner, Generals Carl Spaatz and George C. Kenny; Vice-Admirals John S. McCain, John H. Towers and Charles Lockwood; Lieutenant Generals Robert L. Eichelberger, Richard K. Sutherland, Barney Giles, James Doolittle, Roy S. Geiger, and Nathaniel Twining; Rear Admirals Jack Shafroth, Carey Jones, Don Beary, Jerry Wiltse, Oscar Badger and many others. All the American officers were in khaki shirts without ties, with no coats, and wearing no decorations. This had been our uniform during the fighting, and it was deliberately prescribed for this occasion to impress the Japanese with the fact that no honors were being given them. The foreign officers wore their blouses.

About 8:45 General MacArthur, with his Chief of Staff, Lieutenant General Richard K. Sutherland, arrived on a destroyer which came alongside the portside. They disappeared into Admiral Halsey's cabin to await the arrival of the Japanese emissaries. About five minutes later the enemy party came alongside the starboard gangway in a small motorboat. A pompous little man garbed in a high silk hat, frock coat and striped trousers, and carrying a cane, was the first to get out of the boat and arrive at the top of the ladder. It was Mamoru Shigemitsu, Japanese Foreign Minister. He was followed by two other men in top hats and frock coats, another in a civilian white sack suit, and six others in army field uniforms of olive green with red trimmings. No honors were rendered the enemy delegation. Nobody offered to shake hands with them, and they were greeted by a stony silence. Only stares of curiosity were directed at these men who represented a nation which had descended into the depths of barbarism in conducting the war.

Shigemitsu had difficulty negotiating the ladder and was helped by one of his party. This was the only evidence of his artificial leg, except that he limped and used a cane. The number two man of the delegation, a short stocky individual in uniform, was General Yoshijiro Umezu, Chief of the Japanese Imperial General Staff. All of the party wore grim expressions, as if they were tasting the bitterness of defeat.

The Japanese party was ushered to a small open square in front of the table upon which lay the documents to be signed. All around them, the ship was crowded with spectators, the high-ranking Allied officers lined up inboard of the central table and behind it, and other officers and bluejackets jamming every inch of space from which the spectacle could be viewed. The tops of the turrets, the bridges, and the mast overhead were all crowded with men in uniform.

General MacArthur, Admiral Nimitz and Admiral Halsey, in the latter's cabin, allowed the Japanese representatives to await their presence for an appreciable time. As I looked at the Japanese party, I presume I shared my mixed feelings with the hundreds of other watchers. My heart thrilled at the thought that the war was over and that now, at last, we could get back to normal and resume peacetime living. On the other hand, my mind went back to the hundreds and thousands of fellow Americans, many of them close personal friends or their sons, who had given their lives that this day might come.

After an appropriate interval, General MacArthur, Admiral Nimitz and Admiral Halsey came out of the cabin and stood behind the table facing the Japanese delegation. Microphones had been set up for broadcasting the proceedings to the world. The ears, if not the eyes, of mankind were concentrated on that scene.

With a stern expression General MacArthur stepped forward and made the following speech:

"We are gathered here, representatives of the major warring powers, to conclude a solemn agreement whereby peace may be restored. The issues involving divergent ideals and ideologies, have been determined on the battlefields of the world and hence are not for our discussion or debate. Nor is it for us here to meet, representing as we do a majority of the peoples of the earth, in a spirit of distrust, malice or hatred. But rather is it for us, both victors and vanquished, to rise to that higher dignity which alone befits the sacred purpose we are about to serve, committing all of our peoples unreservedly to faithful compliance with the undertakings they are here formally to assume.

"It is my earnest hope and indeed the hope of all mankind that from this solemn occasion a better world shall emerge out of the blood and carnage of the past,—a world founded upon faith and understanding,—a world dedicated to the dignity of man and the fulfillment of his most cherished wish—for freedom, tolerance and justice.

"The terms and conditions upon which the surrender of the Japanese Imperial Forces here to be given and accepted are contained in the instrument of surrender now before you.

"As Supreme Commander for the Allied powers, I announce it is my firm purpose, in the tradition of the countries I represent, to proceed in the discharge of my responsibilities, with justice and tolerance, while taking all necessary dispositions to insure that the terms of surrender are fully, promptly and faithfully complied with.

"I now invite the representatives of the Emperor of Japan and the Japanese Government and the Japanese Imperial General Headquarters to sign the instrument of surrender at the places indicated."

Shigemitsu signed first and had a little difficulty with his pen. There were two documents, bound in large books, side by side, one in English, the other in Japanese. Each man signed twice, once in each book. Only the page of signatures was exposed. Following the Japanese Foreign Minister, General Umezu signed and the enemy representatives stepped back.

Then General MacArthur announced that he would sign for all the Allied powers. He used five pens, making part of his signature with each one. He asked General Jonathan M. Wainwright and British General Arthur Percival to attend while he signed. Wainwright had surrendered at Corregidor and Percival at Singapore in the early part of the war. Both had since been prisoners of the Japanese and had only recently been released. Their physical appearance showed signs of their long incarceration. General MacArthur presented each of them with one of the silver-tipped pens he had used. I learned later that of the three others, one had been presented to the battleship *Missouri* and one to President Truman, and the other retained by General MacArthur himself.

Admiral Nimitz was then called to sign for the United States. He asked Admiral Halsey and Rear Admiral Forrest P. Sherman, his Operations Officer, to attend while he signed, and gave each of them one of the pens he used.

The Chinese delegation signed next, somewhat to my surprise. General Hsu Yung Chang was their signatory. Admiral Sir Bruce Frazer was next, for the British, then Lieutenant General Kuzma Derevyanko for the Soviet Union, General Sir Thomas Blamey for Australia, Colonel Laurence Cosgrove for Canada, General Jacques LeClerc for France, Admiral C. E. L. Helfrich for the Netherlands, and Air Vice-Marshal Leonard Isitt for New Zealand.

With perfect timing, just at this time, thousands of American planes began passing in stately formation overhead in further demonstration of the power that had won the war. They were planes from the carriers off the coast and formations of the Army's B-29's which had been bombing Japan only a short time before.

General MacArthur then said: "Let us pray that peace be now restored to the world and that God will preserve it always. These proceedings are now closed." With these remarks, he walked off to Admiral Halsey's cabin, accompanied by Admirals Nimitz, Halsey and Fraser and other high-ranking officers. Thus ended the most thrilling episode of my life.

In a glass case on the bulkhead alongside the spot where the ceremony had occurred, was an American flag which had been flown by Commodore Perry when he opened Japan to the commerce of the world in 1854. At the masthead of the *Missouri* that day flew the same American ensign which had flown over the White House in Washington on December 7, 1941.

After the ceremony, the Japanese were ushered to the gangway and left. Nobody saluted them or shook hands with them. They just left.

Thus ended the greatest war in history. The naval part of that war had seen the concentration in the United States fleet of greater power than the world ever dreamed possible. This fleet was more than twice as strong as the second largest navy, that of Great Britain, no longer the mistress of the seas.

The war had witnessed a revolution in high-seas fighting in which the weight of naval strength had passed from the battleship of yore to the aircraft carrier. Submarines, cruisers, destroyers, PT boats, tankers, auxiliaries, yes, even battleships, as well as the amphibious troops of the Army and the Marine Corps, the Army Air Force, and all the arms of our Allies—the British, Australians, New Zealanders, Dutch, Chinese, Free French, and Filipinos—all were part of the team. But the ships which secured and held control of the sea and made all the other operations possible were the United States Navy's aircraft carriers and their aircraft squadrons. The winning of the control of the Pacific was their accomplishment and the recognition of this job, well done, is their reward.

21

CONCLUSIONS AND LESSONS

Before discussing the conclusions and lessons of the Pacific war from the American standpoint, it seems well to take up the reasons for Japan's downfall from the standpoint of her own mistakes. Her naval strategy achieved wonderful success at the beginning of the Pacific war. Why did it fail over the longer period, and what were the errors which contributed most to Japan's ultimate defeat? Whereas the main cause of that defeat was the vast difference in material and industrial resources between the United States and Japan, nevertheless the Japanese made serious mistakes which played a large part in their downfall.

The basic war plan comprised, first, the seizure of the Dutch East Indies and Malaya, which contained the oil, tin, rubber, foodstuffs and other resources which were vital to Japan for carrying on the war; second, the attack on the United States fleet in Hawaii to prevent it from interfering with their operations in the western Pacific; and third, the establishment of a defensive perimeter of outlying islands behind which they could develop their resources and conduct their economy undisturbed by external forces.

Under these plans, all that remained for the Japanese to do after these three initial undertakings were completed was to consolidate and destroy any attacking force which might threaten that line. They estimated that the United States would take little interest in fighting a war so far from home and, rather than accept the losses required to breach the Japanese defense line, would be willing to make peace on the basis of the *status quo*.

The Japanese concept was undoubtedly based on the belief that Hitler would win the war in Europe, or at least force a compromise peace in that area. It is inconceivable that Japan would have undertaken a war against the combined might of the United States, the British Empire and the Netherlands unless her leaders had thought that Germany would keep the armed strength of the Allies preoccupied in other regions than the Orient. From the beginning of the Pacific war, I cofsistently predicted that Japan would collapse within six months after the fall of Germany. This prediction was based primarily on psychology, in the belief that the entire Japanese estimate must have rested on the fundamental assumption that Germany would win or at least achieve a stalemate. If Germany lost, the whole foundation of the Japanese decision would disintegrate. Actually Japan surrendered a little more than three months after Germany succumbed.

The initial successes of the Japanese forces went to their heads. Instead of being content with the defensive line originally contemplated, they proceeded to attempt further expansion. With their limited resources, they even delayed consolidation and strengthening of the planned defensive perimeter.

The original line was to be one joining the Kuriles,

Marshalls, Bismarcks, Timor, Java, Sumatra, Malaya, and Burma. When their first operations were successfully completed with such unexpected ease, the Japanese attempted to extend their control to Port Moresby, on the southern coast of New Guinea; to Midway in the central Pacific, in order to strengthen the defenses of that area, where they also hoped to force a decisive engagement with the United States fleet; and to the western Aleutians, in order to buttress the defenses of the northern area. If these operations were successful, they then intended to seize New Caledonia, Fiji and Samoa, for the purpose of cutting the lines of communication between the United States and Australia.

One of the gravest mistakes in the Japanese strategy was their failure to realize that overseas bases can be held only by control of the sea. When this is lost, the bases can no longer obtain the supplies and reinforcements vital to their continued existence. For the Japanese to hold their defensive line, they would ultimately have to meet and defeat the United States fleet in a contest for control of the sea. In such a clash, the attacker has the advantage of choosing the point of attack, and the defender cannot be strong everywhere.

Although the Japanese displayed an early recognition of the vital role of aircraft carriers in exercising control of the sea, it is doubtful whether they fully appreciated the ability of the United States to build up its strength in this important class of ships. Had they done so, the hopelessness of their position against our superior sea forces would have been apparent, and they might have refrained from challenging our power.

The first setback the Japanese received was in the Battle of the Coral Sea in May, 1942, which turned back their attempt to capture Port Moresby by sea. In this battle they lost one carrier and almost all of the planes and pilots from the two other carriers engaged. We lost the *Lexington*, but the American task force still included the slightly damaged *Yorktown*, with a full complement of her own planes and additional ones recovered from the *Lexington*. Potentially she dominated the situation.

In spite of the advantage we held, the American commander withdrew from the Coral Sea. Had the Japanese but known it, with the withdrawal of our task force they could have continued on and Port Moresby would have fallen within 48 hours, since there were no other forces then available to stop them. But the enemy were unaware of these facts, and themselves retired to what they considered safer waters. This tactical defeat by inferior forces was the first naval repulse that Japan had experienced in all its modern history.

A month later, in their attempt to capture Midway, the Japanese had a greatly superior carrier force to repel our weaker force of only three carriers. Even though their plans contemplated seeking a decisive engagement with the American fleet, they neglected to guard their security by sending scouting planes ahead of their ships to find out what American forces were within the area and in a position to threaten them. This failure resulted in the loss of four of their carriers as compared with only one of ours, and brought about a change in the existing ratio of naval power in the Pacific. Whereas the Japanese had previously possessed superiority in aircraft carriers, they were now reduced to a level of approximate equality.

The new situation beginning in the summer of 1942 was one in which neither side had sufficient superiority to take the offensive. More than a year later, in the fall of 1943, the newly built American aircraft carriers of the *Essex* type started arriving in the Pacific in ever-increasing numbers, and the United States fleet achieved sufficient superiority to take the offensive in its march across the Pacific which was ultimately destined to end at Tokyo less than two years later.

This offensive never stopped, but relentlessly rolled on in such rapid advances that the Japanese were never able to get set for the next blow. The success of the offensive was due mainly to our control of the sea through the power of our carriers. Having that control, we were able to keep our supplies moving wherever we desired and to cut the enemy's lines of communication to all their outlying bases.

There were other errors in the Japanese strategy. They failed to provide an adequate replacement program to take care of their losses in aviation pilots. They failed to realize the enormous quantity of merchant shipping which would be required to exploit their gains in the southern area and to supply their bases in their defensive perimeter. They further failed to make sufficient provision for protection of their shipping lanes against the attacks of our submarines.

The Japanese made many tactical errors which undoubtedly had some effect on strategy. Among these were the failure to go in and destroy our transports off Guadalcanal after the First Battle of Savo Island; their failure to continue on to Port Moresby in spite of their repulse in the Battle of the Coral Sea; their withdrawal from the action of the Komandorskis when they had our inferior forces helpless and at their mercy; and their failure to enter Leyte Gulf after the action off Samar.

In retrospect, it is amazing that Japan ever thought she could be successful in a war against the United States. It is evident that the Japanese failed to estimate properly their own military and economic requirements for such a war, and grossly underestimated the potential of the United States.

But perhaps their greatest error was their failure to appreciate the will to fight of the American people. It is said that many Japanese considered the United States a nation of pacifists. It is impossible to say how far such opinions influenced their decision to initiate the war. Fundamentally, their naval strategy failed not only because of their inadequate resources as compared with ours, but also because of their faulty appraisal of American psychology.

But there are also conclusions to be drawn and lessons to be learned from the American side of the picture. We have been prone to think of the Japanese attack on Pearl Harbor on December 7, 1941, as the greatest naval disaster in our history. Actually it had little effect, from a material standpoint, on the control of the Pacific Ocean. Although the fact was not fully recognized by many high-ranking officers at the time, battleships were already out of date and were destined to play only a small part in the outcome of the war.

Psychologically, however, the attack on Pearl Harbor had profound effects. First, it united the American people in a willingness to go to war, and in an all-out prosecution of the war effort, as nothing else could have done. The second psychological effect of the attack on Pearl Harbor was to disrupt, instantaneously, the previous conceptions of naval authorities as to the supremacy of the battleship. It was probably well that we learned this lesson at the very beginning of the war rather than later. If the battleships sunk at Pearl Harbor had gone down later in the open sea, as did the *Prince of Wales* and the *Repulse,* the loss of life and the strategic disaster would have been much more serious. The sinking of these battleships in the shallow waters of Pearl Harbor forced a reconsideration of the stereotyped plans then in effect for fighting a war with Japan.

The Japanese attack which opened hostilities was made possible by their superiority in large aircraft carriers. At this time, they had approximately ten carriers in commission, compared with our seven, of which only three were in the Pacific. Although they were well in advance of most naval thinking, the Japanese themselves did not realize fully the potential dominating role of carriers. But thenceforth aircraft from carriers were destined to rule the sea from the sky overhead.

Our weakness in carriers would have forced us to take the defensive in the early part of the war, even if there had been no Pearl Harbor. It was primarily responsible for the loss of the Philippines, Guam and Wake. Another condition which made the early days of the Pacific campaign so desperate was the decision to give the war in the Atlantic first priority and to channel the bulk of men and matériel to that theater.

Contrary to the general impression, Alaska and the Aleutians were never a very critical theater. The idea that these areas could be used as steppingstones for an invasion of the continental United States is hardly tenable. Alaska is a country that offers almost no resources to sustain an invading army, and all supplies and equipment for its invasion would have to be brought overseas. In addition, the severe weather in that region makes nature herself a formidable opponent there. As a practical matter, invasion routes in more temperate climates are more feasible, and our own invasion routes to Japan took the much longer but much more favorable way across the South and Central Pacific.

The tremendous distances of the Pacific necessitated a completely new kind of naval warfare. Our first offensive operation, in the Solomon Islands, was conducted roughly 5,000 miles from our Pacific Coast bases. The logistics of our campaigns in those far-off areas necessitated colossal amounts of shipping to transport the vast quantities of essential supplies. Port facilities for unloading these materials were nonexistent, and their lack resulted in long delays at the terminals and added to the tonnage of shipping required.

An amazing accomplishment of the United States Navy was the development of the service squadrons, those groups of ships which furnished food, ammunition, and supplies of every description to our fighting ships at sea, thus enabling them to remain in combat areas almost indefinitely. These squadrons were floating bases in almost every sense of the word, and lacked only the ability to dry-dock ships to be able to furnish every requirement. To a large extent, only the necessity for giving rest and relaxation to the personnel required our combatant ships ever to return to port.

The war in the Pacific, while fundamentally naval in character, illustrated the necessity of teamwork between all branches of the service. Naval aviation spearheaded the advance and gained control of the sea, but its effort would have gone for naught had our amphibious forces not been able to seize the advance bases from which our power could gradually be extended to the enemy's homeland. The tasks of all these services would have been rendered much more difficult had it not been for the enormous destruction of enemy shipping by our submarines, which helped defeat the Japanese efforts to exploit their conquests.

The advantage of unity of command was one of the great lessons of the Pacific war. In a campaign requiring participation by many branches of the Army and Navy, unity of direction of effort is essential. This can be accomplished only by unity of command *in the operating theater*. It was secured at the top by the over-all direction of the Joint Chiefs of Staff in Washington, who, in effect, became a general staff. In the lower echelons, unity of command was not as complete as it might have been, as shown by the separate operations conducted by General MacArthur in the Southwest Pacific and those in the contiguous area of the South Pacific under Admiral Halsey. Lack of unity of command also affected the Second Battle of the Philippine Sea, or the Battle for Leyte Gulf, where the Japanese Central Force passed through San Bernardino Strait without opposition when Admiral Kinkaid, commanding the Seventh Fleet under General MacArthur, and Admiral Halsey, commanding the Third Fleet under Admiral Nimitz, each thought the other was taking care of the situation.

Whereas mistakes of omission and commission played their part in the Pacific war, it should not be overlooked that after the attack on Pearl Harbor and the loss of Wake, Guam and the Philippines, America never lost a campaign in the Pacific. Such results could not have been obtained had not the basic planning been sound, and had not the execution of these plans been carried out intelligently and aggressively. Individual exploits of heroism and devotion to duty were legion. The leadership of the officers in all echelons could not have been other than brilliant to win the victories which our forces achieved against one of the most fanatical and determined enemies in history. In finding fault with the conduct of any specific operation, these basic facts should be kept in mind.

The war in the Pacific will be known to future generations as one of the greatest undertakings in all the long history of conflicts between nations for supremacy. It will achieve this distinction because of the magnitude of the distances involved, the enormous numbers of men and ships employed, the undeveloped nature of much of the territory over which the campaigns were fought, and the decisiveness of the results obtained. It will also be recorded as the first occasion when man used the terrible energy of the atomic bomb to destroy his fellow men.

As the Pacific war differed from all previous wars, so will the next war differ from the last one. Over the horizon we can see the approaching developments in the fields of atomic science, guided missiles, and pilotless aircraft. If America is to be preserved, we must maintain our preparedness for war. The most vital lesson for the future leaders of our air, naval and ground forces is that no two wars are ever alike. They must keep their minds wide open in applying the new developments of science to the art of war. The principles of warfare do not change, but the weapons do, and our civilization could be destroyed should we fail to keep abreast of new possibilities.

Man has always dreamed of universal peace. Yet history would indicate that for the foreseeable future, at least, it is a vain hope. If we desire to preserve what our civilization has developed, if we wish to retain our right to life, liberty and the pursuit of happiness, we must continue to be prepared spiritually and materially to defend our destinies on the field of battle.

BIBLIOGRAPHY

Following is a selected bibliography of works bearing upon the operations of the United States Navy in the war against Japan, or the background of the war. In addition to my own records and observations, official reports of action, and interviews with naval personnel of all ranks, all of these publications have been consulted during the preparation of the present volume.

Aviation History Unit OP-519B, DCNO (AIR), *The Navy's Air War* (New York: Harper & Brothers), 1946.

Charles A. Beard, *President Roosevelt and the Coming of the War, 1941* (New Haven: Yale University Press), 1948.

Lieut. General Lewis A. Brereton, U.S.A., *The Brereton Diaries* (New York: William Morrow & Company), 1946.

James A. Field, Jr., *The Japanese at Leyte Gulf: the Sho Operation* (Princeton: Princeton University Press), 1947.

Fleet Admiral William F. Halsey, U.S.N., and Lieutenant Commander J. Bryan, III, U.S.N.R., *Admiral Halsey's Story* (New York: Whittlesey House), 1947.

Frank O. Hough, *The Island War: The United States Marine Corps in the Pacific* (Philadelphia: J. B. Lippincott Company), 1947.

Clive Howard and Joe Whitley, *One Damned Island After Another* (Chapel Hill: University of North Carolina Press), 1946.

Jane's Fighting Ships, 1946–47 (New York: The Macmillan Company).

Stanley Johnston, *Queen of the Flat-Tops: The* U.S.S. Lexington *and the Coral Sea Battle* (New York: E. P. Dutton & Co., Inc.), 1942.

Roger Kafka and Roy L. Pepperburg, *Warships of the World* (New York: Cornell Maritime Press), 1946.

Commander Walter Karig, U.S.N.R., and Lieutenant Welborn Kelley, U.S.N.R., *Battle Report: Pearl Harbor to Coral Sea* (New York: Farrar and Rinehart, Inc.), 1944.

Commander Walter Karig, U.S.N.R., and Commander Eric Purdon, U.S.N.R., *Battle Report: Pacific War, Middle Phase* (New York: Rinehart & Company, Inc.), 1947.

Commander Walter Karig, U.S.N.R., Lieutenant Commander Russell L. Harris, U.S.N.R., and Lieutenant Commander Frank A. Manson, U.S.N.R., *Battle Report: The End of an Empire* (New York: Rinehart & Company), 1948.

Fleet Admiral Ernest J. King, U.S.N., *The United States Navy at War, 1941–1945: Official Reports by Fleet Admiral Ernest J. King, U.S.N.* (United States Navy Department), 1946.

Donald W. Mitchell, *History of the Modern American Navy* (New York: Alfred A. Knopf), 1946.

George Morgenstern, *Pearl Harbor: The Story of the Secret War* (New York: The Devin-Adair Company), 1947.

Samuel Eliot Morison, *The Rising Sun in the Pacific, 1931—April, 1942* (Boston: Little, Brown and Company), 1948.

General Joseph W. Stilwell, *The Stilwell Papers*. Arranged and edited by Theodore White (New York: William Sloane Associates), 1948.

United States Marine Corps, Historical Section, Division of Public Information, *The Defense of Wake* (United States Marine Corps), 1947.

United States Marine Corps, Historical Section, Division of Public Information, *The Marines at Midway* (United States Marine Corps), 1948.

United States Strategic Bombing Survey (Pacific). Naval Analysis Division, *Interrogations of Japanese Officials* (Washington: United States Government Printing Office), 1946.

United States Strategic Bombing Survey (Pacific), Naval Analysis Division, *The Campaigns of the Pacific War* (Washington: United States Government Printing Office), 1946.

Allan Westcott, Editor, *American Sea Power Since 1775* (Philadelphia: J. B. Lippincott Company), 1947.

C. Vann Woodward, *The Battle for Leyte Gulf* (New York: The Macmillan Company), 1947.

INDEX

Aaron Ward (destroyer), 147

ABDACOM (American - British - Dutch - Australian Command), 32

"A" Plan of Japanese, 200

Abukuma (light cruiser), 13, 113, 117, 123, 256–257

Acuff, Capt. Jasper T., 278

Adak, 113, 114–115, 122–123

Admiral Halsey's Story, Fleet Admiral Wm. F. Halsey, U.S.N. and Lt. Commander J. Bryan, III, U.S.N.R., xv, *Bibliography* 335

Admiralty Islands, 269

Agana (Guam), 218–219

Agana Field (Guam), 204

Agano (light cruiser), 171, 172

Agattu (Aleutians), 116

Ainsworth, Rear Admiral Walden L., 156, 157–158

Air attacks, training for, 1, 2, 4, 24, 182

Air Forces, *see* U.S. Army

Air Power: growing importance, 181, 306, 327; shortage of carriers, 181; *see also* Battleships *vs.* Air Power

Air reconnaissance, 29–31; at Truk, 192

Air Support Force, under Rear Admiral Noyes, 131

Air-search mission, 113

Air warfare, xiii, 2, 3, 23–28, 45, 86, 292; dominance of aircraft carrier, 93–94; flying fortresses, 97, 106; *see also* Aircraft Carriers; Army Air Forces; Naval Air Forces

Aircraft, land based, 277

Aircraft Carriers, ix-xi, xiii-xiv, 2–4, 10, 13–14, 20, 22, 172, 198; *Akagi; Amagi; Ark Royal; Astoria; Bataán; Belleau Wood; Bennington; Bismarck Sea; Bunker Hill; Cabot; Cowpens; Enterprise; Essex; Gambier Bay; Hancock; Heron; Hiryu; Hiyo; Hornet; Independence; Indomitable; Intrepid; Junyo; Kaga; Katsuragi; Lexington; Lunga Point; Manila Bay; Monterey; Nassau; Ommaney Bay; Princeton; Ranger; Ryujo; Saint Lo; San Diego; San*

Aircraft Carriers (*cont*.)
Jacinto; Santee; Saratoga; Shoho; Shokaku; Soryu; Suwanee; Taiho; Ticonderoga; Wasp; White Plains; Yorktown; Zuiho; Zuikaku; see under individual names

Aircraft Tenders, *Seawitch* (British), 36

Airfields: Aleutians, 123; at Eniwetok, 182; at Iwo Jima, 285; at Okinawa, 293; 301; at Peleliu and Angaur, 228; in Gilbert Islands area, 188; Kadena, 296; Kanoya (Japanese Kyushu base) 308; Machinato, 297; Naha, 298; on Kiska, 116; on Mindanao, 230; on Umnak, 113; Orote Peninsula, 218; Yonabaru, 298; Yontan, 296

Akagi (aircraft carrier), 13, 103, 104, 106

Akatsuki (destroyer), 147

Akebone (destroyer), 48

Akagane Maru (Japanese supply ship), 117

Alabama (battleship), 187, 205, 230

Alameda (Calif.), 67

Alaskan area, defense, 113

Albacore (submarine), 203, 210

Aleutians, 14, 94–96, 113–115, 123; tundra, 115; volcanic islands, 115; weather conditions, 114–116

Alifan Ridge, 220

Allied Forces in Java, 34

Allied Naval Forces, 32, 43

Allies, ship losses, 45

Amagi (aircraft carrier), 312

Amami O Shima, 234

Ambon (south of Molukka Passage), 33, 44

Amboina, 34

Amchitka (Aleutians), 116, 121

American Bases in the Aleutians, 113

American, British and Dutch naval forces, 29

Americal Division, 142, 145, 152

American Forces, at Saipan, 200; in Philippine Sea, 202–203; losses at Midway, 108; position in Battle of the Coral Sea, *diagram*, 72–73

American Groups, location of, *diagram*, 242–243

American-Japanese relations, 6–7

American Joint Chiefs of Staff, 112

Ammunition, tracer, 195

American troops, responsible in the main for ground conquests in Japan, 316

American Sea Power, *Bibliography*, 337

Amoy (China), 279

Amphibious forces, 183, 197, 237, 333; bombers, 113; command of Rear Admiral Barbey, 128; command of Rear Admiral Turner, 130–131, 190; expedition to expel Japanese, 119; Fifth Amphibious Corps, 200, 287; flying boats, 113; Fourth Marine Division, 287; Geiger's Third Amphibious Corps, 225; in Philippine campaign, 282; Okinawa, largest amphibious operation in Pacific, 293; Russell Islands, 155; Third and Fifth Amphibious Corps, 200, 219, 294

Amphibious Support Force, under Admiral W. H. P. Blandy, 295

Amphtracks (water and landcraft for amphibious operations), at Iwo Jima, 287, 295

Anderson (destroyer), 71; in Task Force 17, 96

Angaur (The Palaus), 225, 227

Antiaircraft guns, 70, 111, 175

Antisubmarine patrols, 116; *see also* Navy Patrol

Aoba (heavy cruiser), 70, 134, 140, 312

Apamama Island, 187

Aparri (Luzon), 26

Apra (Guam), 53

Apra Harbor (Guam), 218, 220

Arare (destroyer), 116

Arashi (destroyer), 160

Arashio (destroyer), 107, 125

Arizona (battleship), 15, 18, 19

Ark Royal (aircraft carrier), 27

Army, *see* U.S. Army

Army Air Forces, 8–9, 12–13, 26, 44, 171, 181; B-17 Flying Fortresses at Midway, 96–97, 102, 107; B-26, torpedo attack at Midway, 101; losses at Oahu and Luzon, 45; major defense in Aleutians, 112–113; shore based planes, 313; units under Brig. Gen. Butler, 113

Army B-17 Flying Fortresses, 106, 138

Army B-24's, 124–125, 257; *see also* U.S. Army

Army B-29 Superfortresses, 291; based on Saipan, 283; based on Marianas, 292; *see also* U.S. Army

Army bomber squadrons, 113, 115; fighter squadrons, 113; *see also* U.S. Army

Army fighter planes, 157; *see also* U.S. Army

Arnold, Gen. H. H. ("Hap"), 112, 171; head of Army Air Force at Washington, 284

Arundel, 162

Asakumo (destroyer), 125–127

Asashio (destroyer), 107, 125

Asheville (gunboat), 43, 45

"Asia for Asiatics," 4

Asiatic Fleet, 26, 29, 180

Aslito, airfield, 200

Assault forces, 200

Astoria (heavy cruiser), 61, 64, 70, 74, 134; flagship of Rear Admiral W. W. Smith, 96; in Task Force 17, 96

Asaka Maru (light cruiser), 113, 117

Ashigara (heavy cruiser), 70

Ashigura (cruiser), 257

Astoria (aircraft carrier), 304

Atago (heavy cruiser), 171, 210, diagram, 242–243, 247

Atlanta (antiaircraft cruiser), 137, 146; in Task Force 16, 96, 131

Atolls, fortified; carrier strikes against, 189–190

Atom bomb, 314; moral and political implications, 315

Atsugi (near Tokyo), airfield, 321

Attack squadrons, 71

Attu (Aleutians), 113, 114, 115, 117–120, 122; Jones, Mr. and Mrs., prisoners of Japanese, 114; weather station, 114

Ault, Commander William B., 62, 64, 82–83; death of, 83

Austin, Commander B. L., 168

Australia, 32, 35, 41, 43, 53, 79, 95; assistance in war on Japan, 316; represented at signing of Japanese surrender, 326; ships arrive from Philippines, 45

Australia (cruiser), 61, 64, 74, 79, 131, 134, 136, 240, 277

Australian Barrier Reef, 93

Australian troops, 124

Auxiliaries, 119

Aviation unit under command of Major Paul Putnam, 48

Axis, Japan sympathetic to, 5

Ayashi (destroyer), 104

Aylwin (destroyer), 58, 74; in Task Force 16, 96

Ayres, Col. R. G., 191

B-17's (Army flying fortresses), 96, 138; at Manila, 25

B-24's bombers (Army), 124–125

B-25's bombers (Army), 66, 67

B-29's bombers (Army), 218, 223, 284, 291, 313; demonstration at Japanese surrender, 326; Marianas based, 292; mined Inland Sea, 313

Babelthaup (The Palaus), 224, 228

Badger, Rear Admiral Oscar, at Japanese surrender ceremony, 323

Badoeng Strait, 35

Bagley (destroyer), 58, 134

Baguio (Philippines), 282

Bailey (destroyer), 117, 119

Bairoko-Enogai area (New Georgia), 156, 157

Bairoko Harbor, 159

"Baka" bombs (Japanese word for fool), 303

Balabac Straits (between Borneo and Palawan), 271

Balch (destroyer), 55, 56, 67, 79; in Task Force 16, 96, 108

Bali (Dutch East Indies), 35, 37

Bali Strait, 42

Balikpapan (Dutch Borneo), 32; scene of Japanese rout by Talbot forces, 32–33

Balintang Channel, 280

Balle (Bougainville), 160

Ballale Island, airfields, 164

Banckert (destroyer), 44

Bandoeng, 43

Bangka Strait, 35

"Banzai boys," 245, 270–271

Barakoma (Vella-Lavella), 161, 162

Barbey, Rear Admiral Daniel E., 128

Barton (destroyer), 147

Bases in Pacific, American and British, 5, 24; American, in the Aleutians, 113; on Eniwetok, Kwajalein, and Majuro, 196

Bashi Channel, 278

Bataán (Luzon, P.I.), 44, 301

Bataán (aircraft carrier), 307

Bataán Peninsula, 29

Batangas, 231

Batavia (Sumatra), 34, 45

Battle for Leyte Gulf, 236, 238, 239–240; *diagram*, 242–243, *Bibliography*, 337

Battle of Badoeng Strait (Java area), 35, 61

"Battle of Bull Run" (Second Battle of the Philippine Sea), 265

Battle of Cape Esperance, 139

Battle of Cape St. George, 173

Battle of Empress Augusta Bay, 167

Battle of Formosa, 236

Battle of Guadalcanal, 145

Battle of Jutland, 256

Battle of Kula Gulf, first, 157; second, 158

Battle of Makassar Straits, 32

Battle of Midway, 47, 84, 93, 108, 110, 112; position of American and Japanese Forces, *diagram*, 98–99; stalemate following, 129

Battle of Santa Cruz, 141, 144

Battle of Savo Island, 331

Battle of Surigao Strait, *diagram*, 242–243

Battle of Tassafaronga, 149

Battle of Vella Gulf, 159

Battle of Vella-Lavella, First, 160

Battle of the Bismarck Sea, 125, 152

Battle of the Coral Sea, 45, *diagram*, 72–73, 94, 105; air group, 74; attack group, 74; Japanese first setback, 329; support group, 74; tactical and strategic victory, 93

Battle of the Eastern Solomons, 137, 139

Battle of the Java Sea, 38, 43, 61

Battle of the Komandorskis, 117

Battle of the Philippine Sea, First, 202, *diagram*, 206–207

Battle of the Ridge, 142

Battle of the Tenaru, 142

Battle off Cape Engano, *diagram*, 242–243

Battle off Samar, *diagram*, 242–243

Battleships: *Alabama, Arizona, California, Fuso, Haruna, Hiei, Hiyei, Hyuga, Indiana, Iowa, Ise, Kirishima, Kongo, Maryland, Mississippi, Missouri, Musashi, Nagato, Nevada, New Jersey, North Carolina, Oklahoma, Pennsylvania, Prince of Wales, Revenge, Royal Sovereign, South Dakota, Tennessee, Utah, Vestal, Washington, West Virginia, Yamashiro, Yamato*

Battleships vs. Air Power, 2–3, 8–9, 15, 20, 21–22, 29, 45, 110–111, 113, 327

Bawean Island, Bombardment, 43

Beary, Rear Admiral Don B., 294; at Japanese surrender ceremony, 323

Beck, Lt., Comdr. Edward L., 74

Beightler, Major Gen. Robert S., 165

Belete Pass, 282

Bell (destroyer), 174

Belleau Wood (aircraft carrier), 204, 269, 301

Bellinger, Rear Admiral Patrick N.L., 3

Bellows Field, 19

Benham (destroyer), 67, 149, 320; in Task Force 16, 95, 108

Bennington (aircraft carrier), 301

Betio, Japanese troops on, 186

Betty snoopers, 174–176

Biloxi (cruiser), 266

Binford, Comdr. Thomas H., 40–41

Birmingham (cruiser), 230, 252

Bismarck Archipelago, 94

Bismarck Sea (aircraft carrier), 290

Bittern (Mine sweeper), 45

Blamey, Gen. Sir Thomas (Australia), represented Australia at signing of Japanese surrender, 326

Bloch, Admiral C. C., 1, 3

"Bloody-Nose Ridge" (Peleliu), 226–227

Blue (destroyer), 55, 135; surrender of the Japanese submarine I-400, received, 322

Bode, Capt. Howard D., 74

Bogan, Rear Admiral Gerald F., 229; *diagram*, 242–243, 249, 265, 266, 269, 273; succeeded Admiral Sherman in command of Task Group 38.3, 309

Bohel, 231

Boise (cruiser), 32, 140

Bombay Shoal, 248

Bomber fields, on Attu, 124; on Shemya, 124

Bombers, 36, 66–67, 81, 86, 96, 124–125, 138, 218, 223, 284, 291–292, 313, 326

Bombing, dive, ix, 9, 13, 15, 18; horizontal, x, 13, 109, 284; "saturation" or "pattern" type, 284

Bombing survey, U.S. strategic, 36, 337

Bombs, fragmentation, 49

Bonin Islands, 236, 284

Bonis, airfield, 166

Borneo (Malay Archipelago), 32–33, 38

Bougainville, ix, 61, 151, 155, 158, 164, 165–166, 174

Bowling, Comdr. Selman S., 253

Bradford (destroyer), 174

Brereton Diaries, The, Lt. Gen. Lewis H., Brereton, 25, 335

Brereton, Lt. Gen. Lewis H., *The Brereton Diaries*, 25, 335

Brett, Lt. Comdr. Jimmie, 64, 83

British carrier force, 3, 294, 308

British naval forces, 29; in the Orient, 27

British Pacific Fleet, commanded by Vice-Admiral Rawlings, 314

Brown (destroyer), 174

Brown, Major Gen. A.F., 119–120

Brown, Vice-Admiral Wilson, 50, 58, 61, 65, 70

Brunei, diagram, 242–243

Brunei Bay (Borneo), 246, 259

Buchanan (destroyer), 146, 166

Buckmaster, Capt. Elliott, 74, 102

Buckner, Lt. Gen. Simon Bolivar, commander of the Tenth Army, 293, 294; death of, 299

Buckner Bay (earlier, Nakagusuku Wan), 293

"Buffalo" F^2A fighter planes, 54, 100

Buin-Faisi area, 145

Buin-Shortland area of Bougainville, 156

Buka, 173; airfield, 164–165

Buka-Bonis airfields, 166

Buku Island, 164

Bulkeley, Lt. John D., 31

Bullard (destroyer), 307

Buna, 62, 128

Bunker Hill (aircraft carrier),

172, 174, 187, 196, 205, 292, 301; hit by *kamikaze planes*, 307

Burford, Lt. Comdr. William P., 74

Burke, Capt. Arleigh, 167, 173

Burma, 32, 94

Burns (destroyer), 187, 193

Butler, Brig. Gen. W. C., 113

Byrnes, Secretary of State James F., accepted for Allied powers Japanese surrender, 316

Cabot (aircraft carrier), 246, 249, 273, 301, 304

California (battleship), 15, 19, 245, 253, 255, 259

Callaghan, Rear Admiral Daniel J., 146

Camranh Bay (Indo-China), 278

Canada, represented at signing of Japanese surrender, 326

Canadian fighter squadron, 113

Canberra (Australian cruiser), 131, 134, 135, 236

Cap St. Jacques, 278

Cape Engano, *diagram*, 242–243, 245, 263

Cape Esperance, 140, 142, 152, 153

Cape Gloucester (New Britain), 173

Cape St. George, 171

Cape Torokina, 165, 172

Carlson's Raiders, 155

Caroline Islands (in Pacific Ocean), 23, 198, 223

Carrier Division One, 198; planes, 88

Carrier duel, first in history, 86

Carrier group disposition, *diagram*, 63

Carriers, *Essex* type, 128, 178; importance of, 180; *Independence* class, 178; *see also* Aircraft carriers

Cassin (destroyer), 18, 19

Catalinas, 100

Cates, Major Gen. Clifton B., 287

Cavalla (submarine), 203, 210

Cavite naval yard, 272

Cebu, 199, 231, 233, 281

Cebu Harbor, 231

Cecil, Capt. C.F., 158

Celebes (Malay Archipelago), 34

Celebes Sea, 26

Censorship, xiii

Central Force (Japanese), 246–248, 251–253, 258, 261–263, 266–267

Central Pacific campaign, x, 167, 185, 221, 229

Central Pacific defenses of the Japanese, 95

Central Pacific Forces, 221, 223–224, 229, 239–

Central Pacific German held islands, 4

Central Philippines, 232–233

Central Solomons campaign, 164

Ceram (Malay Archipelago), called by natives Serang, 34, 44

Ceylon, 36

Chappel, Lt. W. G., 30

Charles Ausburne (destroyer), 165

Charrette (destroyer), 174, 187, 193

Chennault, Major Gen. Claire L., American combat air force in China commanded by, 181

Chester (heavy cruiser), 55, 70, 74, 93, 141

Chevalier (destroyer), 157, 162–163

Chiang Kai-shek's Troops, 181

Chicago (cruiser), 64, 70, 74, 134–136, 152

Chicago Harbor, 121

Chichi Jima (near Japan), 201, 285, 290

Chikuma (heavy cruiser), 13, 106, 144, 266

Chillingworth, Lt. Comdr. Charles F., Jr., 74

China, 5; activity in war, 47, 181; air-bases in, 67; represented at signing of Japanese surrender, 326

China Sea venture ("Plan Gratitude"), 278

Chitose (seaplane carrier), 137, 138, 265

Chiyoda (light carrier), 116, 264

Choiseul, Marines at, 165

Chokai (heavy cruiser), 134, 136, 148

Chonito Cliff, 219

Christmas Day, 1943, 174; at Ulithi, 276

Christmas Island (in Indian Ocean), 37

Churchill, Prime Minister Winston L. S., 229

Clapper, Raymond (newspaper columnist), killed in plane collision, 191

Clark (destroyer), 58

Clark, Rear Admiral J. J., 300, 305, 308

Clark Field (Manila), 26, 231, 273

Claxton (destroyer), 165, 169

Cleveland (cruiser), 156, 165, 168

Codes, Japanese, 7–8, 9, 96

Coghlan (destroyer), 117

Cold Bay (Alaska), 119

Colombo (Ceylon), 46

Columbia (cruiser), 156, 165, 168

Combat Air Patrol, 321

Combat fatigue, 183

Combat losses; at Palau, 199

Combined Chiefs of Staff, 112

Command of American, British and Dutch naval forces, 29

Communications: cut between Rabaul and north New Guinea, 128; experts broke Japanese code, 96; Japanese, 199

Congressional Investigating Committee (Pearl Harbor), 8

Congressional Medal of Honor, awarded to Lt. "Butch" O'Hare, with promotion to rank of Lt. Comdr., 60; Capt. Cassin Young, 147

Connor (destroyer), 174, 187

Converse (destroyer), 165

Conyngham (destroyer), in Task Force 16, 96

Coral Sea, 62, 70, 75, 203

Coron Bay, 233

Coronado, x

Corregidor fortress (Manila Bay), 23–24, 29, 238; evacuation of personnel, 43–44; Gen. Wainwright, surrendered to Japanese at, 326

Corsair, F⁴U fighter planes, 181, 281

Cosgrove, Col. Laurence, represented Canada at signing of Japanese surrender, 326

Coward, Capt. J. G., 254

Cowell (destroyer), 174

Cowpens (light aircraft carrier), 189, 194, 195, 208; in typhoon, 275

Crace, Rear Admiral John Gregory, R. N., 64, 74, 76

Cruisers: *Abukuma, Agano, Aoba, Astoria, Asaka Maru, Ashigara, Atago, Atlanta, Australia, Biloxi, Birmingham, Boise, Canberra, Chester, Chicago, Chiyoda, Chokai, Cleveland, Columbia, Danae, De Ruyter, Denver, Dragon, Exeter, Furataka, Guam, Haguro, Hawaii, Helena, Hobart, Honolulu, Houston, Indianapolis, Isuzu, Iwate, Izumo, Java, Jintsu, Juneau, Kako, Kalinin Bay, Kinu, Kinugasa, Kiso, Kitkun Bay, Kumano, Lamotte-Picquet, Leander, Louisville, Marblehead, Maya, Miami, Mikuma, Minneapolis, Mobile, Mogami, Montpelier, Myoko, Nachi, Nashii, Nashville, New Orleans, Northampton, Nashiro, Oyodo, Pensacola, Perth, Pittsburgh, Portland, Quincy, Raleigh, Reno, Repulse, Richmond, St. Louis, Salt Lake City, San Francisco, San Juan, Santa Fe, Sendai, Settu, Takao, Tama, Tatsuta, Tenryu, Tone, Tromp, Vincennes, Wichita, Yahagi, Yubari*

Crutchley, Rear Admiral V. A.

C., British Admiral in command of screening force, 134

Cunningham, Comdr. Winfield Scott, 48, 52

Curtiss (seaplane tender), 15, 19

Curtiss-Wright F⁴U Corsair planes, 181

Cushing (destroyer), 147

Cushioning missile devices on Japanese planes, 88

D-Day, 119–120, 130; Bougainville landing, 165; Saipan landing, 200

D plus 5 day, 288

Dace (submarine), 245, 247

Dale (destroyer), 58, 117

Danae (British cruiser), 37

Darien (southern Manchuria), Admiral Nimitz to occupy port; later occupied by Russia, 320

Darter (submarine), 245, 247

Darwin (Australia), 35

"Dauntless" SBD dive bombers, 54, 56, 86, 281–282

Davao (Philippine Islands), 31, 198, 281

Davison, Rear-Admiral R. E., 229, 245, 265, 269, 300–301

De Ruyter (Dutch cruiser), 33, 34, 36, 38–41, 45

"Deckloads" (small groups of attack planes), 271

Defense Battalions, 14th, 219

Defensive forces (Philippines), 24

Denver (cruiser), 156, 165, 168, 169

Derevyanko, Lt. Gen. Kuzma, at Japanese surrender signed for the Soviet Union, 326

Destroyer Division, 32

Destroyers: *Akatsuki, Akebone, Anderson, Arare, Arashi, Arashio, Asakumo, Asashio, Ayashi, Aylwin, Bagley, Bailey, Balch, Banckert, Barton, Bell, Benham, Blue, Bradford, Brown, Buchanan, Bullard, Burns, Cassin, Charles Ausburne, Charrette, Chevalier, Clark, Claxton, Coghlan, Conner, Converse, Conyngham, Cowell, Cushing, Dale, Dewey, Downs, Drayton, Duncan, Dunlap, Dyson, Edsall, Edwards, Electra, Ellet, Encounter, Evertsen, Express, Fanning, Farenholt, Farragut, Fletcher, Foote, Frazier, Fubuki, Fuginami, Grant, Grayson, Gwin, Hagikaze, Hamakaze, Hammann, Haraden, Hatsukukaze, Hatsushimo, Helm, Henley, Hoel, Holloran, Hughes, Hull, Ikazuchi, Isasuma, Isokazi, Izard, John D. Ford, Johnston, Jupiter, Kagero, Kasumi, Kawakaze, Kidd, Kisaragi, Kishinami, Kortenaer, Laffey, Lang, Lansdowne, Lardner, Lavallette, McCall, MacDonough, Maddox, Makigumo, Maury, Meredith, Michishio, Minegumo, Mitsuki, Monaghan, Monssen, Morris, Murakumo, Murasame, Nagamami, Nagatsuki, Natsubio, Natsugumo, Nenobi, Nicholas, Niizuki, Nowake, O'Bannon, O'Brien, Parrott, Patterson, Paul Jones, Peary, Perkins, Phelps, Philip, Piet Hein, Pillsbury, Pope, Porter, Preston, Pringle, Rall, Ralph Talbot, Renshaw, Roberts, Russell, Samuel B. Roberts, Saufley, Scout, Selfridge, Shaw, Shigure, Shikinamie, Shiranubi, Shiratsuyu, Shirayuki, Sims, Smith, Spence, Stack, Stanly, Sterrett, Stewart, Strong, Suzunami, Tenedos, Thatcher, Tokitsukaze, Ukikaze, Umikaze, Urakaze, Uranami, Ushio, Vampire, Van Ghent, Wakaba, Wakatsuki, Walke, Waller, Whipple, Wilson, Witte De With, Woodworth, Worden, Yudachi, Yugumo*

"Devastator," TBD torpedo plane, 54, 56

Devereaux, Major James P. S., 48, 51–52

Dewey (destroyer), 58, 74

Deyo, Rear Admiral M. L., 295

Diatsu boats, 161

Diplomatic exchanges between Japan and the United States, 6

Disarmament Conference (1922), 5

Disarmament Treaties (1936), 24

Dive bombers, x, 9, 13, 15, 18, 71, 86, 101, 103–105; Douglas SBD "Dauntless," 54, 56

Divided command, 154, 253

Dixon, Lt. Comdr. Bob, 78, 81

Dobadura, 127

Doolittle, Lt. Gen. James H., 67, 94, 286; at Japanese surrender ceremony, 323

Doorman, Rear Admiral Karel

W. F. H., 33–36, 38–40; tactics examined, 47

Douglas Dauntless dive bombers, 281–282

Downs (destroyer), 18, 20

Dragon (British cruiser), 37

Drayton (destroyer), 58

Dublon Island (Truk Atoll), 192

Duckworth, Comdr. H. S., 87–88; in command of Yokosuka airfield, 323

Duncan (destroyer), 140

Dunlap (destroyer), 55

Dutch East Indies, 24, 34, 48, 61, 94, 238; fall of, 180

Dutch Harbor (Unalaska), seaplane base, 113

Dutch naval forces, 29

Dyson (destroyer), 165

Early, Capt. Alexander R., 74, 96

Eastern Solomons, 153

Edsall (American destroyer), 36, 43

Edwards (destroyer), 36

Efate airfield, 166

Eichelberger, Lt. Gen. Robert L., at Japanese surrender ceremony, 323

XVIII Army under Lt. Gen. Hyakutake, 141

Eighth New Zealand Brigade Group, 165

81st Infantry Division (U. S. Army), 225

Electra (destroyer), 27, 38–39; survivors, 43; loss of, 45

Eleventh Airborne Division, first occupation force, 321

11th Bombardment Squadron at Espiritu Santo, 138

Ellet (destroyer), 67; in Task Force, 16, 96

Emirau Island, 178

Emperor of Japan, representative of, signed the Japanese surrender, 325

Empress Augusta Bay, ix, 165–166, 169

Encounter (British destroyer), 38, 39, 40, 45, 66

"End run" message of Admiral Spruance, 204

Engebi Island, 191

Eniwetok Atoll, 189, 191, 230

Enogai Inlet, 157

Enterprise (aircraft carrier), 110, 131, 137–139, 143, 148, 151, 230, 246, 302, 307; at Midway, 102, 104, 106; at Okinawa, 301; damaged at Guadalcanal, 139; in Task Force 16, 95; raid on Tokyo, 286

Erskine, Major Gen. Graves B., 287

Escort carriers, (*see* under individual names), *Nassau*

Espiritu Santo, 149, 151, 154, 172, 189; Bombardment Squadron at, 138, 141, 172

Essex (aircraft carrier), 111, 172, 178, 208, 230, 269–270, 273, 292, 302, 306–307; flagship of Admiral Sherman; later of Rear Admiral Bogan, 310

Essex Air Group, 250, 301

European War, 1914-1918, 5

Evertsen (Dutch destroyer), 41–42, 45

Ewa, marine air base (Oahu), 12, 20

Exeter (British heavy cruiser), 34, 37–40, 45

Explosion from gasoline vapor, 84, 91; central station report, 89–90

Express (destroyer), 27

F²A fighter planes ("Buffalo"), 54

Fais, 223

Fanning (destroyer), 67

Far Eastern Air Force (*The Brereton Diaries*), 25

Farenholt (destroyer), 140, 166

Farncom, Capt. H. B., RAN, 74

Farragut (destroyer), 74, 76

Fast Carrier Task Force, 183–184, 223, 229, 236–237, 239, 240, 244, 261, 263, 271, 280, 294; at Iwo Jima, 290; at Kyushu, 310; at Leyte Gulf, 309; at Okinawa, 300–301; became Task Force 58, 283; compared with "Pony Express," 283; Group 38.4, 230; in South China Sea, 278; Task Force 38, four groups, 239; Truk attack, 192

Felt, Commander Don, 138

Ferries for Japanese coal trains at Hokkaido; bombardment of, 311

Fifth Air Force, 125, 127

Fifth Amphibious Force, 287

Fifth Fleet (Japanese), 253, 256

Fifth Marine Division, 143, 287

Fighter direction, early development of, 85; methods need improvement, 94

Fighter planes, 11–12, 13, 20, 71, 86, 93, 111, 208; "Buffalo" F²A, 54; Canadian, 113; Nakajima, 78; on Iwo Jima, 292; protection of, 109; speed of, 181; Zero, 78

Fighting Squadron Two, 58

Fighter squadrons, Army; Navy, 113

Fiji (Oceania), 95

Fiji Islands, airfields on, 131

Filipino guerrillas, 238, 281–282

Filipinos, hail American forces, 278

Finch (mine sweeper), 45

Finschhafen (Huon Peninsula), 128

Fire-fighting equipment inadequate, 94

First Battle of Kula Gulf, 157

First Battle of the Philippine Sea, 202, *diagram*, 206–207, 241

First Marine Air Wing, 281–282

First Marine Amphibious Corps, under Lt. Gen. Roy S. Geiger, 299; under Gen. Vandergrift, 165

First Marine Division, under Major Gen. Vandergrift, 130, 142, 145, 294, 297

First Seaborne Brigade, commanded by Major Gen. Nishida, 191–192

Fitch, Rear Admiral Aubrey Wray, 70, 74, 78, 91, 93

Flashless powder, 195

Fifth Marine Division, 143, 287

"Flattops," 78

Fleet oiler (*see* under individual name) *Neches*

Fleet units, security of, 4

Fletcher (destroyer), 147, 150, 156

Fletcher, Rear Admiral Frank J., 49–50, 53, 55, 70, 76–78, 80, 96, 106, 131; ordered the *Phelps* to sink damaged *Lex-*

ington, 92; recommended withdrawal of carrier task force, 136

Florida Island, 133

Flying Fish (submarine), 203

Flying Fortresses, 97, 106

Foote (destroyer), 166, 169

Ford, Lt. Comdr. Walter C., 74

Ford Island Naval Air Station (Pearl Harbor), 13–14, 15, 20

Formosa, 25, 46, 234, 237, 279; carrier strike against, 276, 277; Japanese air base, 308

Forney, Lt. Col. E. H., 165

Fourth Marine Raider Battalion, 287; went ashore at Segi Point, 156

France, represented at signing of Japanese surrender, 326

Franklin (aircraft carrier), 269, 301

Fraser, Lt. Comdr. Thomas E., 74

Frazer, Admiral Sir Bruce (British), at Japanese surrender, signed for Great Britain, 326

Frazier (destroyer), 122

Fubuki (destroyer), 140

Fujinami (destroyer), 171

Funafuti airbase, 186; Marshall's assault forces, 189

Furataka (heavy cruiser), 70, 134, 140

Fuses, proximity, 195

Fuso (battleship), 246, 254–255

Gambier Bay (aircraft carrier), 260; survivors of, 262

Gamma rays in the atomic bomb, 315

Gardner, Rear Admiral M. B., 301

Garipan, 201, 213

Gasmata (New Britain), 61–62

Gavutu Harbor, 71

Gavutu-Tanambogo, 133

Gay, Ensign G. H., 103

Gaylor, Comdr. Noel, 65, 83, 323

Gehres, Capt. Leslie F., 113, 302

Geiger, Lt. Gen. Roy S., 165, 200, 219, 225, 294; outstanding aviator, 299; succeeded Gen. Buckner in command of expeditionary troops, 299–300; at Japanese surrender, 323

George F. Elliott (transport), 134, 135

Germans, 4

Germany, loss of Marshall Islands, 189; submarine campaigns by, 180

Gertrude Cove, 122

Ghormley, Vice-Admiral Robert L., 130–131, 136

Giffin, Vice-Admiral R. C., 151

Gilbert Islands, 55, 185–186; cost of taking high, 188

Giles, Lt. Gen. Barney, at Japanese surrender ceremony, 323

Gill, Lt. "Red," fighter-direction officer, 85

Gilmore, Comdr., paymaster on the *Lexington*, 88

Ginder, Lt. Comdr. John K. B., 74

Glassford, Rear Admiral William Alexander, 32, 41, 43, 45

Good, Capt. Howard H., 74

Goodenough Island, 127

Goto, Rear Admiral, 140

Graf Spee, 37

Grant (destroyer), 255

Grayson (destroyer), 67, 166

Great Britain, alliance with Japan, 4; assistance in war on Japan, 316: represented at signing of Japanese surrender, 326

Green Island, 178

Grew, Ambassador Joseph Clark, 6

Growler (submarine), 116

Grumman, F⁴F Wildcat fighter planes, 48, 52, 54, 100, 181; superseded by F⁶F Hellcats, 182

Guadalcanal (Solomons), 70–71, 125, 129, 132, 137, 139–140, 147–148, 149, 154, 155; Japanese airfield, 130; Marines landed, 133; Navy losses, 153

Guam, 53, 197, 198, 200, 204, 205, 208, 216, 218–220, 300; Admiral Sherman at, 310; recapture of, 221

Guam (cruiser), 301

Guided missiles, 334

Guimaras, 203

Guitarro (submarine), 246

Gulf of Davao, 26

Gulf of Papua, 62–64

Gunboats, *Asheville*, 43; *Oahu*, 45; *Panay*, 5; *Wake*, 45

Gunfire and Covering Force, under Rear Admiral M. L. Deyo, 295

Gunnery ships, assigned to bombardment missions, 295

Guns, antiaircraft, 111; sky, 111

Gunto, Japanese air base, 308

Gwin (destroyer), 67, 158

Hagikaze (destroyer), 160

Haguro (heavy cruiser), 70, 167–169, 211

Haha Jima, 290

Halibut (submarine), 266

Halsey, Fleet Admiral William F., ix–xi, xv, 21, 55, 65, 67, 97, 148–149, 155, 158, 166, 172, 228, 239, 244, 261, 263, 264, 267, 269, 272, 275, 309, 317, 333; addressed ships over voice radio, 317–318; at Formosa, 235–236; at Japanese surrender ceremony, 323–326; at Ulithi, 271; attack on Karieng, 175; headquarters at Yokosuka, 322; in South China Sea, 278; message to task force, 277; on the *Missouri*, 323; ordered attack on Central Force, 246, 248; ordered precautions against Japanese treachery, 318; relieved Admiral Ghormley at Noumea, 143; Admiral Spruance as Fleet Commander, 308; Visayas strike, 231

Hamakaze (destroyer), 305

Hammatsu (Honshu), coastal target, 313

Hammann (destroyer), 71, 108; in Task Force 17, 96, 108

Hancock (aircraft carrier), 273, 301, 304, 306

Haraden (destroyer), 274

Harbor development in Aleutians, 123

Harder (submarine), 203

Hart, Admiral Thomas C., 27–31, 34

Hartwig, Lt. Comdr. Glenn R., 75

Haruna (battleship), 106, 143

Haschke, Ensign, 83

Hatsukaze (destroyer), 169

Hatsushimo (destroyer), 117

Hawaii *see* Oahu; Pearl Harbor

Hawaii (cruiser), 301

Hawaiian Detachment, Pacific Fleet, 6

Hayo Maru (transport), 31

Healy, Lt. Comdr. H. R. ("Pop"), Damage Control Officer, 89–90

Helena (cruiser), 19, 37, 140, 146, 155, 158

Helfrich, Admiral Conrad E. L., 34, 37, 41, 43; represented Netherlands at signing of Japanese surrender, 326

Hellcat F^{6}F fighter planes, 181, 250, 302

Helm (destroyer), 134

Henderson, Major Loften R., Marine flyer, died at Midway, 133

Henderson Field (Guadalcanal), 137, 138, 139–142, 145, 147, 155

Henley (destroyer), 79

Heron (aircraft carrier), 26

Hickam Field, 13

Hideout areas, 26

Hiei (battleship), 13, 137, 143, 146–147

Hiroshima (Honshu), atom bomb dropped on, 314; effects of atom bomb, 315

Hiryu (aircraft carrier), 13, 50–52, 104; destruction of, 106

Hitokappu Bay (Kuriles), 14

Hiyei (battleship), 183

Hiyo (aircraft carrier), 209

Hobart (Australian light cruiser), 34, 37, 74, 131

Hodge, Lt. Gen. John R., USA, 294

Hoel (destroyer), 260; survivors of, 262

Hokkaido, air strikes on, 311–313

"Holiday Inn" (carrier *Bunker Hill*), 176

Hollandia, 128, 198, 200, 239

Holloran (destroyer escort), 272

Holtz Bay, 120

Hong Kong, fall of, 32; plane losses, 279

Honolulu (cruiser), 31, 151, 157–158, 240

Honshu, air strikes on, 311–313

Hoover, Herbert Clark, 5

Hornet (aircraft carrier), 66–67, 106, 110, 139, 144, 181, 286; at Okinawa, 301; at Midway, 102; in Task Force 16, 95

Hosogaya, Vice-Admiral Moshiro, 117–119

Hospital Point, 19

Houston (heavy cruiser), 33–35, 37, 40–42, 45, 236

Hovey (mine sweeper), 277

Howden, Capt. H. L., 74

Hsu, Gen. Yung Chang, at Japanese surrender signed for China, 326

Hughes (destroyer), 55, 105; guarded damaged Yorktown, 107; in Task Force 17, 96

Hull (destroyer), 58; in typhoon, 275–276

Hump air route from India, 181

Hunter, Lt. Comdr. George P., 74

Huon Gulf, 127, 128

Hyakutake, Lt. Gen., 141

Hyuga (battleship), 278, 312

I-7 (Japanese submarine), 122, 123

I-9 (Japanese submarine), 122

I-31 (Japanese submarine), 122

I-168 (Japanese submarine), sank the *Hammann* and *Yorktown*, 108

IFF (Identification of Friendly Forces), 80

Idaho (battleship), 119

Ie Shima, 297

Ijuin, Rear Admiral M., 161, 163

Ikazuchi (destroyer), 117

Immigration laws affecting Japanese, 4

Imperial Navy, 157

Imperial Palace, Japan, 68

Independence (light aircraft carrier), 112, 172, 178, 187, 301

India, 34

Indian Ocean, Japanese action in, 46

Indiana (battleship), 205

Indianapolis (heavy cruiser), 58, 117, 203

Indispensable Straits, 141

Indo-China, 26

Indomitable (aircraft carrier), 27

Infantry Divisions: 7th Division, 27th Division, 294; 77th Division, 294; 96th Division, 294; 106th Division, under Col. R. G. Ayres, U.S.A., 191

Inland Sea, 236, 301; mined heavily, 313

Intrepid (aircraft carrier), 194, 230, 249, 269, 301, 307

Invasion routes, 332

Iowa (battleship), 189, 193, 266

Isasuma (destroyer), 117

Ise (battleship), 278, 312

Isely Field (Saipan), 223

Isitt, Air Vice-Marshal Leonard, represented New Zealand at signing of Japanese surrender, 326

Isukazi (destroyer), 161

Isuzu (heavy cruiser), 148

Italian fleet, 3

Ito, Vice-Admiral, of the Imperial Japanese Navy, 305

Iwate (cruiser), 312

Iwo Jima, 201, 280, 284, 287, 290; Airfield No. 1, 288, 293; Airfield No. 2, 204; called the "Inevitable Island," 284–285; Hill 382 ("meat grinder"), 289; Marine cemeteries at, 320; target date, 285

Izard (destroyer), 187, 193

Izumo (cruiser), 312

Jaluit (Marshall Islands), 21, 50, 55, 189, 223

Japan: at Guadalcanal, 139; bombed the *Panay*, 5; bombing of, 66, 310–313; carriers, number of, 112; combat ships, loss of, 268; conquest at Corregidor and elsewhere, 45, 69, 94, 110; conquest of Dutch East Indies, Malaya, Borneo and the Philippines, 179; defense headquarters on Kiska, 116; expansion plans, 94–95; hostilities with China (1937), 5; imports essential to, 179; in the Solomons, 178; internal forces, 6; invasion of Alaskan waters, 113; preparations, 309; losses, at Battle of Formosa, 236; losses, at Guam,

208; losses at Midway, 108–109; losses at Tulagi, 133; losses, in aircraft, at Midway, 104; losses, naval, 45, 94; naval policy, 241; policy at Midway, 112–113; shortage of gasoline and oil, 241; Tarawa loss began defeat, 179; terms at Naval Disarmament Conference, 5; took *Houston* men prisoners, 42; war with anticipated, 2–3, 8, 23–24

Japanese, "A" Plan, 200

—affected by U.S. legislation, 4

—aircraft losses in New Guinea campaign, 128; fighters destroyed at Tinian, 196; *see also* Japan

—airfield at Guadalcanal, 130; at Orote Point, 196

—Army aviation units at Rabaul, 157

—Army garrison, 285

—bases: Mashall Islands, 24, 49, 56; Orote Point, 196; Saipan and Tinian (Mariana Islands), 194; *see also* Aleutians; Hollandia; Wewak

—carrier raiding force, 10, 20, 24–28, 35, 36, 45–46, 81, 242–243, 263; attack on Wake, 48–53; losses at Midway, 104–105; Battle for Leyte Gulf, *diagram*, 242–243; planned attack on Midway, 48

—Central Force, 246–248, 251, 253, 257–258, 261–263

—Combined Fleet, 202

—Communications, cut from

Mundato Bairoko Harbor, 157

—convoy, 33

—Emperor, 316–317

—evacuation of troops, from Guadalcanal, 152; from Vella-Lavella and Kolombangara, 164

—expeditions from Davao and Jolo, 31–32

—Fleet, 13, 20, 114, 183, 198, 202–203, 204, 244, 272; destruction of, 313; U.S. air attack on, *diagram*, 206–207

—Forces: *diagram*, 72–73, 127–128; air force units, 155; attempted to cross Owen Stanley Mountains, 124; main, 96–97; mobile, 96–97, 106; occupation, 97; Second Mobile Force, 114

—Fourth Air Army, 127, 129

—garrison on Kolombangara, 164

—Government, representative of, signed Japanese Surrender, 325

—harbors, mined by B-29's, 313

—High Command: alarmed at conquest of Marshalls, 198; report on Guadalcanal campaign, 152

—Imperial Forces, *diagram*, 242–243, 268, 271; surrender of, on battleship *Missouri*, 324–326; *see also* Central Force

—Imperial Headquarters decided to evacuate Kiska, 122, 241; representative of,

Japan (*cont.*)
  signed the Japanese surrender, 325
  —lack of trained aviators, 325
  —midget submarines, 372
  —Military characteristics, 154
  —morale, 299, 313
  —naval air forces, 127, 130
  —Navy, 241, 267, 268, 311–313; dwindling, 304; suffers first defeat, 93
  —prison camps, 42
  —reply to Allied surrender ultimatum issued at Potsdam, 316–317
  —Second Destroyer Squadron, 141
  —Second Fleet, 305
  —Southern Forces, 244, 246
  —Stockades in Manila, 278
  —Strategy, 203, 327; failure due to inadequate resources and faulty appraisal of American psychology, 331
  —submarine *I-168* sank the *Hammann* and *Yorktown*, 108
  —submarine I-400, 322
  —Tanks, 226
  —Tony pursuit plane, 286
  —Troops: at Peleliu, 225; at Rabaul, 152; at Iwo Jima, 285; combat and labor, 115; in Leyte, 271; in the Palaus, 224
  —war policy, 327–331
Japanese-American relations, 6
Jarman, Major Gen. Sanford, U.S. Army, 213
Jarrett, Comdr. Harry B., 74
Java (Dutch East Indies), 34–35, 36–38, 41, 44, 94; surrender of American, British, Dutch troops, 45
Java (Dutch cruiser), 34, 36, 38–40, 45
Java Sea, 35; submarines in, 43
"Jeep" carriers, 229, 239, 240, *diagram*, 242–243, 245, 257, 260, 261, 267, 292; at Okinawa, 300
Jintsu (cruiser), 138, 159
John D. Ford (destroyer), 32
Johnson Island, 310
Johnston (destroyer), 260; survivors of, 262
Joint Chiefs of Staff: Central Pacific plans, 184, 229, 333; set date for Tulagi landing, 130; shift boundary line to include Russell Islands, 155; authorized independent strategic bombing force, 284
Joint Expeditionary Force, under Admiral Richard K. Turner, 294
Jolo (Philippines) 31, 44, 282
Jomard Passage, 70, 77, 79
Jones, Rear Admiral Carey, at Japanese surrender, 323
Jones, Mr. and Mrs. Charles F., prisoners of Japanese at Attu, 114
Juneau (Antiaircraft cruiser), 143, 146, 147
Jungle "rain forest," 132
Junyo (aircraft carrier), 113, 143
Jupiter (British destroyer), 38, 40, 45

Kadena, 296; airfield, 296
Kaga (aircraft carrier), 13, 102, 103
Kagero (destroyer), 138

Kagoshima Bay, 304

Kahili (Bougainville), 160; airfields, 164; largest Japanese air base in the Solomons, 161, 163

Kajioka, Rear Admiral, 50

Kako (heavy cruiser), 70, 134, 136

Kalinin Bay (escort carrier), 261

Kamaishi (in northern Honshu), gunfire bombardment of, 311

Kamchatka, 117

Kamikazes (Special Attack Corps), 240, 252, 261, 267, 269–270, 273, 274, 277, 280, 295, 300, 307; attack carrier *Saratoga*, 291; attacks on Kyushu, 310

Kamoi (seaplane tender), 65

Kaneohe Naval Air Station, 12–13

Kanoya, 360; Japanese airfield, 308

Kanoya Airfield (Japanese Kyushu base), 308

Kara, airfields, 164

Kasumi (destroyer), 116

Katsuragi (aircraft carrier), 312

Kavieng (New Ireland), 34, 136, 166, 189; carrier raids on, 173–174

Kawakaze (destroyer), 160

Kawanishi four-engine flying boat, 85

Keise Shima (near Okinawa), 295

Kelleher, Ensign David, fighter pilot from the *Cabot*, 304

Kema (Celebes), 33

Kendari (Celebes), 34

Kenny, Gen. George, 125, 269; at Japanese surrender, 323

Kerama Retto Islands, 295

Khabarovsk (Siberia), 68

Kidd (destroyer), 306

Kieta, airfield, 164

Kimmel, Admiral Husband E., 2–4, 8, 10, 51

King, Admiral Ernest J., 34, 53, 70, 112, 278, 292

Kingfisher seaplane, 234

Kinkaid, Vice-Admiral Thomas C., 74, 96, 119, 143, 229, 239, 246, 253, 257, 258, 261, 265, 267, 269, 333

Kinryu Maru (transport), 135

Kinu (light cruiser), 267

Kinugasa (heavy cruiser), 70, 134, 140, 148

Kirishima (battleship), 13, 137, 143, 146, 148–149, 183

Kiriwina Bay (New Guinea), 127

Kisaragi (destroyer), 50

Kishinami (destroyer), 248

Kiska, 113; evacuation of, 122; weather station, 114–115

Kiska Garrison Force, 122

Kiska Harbor, 116, 123

Kiso (cruiser), 113

Kitkun Bay (escort carrier), 261, 277

Kitts, Capt., 151

Knox, Col. Frank, 1

Kobayashi, Vice-Admiral, 193

Kobe (Japan), 301, 302

Kodiak, naval base and airfield, 113

Koga, Admiral, Commander in Chief of Japanese Fleet, 198, 199

Koisumi aircraft plant, 291

Kolombangara plantation establishments, 156, 160

Komura, Admiral Keizo, 145

Kondo, Vice-Admiral N., 148

Kongauru, 227

Kongo (battleship), 144, 273

Konoye, Fumimaro, Prime Minister of Japan, 6

Korea, annexed by Japan (1910), 5, 180

Korean laborers, 153

Koro (Fiji Islands), 131, 224

Koror (the Palaus), 228; naval base, 225

Kortenaer (Dutch destroyer), 39–40, 45

Koshun, Japanese air base, 278

Kossol Roads anchorage (The Palaus), 225, 234

Krueger, Lt. Gen. Walter; Sixth Army, 239, 282

Krulak, Lt. Col. V. H., 165

Kula Gulf, 158–159

Kumano (heavy cruiser), 260

Kunisi Ridge, 299

Kure (Japan), 301, 302; fast carrier strikes on, 313; Naval Base, 312

Kuribayashi, Lt. Gen. Tadamichi, 285

Kuriles, 14, 94, 113, 124, *diagram*, 242–243

Kurita, Vice-Admiral Takeo, 246 253, 259, 261–262, 264, 267–268; commander of forces from Singapore, 253

Kurusu, Saburo, Special Envoy to the United States, 6

Kusaie, Japanese bases target for land-based aircraft, 188

Kushiro, destruction of 20 city blocks, 311

Kwajalein (Marshall Islands), 50, 55, 56, 189

Kwajalein Lagoon is largest in the world, 190

Kwantung Army from Manchuria, 225

Kyushu (Japan), 284, 294, 300, 303, 310; airfields attacked by task groups, 308

LCI's, 263

LST's, 274

Lae (New Guinea Territory), 61, 62–64, 69, 125, 128

Laffey (destroyer), 147

Lamotte-Picquet (French cruiser), 279

Land-based planes, 203, 313

Landrum, Major Gen. Eugene, 121

Lang (destroyer), 187

Langley (Seaplane Tender), 36, 208, 230, 250, 269, 280, 301

Lansdowne (destroyer), 139, 166

Lardner (destroyer), 166

Larsen, Commander Harold O., 163–164

Lavallette (destroyer), 152, 163

Le Clerc, Gen. Jacques, represented France at signing of Japanese surrender, 326

League of Nations, 5; mandated Marshalls to Japan, 189

Leahy, Admiral W. D., 112

Leander (British cruiser), 158

Leary, Vice-Admiral Herbert F., 58, 130

Lee, Vice-Admiral W. A., 148–149, 176

Lexington (aircraft carrier), x, 1, 4, 6, 8, 15, 21–22, 70, 74, 75, 78, 80–84, 210, 230, 250, 269, 271, 329; bombed, 88; central station report of explosion, 89; fighter direction, 85; new carrier of that name,

320; order to abandon ship, 91; prepared for attack by Japanese, 84; sunk by Torpedoes, 92, 110; survivors return to United States, 93; with Admiral Brown's task force, 50

Leyte Gulf, 234, 239, 240, 246, 247, 253, 267, 269–271; Admiral Sherman's task group at, 308; Fast Carrier Task Force at, 309

Leyte Island (Eastern Philippines), 229, 238, 239–240, 269, 270–271, 274, 281

Lingayen, 281

Lingayen Gulf (Philippine Islands), 30; MacArthur's forces at, 276, 277

Liscome Bay (escort carrier), 187

Lockwood, Vice-Admiral Charles, at Japanese surrender, 323

Logistic problems, 24, 284, 293, 332; British, 314

Logistics Supply Group, 294

Lombok Strait, 43

Long (mine sweeper), 277

Louisiades Islands, 62, 64, 70

Louisville (cruiser), 55, 61, 64, 151, 253–254, 277

Lowry, Capt. Frank J., 74

Lunga Channel, 150

Lunga Point, 145

Lunga Point (aircraft carrier), 290

Luzon (P. I.) 29, 231, 234, 237, 245, 250, 269, 270, 281; airfields, 274; carrier raids on, 274

Lytton Commission, 5

MacArthur, Gen. Douglas, 23, 25, 29, 112, 155, 171, 180, 224, 229, 238–239, 269, 274; appointed Supreme Commander for the Allied Powers in the Pacific, 319; arrival at Yokohama on the Missouri, 321; headquarters, Grand Hotel, Yokohama, 322; in Australia, 124; in Southwest Pacific, 333; invasion of Mindanao, 281; Japanese surrender ceremony, 324–326; liberation of the Philippines, 238; Lingayen landing, 276, 277; New Guinea campaign, 184; return to Philippines, 238–239

McCain, Vice-Admiral John S. 131, 229, 235, diagram, 242–243, 245, 261, 266, 271–272; at Japanese surrender ceremony, 323; authorized to bring all flag officers to surrender ceremony on the Missouri, 322; message to his force on further attacks on Japan, 317; relieved Admiral Mitscher, 308; relieved as Task Force Commander, 283; strikes at airfields and industrial plants in Tokyo, 311

McCall (destroyer), 55

McCampbell, Comdr. David, 250, 264

McCawley (Admiral Turner's flagship), 134; ex-passenger liner Santa Barbara, 156

MacDonough (destroyer), 58

McInerny, Comdr. Francis X., 74

McKenzie, Chief Quartermaster, 87

McManes, Capt. K. M., 254

McMorris, Rear Admiral Charles Horatio, 117, 118

Machinato, airfield, 297

Mactan Island, 231

Maddox (destroyer), 280

Main Force, Japanese, 97

Majuro Atoll, 190, 192, 200; Sea Bees active on, 190–191

Makassar city, 33

Makassar Straits, 33

Makigumo (destroyer), 106

Makin (Gilbert Islands), 55, 56, 185

Makunsho village, 214

Malaita Island, 140

Malay Barrier, 43

Malay Peninsula, 27, 32, 94, 240

Maloelap (Marshall Islands), 55, 189, 223

Manchukuo, 180

Manchuria, occupied by Japan (1931), 5; Russian Army in, 316

Manchurian Army, 29th Division, 218, 225

Maneuverability improved in later carriers, 87

Manila, 23–25, 29, 231–232, 237, 249, 270, 281; arrival of Vice-Admiral Sir Tom Phillips, 27; Japanese emissaries arrive for instructions on surrender, 321

Manila Bay, 23, 270

Manila Bay (escort carrier), 277

Manila Harbor, 232, 270

Mansbergh, Capt. C. A. L., RN, 158

Manus, 234, 269; British supply base, 308

Marblehead (cruiser), 32–34

Marco Polo Bridge (Peiping) incident, 1937, 5

Marcus, 66, 185

Mariana Islands (in Pacific Ocean), 23, 196, 203, 208, 211, 223; Japanese bases, 194; air strength in, 200; shore based aircraft, 285

"Marianas Turkey Shoot," 205

Marine Aviation Groups, 281; Air Groups (12, 14, 24, 32), 281, 309; commemorative plaque from Forty-First Infantry Division, 282; won high accolades from army commanders, 281; C-47 Transports, 142; Dive Bombing Squadron 24, 101; Fighter Squadrons, 157; Squadron *21*, 48; Squadron *221*, 100; Flying Artillery (name given dive bombers), 281; Parachute Battalion, 165; Raider Regiment, 165; Marine III Amphibious Corps, under Maj. Gen. Roy S. Geiger, USMC, 294, 297; 22nd combat team under Col. J. T. Walker, 191; Units, 288

Marines, *see* U.S. Marine Corps

Marines at Midway, The, USMC, Hist. Sec., Div. of Pub. Information, *Bibliography*, 337

Marshall, Gen. George C., 7–8, 112

Marshall Islands, 21, 23, 49, 55, 61, 94, 185–186, 188–189, 198, 218; campaign ended, 197; successful raid, 69

Martin, Major General Frederick L., 2

Maryland (battleship), 15, 19, 245, 253

Masbate Island, 233

Massachusetts (battleship), 230

Massacre Bay (on Attu), 120

Massacre Valley, 121

Masthead bombing, 126

Maury (destroyer), 55; in Task Force 16, 96

Maya (heavy cruiser), 113, 117, 171, *diagram,* 242–243, 247

Menado (Celebes), 32

Merchant Vessels, 35

Meredith (destroyer), 67

Merrill, Admiral Aaron Stanton ("Tip"), ix, 156, 165–166, 167

Metals essential to Japan, 179

Miami (cruiser), 266

Michishio (destroyer), 148

Midway, 1, 9, 14, 21, 66, 96, 102, 106, 203, 215; Japanese seek possession, 94–95; plane base of Army, Marines, Navy, 103; radar report on approaching planes, 100

Mikawa, Rear Admiral, 134–135

Mikuma (cruiser), 106–107

Mille (Marshall Islands), 55, 188–189, 223

Miller, Lt. Henry L. (Navy), 67

Milne Bay, 128

Mindanao (Philippine Islands), 29, 229; invaded by Gen. MacArthur, 281; Marine bomber support, 282

Mindoro, 246, 274

Mine laying, 4

Mine layer, (*See* under individual names), *Oglala*

Mine sweepers, 131, 295; *Bittern,* 45; *Finch,* 45; *Hovey,* 277; *Long,* 277; *Palmer,* 277; *Quail,* 45; *Tanager,* 45

Minegumo (destroyer), 156

Mines, "unsweepable" type, 313

Minneapolis (heavy cruiser), 58, 74, 92, 131, 137, 150, 205; at Truk, 193; in Task Force 16, 95

Misaki (Honshu), coastal target, 313

Misima Island, 77–78

Missions assigned to Navy, 112

Mississinewa (Japanese Tanker), 272

Mississippi (battleship), 245, 253, 256

Missouri (battleship), Japanese surrender signed on, 321–327

Mitscher, Admiral Marc A., 66, 183, 194–195, 203–204, 205, 209, 265, 301, 305; ordered the Princeton sunk, 252; relieved by Admiral F. C. Sherman, 310; transferred from *Bunker Hill* to *Enterprise,* 307; transferred to the *Randolph,* 308

Mitsuki (destroyer), 138

Mobile (cruiser), 230, 272

Mobile Force, Japanese, 97, 106

Mog Mog (Ulithi Lagoon), recreation area, 228

Mogami (cruiser), 106–107, 171, 246, 255–257

Monaghan (destroyer), 74, 117, 123; in Task Force 16, 95; in typhoon, 275–276

"Monroe Doctrine of the Orient," 4–5

Monssen (destroyer), 67, 147

Monterey (light carrier), 174, 177, 187; in typhoon, 275

Montgomery, Rear Admiral A.E., 172, 192, 194

Montpelier (cruiser), 156, 165, 169

Moosbrugger, Comdr. Frederick, 160

Morale effect of Allied resistance, 47

Morotai (south of Mindanao), 224

Morris (destroyer), 71; in Task Force 17, 96

Motobu Peninsula, 297

Mount Suribachi (Iwo Jima), 285, 288

Mount Tapotchau (Saipan), 200

Mudge, Major Gen. Verne D., tribute to the Marine dive bombers, 281–282

Mueller, Major Gen. Paul J., U.S. Army, 225

Mullinnix, Rear Admiral Henry, M., Commander, Escort Carrier Group, 188

Munda airfield, 157, 160, 165

Munda Point (New Georgia), 158; airfield of Japanese bombarded, 155

Murakumo (destroyer), 140

Murasame (destroyer), 156

Muroran (in Hokkaido), gunfire bombardment of, 311

Murray, Vice-Admiral George D., 102

Musashi (battleship), flagship of Admiral Koga, 184, 198, 202, 258, 262, 305; sunk, *diagram*, 242–243, 268

Myako Jima, 234

Myoko (heavy cruiser), 70, 167–169

Nachi (heavy cruiser) flagship of Vice-Admiral Moshiro Hosogaya, 113, 256–257, 270

Nadzab, 128

Nagamami (destroyer), 172

Nagasaki, atom bomb dropped on, 314; effects of bomb, 315

Nagato (battleship), 249, 259

Nagatsuki (destroyer), 158

Nagoya, 342; air attack on, 291

Nagumo, Vice-Admiral Churichi, 13, 143, 214

Naha (capital city of Okinawa), 234, 295, 299

Naha Harbor, 291

Nakagusuku Wan (Okinawa), renamed Buckner Bay, 293

Nakajima Airplane Plant, 286; 97 fighters, 78; Tama Engine Plant, 286

Namur, 190

Nansei Shoto Islands, 234, 237, 276, 293

Napalm (jellied gasoline), 230

Nashii (Japanese light cruiser), 279

Nashville (cruiser), 67, 155, 274

Nassau (escort carrier), 119–120

Nassau Bay (New Guinea), 127

Natsubio (destroyer), 34

Natsugumo (destroyer), 140

Nauru Island, 173, 188–189

Nautilus (submarine patrol), 104, 187

Navajo (tug), 152

Naval air forces, ix–xi, 2–4, 9, 103; carrier dominant factor in control of sea, 110; in Aleutians, 113; base at Pearl Harbor, 1–2, 9; battles, 153; *see also* under Battle; Bureau of Aeronautics, under Rear Admiral J. H. Towers, 182; Flotilla at Saigon, 27; policy, 24, 53; *see also* American Joint Chiefs of Staff; combined Chiefs of Staff; tactics, new, 22, 332; *see also* American Joint Chiefs of Staff; combined Chiefs of Staff; units of other nationalities, 29; War college (Newport), 23

Navy, *see* U. S. Navy

Navy Unit Citation, x

Navy Yard at Cavite, 26

Navy's Air War, The, Bibliography, 335

Neches (fleet oiler), 50–51

Negros, 229, 281–282

Nenobi (destroyer), 116

Neosho (tanker), 70, 75, 79; loss of, 93

Neptuna (British ammunition ship), 35

Netherlands, represented at signing of Japanese surrender, 226

Netherlands East Indies, 13; defense of, 42

Nets, anti-torpedo, 3

Nevada (battleship), 15, 19, 119

New Britain, 58, 75; Japanese position, 125

New Caledonia, 75, 95

New Georgia (Island), Admiral Halsey's forces established on, 128; airfield built, 155; occupation planned, 156; PT boats at, 162; troops at, 161

New Guinea, 69–70, 75, 95, 158, 165, 173, 199, 222; campaign, 125, 129; Gen. MacArthur's forces, 152

Nojima (special service vessel), 125

New Hanover, 178

New Ireland, 58, 173

New Jersey (battleship), 189, 193, 229, 266, 269

New Orleans (cruiser), 74, 131, 137, 150; at Truk, 193; in Task Force 16, 95

New Zealand, 129–130, 161; aircraft units, 131; assistance in war on Japan, 316; represented at signing of Japanese surrender, 326

New Zealand Brigade, 165

Newton, Rear Admiral John H., 20

Ngesebus (small island connected with Peleliu), 227

Ngulu, 223

Nicholas (destroyer), 157, 161

Nicholas Field, 271

Night landings, 80

Niizuki (destroyer), 158

Nine Power Treaty, 5

96th Marine Division, 297

Nimitz, Admiral Chester W., 51, 53, 65, 70, 75, 154, 221, 228, 239, 241, 244, 265, 272, 293; at Japanese surrender signed for the United States, 324–326; Central Pacific Forces, 239; Commander in Chief of Pacific Fleet and Pacific Ocean Area, 112, 184; directed Okinawa capture, 294; ordered by President to occupy port of Darien, 320;

Nimitz, Admiral (*cont.*)
ordered cancellation of strikes on Japan, 317; use of Japanese codes, 96

Nishida, Major Gen., headquarters at Parry Island, 191–192

Nishimura, Vice-Admiral Shoji, *diagram*, 242–243, 246

Nojima (special service vessel), 125

Nomura, Ambassador Kichisaburo, 6

"Nonrecognition" policy towards Japan, 5

Normandy landing in Atlantic, 293

North Carolina (battleship), 131, 137–138

Northampton (cruiser), 55, 65, 67, 144, 151; in Task Force 16, 95

Noshiro (light cruiser), 171, 176, 266

Noumea (New Caledonia), 75, 79, 93, 139; airfield, 131

Nowake (destroyer), 104, 266

Noyes, Rear Admiral Leigh, 131

Nurses (American) at Guam later returned to U.S. on S.S. *Gripsholm*, 53

Oahu, 3, 12, 15, 20, 21

Oahu (gunboat), 45

Oakland (California), 310

O'Bannon (destroyer), 147, 156, 157, 163

O'Brien (destroyer), 139

Occupation Force, Japanese, 97, 321

Offensive operations ordered suspended, 317

Oglala (minelayer), 19

O'Hara, Lt. "Butch," 60

Okinawa, 234, 237, 280, 284–286, 291–294, 304; carrier strikes against, 276; Japanese counterattack, 304; natives, primitive, 294; suicide attacks at, 300; typhoon crossroads, 293

Okinawa campaign, 308; losses, 309

Okinawans, 294; amphibious assault; loading of troops and cargo, 295

Oklahoma (battleship), 15, 18, 19

Oldendorf, Rear Admiral Jesse B., 253, 255–257, 267

Ommaney Bay (escort carrier), 277

Omori, Rear Admiral S., 167

Omura (Honshu), coastal target, 313

164th Infantry Regiment, Americal Division, 141–142

Opinions of a combat commander, x–xi

Ormoc Bay (on west coast of Leyte), 271, 274

Orote Peninsula, airfield, 218–219, 220

Orote Point, 196

Oruku Peninsula, 299

Osaka, British target, 314

Ota aircraft plant, 291

Owen Stanley Mountains (New Guinea), 62, 95

Oyodo (cruiser), flagship of the Commander in Chief of the combined Fleet, 312

Ozawa, Admiral, 210–211, 261, 264, 266

P-35's at Manila, 26

P-38's, 121, 169

P-40's at Manila, 26
PBY's (Navy), 44, 100, 113, 114
PC-487, 122
PT boats (Navy), 31, 127, 162, 253, 254; No. 137, 256
PV planes (Navy), 124
Pacific campaign, 22–23, 109
Pacific Fleet, *see* U.S. Pacific Fleet
Pacific Ocean, control of by U.S. Navy Air force, 327; war conditions in, xiii
Pacific war, grand strategy, 183; Japanese losses in, 208; new phases, 268; results of, 332; shift of power in, 229; *see also* Air Power, Japan, and under headings Japanese, U. S. and names of ships
Palau Islands, 26, 198, 199, 222, 228, 229, 234, 237; invasion of, 230; occupation of, 222, 224; position of, 224–225
Palaus (*see* Palau Islands)
Palawan Island (Philippine Islands), 26
Palembang (Sumatra), 34
Palliser, Admiral, 41, 43
Palmer (mine sweeper), 277
Panama Canal, 2, 53
Panay, 266, 281
Panay (gunboat), 5
Papuan Peninsula (eastern New Guinea), 125
Paramushiro (Kuriles), 117, 119, 124
Parrott (American destroyer), 32, 36
Parry Island, 191
Pasig River, 281
Patch, Lt. Gen. A. M., 151

Patterson (destroyer), 58, 134
Paul Jones (destroyer), 32
Peale (Wake atoll), 49
Pearl Harbor, ix, 1–4, 7–11, 20–21, 22, 47; attack on, 24, 27, 48; Doolittle command arrives, 68; lessons from, 331; minimum depth, 3; official investigation, 9–10; retaliation for, 312; sneak attack on, 180; submarines based at, 180
Peary (destroyer), 26, 35, 45
Pecos (Navy tanker), 37, 45
Peleliu (the Palaus), 225, 227–228, 230
Pennsylvania (battleship), 15–20, 119, 245, 253, 256, 259
Pensacola (heavy cruiser), 58, 143, 151; flagship of Rear Admiral T. C. Kinkaid, 96; in Task Force 16, 95
Perch (submarine), 45
Percival, Gen. Arthur (British), at Japanese surrender ceremony, 326
Perkins (destroyer), 70, 74
Perlman, Capt. Benjamin, 74
Perry, Commodore Matthew Calbraith, 326
Perth (Australian light cruiser), 37–42, 45
Pescadores Islands, *diagram*, 242–243, 279
Petroleum products essential to Japan, 179
Peyton, Marine Sergt., 92
Phelps (destroyer), 58, 74, 92; in Task Force 16, 95
Philip (destroyer), 156
Philippine Islands, 13, 237–238, 275; defenses, 24, 29; Japanese defense of, 240; liber-

Philippine Islands (*cont.*) ated July 9, 1945, 281; raids on, 224, 228, 230–231

Philippine Sea, 203, 241

Phillips, Vice-Admiral Sir Tom, 27–29

Pickets, *see Takanami*

Piet Hein (Dutch destroyer), 36, 45

"Pig boats," 245

Pillsbury (American destroyer), 36, 43, 45

Pilotless aircraft, 334

Pilots on U. S. carrier planes best in the world, 93, 211; Japanese, poorly trained, 212

Pintado (submarine), 266

Pittsburgh (cruiser), 302

"Plan Gratitude" (China Sea venture), 278

Planes, *see* Aircraft carriers; Air warfare; Army Air Forces; Bombers; Fighter planes; Flying Fortresses; land-based planes; Naval Air Forces; Scouting Squadron Two; Seaplanes

"Pony Express" compared with Fast Carrier Task Force, 283

Pope (destroyer), 32, 41, 45

Port Moresby (New Guinea), 62, 64–65, 75–77, 93; Japan plans to capture, 95; miscalculation of situation by Japanese at, 329

Porter (destroyer), 144

Portland (heavy cruiser), 70, 74, 131, 137, 143, 146; in Task Force 17, 96

Preston (converted destroyer), 26, 149

Prince of Wales (British battleship), 27–28, 45–46, 111, 331

Princeton (aircraft carrier), ix, x, 166, 230, 250; sunk, *diagram,* 242–243, 251–252

Pringle (destroyer), 156

Prison camps, Japanese, 42

Prisoners, from the *Houston* recovered, 42

Prisoners of war, relief flights to Allied personnel, 319

Production in U. S. important factor, 112, 182

Projectiles, *see* Bombs; Bombing

Purvis Bay, 154

Putnam, Major Paul, in command of aviation unit, 48

Pye, Vice-Admiral William S., 51

Pyle, Ernie (famous war correspondent), killed by a Japanese shell, 297

Quail (mine sweeper), 45

Quezon, President Manuel, 29

Quincy (cruiser), 134–135

Rabaul (New Britain), ix, 34, 58, 70, 151, 154, 164–165, 178; attack on, 61–62, 75, 79; Japanese headquarters at, 133, 164; position at, 125; troops at, 173; second carrier strike on, 172

Rabaul Harbor, 172

Radar, 22, 59, 80, 85, 149, 278; fire control, 195; Japanese planes lacked, 195; patrol line, 306; U. S. equipment superior to Japanese, 168

Radford, Rear Admiral A. W., 300–301

Radio, 40, 81, 96; on Aleutians, 124; Russian stations in Kamchatka, 124

Radio Tokyo, 152, 166, 235, 280

"Rain forest" (jungle), 132–133

Raleigh (cruiser), 15, 19

Rall (destroyer escort), 272

Ralph Talbot (destroyer), 55, 134–135, 159, 163

Ranger (aircraft carrier), 110

Rangoon (Burma), 32

Rawlings, Vice-Admiral H.B., RN, 295; commander of the British Pacific Fleet, 294

Reeves, Admiral, 192

Rendova (near Munda Point), 156

Rennell Island, 152

Reno (cruiser), 230, 236, 251, 270; sank the *Princeton*, 252

Renshaw (destroyer), 156

Repulse (battle cruiser), 27–29, 45–46, 111, 331

Revenge (battleship), 27

Rice Anchorage, 157

Richardson, Admiral James Otto, 1–2

Richmond (light cruiser), flagship of Admiral McMorris, 117–118

Roberts (destroyer), 262

Rockey, Major Gen. Keller E., 287

Rockwell, Rear Admiral F. W., 119, 121

Rogers, Lt. Comdr. Robert H., 74

Roi (Marshall Islands), 56, 190

Rooks, Capt. Alfred H., 34, 41–42

Roosevelt, Franklin D., 6, 69, 228; death reported, 307; orders to Gen. MacArthur, 29

Roosevelt, Theodore, 4

Rosenthal, Joe, (Associated Press photographer), stars and stripes raising on Iwo Jima photographed by, 288

Rota, base at, 208

Row, Brig. R. A., 165

Royal Navy, 64

Royal Sovereign (battleship), 27

Rupertus, Major Gen. William H., of the marines, 225

Russell Islands, 155

Russell (destroyer), 55; in Task Force 17, 96

Russian radio stations in Kamchatka, 124

Ryan, Capt. T. J., 161

Ryujo (aircraft carrier), 113–114, 137, 181, 183, 312

Ryukyu Islands (southwest of Japan), 293

S-36 (submarine), 45

S-37 (submarine), 33; rescued *DeRuyter* sailors, 43

S-38 (submarine) sank the *Hayo Maru*, 31; gun bombardment of Bawean Island, 43

S-44 (submarine), 136

SBD planes, 61, 84, 194

Sabotage, 4, 8

Saigon (city of Cochin China), 27

St. George's Channel, 173

Saint Lo (escort carrier), 258, 261; survivors of, 262

St. Louis (cruiser), 55, 155, 157–159

St. Nicholas Point (Java), 42

Saipan, 176, 197–198, 200–201, 212–213, 217, 234, 241; base for Army B-29 superfortresses, 283

Saito, Gen., 214

Sakashima, Japanese air base, 308

Sakito Maru (transport), 117

Salamaua (New Guinea Territory), 62, 64, 69, 125; Japanese at, 128

Salt Lake City (cruiser), 55, 65, 67, 117–119, 139, 140

Samar, 261, 265, 267, 269; Naval Air Station, 310

Samoa, vital to supply routes, 53, 95, 131

Samuel B. Roberts (destroyer escort), 260

San Bernardino Strait, 203, *diagram*, 242–243, 244, 246, 257, 259

San Diego (California), 310

San Diego (antiaircraft cruiser), 143, 166, 174

San Fernando Harbor, 273

San Francisco, 1; base for U.S. battleships, 95; *Hornet* departs from, 67

San Francisco (heavy cruiser), 58, 131, 140, 146–147

San Jacinto (aircraft carrier), 275, 301

San Juan (antiaircraft cruiser), 143–144, 166, 174

Santa Barbara, passenger liner that became the *McCawley*, Admiral Turner's flagship, 156

Santa Cruz Islands, 143, 153, 273

Santa Fe (cruiser), 230

Santee (jeep carrier), 260

Saratoga (aircraft carrier), ix, x, 49, 51, 52, 110, 131, 137–138, 166, 171, 174, 187, 290; conference of officers on, 131; under repair in Puget Sound, 97

Sargo (submarine), 43

Saufley (destroyer), 156

Savo Island, 132, 134, 136, 141, 146, 149, 153

Sayre, High Commissioner Francis B., 29

Scanland, Capt. Francis W., 74

Schmidt, Major Gen. Harry, 287

Scott, Rear Admiral Norman, 140, 146

Scott, Ensign O. L., rescue of, 233

Scout (British destroyer), 37

Scout planes, 71, 77–78, 84

Scouting Squadron Two, 78, 81

Screening Force at Guadalcanal, 134

"Sea Bee" construction battalions, 155, 160–161, 213

Sea Lion (submarine), 26, 272

Seal (submarine), 43

Seaplane base, Dutch Harbor, (Unalaska), 113

Seaplane carriers (*see* under individual name), *Chitose*

Seaplane tenders, *Curtiss*, 15, 19; *Kamoi*, 65; *Langley*, 36–37, 45, 61; *Tangier*, 50

Seaplanes, Japanese, 116

Seattle, amphibious bombers at, 113

Seawitch (aircraft tender), 36

Seboekoe Island, 42

Second Battle of the Philippine Sea, officially designated Battle for Leyte Gulf, 241; *diagram*, 242–243, 265, 267, 268

Second Marine Division, 145, 152, 186

Second Marine Parachute Battalion, 165

Segi Point (New Georgia), 156

Selfridge (destroyer), 163

Sendai (light cruiser), 167–169

Seligman, Comdr. Mort, executive officer on the *Lexington*, 90, 92

Serang, native name for Ceram, 34

Service squadrons of U. S. Navy, 332

Seventh Fleet, under Vice-Admiral Kinkaid, 229, 236, 239, 240, 245, 247, 253, 258–259, 263–264, 274; bombardment and mine sweeping units, 277

77th Marine Division, 239; at Ie Shima, 297

Shafroth, Rear Admiral Jack, at Japanese surrender, 323

Shantung Peninsula, 4

Shapley, Col. Alan, 165

Shark (submarine), 45

Shaw (destroyer), 19

Shemya airfield, 124

Shemya Island, 122

Sherman, Rear Admiral Forrest P., 139; received pen used at signing of Japanese surrender, 326

Sherman, Admiral Frederick C., ix–xi, 9–10, 20–21, 74, 166, 172, 189, 229–232, 245, 250, 269, 273, 305; at Kossol Roads, 225; at Tarawa, 187; at Truk, 191–192, 194; at Yontan, 283; attack on Kyushu airfields, 308; attack on Tokyo, 286–287; attendance at Japanese surrender ceremony, 323; Commander of Fast Carrier Force, 300, 310; congratulations received on Task Force achievement, 272; *Cowpens* carrier added to his Task Force, 189; Fleet Air Commander, 230; order to abandon *Lexington*, 91; reported to Admiral Halsey and hoisted flag on new carrier *Lexington*, 320; returned to Kyushu, 303; returned to United States on the *Chester*, 93; Task Group 38.3 at Leyte Gulf, *diagram*, 242–243; to Leyte Gulf for rest period, 308; transferred to cruiser *Minneapolis*, 92; carrier *Bunker Hill*, 308

Sherman tanks in the Palaus, 226

Shigernitsu, Mamoru, Japanese Foreign minister; as representative of Japanese Government signed at surrender ceremony, 324

Shigure (destroyer), 160, 257

Shikinamie (destroyer), 125, 127

Shima, Vice-Admiral Kiyohide,

Shima (cont.)
in command of Japanese Eighth Fleet, diagram, 242–243, 244, 246, 256; divided command, 253

Shimizu (Honshu), coastal target, 313

Shimonoseki Strait (Inland Sea), 313

Shiono (Honshu), coastal target, 313

Ships constructed by U. S. Navy, 112

Shiranubi (destroyer), 116

Shiratsuyu (destroyer), 169

Shirayuki (destroyer), 125

"Sho No. 1" operation, 239

Shock, Capt. Thomas M., 56, 74

Shoho (aircraft carrier), 70, 78

Shokaku (aircraft carrier), 13, 70, 78, 81, 84, 95, 137–138, 143, 210; loss of pilots, 110

Short, Major Gen. Walter C., 3, 8

Shortland Islands, 139, 149, 162, 164, 167

Shuri (Okinawa), 298

Sibuyan Sea, 246, 248, 251, 258, 263, 305

Silber, Comdr. Sam, 196

Simkuna, Lt. A. C., U.S.M.C., 292

Simpson, Cmdr. Roger, 160

Sims (destroyer), 55, 71, 75, 79; loss of, 93

Singapore, 5, 24, 27, 32, 198; Gen. Percival surrendered to Japanese at, 326; Japanese Force, 253

Sixth Army, 239, 240, 282

Sixth Marine Division, 294, 298

Sky guns, 111

Slot, 156, 158, 159

Smith (destroyer), 144

Smith, Lt. Gen. Holland M., 200, 213, 287

Smith Lt. (j. g.) Joseph, of Scouting Squadron Two, 81

Smith, Gen. Julian C., 186

Smith, Major Gen. Ralph, U. S. Army, 213

Smith, Cmdr. Walton W., 62

Smith, Rear Admiral William W., 74, 96

Smoot, Capt. Roland N., 255

Soerabaja (Java), 29, 32, 34, 38, 40, 42; reached by survivors, 44

Solomon Islands, 13

Solomons campaign, x, 58, 61, 75, 77, 164, 171–172, 178; carrier operations, 178

Solomons Sea, 77

Somerville, Lt. (j. g.) Ronald Lee, dive-bomber pilot from the Hancock, 304

Sorol, 223

Soryu (aircraft carrier), 13, 50–52, 103, 104

South China Sea, 276, 278, 280; Fast Carrier Force in, 278

South Dakota (battleship), 143–144, 148, 149, 187, 205, 230, 292

South Pacific Area Command under Vice-Admiral Ghormley, 130

South Pacific forces, 156, 178, 189

Southern Force (Japanese), 246–247, 253

Southwest Pacific, 184, 229, 238, 244; as stalemate ended,

128; forces of Gen. Mac-Arthur, 178, 222; ships organized as two fleets, 229; submarine activity in, 180

Soviet Union, declared war on Japan, 316; represented at signing of Japanese surrender, 326

Spaatz, Gen. Carl, at Japanese surrender ceremony, 323

Special Attack Corps (Kamikaze), 240, 252, 261, 267, 269

Spence (destroyer), 165, 169; in typhoon, 275–276

Sprague, Rear Admiral C. A. F., 258–260

Sprague, Rear Admiral Thomas L., 260

Spruance, Rear Admiral Raymond A., 56, 65, 67, 95, 97, 106–107, 208; at Truk, 192–193; Commander of the Fifth Fleet, 294; relieved Admiral Halsey, 283

Stack (destroyer), 166, 187

Stalemate period, 111

Stanly (destroyer), 166

Staring Bay (Celebes), 34, 35, 46

Stark, Admiral Harold Raynsford, 3

"Step-by-step" method, 23

Sterrett (destroyer), 147, 166

Stewart (American destroyer), 36, 45

Stilwell, Gen. Joseph W., 69; relieved Lt. Gen. Roy S. Geiger, 300

Stilwell Papers, The, Ed. by Theodore White, *Bibliography*, 336

Stimson, Henry L., 1, 5

Stingray (submarine), 29

Strategic Bombing, *Bibliography*, 236–237

Strategy in the Pacific, xiii, 27, 48, 119, 129, 183, 311; blockade major feature, 179–180; conflicting theories, 23, 46; Japanese, 94, 203; *see also* Combined Chiefs of Staff

Strong (destroyer), 157

Subic Bay (Luzon), 280

Submarine Warfare, against Japan, 180; international law, 180

Submarines, ix, 4, 19, 29–30, 33, 37, 97; in Philippine waters, 244; Japanese, at Ulithi, 272; of Asiatic Fleet based at Freemantle (southwest Australia), 180; used in Pacific War (*see also* under individual names); *Albacore; Cavalla; Dace; Darter; Flying Fish; Growler; Guitarro; Halibut; Harder;* I-7; I-9; I-31; I-168; *Kongo; Nautilus; Perch; Pintado;* S-36; S-37; S-38; S-44; *Sea Lion; Seal; Sargo; Shark; Stingray; Tambor; Triton*

Sulu Archipelago, 196

Sulu Sea, *diagram*, 242–243, 246

Sumatra (Dutch East Indies), 35, 37, 94

Sunda Strait (near Java), 41

Supply ships, *Akagane Maru*, 117

Surigao Strait, *diagram*, 242-243, 244, 246, 253, 257, 267

Surrender of Japan, 320–326

Sutherland, Lt. Gen. Richard K., 25; at Japanese surrender, 323

Suwanee (jeep carrier), 260, 267

Suzunami (destroyer), 172

Swatow (China), 279

Sweeney, Lt. Col. Walter C., 97

Swiss Government relays Japanese surrender note, 316

Tactics: errors in Indian Ocean defense, 46–47; masthead bombing 126; new, for Pacific War, xiii; of other nations, 29; Pearl Harbor, 48; Rabaul, 62

Taiho (aircraft carrier), flagship of Admiral Ozawa, 210

Taiwan Strait, 279

Takagi, Vice-Admiral, 70, 84

Takanami (picket), 150

Takao (cruiser), 113, 171, *diagram*, 242–243, 247–248

Talbot, Cmdr. Paul H., 32–33

Tama (cruiser), 113, 117, 266

Tambor (submarine), 106

Tanager (mine sweeper), 45

Tanaka, Admiral, 137–138, 150

Tanapag Harbor, 213

Tandjoeng Priok (Java), 38, 41

Tangier (Seaplane Tender), 50

Tankers, 278, 294; *Mississinewa*, 272; *Neosho*, 70, 75, 79, 93; *Pecos*, 37, 45; *Tippecanoe*, 70

Tarakan (Borneo), 31, 44

Taranto (Italy), 3

Tarawa (Gilbert Islands), 173–174, 179, 185–186

Targets in raid on Japan, 68

Taroa (Marshall Islands), 56

Task Force Commanders, 116, 131, 229–230, 266, 308; *see also* under individual names

Task Force Divisions, 237; Group 12, 160; Group 15, 160; Group 16, 95–96, 108, 135; Group 17, 96, 105; Group 34, 245, 263, 265–266; Group 38, 229, 231–232, 245–246, 248, 263–264, 268, 275, 277, 278, 280, 283, 308, 317; Group 38.1, 230, *diagram*, 242–243, 270, 272; Group 38.2, 230, 270; Group 38.3, *diagram*, 242–243, 249, 273, 309; Group 38.4, 230, *diagram*, 242–243; Group 58, *see* Fast Carrier Task Force; U.S. Task Force 58

Tassafaronga, 148, 149–150, 153

Tatsuta (light cruiscr), 70, 134

Tawi Tawi (Sulu Archipelago), 196, 198–199, 202

Taylor (destroyer), 163

Tenedos (destroyer), 27, 37

Tennessee (battleship), 15, 18, 19, 245, 253, 256, 259

Tenryu (light cruiser), 70, 134

Tenth Army, 295; Gen. Buckner's expeditionary troops, 294

Thatch, Lt. Comdr. Jimmie, 55, 58

Thatcher (destroyer), 165

Theater Commanders, 112

Theobald, Rear Admiral Robert Alfred, over-all command in North Pacific, 113, 119

III Amphibious corps, 298

Third Fleet, under Admiral Halsey, 228–229, 239, 240, 246, 253, 257–258, 261, 263–264, 269, 274, 310; attacks continued after Japanese surrender, 317; becomes the Fifth Fleet, 283; raids on Japan, 314

Third Marine Defense Battalion, 165

Third Marine Division, 165, 287

13th Troop Carrier Squadron (Air Force), 142

Thirty-Seventh (Army) Infantry Division, 165

Thomas, Lt. Comdr. Francis J., 18

Ticonderoga (aircraft carrier), 269, 271, 276, 280

Timor (Malay Archipelago), ferry station for fighter planes, 34, 35, 94

Tinian, 176, 196–197, 200, 217

Tippecanoe (tanker), 70

Tjilatjap (Java), 34, 36, 41, 43

Todd, Comdr. Carlton R., 265

Tojo, General, 222

Tojo Cabinet, resignation of, 222

Tokitsukaze (destroyer), 125

Tokyo, 1, 47, 178, 317; bombing expedition to, 66–69, 283, 286, 311–314; island bases, 284, surrender at, 320

Tokyo Bay, x

"Tokyo Express," 142, 149, 158

Tone (heavy cruiser), 13, 106, 312

Tonga Tabu (Friendly Islands), 93; airfield, 131

Torpedo planes, ix, 1–2, 3–4, 11–13, 15, 71, 81, 86; "Devastator" (TBD), 54, 56; protection of, 108

Torpedo Squadrons, 64; Squadron Eight, 102; Squadron Six, 103; Squadron Three, 103

Torpedoes, 36, 39–40, 87–88; Japanese, 150, 193; method of dropping, 86; performance disappointing, 30, 43; use in shallow water, 3

Towers, Rear Admiral John H., 182; at Japanese surrender, 323

Townsville (Australia), 62, 75, 93

Toyoda, Admiral (Japanese Naval Commander in Chief), 239, 253, 305; succeeded Admiral Koga, 199, 202; viewpoint on atomic bomb and Russia's entry into war, 316

Transports, 35, 38, 42, 97, 119–120; at Wellington, New Zealand, 131; *George F. Elliott*, 134, 135; *Hayo Maru*, 31; *Kinryu Maru*, 138; Marine C-47, 142; off Bougainville, 171; *Sakito Maru*, 117

Treasury Islands, 165

Trincomalee (Ceylon), 46

Triton (submarine), 116

Trojalkowski, Comdr., dentist on the *Lexington*, 88

Tromp (small cruiser), 34

True, Comdr. Arnold, 75, 96

Truk (Oceania), 70, 141, 171, 218, 223; air attacks on, 194, 197

Truman, President Harry S., directed Admiral Nimitz to occupy port of Darien, 320; received a pen used in signing of Japanese surrender, 326

Tsingtao (China), 4

Tsushima Strait, 180

Tugs (*see* under individual names), *Navajo: Vireo*

Tulagi (Solomons), 70, 71, 132–133, 154

Tundra (swamp) in Aleutians, 114, 121

Turnage, Major Gen. A. H., 165

Turner, Admiral Richmond K., 130–131, 134, 136, 153, 162; amphibious forces under his command, 190; at Japanese surrender, 323; Commander of Fifth Fleet, 294

20th Air Force, 284, 291

XXIV Army Corps, 239, 294, 297

27th Marine Division, 297

Twining, Lt. Gen. Nathaniel, at Japanese surrender, 323

Typhoons, 275–276, 279, 321

U. S. Army, Air Forces, 171, 181, 269; aircraft units, 131; B-17 Flying Fortresses, 106, 138; B-24's, 124–125; B-26's, 79; bomber squadrons, 113, 115; 81st Infantry Division, 225, 227; fighter planes, 114, 156; First Cavalry Division, 281; in the Philippines, 239; infantry divisions, 200; occupation of Kwajalein, 190; responsible in the main for ground conquests in Japan, 316; 77th Army Division, 219, 221; Sixth Army, 239; troops on Makin, 185; 27th Division, 213; *see also* under Air; Army

U. S. Far Eastern Air Force, 26

U. S. Fifth Fleet, 203; earlier, Third Fleet, 283

U. S. Fleet Command, 53, 203, 318

U. S. Pacific Fleet, xiii, 1, 2, 6, 8–10, 11, 13–14, 95, 198; Carrier Task Forces, 174; Commander in Chief orders suspension of attacks, 317; counter attack by, 56; in Pearl Harbor, 1, 9; *see also* under Air

U. S. Seventh Fleet, 128

U. S. Strategic Bombing Survey, 36, 337

U. S. Task Force 58, 203, 208, 285, 291; at Palau, 198; at Saipan, 201, 202; became Task Force 38, 308; earlier, Fast Carrier Task Force, 283; in Philippine Sea, *diagram*, 206–207

Ukikaze (destroyer), 125–127

Ulithi, 199, 223–224, 227–228, 269, 274, 280, 285

Ulithi Lagoon anchorage, 228, 234, 236, 269, 272, 283, 292

Umezu, Gen. Yoshijiro, Chief of the Japanese Imperial General Staff, at Japanese surrender ceremony, 324

Umikaze (destroyer), 172

Umnak (Fox Islands, Alaska), Army airfield, 114

Underwater demolition teams, 295

Urakaze (destroyer), 172

U. S. Marine Corps, 12, 21, 23, 48–49, 51–52, 132, 166, 215, 219–220; air group at Midway, 97; aircraft units, 131; Apamama Island landing, 187; at Guadalcanal, 138, 152; at Namur and Roi, 190; at Saipan, 200, 213; at Shuri, 299; at the Palaus, 227; C-47 transports, 142; Dive Bombing Squadron, 24, 101; Fifth Marines, 226–227; Fighter Squadron 21, 48, 52; Fighter Squadron 221, 100; First Marine Air Wing, 281–282; First Marine Amphibious Corps, 165; First Marine Division, 225–227; First and Sixth Divisions, 294; Fourth Marine Raider Battalion, 156; in the Philippines, 238–239; losses at Iwo Jima, 289–290; Marine aviation at Leyte, 240; Marine Divisions, 6th, 294–298; Marine Divisions 27, 297; Marine Division, 77, 239, 297; Marine Division 96, 297; Parachute Battalion, 165; Raider Regiment, 165; Second Marine Parachute Battalion, 165; Second and Fourth Divisions, 217; III Amphibious Corps, 298; Third Marine Defence Battalion, 165; 22nd Combat Team, 191; Units at Iwo Jima, 287–288

U. S. Navy, air control over Pacific by Navy carriers a revolutionary chapter in naval warfare, 316; aircraft units, 131; Catalinas, 116; fighter squadron 113, 157; Guam, 53; losses at Guadalcanal, 153; losses at Pearl Harbor, 21; occupation force at Yokosuka naval base (near Tokyo

Bay), 321; PBY's, 100; PT boats, 127; PV planes, 124; Pacific area, 149; Pacific Ocean control won mainly by, 316; patrol planes, 96, 115, 313; Patrol Wing Four, 113; Patrol Wing Ten, 27, 32, 44–45; TBF's of Torpedo Squadron Eight, 101; see also under Navy; Naval

Unity of command, lesson of the Pacific War, 333

Uranami (destroyer), 125–127, 267

Ushio (destroyer), 48

Utah (battleship target vessel), 15, 19

Vampire (destroyer), 27

Vandergrift, Major Gen. A. A., 130, 134, 151, 165, 299

Van Ghent (Dutch destroyer), 35, 45

Vella Gulf, 159–160

Vella-Lavella Island, 159–161, 164, 165

Venturas (Navy planes), 124

Vestal (repair battleship), 15, 18, 19, 147

Vigan (Luzon), 26

Vila-Stanmore (Kolombangara), 157; garrison, 159; Japanese airfield at, 156

Vincennes (cruiser), 67, 266; in Task Force 16, 95, 134–135

Vireo (American tug), Yorktown salvage attempted by, 107–108

Visayas, 231, 234, 237

Vitiaz Strait, 128

Volcano Islands, 284

Wagner, Rear Admiral Frank D., 43

Wainwright, Gen. Jonathan D., 45; at Japanese surrender, 323–324

Wakaha (destroyer), 117

Wakatsuki (destroyer), 171

Wake (gunboat), 45

Wake Island, attack on, 65, 185, 188; fighter planes on, 8, 48–49; relief withdrawn, 50–51; surrender at, 51–52; use as operating base, 66

Waldron, Comdr. John C., 102

Walke (destroyer), 55, 71, 74, 149

Walker, Capt. Frank R., 162

Walker, Col. J. T., 191

Waller (destroyer), 156

War games, Naval War College, 23

War Plans Division of Naval Operations at Washington, 112, 130

Warships of the World, Roger Kafka and Roy L. Pepperburg, *Bibliography*, 336

Wasatch (flagship of Vice-Admiral T. C. Kinkaid), 258

Washington (D.C.), Admiral Sherman in conference with Navy Dept., 310

Washington (battleship), 139, 148, 149, 187, 230

Washington Naval Disarmament Conference (1922), 5

Wasp (aircraft carrier), 110, 131, 139, 181, 205, 301

Wavell, Gen. Sir Archibald, 32, 34

Wellington (New Zealand), transports at, 131

West Virginia (battleship), 15, 19, 245, 253, 255

Western Pacific, 224; Air Forces, 3

Wewak (New Guinea), 127–128

Weyler, Rear Admiral George L., 253

Wheeler Field, 13

Whipple (American destroyer), 36

White Plains (escort carrier), 258, 261

Whittaker, Lt. Comdr. Frank M., killed in plane collision, 191

Wichita (heavy cruiser), 235

Wildcat F⁴F fighter planes, 48, 52, 54–55, 100, 181

Wilkes (Wake atoll), 49, 51

Wilkinson, Vice-Admiral Theodore S., 162; commanded Third Amphibious Force, 322

Williwas (squalls of gale force), 114

Wilson (destroyer), 134, 166, 187

Wiltse, Rear Admiral Jerry, at Japanese surrender, 323

Witte De With (Dutch destroyer), 40, 45

Woleai, 199

Woodlark Island (Louisiade Archipelago), 127

Woodworth (destroyer), 166

Worden (destroyer), in Task Force 16, 96

World War, 1914–1918, 4; Japanese took Marshalls from the Germans, 189

World War, 1939–1945, 5

Wotje (Oceania), 189, 223; gun bombardment, 56–57

Wright, Rear Admiral C. H., 149

Y-Day, 143
Yahagi (light cruiser), 305, 306
Yamamoto, Admiral Isoroku, 13, 106, 114
Yamashiro (battleship), 246, 254
Yamashita, Gen. Tomoyuki, 240
Yamato (battleship), 184, 202, 248, 258, 305, 306
Yangtze River incident, 5
Yap, 199, 223–224, 228, 229
Yellow Sea, 180
Yokohama, 286, 313
Yokosuka airfield, commanded by Capt. H. S. Duckworth, 322
Yokosuka Navy Yard, target in raid, 68; U. S. Navy occupation force at, 321
Yonabaru (Okinawa), airfield, 298
Yontan, 296; airfield, 296
Yorktown (aircraft carrier), 53– 55, 61, 65, 69–70, 74, 76–78, 80–84, 93, 102–105; at Okinawa, 301; damaged, 88, 92, 105–106, 329; fighters on, 85; flagship of Rear Admiral F. J. Fletcher, 96; sunk by torpedoes, 108, 110; Task Force 17, 96
Young, Capt. Cassin, 147
Yubari (light cruiser), 50, 70, 172
Yudachi (destroyer), 147
Yugumo (destroyer), 106, 163

Zealandia (British ammunition ship), 35
"Zeke" fighters, 261
"Zeros," Japanese fighter planes, 55, 56, 80, 82, 86, 100
Zuiho (small carrier), 97, 107, 143, 265
Zuikaku (aircraft carrier), 13, 70, 78, 81, 84, 95, 137–138, 144, 210–211, 264, 265; loss of pilots, 110

ABOUT THE AUTHOR

FREDERICK CARL SHERMAN was born in Port Huron, Michigan and attended the U.S. Naval academy in Annapolis, Maryland.

After graduation on June 3, 1910, he had consecutive duty in the battleships *Montana, Ohio,* and *Maryland* and, upon completion of the two years of sea duty, then required by law before commissioning, was commissioned Ensign to rank from March 7, 1912. He progressed in rank to that of Captain, effective June 23, 1938. He was appointed Rear Admiral, for temporary service, to rank from April 3, 1942, and on July 13, 1945, was appointed to the rank of Vice Admiral. He was transferred to the Retired List of the U.S. Navy, in the rank of Admiral, on March 1, 1947.

He served valiantly during two World Wars, and during World War II, he had active combat duty in the Pacific during the entire War period with the exception of two brief shore assignments totaling seven months.

In addition to the Navy Cross with two Gold Stars, the Distinguished Service Medal with two Gold Stars, the Legion of Merit with Combat "V," and the Commendation Ribbon, Admiral Sherman had the Nicaraguan Campaign Medal; the Mexican Service Medal; the Victory Medal, Submarine Clasp (World War I); the American Defense Service Medal, Fleet Clasp; the American Campaign Medal; the Asiastic-Pacific Campaign Medal; and the World War II Victory Medal. He also had the Order of the British Empire awarded him by the Government of Great Britain.

Admiral Sherman died on July 27, 1957.

Join the Allies on the Road to Victory
BANTAM WAR BOOKS

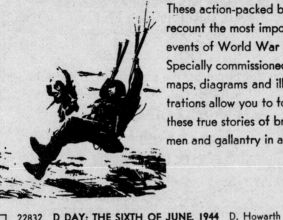

These action-packed books recount the most important events of World War II. Specially commissioned maps, diagrams and illustrations allow you to follow these true stories of brave men and gallantry in action.